BLOCKLAND

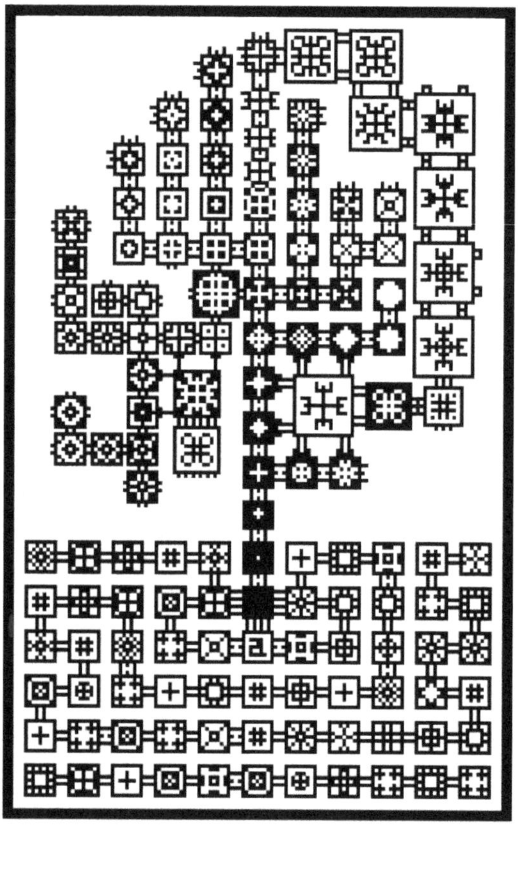

'Blockchain Tree', 2020, symbolizing cryptography, and nature of blockhains and their evolution, made in the imagined traditional style of the people of Blockland.

Previous titles by Elias:

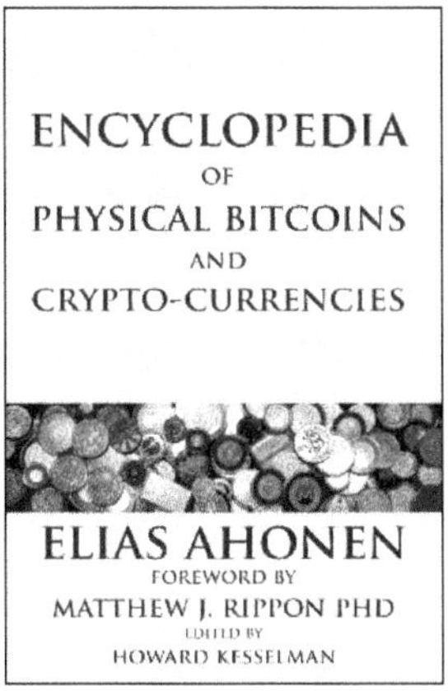

Encyclopedia of Physical Bitcoins and Crypto-Currencies
6x9 Paperback – Apr. 2016
ISBN 978-0995089907

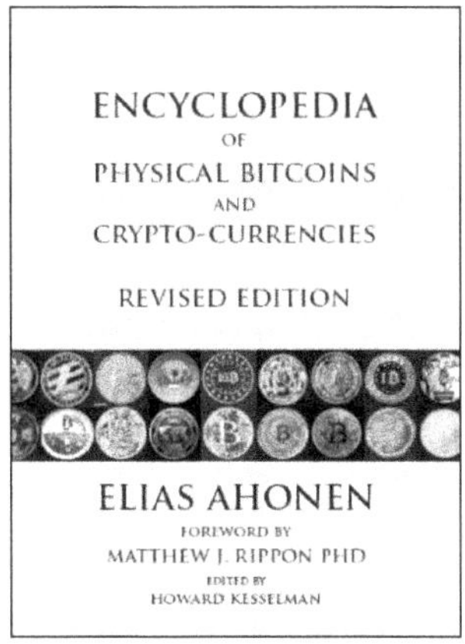

Encyclopedia of Physical Bitcoins and Crypto-Currencies, Revised Edition
8.5x11 Hardcover – Nov. 2016
ISBN 978-0995089921

Orders: cryptonumist.com

ɃLOCKLAND

21 STORIES OF BITCOIN, BLOCKCHAIN AND CRYPTOCURRENCY

ELIAS AHONEN

Cryptonumist (Elias Ahonen Inc.)
Ontario, Canada
January 3rd, 2021 (12th anniversary of the Genesis Block)

Contact: **elias@cryptonumist.com**

Ordering Information:
Contact Cryptonumist at the email address above to order books.

Paperback, hardcover, and/or digital copies available directly from the publisher and/or approved distributors. Quantity discounts may be available.

Ahonen, Elias.
Blockland: 21 Stories of Bitcoin, Blockchain, and Cryptocurrency / Elias Ahonen

ISBN 978-0-9950899-6-9

Subjects:
BUSINESS & ECONOMICS / Bitcoin & Cryptocurrencies
SOCIAL SCIENCE / Technology Studies
POLITICAL SCIENCE / Comparative Politics

Thema Subjects:
Digital or internet economics; Economic theory & philosophy; Comparative politics; Social & political philosophy; Philosophy & Religion; History: specific events & topics; Biography & non-fiction prose; Memoirs; Economic History; History of engineering & technology; Inventions & inventors; Ownership & organization of enterprises; Business innovation; Laws of specific jurisdictions & specific areas of law; Media studies: Internet, digital media & society; Political control & freedoms

Cover art by Trevor Jones.
Updated June 2021 with minor corrections.
Hidden private keys enclosed — good luck.

To my mother Heidi –
to explain this brave new world of Blockchain

This 2014 image envisions *chains* pulling down a burning bank.
A new technology is shifting our economic, political, and societal models – the winds of change are upon us.

ACKNOWLEDGMENTS

There is no shortage of people to whom I owe gratitude. In both failure and success, these include the many business partners, friends, and acquaintances made along the way. They together have defined my journey to Blockland, leading me to its treasures.

Alanthea C.
Andre H.
Aziz K.
Blal H.
Christy O.
Dane A.
Daniel M.
David A.
Erik P.
Ethan L.
Gary L.
Griff G.
Howard K.
Jim M.
JJC
John. T.
Josh G.
KLB
Kenny A.
Kieran M.
Leo F.
Liz J.
Luke W.
Manuel Z.
Maria
Matthew R.
Max W.
Nav D.
Onomor E.
Prab L.
Ray H.
Roland H.
Ron P.
Steve W.
Torrie
Trevor C.
Vizique
Yasong C.
Zachary K.

And many others, perhaps especially those who have played the roles of adversaries and thus added flavour to my adventures.

Special thanks to editors, proofreaders, formatters, and designers:

Daniel M.
F. Frankie
John Li
Mopar Mining LLC
Naleen
PA Studio
Saima
Sam Oliver
Sandi M.
Santosh S.
Toke Groth
Usman G.

Trevor Jones Art for the beautiful cover image, *Bitcoin Ecstasy.*
Jack Martin of *Cointelegraph* for writing the first book review,
The artists and creators behind the symbolic art and objects pictured,
And to my early supporters whom I have kept waiting for years.

After seven years of trekking the Finnish-Karelian swampland
Recording its ancient oral histories, legends, and rituals,
The anthropologist Elias Lönnrot created in 1835 The Kalevala,
The mythology and national epic of Finland.

According to this legend, a mystical shamanistic bard
directs the archetypal god of invention to forge the Sampo,
which he then defends from evil forces that seek to control it.
This Sampo, a magical mill that produces gold from thin air,
Brings security and prosperity to the land of Kalevala.

After seven years of surfing the cryptic jungles of blockchain,
Peering Bitcoin's depths for epic tales and foundational stories.
Flying through five continents exploring all that it has inspired,
I bring you the 21 Legends of Blockland.

Elias Lönnrot's work not only inspired The Lord of the Rings,
But established the Finnish language and cultural identity,
Ultimately leading to the nation's independence in 1917.
I am named after him.

TABLE OF CONTENTS

INTRODUCTION

This is an account of events set on and surrounding blockchain, a new digital realm beyond the internet. In these first years of this daring frontier, there are no rules and limitless opportunity to both find fortune or to steal it. Such an untamed land attracts only the most interesting of heroes and outlaws, for it is no country for the old or the meek. This collection of true tales is the 2010's canon of Bitcoin and its descendants.

For millennia we have gathered to share stories and myths. Tales of fantastical lands where adventures battle for the highest of stakes. For as long as we have been able to convey thoughts, those who ventured far from their homes have taken on near-mythical personas in the eyes of their land-lubber peers. Sailors on years-long voyages formed traditions of passing on the legends of the seas, just as soldiers, explorers, merchants, and missionaries have long returned with tales that have left their homely hamlets in awe.

I, your storyteller, am one such minor adventurer who upon returning home, was left to ponder the meaning of his journey. The following is an account of the workings and culture of this ethereal wilderness, punctuated by recllections of my travels through it and the colorful characters encountered upon the way.

It is my conviction that the collective adventures of those involved in this brave new world, in its decade of infancy, are ones that will outlive them. Indeed, some stories to come out of this "*space*" are so fantastical and strange that they read like fantasy. This is perhaps due to a disorienting fog which rolls across the land and causes many visitors to question the validity of even their own experiences.

As with ancient mythologies, we do not quite know when this story begins nor with whom nor where. Nevertheless, you will see that concepts of neither time, place, nor person hold as much importance as we might think. Indeed, many of the interactions in this book have not taken place between physical persons in our geographic world, but between digital personas interacting across a collection of virtual platforms. These have of course led to real-world outcomes ranging from mere untold transfers of wealth to perhaps the evolution of the very foundations of our societal systems as we know them. Bitcoin and its base technology, Blockchain, are the most transformative concepts since the internet came around. Nothing will ever be the same.

Especially fascinating is that the Bitcoin phenomenon, along with its elements of blockchain and cryptocurrency, mean entirely different things to different groups of people. Like many blind people feeling different parts of an elephant, not one seems to form a complete image of the whole. Interpretations vary, with the technology seen in a different yet positive light by all manner of people and groups with a broad range of motivations and even wholly contradictory worldviews. Others, however, see the technology as mere foolishness or worse, as a harbinger of doom. None are wrong.

These groups are not divided by race or religion, but most often by occupation and expertise. Not only is blockchain a whole new animal in fields such as computer science, economics, political science, law, and even philosophy, but it is ultimately a tool which, much like the internet, can be used to advance and promote the interests of practically any group no matter their ideas, purpose, or political persuasion. There is essentially no consensus reality regarding what this is all about and where it is or should be going.

Every revolution needs a cohesive story, a mythology of sorts. Every society, sect, movement, family, nation, religion, company, culture, and individual have some sort of collective history which unites and galvanizes them. These collective sagas explain the consensus origin, understood present state, and imagined future direction of each entity. These myths of adversity and triumph evoke feelings of pride and identity as well as the transmission of genuine life lessons and advice.

In this book, I introduce to you the stories and their people that both made Bitcoin and Bitcoin made. These 21 stories offer a lasting glimpse into the many facets of the fantastical wild-west first decade of Bitcoin, Blockchain, and Cryptocurrency.

Welcome to Blockland.

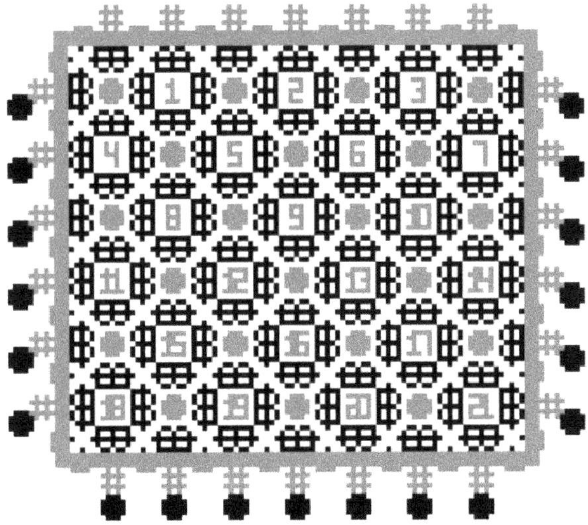

1 TROY OZ .999 FINE GOLD
VIRES IN NUMERIS
2012 CASASCIUS
1000 BITCOINS

AUTHOR'S FOREWORD

Art of Bitcoin

The dust storm settled as I lay on a mattress in the open Nevada desert. I felt a shadow come over me and opened my eyes to see him towering above, blocking the sun: *"We're about to roll out of here in two, Elias. Hop on into the Purple People Eater!"* I sat up to see what Brock, the last Chairman of the Bitcoin Foundation, was gesturing at. I saw a one-eyed, purple, and strangely furry golf cart which had arrived to take me to a party. Soon on our way, I took my bearings. In the driver's seat with one hand around his wife Crystal, their marriage registered on the blockchain, sat crypto billionaire Brock Pierce, co-founder of Tether and EOS, who told me that it was his first time experiencing Burning Man without psychedelic drugs. To their left was the red-haired, sword-carrying, nipple-tassel-wearing Brittany Kaiser, the Cambridge Analytica whistleblower known for leaking controversial information about the firm's harvesting of Facebook data for political ends as told in The Great Hack, for which she had been filming hours earlier. In the backseat sat the manager of the Ethereum launch on one side and to my other was the Santa-suit wearing Griff Green, who had led the industry-defining DAO hacker war against Mr. Popescu, a shadowy Romanian crypto super-villain. I was the odd one out; unremarkable.

Though no cyber-warrior, shadowy tycoon, technical genius, or international newsmaker, my life was at least far from boring. Allow me to rewind by one month and show you how I became entangled in the most fascinating of industries since rock'n'roll.

The 2018 Calgary Stampede was in full swing as the day began at a downtown bank vault where I had invited a small group of conference guests from across the continent to view a unique coin collection. Despite having just broken up with a girlfriend the previous day while we both worked a blockchain art booth at said Bitcoin conference, I had to sit with her for hours at the airport waiting for my company's co-founder who had been detained at the border. While attending a client's investor gala that evening, we began to suspect that a mutual friend had betrayed the company we were consulting for with an aim to bring it down in revenge for a percieved slight by the CEO. Though shocking it was par of the course in our time and place, seeing as earlier that very same day while preparing for the gala, I had slipped into another blockchain event down the street where I would help an enemy of an enemy, thus a friend, to serve their rival with a massive lawsuit. Blackmail, covert ops, fraud, and even police investigations amid threats of violence. Things were getting too hot, and I spent the cab ride to the airport helping a local reporter piece together the story of a city whose blockchain industry was split into tribal groups engaged in a near-literal western shoot-out.

I land in Vancouver at 4pm, and just make it to the Bitcoin exchange's office where I am scheduled to discuss a high-volume client who I've introduced to them. The Dubai-based buyer wants to buy one to two million dollars' worth of Bitcoin every day for a year, and I stand to make a substantial commission. We discuss flying to the buyer for an in-person meeting next week, but my schedule is full. I leave the office by 5:30pm for my next appointment at a nearby Starbucks. I'm somewhat lost, as it's my first time in this city and I'm lugging around a large suitcase. The Starbucks meeting with a potential business partner goes on for an hour, and then I am off to meeting number three at a pizzeria. By 10pm, I'm back at the airport to continue to China.

It's apparent that I've gotten a hero's welcome, as that night I find myself taking shots on-stage at a huge rap concert in Shanghai. This impromptu adventure came about after I struck up a conversation with BBNO$, a lead artist, at the airport luggage claim. Excited about my work and telling me of a friend creating a blockchain solution for recording artists to get paid for their music, he invited me to join his crew backstage. Remember kids; always talk to strangers. Despite having a great time, I leave the party early to get my jet-lagged self to a business lunch the next day. On my way out I see two fans get turned away after unsuccessfully trying to convince security that they belonged backstage. *"Hey Cindy, there you are! They are waiting for you back there!"* I yell out with a wink as I guide them both past the bouncers. They are ecstatic and rush to find their idol. As I make my exit, I chuckle at the disorder I've caused. Crypto is, after all, all about beating the system.

I'm running some minutes late for a corporate event where I'm due to give a presentation on *Crypto-Currency in North America.* I arrive at the Chinese cryptocurrency exchange's office to find the door locked and the lights off. "*Not another Mt.Gox."* I think as I call the secretary to whom I had sent my presentation the previous day. "*Oh no!"* she exclaims as she sends me the address to the Ritz-Carlton. I desperately hail a cab in the sweltering heat. As I am greeted by tiara-clad models in flowing dresses who walk me to a massive stage with rock music playing to herald my entrance, I notice large banners with my name, photo and translated biography pulled from LinkedIn strewn throughout the lavish ballroom. The 500-some audience is difficult to see due to the dozens of moving lights that remind me more of the concert from three days before than any keynote I've ever seen. My simplistic PowerPoint suddenly feels inadequate for the screen three times my height, though to be fair I had expected a bland boardroom with less than a tenth of the audience. This was stop number three of six on this oddly routine jet-lagged 10-day round-the-world errand-run, and the next day I was off to South Korea. Welcome to life in Blockland.

Supercars abound as crypto big shots from around the world converge at a luxury resort overlooking Seoul. The following three days are a blur. The conference itself goes 9-5 each day, but is followed by events around the city, champagne receptions, parties, after parties, and a billionaire-studded pool party that would earn accolades from Hugh Hefner himself. In addition to making new contacts for my company and clients, I'm here to finally meet colleagues who I'd been working with for months. The conference was a success, and I'm lucky to get a few hours of sleep after the last party before I'm off to London to make a special pick-up.

Physical Bitcoins

"*I'm sitting at the corner table at Costa Coffee. Green shirt*" I email my pseudonymous contact, and the reply comes back as "*2 minutes away. Orange sweater.*" It is 10am in the terminal, and just an hour ago I was asleep and in the air. Orange Sweater arrives and places a small suitcase on the table. After pleasantries, the suitcase clicks open and I see what look like two film canisters. I spread their contents on the airport coffee-shop table. In front of me are 50 brass coins worth more than most houses. I roll up my sleeves like an oldschool casino dealer, carefully counting and examining the coins as groggy travelers line up for coffee behind me. I'm satisfied, and I turn my Wi-Fi-connected laptop to Orange Sweater who nods to indicate that the transaction is correct. I press enter, and figurative Lamborghinis zoom from my computer to his smartphone which he checks to confirm receipt. I slide the film canisters into the breast pocket of my nondescript leather coat and grab the next train to the city like any other commuter where I meet an old classmate for an afternoon at the British Museum. The next day I'm back at the airport to make a delivery across the Atlantic.

These coins were Casascius Physical Bitcoins, and you are not likely to find them in your change. On the back side of each metal coin, there is a tamper-evident holographic seal which can be peeled away to reveal a *private key* to access a Bitcoin wallet. These were developed by Mike Caldwell of Utah in 2011 as an educational gimmick to introduce the heavily theoretical (at the time) concept of Bitcoin to his friends who had no expertise in computer science. The idea is that each coin is in effect a *paper wallet*, meaning that it contains both the private key and public key on a physical object (usually a piece of paper). By handing the coin to someone, one could demonstrate that *"I control this bitcoin, and when I hand it to you, you now control it and can freely give it to someone else and I cannot take it away from you or replicate it. If you throw it in an ocean it does not get destroyed, but no one can ever use that bitcoin again."*

Mr. Caldwell worked with a company that made tokens for car washes and amusement parks to design a brass token that featured the Bitcoin logo and the denomination of "1 Bitcoin". He then printed off thousands of private keys which he placed on the back, covered by a custom tamper-evident hologram sticker that would leave a honeycomb pattern when peeled. The public key was printed on each hologram, meaning that anyone could check the balance of any given coin. Presuming that Mr. Caldwell himself did not keep record of the private keys, this meant that any coin with an intact hologram could be trusted to contain the stated amount of BTC.

When these coins were first offered for sale on September 6th, 2011, each bitcoin was worth around 50 cents. Mr. Caldwell made these coins as a hobby without a profit motive and sold tens of thousands of them in bulk on the Bitcointalk.org forum for an amount that just covered the contained BTC and his expenses. Hundreds of these coins were given away as gifts and tips to encourage people to learn about Bitcoin. Since each bitcoin was relatively cheap, Mr. Caldwell also designed higher value pieces. These included 5 BTC nickel coins, 10 BTC silver coins, 25 BTC gold-plated coins, 100 and 500 BTC gold-plated bars, and even 1,000 BTC coins made of pure gold. As Bitcoin's value increased into the hundreds of dollars, Mr. Caldwell expanded the Casascius coin line with 0.1, 0.5, and 1 BTC coins made of silver.

This is where I entered the Bitcoin game in January 2013. An unremarkable 18-year-old, I had recently purchased my first bitcoins for for $20 apiece through a convoluted method of using a credit card via PayPal to purchase Second Life (a multi-player computer game) in-game currency and converting it to BTC. As I created a Bitcoin wallet on my hard drive, I knew I couldn't trust myself not to screw it up so I chose to use my digital bitcoins to buy *physical* bitcoins that I was less likely to lose. I found a website that re-sold Casascius coins, but they only shipped to Europe so I had them sent to my grandmother's house in Finland where I picked them up a few months later as I left for a 2-month, 27-country backpacking trip across the continent. "*Even if I lose my money and credit cards, I guess I'll always have these bitcoins wherever I go*" I figured as I threw the coins in my backpack and embarked on a grand adventure. Seven years later I still have one of those original coins, which I consider my Number One Bitcoin as a play on the Disney character Scrooge McDuck's *Number One Dime*. True to my prediction, I'm locked out of my original wallet after forgetting its password.

As one might expect, these coins became highly collectible due to their limited quantities and trackable addresses. The coins were widely sold on eBay and even on local classifieds ads in bigger cities, with many people seeing them as easy ways to buy and hold BTC. I had always collected coins, and as a Political Science undergrad I found the "mainstream" Bitcoin community that focused heavily on computer science to be intimidating and inaccessible. Soon, I had quite a collection of physical Bitcoins created by several manufacturers. I began trading these coins and posting about them on forums, with my posts encouraged by other collectors including an industry maverick named Charlie Shrem, who, while wearing an ankle monitor and awaiting sentencing for money laundering, mentored me to create a sort of association of "physical crypto mints":

> CHARLIE: *If you put some work and some money into this, you can really do well and become a major player. ...People who want to release coins would want to become a member first, marketing and legitimacy reasons.*
>
> ELIAS: *Hearing the great feedback from you gives me great hope for this, knowing that it isnt just my optimism talking. I want nothing more then to be a major player in the bitcoin world in this historic time.*
>
> - Email exchange, 13 June 2014.

Things got interesting after Mr. Caldwell received a letter from the US Securities and Exchange Commission (SEC) which asked him to stop producing his coins because their production amounted to *money transmitting*, which required a license.[1] Caldwell ceased operations, and Casascius coins became history.

I had the privilege of writing that history; a 31-page eBook with the history, analysis, metrics, and images of every Casascius coin. It was

---

[1] McMillan, Robert. "U.S. Government Nastygram Shuts Down One-Man Bitcoin Mint." *Wired*, 12 Dec. 2013.

well received and was soon referenced in every eBay ad selling the coins. As new manufacturers of physical bitcoins began to appear around the world, I published the 270-page *Encyclopedia of Physical Bitcoins* in April 2016. Charlie received his copy at the Lewisburg Federal Prison Camp.

> *Physical crypto-currency is worthy of study because it is evidence of the notable technological and social progress relating to the continued development of a new system of value. The concept of a digital currency that is based on mathematical principles is simply revolutionary, and will in one way or another eventually reshape the world and society in which we live.*
> *These coins are the artifacts of that future.*[2]
>
> - Back cover of the book, 2016.

It was while working fulltime at BlackBerry that I began to feel disillusioned with the world I knew, first with academia and then with the corporate life. Days after I signed and shipped the pre-ordered books, I embarked on my first true call of adventure: an internship at a business sustainability consultancy in Johannesburg, South Africa. Later that same year while studying in Nanjing, China and working as a North Korea & South China Sea security analyst, it became apparent that one of the *First Print Edition* books had gotten lost in the mail so I flew to Singapore to personally sign the buyer's replacement copy.

As my computer did the final file conversion before printing the *Revised Edition,* it pulled two of the wrong images from my files which happened to share the same file names. The most memorable of these resulted in the image of a coin featuring a burning bank amid a revolution, being replaced by an image of me holding a Geiger counter in the abandoned and irradiated Ukrainian town of Pripyat near the infamous Chernobyl nuclear reactor which irradiated swaths of the Societ Union after the catastrophic meltdown in 1986. Much like

---

[2] Ahonen, Elias, and Matthew Rippon. Encyclopedia of Physical Bitcoins and Crypto-Currencies. Edited by Howard Kesselman, Elias Ahonen, 2016.

certain 'error coins' which command higher prices, these 'error prints' became popular. I used some of these to create the *Autographs Edition* limited to 20 copies that featured autograph stickers of 25 physical bitcoin manufacturers affixed to the 'error prints', selling them for up to $10,000 each.

Perhaps the most notable physical bitcoin story is that of the 1,000 BTC coins. When they were released in late 2011, the ounce of gold they were made of held about the same value as the 1,000 BTC inside each coin. Less than ten of these fully-loaded coins were made, and even fewer remain un-peeled. The first of these sold for about $5,000 in December 2011, and its buyer re-sold it less than two years later in November 2013 for over a million dollars which was paid in a mixture of US Dollars, Bitcoin, Litecoin, and gold. When Bitcoin's exchange rate soared past $10,000 in 2018, these coins became the most valuable coins in the world. This surpassed the value of the 'Flowing hair dollar' which was the first coin minted by the US government in 1794, with the most valued specimen of these having fetched over $10 million. With Bitcoin peaking at $20,000, each of these gold coins were more than twice as valuable!

There is a certain irony in the first coin of the most influential currency and minted by the world's most powerful government being the most valuable, only to be surpassed by the first coin minted of the world's first de-centralized digital currency that is not controlled by any government. The neat thing about physical bitcoins was not only that they bridged the gap between the digital and physical, but that the symbolism and imagery in them could be interpreted in many interesting ways. By putting leaderless peer-to-peer digital money into the form of coins, bills, and plastic cards like those issued by banks and governments, it would seem that these crypto-mints were sending some type of message. Though Casascius coins were the first *coins* loaded with Bitcoin, BitBills created plastic cards with a similar function in denominations of 1 BTC, 5 BTC, 10 BTC, and 20 BTC a little earlier in May 2011.

While I believe these physical bitcoins will serve as a lasting symbol, there is plenty of other art inspired by Bitcoin, blockchain, and cryptocurrency. This artistic footprint includes paintings, poetry, and music among other media. It is well known that art is the indication of culture and the collective imagination and expression of a related people in their time and place. This art communicates various archetypes and ideals among the people of Blockland, their dreams and fears, while also revealing their internal classes, divisions, and tribalism.

That's the story of how I became a (very) modern art historian and numismatist before my 21st birthday. I launched a website named CoinFirm, later called Cryptonumist.com, on which I shared all the book's content about two years after publishing. The information wanted to be free. This led me to the title of rare coin broker, making numerous international trips to inspect, collect, and deliver coins along with certificates of assessment. This in turn gave me the platform from which to eventually launch an ICO analysis service and consulting firm, the instigator of greater adventures.

From Jungle to Blockland

After dropping by Singapore to sign the replacement book, I took the opportunity to backpack Southeast Asia only to have my ass saved by Bitcoin, which I had just watched cross the $1,000 milestone after a 3-year bear market. Having not informed my bank about my travel plans, I found my accounts locked as I successively attempted to withdraw money in Singapore, Malaysia, and Cambodia within the space of three days. Surely, this person with Elias' bank cards and PIN codes could not be Elias stuck in a foreign country and trying desperately to get his hands on his own money.

As I checked into a grimy 15-dollar-per-night hotel in Cambodia's bustling Phnom Penh, I counted out my remaining cash which was made up of no less than five currencies. Less than $60; enough for a bus ticket to Vietnam for a final desperate ATM attempt, or a few days of staying put while negotiating with the banks back home. Too bad it was the weekend, and that I had left my phone in an unlicensed taxi the day before. My predicament was an unpleasant one. That's when I recalled buying some of my first bitcoins at a campus Starbucks at Wilfrid Laurier University years earlier in Canada. Back then, I met a stranger at a predetermined table and discreetly slid him a manila envelope stuffed with cash before he confirmed the transaction and sped off on a motorbike. Perhaps I could do the same here in Cambodia, only with me being on the receiving end of such an envelope of freedom and safety.

It took less than an hour to find what I needed; someone looking to buy BTC on a site connecting local buyers and sellers of bitcoin. He had a good trust rating and charged only 3%, so I promptly sent him some BTC. Two hours later I recieved a phone number and password, with instructions to present them at a certain cell phone repair shop about a 10-minute drive away. I arrived to find the shop on a dirt road, with chickens and goats scurrying about as my driver assured me that I was in the right place. I incredulously handed my note to the shopkeeper who seemed not beyond thirteen, and he disappeared to the back. Shortly after, a man I perceived as his father arrived and promptly handed me seven crisp $100 bills. I have no idea what happened, but it worked! I was no longer destitute in a third world country: Banks 0, Bitcoin 1.

This sketchy, confusing, yet undeniably functional journey is a pretty good metaphor for the average early cryptocurrency user-experience. This imagery expands to the crypto-investor as we consider my adventure the following day. With cash on hand I promptly treated my driver to dinner, where he agreed to take me to see the memorials for

Khmer Rouge victims the following day. As the somber tour drew to a close, it was apparent that there was another option on the itinerary. *"You wanna try the rocket bomb?"* he asked in broken English, making an exploding-fist hand sign. "*Sure*" I replied. Carpe diem.

Our tuk-tuk pulled up to a gas station at the very edge of the city, from where he made a call. A car arrived 30 minutes later, which sped for about an hour through sparsely populated mountainous terrain. I didn't bother to ask where we were going nor when (or if) I would return, as by now the situation was well out of my hands. I began to ponder how much my 22-year-old organs might be worth. The car turned onto a bumpy, winding jungle road and after perhaps 20 minutes of seeing no buildings or signs of life, we stopped at a small clearing. Now the driver stepped out and made a phone call. I waited. After 15 more minutes, a jeep pulled up and two men in camouflage jumped out. One carried handfuls of machine guns and RPG's to an otherwise idyllic picnic table, and the other handed me a decades-old rusty grenade that was held together with duct tape.

He walked me to the edge of a small cliff at the back of the clearing and instructed me on how to pull the pin and immediately (but very calmly) throw the grenade before ducking behind a rock. The timer was four seconds, after which point the kill-radius would be 15 meters. If for whatever reason I fumbled the throw, I was to throw myself off the cliff instead. Shaking from adrenaline after the powerful *thump*, I walked back towards the picnic table to find the other "soldier" using a hammer to pound a 40-year-old RPG rocket into its tube. I had not quite signed up for this, but I was in too deep and could not say no to such a once-in-a-lifetime opportunity. My foolhardy bravery paid off as I felt the rocket shoot upwards and watched it sail above the treeline. Not quite to the moon, it impacted a faraway mountain face in an explosion that sent deafening echoes across the valley.

Throughout this legally questionable adventure there was the implicit understanding that there were no refunds nor guarantees. The formidably powerful rocket which I wielded could very well explode in my face, in which case I would be humanely dispatched and disposed of in the jungle, never to be heard from again. Not a soul knew where I was, and the soldiers and drivers could all simply evaporate if anyone knew to come looking.

This exciting, lawless, adrenaline-filled, and unofficial grey-market world could metaphorically describe not just rural Cambodia but Blockland, the virtual land that is the frontier of cryptocurrency and blockchain.

The characterization of early-days blockchain as a frontier describes more than merely bleeding-edge technology, but the way frontier-life is often devoid of established authority, convention, or law. It characterizes the law of the jungle or wild west, where ranchers and cowboys depended on their guns and wits to protect their property and deliver swift frontier justice. There is almost no collective, and everyone is an enemy unltil proven otherwise. Frontiers imply great distance from the security of civilization, and in return offer the potential for rich rewards and exhilarating experiences. It is unestablished, with each successive wave of pioneers pushing deeper into the unknown. Here be dragons.

In the following chapters, I introduce you to the stories of Blockland and its early pioneers who have begun to chart and tame the forbidding jungles of this new era.

1700's titlepage of an Icelandic manuscript of Norse mythology.

PROLOGUE

A Mythology of Blockland

You never change things by fighting against the existing reality. To change something, build a new model that makes the old model obsolete.[3]

- Buckminster Fuller

The legend of Blockland begins with a creation story where a mythical, unreachable Creator being creates everything from nothing by setting in place the foundational Genesis Block from which an everlasting and unbreakable chain of reality is forged into the future. It is an entirely new, albeit small, Foundation Stone arising from the world's oceans of chaos. It is upon this rock that the Creator revealed himself to Hal, the first man within this creation, on the ninth day. This small rising pillar of unbreakable truth is soon spotted by Egnassa and Theirblu, powerful phoenix who see it as a secure platform on which to perch while fighting ideological wars against the great Leviathians Stnem Nrevog and Snoita Roproc for transparency and freedom. Though these impassioned and ideological phoenixes are shot down in balls of fire by their enemies, their colossal bodies fall upon the great Foundation Stone. The spirit of

[3] *A Fuller View: Buckminster Fuller's Vision of Hope and Abundance for All*, by Lloyd Steven. Sieden, Divine Arts, 2012, p. 358.

these birds was like an erupting sea volcano, with their remains solidifying and decomposing to form a large, expansive, and untouched wilderness balanced upon the Genesis Block.

It is then that the first men, The Prospectors, arrived on boats seeking adventure. They constructed rudimentary farms to collect this new terrain's magical resource, increasing the complexity of their operations as this initially plentiful, indestructible and everlasting mana become increasingly difficult to extract from the blocky ground. They took residence in the Sacred Golden City of Bit, which was prepared to them by the Creator. As this city grew, grand markets were established as its residents set up all manner of businesses. The people of the land were united by a religion which commanded them to honor their creator, care for the sacred golden city, seek and store the hidden mana that appeared on the land, and welcome all newcomers with outstretched arms. Though much mana was mishandled and thereby lost, it was swallowed up by the ground so that all remaining mana could absorb its power. This marked the beginning of an illustrious age.

With the Creator no longer among them, the people began to bicker. This came to a head when Lee abandoned the City of Gold, establishing the expansive and advanced City of Silver called Lit to compete. There arose also a great seer, Master Will, who prophesized the future of Blockland as a land not only of gold, but of vast settlements of various types that might one day dominate the landscape. This was soon followed by the great year of plenty, which brought many new settlers to the shores of Blockland in search of its special hidden mana as word of its unique value had spread to the ends of the earth.

Greedy for mana, a Ylliw determined to climb the Great Mountain of Xog, which all in the land looked to for guidance and comfort. The land did not look kindly upon Ylliw's climb, and the mountain erupted violently and took many innocent lives as it sank into the sea where it even killed many of the great whales.

With the advanced knowledge, skills, and vision these settlers brought, they began to work the lands both near and far from the Golden City of Bit. On these lands, they established new settlements, cities, and colonies for every people, ideology, and creed under the sun. A great famine of many years struck, through which many settlements failed from mismanagement or outright wickedness while others survived and bore good fruit. Despite struggles, the land of the block was at peace and the farms by which mana was collected grew larger and larger as demand for this magical resource grew.

This peace was not eternal, and soon turned to conflict. A series of battles broke out as powerful wizards fought each other by creating competing holograms of the Golden City. These battles left the once-united capital divided like branches of a tree growing apart, never to be re-united, and its residents to question reality. Charlatans rose up claiming to be the Creator, with some following them to ruin. The Golden City was not the only one to be ravaged by war; a settlement known as the Ethereal City became the victim of a coup by a fearsome dragon. Though this dragon claimed its rightful throne according to the laws of the land, most Etherealites fled their beloved city and rebuilt it in a safer region to undermine the usurping dragon's power.

There arose also a religious conflict, as the newer settlers would not hold strongly to the faith of the forefathers. No longer did they worship only the Creator and collect his golden mana but made their own creations in his image which distributed different kinds of mana. In the eyes of the elders, such man-made imitations made mockery of the True Foundation Stone upon which the land was established by the Creator. The followers of these new religions even believed that the Creator was imperfect, and that they could do better than he. From these conflicts also sprung those who believed that the entire land had a greater purpose than the mere collection and storing of hidden mana; they believed that this new land that they were building would become the new solid foundation upon which the entire universe would one day rest.

Blockland transitioned from a monoculture to a multicultural land with people of varied ideologies and beliefs. No longer was there a common philosophy, creed, or faith; one's mere existence upon the Block Lands was the necessary requirement of natural citizenship. There was no king nor government to rule the land, and anyone was free to arrive and settle. Before long, the riches and freedom of Blockland again reached the distant shores of far-off lands, and new waves of boats arrived. Though this age was fueled by greed, some early settlers took this season of plenty as an opportunity to care for others and the future by pledging their riches to collective causes.

These new arrivals were not quite as hardy as those before them, with many of them meeting ruin as winter overtook their ill-prepared settlements. This led to despair and gnashing of teeth as many lost the lofty birthrights intended for their descendants. Some experienced the shame of failure and took their own lives, while others were killed for the remainder of what they had. This winter brought with it another famine, which decimated many of those who held strong beliefs but rewarded those who cast lots against their neighbors. Especially well-fed were the merchants, who bought and sold plots within the many settlements of the land.

As Blockland grew in wealth and stability, it began to gain legitimacy among other worlds. While initially ignored and scoffed at by the great leviathians of the old lands, the land upheld by the Genesis Block has slowly begun to earn a reputation as a stable foundation on which to build with an eye for eternity. As the lands of the leviathians are sinking in stormy waters of chaos, they too have begun to look toward Blockland as their future homeland. Here, each leviathian might re-establish their kingdom for a new age. For some this is a horror, as the very land was created from a war against the leviathan's rule, far from their influence. If Anihc, Asu, Aissur, and Eporue and their many followers can make the trek to Blockland and fashion their thrones there, some fear that the entire creation will become its own antithesis as it becomes a final battleground between leviathans great and small. Others however believe that it is only by the setting of the ultimate earthly thrones upon the Block that the creation will actualize itself.

There are ultimately two visions for the distant future of this world. In one, it becomes the fortress of the great old leviathans who will rule all the heavens from its secure foundation. The other, that the leviathans will not be able to thrive long in this new land without evolving into smaller, more humble creatures. This is because the mystical Block that is the root of all power and spring of all wealth seeps away the life force of these large beings. It is prophesied that it will be on and for control of the great Foundation Stone and its spring of mana that the great wars of coming ages will be fought. These drawn-out battles will be fought between all manners of forces from men to leviathans, and even the mysterious, unnatural, and immaterial Wise Force which men will soon awaken.

May all who are wise understand this tale, and may they keep safe the mana which springs from the deep wells of the sacred stone. It is the essence of energy and power for the dawning age.

A 0.1 BTC bronze coin discovered in Blockland, depicting a mythical serpant.

1900 re-election poster for US President William McKinley, who campaigned for the gold standard and "sound money".

CHAPTER 1

Satoshi Testament

To understand the origins of Bitcoin, we must understand the concept of cryptography upon which it is based. The word has its origins in Ancient Greek, with *kryptós* meaning "secret" or "hidden", and *graphein* meaning "to write". Cryptography is therefore the art and science of hidden writing and secret messages.

Methods of encrypting secret messages in such a way as to avoid outsiders being able to comprehend them have been employed in contexts of warfare, spying, and diplomacy for millennia. Among the simplest forms of such encryption was the re-arrangement of letters within individual words according to a certain system, or substituting portions of text for corresponding words, numbers, or shapes. Someone with a *key* indicating the meaning of the code could easily decipher the text, whereas anyone without it would have to go to great efforts to crack the code through cryptanalysis.

With the advent of computational machines, cryptography came to be dominated by various branches of mathematics. Cryptography machines such as the Enigma Machine were central to communications in the Second World War, and Cold War era spies relied on various methods of discreetly carrying and transmitting information that could only be decoded with the key held by the sender and receiver. Failing to use adequate cryptography could prove catastrophic within the context of war. This is demonstrable through my paternal great-grandfather Juho Lemetyinen who was a hacker of sorts known for skiing to and intercepting enemy communication lines during the Winter War for the purpose of identifying targets for artillery strikes. For as long as it has existed, cryptography and the cracking of it has been a very serious business. Various luminaries have taken part in and commented about this eternal cat-and-mouse game, including Edgar Allan Poe who in the 1843 short story *Gold Bug* pronounced that *"human ingenuity cannot concoct a cypher which human ingenuity cannot resolve."*

Public Key Cryptography

The weakness of encryption was that the decoding key itself had to be securely delivered to the receiver, with any third party being able to intercept all messages if the key was compromised. This problem was solved in 1976 with Public Key Cryptography, in which two identical keys were no longer required. The sender could now send information to the receivers' *public key* (comparable to an email address), but only the receiver could decrypt it by using their private key. This is comparable to a password to an email account, provided the account is entirely inaccessible to anyone without the password. The receiver could set up their own "email", and even the sender would never have access to the "password".

Another function of this technology was digital signatures, which allowed receivers to verify the origins of messages. In short, the signature would prove that the sender had access to the private key of a specific public key, meaning that the message came from the person associated with the given public key. This can be understood as the "From" line in a received email; the receiver can know that whoever sent the given message had access to the password by which to access that specific email account. Provided both parties keep their private keys secure, communications could remain confidential. In 1994 almost 20 years after its development, the New York Times recounted the discovery:

> *High-tech has created a huge privacy gap. But miraculously, a fix has emerged: cheap, easy-to-use, virtually unbreakable encryption. Cryptography is the silver bullet by which we can hope to reclaim our privacy.... a remarkable discovery made almost 20 years ago, a breakthrough that combined with the obscure field of cryptography into the mainstream of communications policy.*
> *[the co-inventor] Diffie was dissatisfied with the security [on computer systems]... in the 1960s [because] a system manager had access to all passwords.... A perfect system would eliminate the need for a trusted third party.... Diffie and Hellman achieved a stunning breakthrough that changed cryptography forever. They split the cryptographic key.*
> *In their system, every user has two keys, a public one and a private one, that are unique to their owner. Whatever is scrambled by one key can be unscrambled by the other.... It was an amazing solution, but even more remarkable was that this split-key system solved both of Diffie's problems, the desire to shield communications from eavesdroppers and also to provide a secure electronic identification for contracts and financial transactions done by computer. It provided the identification by the use of 'digital signatures' that verify the sender much the same way that a real signature validates a check or contract.*
> *From the moment Diffie and Hellman published their findings in 1976, the National Security Agency's crypto monopoly was effectively terminated.... Every company, every citizen now had routine*

access to the sorts of cryptographic technology that not many years ago ranked alongside the atom bomb as a source of power.[4]

- Steven Levy, 1994.

The Cypherpunks

Nine years after public key cryptography, David Chaum published a 1985 paper *Security without Identification: Transaction Systems to Make Big Brother Obsolete*[5] which led to a fringe movement centered around the idea of using privacy-enhancing technologies to enact social and political change:

In late 1992, three individuals (Eric Hughes a mathematician from University of California, Berkeley; Tim May, a retired businessman who worked for Intel and; John Gilmore a computer scientist who was Sun Microsystems' fifth employee) who had all retired young, invited twenty of their closest friends to an informal meeting to discuss some of the world's seemingly most vexing programming and cryptographic issues.[6]

- Petri B, 26 jan. 2018.

This meeting became a monthly one, and the author and hacker Judith "St. Jude" Milton soon suggested the group call themselves The Cypherpunks. The movement's raison d'être was described by Eric Hughes in *A Cypherpunk's Manifesto* which he published in 1993:

Privacy is necessary for an open society in the electronic age.... We cannot expect governments, corporations, or other large, faceless organizations to grant us privacy... We must defend our own privacy if we expect to have any.... Cypherpunks write code.

---

[4] Levy, Steven. "Battle of the Clipper Chip." *The New York Times*, 12 June 1994.

[5] Chaum, David. "Security Without Identification: Transaction Systems to Make Big Brother Obsolete." Communications of the ACM, vol. 28 no. 10, October 1985 pp. 1030-1044.

[6] PetriB, Medium.com user. "The Untold History of Bitcoin: Enter the Cypherpunks." *The Startup*, 26 Jan. 2018.

> *We know that someone has to write software to defend privacy, and... we're going to write it.*[7]
>
> - Eric Hughes, 9 Mar. 1993.

The group's "Cypherpunk's Mailing List" grew to an estimated 2,000 subscribers by 1997, with participants receiving dozens of emails per day about topics including mathematics, cryptography, computer science, philosophy, politics, as well as personal discussions, attacks, and pranks. Specific issues of discussion included privacy, government monitoring, and the corporate control of information. A significant portion of the list's subscribers were or became notable figures in the computer industry.

> *[This movement], which originated in the late '80s, took Chaum's ideas and ran quite far with them in terms of rhetoric—in an explicitly subversive direction. For cypherpunks, crypto was at the core of a vision of how technology would cause sweeping social and political change, weakening the power of governments and established institutions. A closely related term is crypto-anarchism, a political philosophy that, in its idealized form, recognizes no laws except those that can be described by math and enforced by code....*
> *Anonymous digital cash, one of the key parts of Chaum's proposal, by itself has political significance in that it offers an alternative to government-backed currencies.*[8]
>
> - Arvind Narayanan, 2013.

It was this ideological movement of revolutionary technological elites that provided the fertile soil in which anonymous digital cash could take root and begin its process of development and evolution.[9]

---

[7] Hughes, Eric. "A Cypherpunk's Manifesto." 9 Mar. 1993.
[8] Narayanan, Arvind. "What Happened to the Crypto Dream?, Part 1." *IEEE Security & Privacy*, vol. 11, no. 2, 2013, pp. 75–76., doi:10.1109/msp.2013.45.
[9] Lopp, Jameson. "Bitcoin and the Rise of the Cypherpunks." *CoinDesk*, 9 Apr. 2016.

HashCash

The first seedling of this dream of decentralized money was "*hash cash postage implementation*", proposed by Dr. Adam Back in March 1997 to combat email spam.[10] The concept was that when sending an email, the sender could generate a special "stamp" onto the header of the email. The creation of this stamp required the computer to perform several calculations, expending a modest amount of CPU power (proof-of-work). The idea was that if everyone began to use the system by only opening "stamped" messages, spammer's work of sending millions of messages would not be cost-effective because of the needed computing power. Thus, the stamp was a sort of "cash" with which to pay for emails.

B-money

In November the next year, Wei Dai described a theoretical "*anonymous, distributed electronic cash system*" called B-money on the Cypherpunk's Mailing List:

> *I am fascinated by Tim May's crypto-anarchy [manifesto]. Unlike the communities traditionally associated with the word "anarchy", in a crypto-anarchy the government is not temporarily destroyed but permanently forbidden and permanently unnecessary. It's a community where the threat of violence is impotent because violence is impossible, and violence is impossible because its participants cannot be linked to their true names or physical locations. Until now it's not clear, even theoretically, how such a community could operate. A community is defined by the cooperation of its participants, and efficient cooperation requires a medium of exchange (money) and a way to enforce contracts. Traditionally these services have been provided by the government or govern-*

[10] Back, Adam. "[ANNOUNCE] Hash Cash Postage Implementation." *hashcash.org*, 28 Mar. 1997.

> *ment sponsored institutions and only to legal entities. In this article I describe a protocol by which these services can be provided to and by untraceable entities. ... ...*
> *The protocol proposed in this article allows untraceable pseudonymous entities to cooperate with each other more efficiently, by providing them with a medium of exchange and a method of enforcing contracts. The protocol can probably be made more efficient and secure, but I hope this is a step toward making crypto-anarchy a practical as well as theoretical possibility.*[11]
>
> - Wei Dai, 1 Nov. 1998.

Bit gold

The next innovations in this line came from Nick Szabo, a computer scientist-turned legal scholar who envisioned a future where legal systems and money could be replaced by code.

> *Szabo also realized that free enterprise needs more than just encryption as a security layer. Inspired by another libertarian author – economist Friedrich Hayek – he found that the basis of human society is, to a large extent, based on building blocks, like property and contracts, which are typically enforced by the state. To create a stateless, non-violent cyber alternative, Szabo knew that these building blocks had to be transferred to the online domain.*
> *This is how Szabo, by the mid 1990s, came to propose what he is perhaps best known for today: smart contracts. These (then-hypothetical) computer protocols could digitally facilitate, verify and enforce the negotiation or performance of a contract, ideally without the need of any third party. As Szabo had famously argued: "Trusted third parties are security holes." These security holes would be targets for hackers or criminals – as well as nation states during times of political instability or oppression.*
> *But smart contracts were only part of the puzzle. The second tool Szabo needed in order to realize his [mythical free-trade utopia] was possibly even more important. Money.*
> *... In his essay "Shelling Out: The Origins of Money," Szabo described how – as first hypothesized by evolutionary biologist Richard Dawkins – using money has been embedded in the very DNA*

[11] Dai, Wei. "b money." *Satoshi Nakamoto Institute*, 1 Nov. 1998.

of humans. Having analyzed pre-civilized societies, Szabo found that people across cultures tended to collect scarce, easy-to-carry objects, often to make jewellery out of them. It was these objects that served as money, which in turn allowed humans to cooperate: game theoretical "reciprocal altruism" through trade, at scale and across time.

Szabo also took a keen interest in free banking, a monetary arrangement advocated by Hayek, where private banks issue their own currency not bound to any particular state. Under such a system, it's completely up to the free market to choose which money to use. While a novel idea today (and even more so in the years before Bitcoin), free banking was a reality in the United States of the 1800s, as well as in several other countries.[12]

- Aaron Van Wirdum, 12 July 2018.

This is where Szabo's Bit gold comes in, an idea he first developed in 1998 but only publicized in 2005:[13]

A long time ago I hit upon the idea of bit gold. The problem, in a nutshell, is that our money currently depends on trust in a third party for its value. As many inflationary and hyperinflationary episodes during the 20th century demonstrated, this is not an ideal state of affairs. Similarly, private bank note issue, while it had various advantages as well as disadvantages, similarly depended on a trusted third party.

Precious metals and collectibles have an unforgeable scarcity due to the costliness of their creation. This once provided money the value of which was largely independent of any trusted third party. Precious metals have problems, however. It's too costly to assay metals repeatedly for common transactions. Thus a trusted third party (usually associated with a tax collector who accepted the coins as payment) was invoked to stamp a standard amount of the metal into a coin. Transporting large values of metal can be a rather insecure affair, as the British found when transporting gold across a U-boat infested Atlantic to Canada during World War I to support their gold standard. What's worse, you can't pay online with metal.

---

[12] Wirdum, Aaron Van. "The Genesis Files: With Bit Gold, Szabo was Inches Away from Inventing Bitcoin." *Bitcoin Magazine*, 12 July 2018.
[13] Szabo, Nick. "Bit Gold." *Satoshi Nakamoto Institute*, 29 Dec. 2005.

> *Thus, it would be very nice if there were a protocol whereby unforgeably costly bits could be created online with minimal dependence on trusted third parties, and then securely stored, transferred, and assayed with similar minimal trust. Bit gold. ...*
> *... In summary, all money mankind has ever used has been insecure in one way or another. This insecurity has been manifested in a wide variety of ways, from counterfeiting to theft, but the most pernicious of which has probably been inflation. Bit gold may provide us with a money of unprecedented security from these dangers. ...*[14]
>
> - Nick Szabo, 27 Dec. 2008.

The theoretical Bit gold functioned on "puzzles" which could be solved by computers, with the solution of each puzzle becoming part of the next to create an on-going chain. Though it was never implemented, Szabo made a blog post in 2008 suggesting that he would soon create live version of his concept[15].

Bitcoin

It began on October 31st, 2008. A link to a paper titled Bitcoin: A Peer-to-Peer Electronic Cash System was posted to the Cypherpunk's Mailing List. The author was listed as Satoshi Nakamoto. Not many people took notice.

> *Abstract.*
> *A purely peer-to-peer version of electronic cash would allow online payments to be sent directly from one party to another without going through a financial institution. Digital signatures provide part of the solution, but the main benefits are lost if a trusted third party is still required to prevent double-spending. We propose a solution to the double-spending problem using a peer-to-peer network. The network timestamps transactions by*

---

[14] Szabo, Nick. "An Unending Variety of Topics." *Unenumerated*, 27 Dec. 2008.

[15] Buterin, Vitalik. *"Global Bitcoin Stock Exchange Shuts Down for Good." Bitcoin Magazine*, 10 Oct. 2012.

hashing them into an ongoing chain of hash-based proof-of-work, forming a record that cannot be changed without redoing the proof-of-work. The longest chain not only serves as proof of the sequence of events witnessed, but proof that it came from the largest pool of CPU power. As long as a majority of CPU power is controlled by nodes that are not cooperating to attack the network, they'll generate the longest chain and outpace attackers. The network itself requires minimal structure. Messages are broadcast on a best effort basis, and nodes can leave and rejoin the network at will, accepting the longest proof-of-work chain as proof of what happened while they were gone.

1.0 Introduction

Commerce on the Internet has come to rely almost exclusively on financial institutions serving as trusted third parties to process electronic payments. While the system works well enough for most transactions, it still suffers from the inherent weaknesses of the trust based model. Completely non-reversible transactions are not really possible, since financial institutions cannot avoid mediating disputes. The cost of mediation increases transaction costs, limiting the minimum practical transaction size and cutting off the possibility for small casual transactions, and there is a broader cost in the loss of ability to make non-reversible payments for nonreversible services. With the possibility of reversal, the need for trust spreads. Merchants must be wary of their customers, hassling them for more information than they would otherwise need. A certain percentage of fraud is accepted as unavoidable. These costs and payment uncertainties can be avoided in person by using physical currency, but no mechanism exists to make payments over a communications channel without a trusted party.

What is needed is an electronic payment system based on cryptographic proof instead of trust, allowing any two willing parties to transact directly with each other without the need for a trusted third party. Transactions that are computationally impractical to reverse would protect sellers from fraud, and routine escrow mechanisms could easily be implemented to protect buyers. In this paper, we propose a solution to the double-spending problem using a peer-to-peer distributed timestamp server to generate computational proof of the chronological order of transactions.

The system is secure as long as honest nodes collectively control more CPU power than any cooperating group of attacker nodes.[16]
- Satoshi Nakamoto, 24 May 2009.

Bitcoin was launched on January 3rd, 2009 when Satoshi mined the Genesis Block. It contained an embedded text: "*The Times 03/Jan/2009 Chancellor on brink of second bailout for banks*" in reference to the day's headline in The Times, seemingly used as both a time-stamp and as a statement against both fractional-reserve banking and the printing of new money which he likely saw at the cause of the 2008 recession.

The first normal Bitcoin block was mined on January 9, 2009, six days after the Genesis Block was created. Block #2 followed a minute later, and Block #3 six minutes after that. The blockchain was born. Block #9 soon became the source of the of the first Bitcoin transaction: 10 BTC from Satoshi Nakamoto to Hal Finney, a cypherpunk who had taken an interest in Nakamoto's work. This is the only transaction that can be attributed to Satoshi. Satoshi is understood to have been the first miner, mining around one million bitcoins in 2009, largely alone.[17] [18] [19] [20] While there is no definitive proof of this, it is a reasonable assumption to make considering nobody else is known to have been involved at the time. A 2013 analysis by Sergio Lerner pegged Satoshi's fortune at 1,148,800 BTC,[21] and later work by BitMEX Research makes a very strong case that one dominant miner

---

16 Nakamoto, Satoshi. "Bitcoin: A Peer-to-Peer Electronic Cash System." 24 May 2009.
17 "Does Satoshi Have a Million Bitcoin?" *BitMEX Research*, 20 Aug. 2018.
18 Hamilton, David. "How Rich Is Satoshi Nakamoto Today?" *CoinCentral*, 7 July 2018.
19 Harper, Colin. "New Research Claims Satoshi Mined Far Fewer Bitcoins Than Previously Thought." *Bitcoin Magazine*, 23 Aug. 2018.
20 Fadilpašić, Sead. "How Many Bitcoins Does Satoshi Have?" *Cryptonews*, 22 Aug. 2018.
21 Lerner, Sergio. "The Well Deserved Fortune of Satoshi Nakamoto, Bitcoin Creator, Visionary and Genius." *Bitslog*, 17 Apr. 2012.

received 740,750 BTC between January and August of 2009.[22] The aspect that makes Satoshi particularly mysterious is the fact that the million or so coins attributed to him have never moved from their original wallets.[23]

It is irresistible to note a curious alignment. After he established the *Genesis* block, Satoshi took 6 days to mine the first block before *revealing himself* to prove his creation via block #9. The Book of Genesis (translated as "origin") is the first part of the Jewish Tanakh and Christian Old Testament and features the creation account where God creates the universe in six days and rests on the seventh. This place of creation, according to certain legends, takes place upon the Foundation Stone. It goes on to tell the story of Noah's ark, where Noah saves humanity and every animal from a catastrophic flood.

Genesis' 9th chapter then consists of God telling Noah's family to multiply and take charge of the entire world and then creating the rainbow as a promise to never again send a flood to destroy the world. Some people have speculated whether this might be intentional on Satoshi's part to suggest that he will never "flood the markets" with his coins. Perhaps there is an even deeper meaning at play, with Bitcoin intended to save those with open minds from some symbolic flood such as a financial collapse. Was Hal Finney chosen by Satoshi to complete his ark, recruit a *family of believers*, and spread it to the proverbial ends of the earth? Whatever the intent, the correlation seems far too convenient to have been a mere accident.

In the months that followed, Satoshi conversed regularly with several people involved in the project. Of these early disciples, Gavin Andresen emerged as the project lead. The early days (and later days) of Bitcoin consisted of notable amounts of drama, with core developers

---

22 "Does Satoshi Have a Million Bitcoin?" *BitMEX Research*, 20 Aug. 2018.
23 Hamilton, David. "How Rich Is Satoshi Nakamoto Today?" *CoinCentral*, 7 July 2018.

including Andresen, Peter Todd, Jeff Garzik, and Luke Dashjr grappling towards a rough consensus regarding the project's development.

Hal Finney announced in 2009 that he had been diagnosed with ALS, a degenerative disease that destroys the body while leaving the mind intact. Despite ongoing decline that left him in a wheelchair and unable to talk, he kept working on code for secure Bitcoin wallets for as long as he could.[24] Upon death, he was immediately cryogenically frozen by a stand-by team from the Alcor Life Extension Foundation, which uses liquid nitrogen to store deceased members at -196 Celsius in hopes that they can be revived through the help of advanced methods available in future decades or centuries.[25] Considering the possibility that Finney may have a *brain wallet* (a Bitcoin wallet existing as a memorized collection of words) with kingly amounts of BTC, his successful re-animation may carry serious incentives.

To better organize the Bitcoin project, Finnish computer scientist Martti Malmi founded the Bitcointalk.org forum in November 2009.[26] Here, discussion regarding the project could be archived and participants could interact with each other via pseudonyms. Bitcointalk became the center of not only the Bitcoin experiment, but a sort of public square for the entire blockchain phenomenon and its various offshoots which followed. This marked Bitcoin's spin-off from the Cypherpunk community into a complex and colorful phenomenon and culture of its own.

The earliest Bitcoiners were highly technical, with cryptography and technology as primary interests. As recounted by Gavin Andresen, the some of the first people to get involved were staunch libertarians who were distrustful of the US Federal Reserve. They were followed

---

[24] Finney, Hal. "Bitcoin and Me (Hal Finney)." *Bitcoin Forum*, 19 Mar. 2013.
[25] "Hal Finney Becomes Alcor's 128th Patient." *Alcor News*, 16 Dec. 2014.
[26] Malmi, Martti. "I'm Martti Malmi, Early Bitcoin Developer and the Original Founder of the Bitcointalk.org Forums, AMA!" *Bitcoin.com Forum*, 18 Nov. 2015.

by *gold bugs,* who were focused on investing in precious metals and saw Bitcoin as digital gold. Beginning in early 2013, there was growing interest from "*Silicon Valley venture capitalist folks who [saw] it less as internet currency that might replace fiat currency someday, and more as a low cost payment network.*"[27] With all these voices innovating towards different and even contradictory ends, Bitcoin's ethos, direction, and demographics entered a state of flux. This ongoing friction was not long concentrated under just the Bitcoin banner.

Some of these new participants in the Bitcoin economy soon separated the concept of Bitcoin into two parts; the monetary use of Bitcoin the cryptocurrency, and the base technology called Blockchain. The blockchain industry was born. It would turn out that Blockland had room for all these types and more.

The Nakamoto Identity

There is no consensus on Satoshi's real-world identity, and dozens of theories ranging from ridiculous to highly plausible have been put forth over the years. Nick Szabo[28], Wei Dai, and Hal Finney are considered by many to be prime suspects, though all have denied such assertions. Others consider that Bitcoin must have been created by a group of people or even a government. Many have looked for clues, including Satoshi's characteristic writing style of double-spaces after periods, textual analysis, his normal active hours between 5am and 11am GMT, his use of a British newspaper headline in the Genesis Block, and other circumstantial evidence. These serious speculations

---

[27] Bosker, Bianca. "Gavin Andresen, Bitcoin Architect: Meet the Man Bringing You Bitcoin (And Getting Paid in It)." *HuffPost India,* 16 Apr. 2013.
[28] Gilbert, David. "Who Is Satoshi Nakamoto? Bitcoin's Mysterious Creator Revealed as Nick Szabo." *International Business Times UK*, 1 July 2017.

have implicated all types of people including a Japanese mathematician,[29] a Finnish Economic Sociologist, an Irish grad student, an imprisoned Mexican drug-lord[30], the Silk Road founder, a former police investigator from Florida[31], and many others.

One of the first people to be declared as Bitcoin's creator was Dorian Prentice Satoshi Nakamoto, who used to live only minutes from Hal Finney and whose relatives described him as "*very focused and eclectic in his way of thinking. Smart, intelligent, mathematics, engineering, computers*" and mentioned that he had long worked with classified government projects. Even his ex-wife suggested he may have created Bitcoin after becoming frustrated with the inefficiency of wiring money internationally when buying model trains. He was tracked down by Newsweek reporter Leah McGrath Goodman, who found the police called on her after knocking on Nakamoto's door. The officers were incredulous, with one commenting that "*this is the guy who created Bitcoin? It looks like he's living a pretty humble life.*"[32] With two officers present, Nakamoto asserted that he was no longer involved and that he was not allowed to discuss it. At a later interview however, he clarified that he had confused Goodman's questions as pertaining to his unrelated classified government work, and that he had never been involved with or even heard of Bitcoin. Following the ordeal, Dorian Nakamoto has become somewhat of an unofficially revered symbolic representative of Satoshi in some Bitcoin art.

---

[29] Oremus, Ill. "Newsweek Thinks It Found the Real "Satoshi Nakamoto" … and His Name Is Satoshi Nakamoto." *Slate Magazine*, 6 Mar. 2014.
[30] Ratliff, Evan. "Was Bitcoin Created by This International Drug Dealer? Maybe!" *Wired*, 16 July 2019.
[31] Funcheon, Deirdra. "Riviera Beach Man Helped Invent Bitcoin." *New Times Broward-Palm Beach*, 9 Dec. 2015.
[32] Goodman, Leah McGrath. "The Face Behind Bitcoin." *Newsweek*, 3 June 2014.

Early Days

Early on, the only way to get BTC was through mining or by receiving it as a gift. In addition to the forum, the community developed according to a cryptography-based *Web-of-Trust* in which members would give trust to one another based on positive interactions. Many of these early cryptography geeks insisted on doing things according to an idealized *cryptographic way* which included communicating only via encrypted and digitally signed messages, even considering "non-verified" communications like unsecure email, social media, phone calls, or even in-person meetings to be wholly illegitimate. This Web of Trust became central to early Bitcoin trading, which often took place between individuals over IRC chat clients.[33] One account described mailing a personal cheque from the USA to Japan to pay for bitcoins. Eventually, early exchange markets were created.

The first time that the Bitcoin network was used to purchase any real good was on November 22nd, 2010 after Bitcointalk.org user Lazlo who was known for being an early GPU miner posted about his desire for pizza:

> *I'll pay 10,000 bitcoins for a couple of pizzas.. like maybe 2 large ones so I have some left over for the next day. I like having left over pizza to nibble on later. You can make the pizza yourself and bring it to my house or order it for me from a delivery place, but what I'm aiming for is getting food delivered in exchange for bitcoins where I don't have to order or prepare it myself, kind of like ordering a 'breakfast platter' at a hotel or something, they just bring you something to eat and you're happy!*[34]
>
> - Lazlo Hanyecz, 18 June 2010.

At the time, bitcoins were not recognized as having a legitimate or solid value. This is evidenced by user ender_x, who suggested that the

---

[33] Bertazzi, Ilaria, et al. "The Anatomy of a Web of Trust: the Bitcoin-OTC Market." *Lecture Notes in Computer Science, Springer*, 23 Oct. 2018.
[34] Hanyecz, Lazlo. "Pizza for Bitcoins?" *Bitcoin Forum*, 18 June 2010.

10,000 BTC could be sold for $41 on wordbitmarket.com but rather inconsistently then wished Lazlo "*good luck on getting your free pizza*" within the same comment. Someone named jercos took the offer and had two Papa John's pizza's delivered to Lazlo's home in Florida. Lazlo shared the pizzas with his 1-year old daughter and enjoyed them so much that he invited others to send him more Pizza for the same deal.

Two months later in July, it was apparent that a price of $0.06 per BTC had been established as one commenter inquired whether the offer was still valid considering 10,000 BTC was worth $600. To this Lazlo replied that "*I can't really afford to keep doing it since I can't generate thousands of coins a day anymore... Thanks to everyone who bought me pizza already but I'm kind of holding off on doing any more of these for now.*" In November, the legendary pizza's rose to $2,600 ($0.26 per BTC), and one user speculated whether one day it would become "*become the world's first million-dollar pizza?*" May 22nd became known as Pizza Day in Bitcoin legend; the day Bitcoin first demonstrated real-world utility.[35]

The Wikileaks Story

Bitcoin first entered the public sphere on December 10, 2010, when PC World asked "*Could the Wikileaks Scandal Lead to New Virtual Currency?*" Less than two weeks earlier, The Guardian, El País, Der Spiegel, Le Monde, and The New York Times had simultaneously published 220 of 251,287 confidential diplomatic cables provided by Wikileaks, originally leaked by Chelsea Manning who was later convicted under the Espionage Act. These documents contained explosive material relating to the United States' internal relations and ex-

[35] vlad230, Bitcointalk.org user. "Happy Bitcoin Pizza Day Everybody!" *Bitcoin Forum*, 22 May 2018.

ternal affairs, including unguarded comments about wars, spying, human rights, and foreign officials. Information that was strictly private and confidential was suddenly being read by foreign governments, enemy combatants, researchers, and curious high school students like myself. Considering Wikileaks a threat to national security, the US Department of Justice created a banking embargo to block donations coming in from around the world through Visa, Mastercard, Moneybookers, American Express, PayPal, and most banks.[36] Like Bitcoin, Wikileaks operated in a way that mixed both transparency and anonymity.

The PC World article observed that "*there's no single point of weakness. Nobody can stop the Bitcoin system or censor it, short of turning off the entire Internet. If Wikileaks had requested Bitcoins then they would have received their donations without a second thought.*" [37] It went on to suggest that businesses could potentially accept bitcoins, which were then $0.20 each and noted that "*purely as an intriguing idea that might indicate a possible future in an Internet heavily regulated by government, Bitcoins are worth taking a look at.*" This was the first time a legitimately influential publication mentioned Bitcoin, which at the time was so obscure that its Wikipedia page had recently been removed. While some were upset that Bitcoin was now associated with Wikileaks, Hal Finney said that "*on the bright side, if Bitcoin did get known as the Wikileaks currency, attacked by governments all over the world, at least we'd get our Wikipedia page back!*"[38], and Bitcointalk.org user RHorning encouraged the idea and effectively challenged the world governments to "bring it on" against Bitcoin:

[36] Ball, James. "The bankers' blockade of WikiLeaks must end." *The Guardian*, 24 Oct. 2011.
[37] Thomas, Kier. "Could the Wikileaks Scandal Lead to New Virtual Currency?" *PCWorld*, 10 Dec. 2010.
[38] Finney, Hal. "Wikileaks Contact Info?" *Bitcoin Forum*, 4 Dec. 2011.

For myself, I'm getting to the point to say "bring it on" in regards to Wikileaks. Note that I'm using my real name here instead of a psuedonym and I'm willing to personally say "bring it on" in terms of being associated with Bitcoins as a project. I've had police come into my house without my permission already and do all kind of stupid stuff, so for me that line being crossed has already happened. I am also connected to enough people politically that if something was to happen to me that it would be noted and things would happen too.
It is the morally correct thing to be supporting Wikileaks, and if they'll take a few of my bitcoins, I not only want to donate but to let the world know that they can donate to Wikileaks through Bitcoins as well.
I can't speak for everybody here in the Bitcoins community but I am speaking for myself on this matter, and I'm not afraid of anything that the U.S. government might do to me if I was associated with backing Wikileaks financially. If anything, it would show that I no longer live under a constitutional government any more. If the U.S. government wants to tip their hand to expose themselves in that way, so be it. If the U.S. government kills me or puts me in jail, I'll certainly set a way for this community to find out. I really don't think it would come to that either, but I don't care if it did.
The only possible concern I would have is over how sound the protocol itself is right now. If anything, a major flux of new people into Bitcoins would help there too, and the worst that could happen is that Bitcoins itself would be broken in some way where a new cryptocurrency would have to be created fixing the problems of Bitcoins. It is the idea of cryptocurrency that would then persist, and it is incredibly hard to censor an idea.
Basically, bring it on. Let's encourage Wikileaks to use Bitcoins and I'm willing to face any risk or fallout from that act.
Robert S. Horning, Logan, Utah[39]

- Robert S. Horning, 4 Dec. 2010.

[39] Horning, Robert S. "Re: Wikileaks Contact Info?" *Bitcoin Forum*, 4 Dec. 2010.

Satoshi disagreed with this sentiment.

> *No, don't "bring it on". The project needs to grow gradually so the software can be strengthened along the way. I make this appeal to WikiLeaks not to try to use Bitcoin. Bitcoin is a small beta community in its infancy. You would not stand to get more than pocket change, and the heat you would bring would likely destroy us at this stage.*[40]
>
> \- Satoshi Nakamoto, 5 Dec. 2010

As interest in the technology grew in the days that followed, Satoshi made his penultimate public post, saying that "*It would have been nice to get this attention in any other context. WikiLeaks has kicked the hornet's nest, and the swarm is headed towards us*".[41]

The next day, he was gone.

Years later, Wikileaks' founder Julian Assange revealed that he had read Satoshi's plea, and decided to wait until the technology was more mature six months later before accepting donations in it. That didn't stop Wikileaks from making a strategic investment into the currency. Writing from the Ecuadorian Embassy in London where he was holed up to avoid extradition to the United States, he later sarcastically thanked the US government for "*erecting an illegal banking blockade*" against Wikileaks and thus causing the non-profit to invest in Bitcoin for a 50,000 to % return. Mr. Assange has also said that "*Bitcoin is the real Occupy Wallstreet*"[42] in reference the 2008 protests, but he is a fan of blockchain for much more than its role as virtual currency. According to Assange:

---

40 Nakamoto, Satoshi. "Re: Wikileaks Contact Info?" *Bitcoin Forum*, 5 Dec. 2010.

41 Nakamoto, Satoshi. "Re: PC World Article on Bitcoin." *Bitcoin Forum*, 11 Dec. 2010.

42 Kollmeyer, Barbara. "WikiLeaks Founder Julian Assange: 'Bitcoin Is the Real Occupy Wall Street'." *MarketWatch*, 15 Dec. 2017.

> *Bitcoin is an extremely important innovation, but not in the way most people think. Bitcoin's real innovation is a globally verifiable proof publishing at a certain time. The whole system is built on that concept and many other systems can also be built on it. The block chain nails down history, breaking Orwell's dictum of 'He who controls the present controls the past and he who controls the past controls the future'.*[43]
>
> -Julian Assange, 15 Sept. 2014.

Austrian Roots

To comprehend the ideology of early cryptocurrency users, we must explore Austrian Economics, upon whose principles Bitcoin especially is based.

In short, the Austrian school supports free markets operating on sound money principles which historically consisted of the gold standard, an incorruptible and tangible value upon which all currency was pegged. Theoretically, the resulting lack of inflation supported the idea of long-term saving and the building of wealth. Many Austrians subscribe to a business cycle theory in which regular depressions naturally flush out inefficient businesses, strengthening the economic gene pool. If these cycles are not allowed to happen naturally, a much larger and more destructive crash becomes inevitable.[44]

This view lost popularity after the Great Depression, during which Keynesian economics proposed that governments should act as economic caretakers by regulating economic activity and bailing out businesses and individuals when they would otherwise struggle to survive hardship. As the lack of economic activity during the Great Depression was blamed on the "hoarding" as opposed to spending of gold,

---

[43] Kuhn, Daniel. "Assange: Bitcoin and WikiLeaks Helped Keep Each Other Alive." *CoinDesk*, 16 Sept. 2014.

[44] Ebeling, Richard. "Austrian Economics and Public Policy: Restoring Freedom and Prosperity." Fairfax, VA: The Future of Freedom Foundation. p. 217. 2016

the ownership of both gold and silver was effectively banned in the United States in 1933 with people and businesses required to deposit their precious metals into banks. The gold standard was entirely done away with in 1971, and Americans were only allowed to own physical gold from 1975 onwards. 1971 marked the beginning of the fiat age, with governments now able to "print" money at their discretion. This naturally laid the foundation for inflation and cheap debt, encouraging economic activity by way of consumption and discouraging saving.

It is important to understand that Austrian economic theory is effectively shunned as a pseudoscience by most modern economists. Despite and perhaps because of this, practically all early bitcoiners can be described as bearing loyalty or at least sympathy to the Austrian school as opposed to Keynesian economics, which they are likely to view as something akin to either misguided policy created to coddle the weak, or as an illuminati-type conspiracy to steal people's economic independence and freedom by making them consumers reliant on nurturing governments. The cyberlibertarian is thus likely to view fiat as a sickness, and Bitcoin as the *orange pill* that cures it.

This is a divider: some readers will enthusiastically take the side of the Austrians, whereas others of a more common disposition are likely to feel discomfort and suspicion at such ideals. This again demonstrates the point which differentiates Bitcoin from the average technological advancement in that it clearly came from outside of the establishment, a factor which explains the slow and cautious approach to the technology by mainstream entities. Bitcoin's origin is by all definitions countercultural and for many, revolutionary. For others, it presents an existential threat to the economic system that was established to maintain stability and peace after the carnage of the Great Depression and World Wars. Satoshi seemed to believe that the 2008 financial collapse was effectively caused by a failure of modern economics, proposing Bitcoin to replace a broken system. It is ironic that this modern economic system which he wanted to replace was itself a replacement to the gold standard, which in its time was similarly viewed as flawed due to its perceived role in the far worse collapse of the 1920's. Indeed, a mainstream economist might label the early Bitcoin proponents as a breed of neo-luddites who refused to let go of a system that had passed its prime a whole century ago.

With this context, it is easy to understand why the Bitcoin movement is so strongly associated with ideas like anarcho-capitalism, individualism, libertarianism, small-government, anti-regulation, negative liberty, tax resistance, and protest. Bitcoin is an experiment in Austrian economics and an open challenge to the world order.

From the perspective of the status quo, Bitcoin and blockchain are dangerous ideas and provide fertile breeding ground for challenge and subversion. But is it, as in the words of Victor Hugo, an idea whose time has come? In that case, it may be unstoppable, and it is best to take heed.

Two 1-gram silver coins minted in 2013 by settlers of Blockland, commemorating Pizza Day and The Genesis Block. Mintage: 500

Chinese gold miners during the California Gold Rush.

CHAPTER 2

The Prospectors

Imagine a desert island with 100 inhabitants. This island has a 'bank', and each islander relays messages to the various accountants throughout the day, consisting of things like "*Islander #056 sends 12.50 Island Bucks to Islander #004, [signed, Islander #56]*." At the end of each business day, the accountants reconcile all these letters while ensuring that they are all authentic and that no payments bounced. The accountants then race each other to the quarry (stone-mine), and one of them succeeds in hewing out a large stone block before the others. These accountant-miners then etch it with a record of every transaction that happened that day, along with each islander's end-of-day balance. The lucky accountant-miner that managed to beat the others in the mine that day gets a special honor: their name is added to the block, and their account is credited with 5,000 new Island Bucks created out of thin air. The other accountant-miners go home empty handed, except for small tips given to them by the islanders who wish to ensure that their payments are recorded that same day instead of delayed by up to several days as is sometimes the case.

The large stone block is then inscribed with the date, and it is cemented to the top of a massive pillar, known as The Pillar of True Accounts in the center of the village market in a 'confirmation ceremony' that all the accountant-miners attend. With each new business day, the cement hardens, and new blocks are placed on-top of the previous ones on the pillar. After five or six days, it becomes physically impossible to replace a block, even if all the accountant-miners conspired together. Any islander can become an accountant-miner, but the more accountant-miners there are, the less likely each one is to get paid on any given day. To make the profession more stable and less like a lottery, most accountant-miners have formed competing *pools* which share all the rewards they receive on any given day in order to get a smaller payout more often.

This is essentially what miners do and how Bitcoin works, with each *Bitcoin day* lasting about 10 minutes and being concluded with the finding of a *block*. Each block contains a Bitcoin *reward* which was initially 50 BTC, but the algorithm is designed in such a way that this number drops by half every 210,000 blocks. This happens approximately every four years and is known as a *halving*. These halving's can be thought of as historical eras within Bitcoin and are useful in placing events in relation to the protocol's age.[45] The implication of this continuous halving is that eventually, there will be nothing left to divide. Each bitcoin is divisible by one hundred million, with this smallest atom-like unit known as a Satoshi (0.00000001 BTC). The theoretical maximum number of bitcoins that can exist is 21,000,000. This means that upon the 33rd halving in the year 2140, 2099999.99769000 bitcoins will have been mined and the new block reward would be only a half of one Satoshi.[46]

---

[45] "Bitcoin Block Reward Halving Countdown." *bitcoinblockhalf.com*

[46] Dean, Colin. "When Will the Last Bitcoin Be Mined?" *Stack Exchange*, 2 May 2013.

While some consider this to be the apocalyptic end of Bitcoin, it is only the end of *mining rewards*, and the protocol could theoretically even be changed to allow for extra decimal places by which fractions of Satoshi's could be mined. Blocks could continue to be confirmed, with miners being rewarded with transaction fees only. Indeed, only 6.25% of bitcoins will remain by the 4th halving in 2024, and 99.9% of all BTC will have already been mined in 2048 with the remaining 0.1% taking an additional 90 years. This is the power of exponential decline and engineered scarcity.

Most every company, school, or other institution maintains a private set of servers which are used to store and process the information they possess. Websites you visit often rent server space to accommodate their users, and banks have massive supercomputers to securely (we hope) process every transaction. Not so with Bitcoin. At its core, Bitcoin uses a system called *proof-of-work* as a basis by which to distribute bitcoins. It is exactly what it sounds like; each bitcoin that exists is by virtue PROOF of the fact that WORK was done to create it. As Bitcoin allows users to *be your own bank*, it also allows them to operate the servers of that bank. Simply put, Bitcoin needs constant computing power to operate. On intervals of approximately 10 minutes, one of the computers powering Bitcoin is rewarded a block of BTC. When this happens, the other computers in the network (also mining Bitcoin) confirm that the BTC was found and in doing so arrive at a consensus of all the Bitcoin transactions done within that ~10-minute span.

It is not known if any significance can be ascribed to 21 as opposed to an even number like 20, 50, or 100, but one can attempt to grasp at straws by considering potential meanings that may have inspired Satoshi. For one it is an important element of the Fibonacci sequence of exponential growth and is also associated with gambling as per blackjack, and also bears some visual resemblance to the Mersenne prime number which is the maximum number that 32-

bit computers can process in certain circumstances. The 21-gun salute is seen as the highest honor, and age 21 can represent true adulthood or freedom in the United States considering the legal drinking age. The more far-fetched of associations might derive from religious numerology, though that too seems worthy of glance considering Satoshi's decision to use overt religious parallels such as in the naming of the Genesis Block. In such circles, 21 can be taken to represent rebellion as the sum of 13 (sinfulness) and 8 (a new beginning). It is also derived by multiplying 3 and 7, which are both seen to symbolize completeness, stability, and perfection. In the science fiction *Hichikers Guide To The Galaxy*, 42 is humorously presented as the answer to "*The Ultimate Question of Life, the Universe, and Everything*", a logic by which 21 would be half the answer. It is of course also possible that the number was simply convenient for the chosen mining algorithm or held personal meaning, and any associations are mere coincidence or otherwise magical thinking.

The Halvings

The First Halving

The first halving occurred when block #210,000 was mined on November 28th, 2012. The reward dropped from 50 BTC to 25 BTC, effectively cutting every miner's daily income by half. This block consisted of 457 transactions, the majority of which related to automated gambling on a game called SatoshiDICE. It was mined by LaughingBear, a member of SlushPool which was the first *mining pool* launched 2 years earlier in October 2010. Any Bitcoin miner could connect to SlushPool, with all participants in the pool sharing the mined BTC according to the computing power contributed by each member, minus a 2% administration fee. That means that the

25 BTC block reward was not received by any individual person or company but shared by thousands, making each mining pool a sort of *decentralized company* or collective whose shares were allocated according to (computing) work completed. 10,500,025 BTC had now been issued. At this point one bitcoin was worth $12.35 (already up from $2.55 12 months earlier), and began a major bull run six weeks later which cumulated at a peak of $230 about five months later in April 2013.

The Second Halving

The second halving took 3 years, 7 months, 11 days, 1 hour, 21 min, and 35 seconds later – on July 9th, 2016, when F2Pool mined Block #420,000 and the block reward dropped from 25 BTC to 12.5 BTC. Even at 12.5 BTC, the block reward stood at $8,125 which was nearly 27 times that of the reward in the 1st halving. The four-year growth of the Bitcoin network was clear, as every metric including the number of transactions and the value of transactions saw exponential growth. Perhaps most shocking was the 63,000-fold increase in hash-rate from 24,616 Giga-Hash per Second to 1,553,893,736 GH/s. This refers to is the total amount of computing power directed at mining. For reference a standard 2019 MacBook has a 1.3 GH/s processor, meaning that someone with the computing power of 200 MacBooks (say, the computing capacity of a well-equipped high school's computer lab) might mine 1% of all bitcoins in 2012 but be left with sub-1 BTC annual earnings four years later.

The hash-rate increase went hand-in-hand with the increase in *difficulty*, which is simply put the amount of computing required to mine a block. Difficulty gets automatically adjusted every two weeks according to the amount of hashing power dedicated to the network. Due to the increased hash-rate and resulting difficulty, virtually any machine mining Bitcoin in 2012 would be utterly useless in 2016 because their electricity consumption alone would far eclipse any BTC they might generate.[47] [48] [49] [50]

The Third Halving

Block 610,000 which heralded the Third Halving was mined by AntPool on May 11th, 2020 causing the block reward to further drop to 6.25 BTC which now accounted for $53,000. Despite the ever-decreasing number of bitcoins being mined, a macro-level comparison between halving's so far supports the long-held Bitcoin supply and demand thesis which asserts that as bitcoins become increasingly rare and difficult to obtain, their value will rise exponentially. And how much more difficult had Bitcoin mining become? About 120,553,893,736 GH/s – an 80-fold increase from 2016.[51]

A fascinating new aspect was that of Bitcoin *forks*, meaning versions of Bitcoin that had split off (with each of these splinters considering themselves the "legitimate Bitcoin." Since each of these new Bitcoin chains were separate and with slightly different technological specs which naturally influenced mining, they celebrated their "third halving" on somewhat different days. Bitcoin Cash (BCH)

---

[47] Quentson, Andrew. "The Bitcoin Community Celebrates the Second Halving." *CCN*, 9 July 2016.
[48] "Dissecting Bitcoin Block 420,000." *MineForeman*, 10 July 2016.
[49] Van Wirdum, Aaron. "How Bitcoin's Second Halving Came and Went, And Not Much Happened." *Bitcoin Magazine*, 18 July 2016.
[50] Tuwiner, Jordan. "What Is Hash Rate?" *Buy Bitcoin Worldwide*, 24 Apr. 2020.
[51] Redman, Jamie. "Bitcoin's Third Halving Complete: Reward Cut Surprisingly Faster Than Previous Time Estimates." *Bitcoin.com*, 11 May 2020.

halved on April 8th[52] with Bitcoin SV (BSV) following on the 10th.[53] As the combined market value of BCH and BSV was only a small fraction of BTC's market cap at the time of the halving's, the difficulty levels and dollar-denominated mining rewards were naturally much lower.

CPU Mining

The first miners used normal computers to run the network. Hal Finney began mining around block #50, doing so for a few days before stopping due to the heat and noise that it caused his computer to generate.[54] Throughout 2009, a CPU (Central Processing Unit) of a normal computer could mine hundreds of bitcoins per day. The first innovation in mining was the use of much faster GPU's (graphics cards), the optimization of which required customized software. Bitcointalk.org user ArtForz wrote such software for himself and became one of the first to mine with a GPU starting on July 18, 2010, after which he/she contributed up to ~25% of the whole network's computing power meaning that he/she received around 1,800 BTC per day.[55] This came as a shock to many people who considered ArtForz to have broken Bitcoin and there were instances of people losing their faith in the project due to this, at least temporarily. Weeks later, Bitcointalk.org user puddinpop developed GPU mining software for NIVIDIA (video card manufacturer) graphics cards, which was made open source on September

---

52 Avan-Nomayo, Osato. "Bitcoin Cash Halving Results in Miner Exodus and Profitability Decline." *CoinTelegraph*, 9 Apr. 2020.

53 Zhao, Wolfie. "Bitcoin SV's First Halving Crimps Profits for BSV Miners." *CoinDesk*, 10 Apr. 2020.

54 Nash, Gerald. "Beginnings of Bitcoin: The First 3000." *Crypto Currently*, 7 May 2018.

55 "ArtForz." *Bitcoin.it*. (Note: The source contains an uncited statement regarding 25% network share, which ArtForz acknowledges on a there-cited discussion about the statement. As such, it can be deduced as factual.)

18th after he/she agreed to accept a payment of 10,000 BTC (~ $625) from Jeff Garzik for doing so. Another open-source GPU miner called *the poclbm* (Python OpenCL bitcoin miner) came online only two weeks later, on October 1st, 2010. This is where mining started to take off.[56] [57] [58]

GPU Mining

While using a singular graphics card (GPU) in a gaming computer was all well and good, many people started tinkering. Hobbyists built *mining rigs* of varying sizes, using fans to cool large arrays of graphics chips in their basements and garages. These contraptions came in all shapes and sizes, using materials such as old vegetable crates and zip-ties to create shelving, mount the processors, and organize the wires. Some placed them outside to avoid the loud buzzing of fans and help the heat dissipate, while others allowed them to add heat to their homes in the winter. As these rigs were quite literally printing money by the hour, miners built larger and larger set-ups and sold off their old equipment for more powerful miners whenever they became available. As more GPU's were added, their power consumption increased to the point that it was impractical to run them in normal houses, leading the most ambitious miners to relocate their operations to rented industrial space which were also

[56] pdxdrumtech, Reddit.com user. "The Stories of Miners from 2012 and the Early Days of Bitcoin, Pulling out Hundreds of Coins off Their Home PCs and Then Suddenly Finding Themselves Millionaire by Becoming Accidental Long-Term Holding Investors Are All but Gone." *Reddit r/Bitcoin*, 7 Sept. 2018.

[57] blazing, Bitcointalk.org user. "The First Miners." *Bitcoin Forum*, 8 Aug. 2012.

[58] desired_username, Bitcointalk.org user. "History of Mining Hardware." *Bitcoin Forum*, 11 Oct. 2013.

much easier to cool and made noise a non-issue. This was the beginning of industrial mining farms.[59]

FPGA Mining

The next innovation in mining came in mid-2011 with the FPGA, which stands for Field Programmable Gate Array. FPGA's are made up of millions of programmable *logic gates* (which are the fundamental building blocks for digital circuits) and can therefore be programmed to do all kinds of calculations when these gates are combined. The first known open-source software to allow for FPGA mining was released on GitHub by Bitcointalk.org user fpgminer on May 20, 2011, which allowed existing FPGA chips to mine at rates between 100 and 400 MH/s.[60] Interestingly, while one of these cards were capable of mining at 109 MH/s, fpgminer's software only allowed for 50 MH/s because he feared that users would run the code without installing proper cooling fans resulting in their chips being destroyed from overheating.[61] A few companies positioned themselves as leaders in the mining field; one of these was Butterfly Labs which sold a 830 MH/s FPGA miner for $599.[62] [63] [64]

---

[59] Moore, Chris. "When was the first GPU miner made available publicly?" *Stack Exchange*, 5 May 2012.
[60] Fpgaminer, Bitcointalk.org user. "The Open Source FPGA Bitcoin Miner." *Bitcoin Forum*, 20 May 2011.
[61] Ltcmaxmyr, Bitcointalk.org user. "The Risk of FPGA Mining." *Bitcoin Forum*, 8 June 2018.
[62] Taylor, Michael Bedford, University of Washington "The Evolution of Bitcoin
Hardware." IEEE *Cloud Computing*, Sept. 2017.
[63] Greene, Tristan. "A Brief History of Bitcoin Mining Hardware." *The Next Web*, 2 Feb. 2018.
[64] "FPGA Mining Overview." *Zetheron Technology*.

1st Generation: ASIC Emergence

ASIC (application-specific integrated circuit) chips are computer chips designed to serve a specific function, which meant that they were made to be extremely efficient at mining Bitcoin. Development costs for ASIC chips were several hundred thousand dollars, and ASIC's were the natural next step in Bitcoin mining. Three companies raced to take over the market, and miners knew that ASIC's would dominate the industry. Some bet on one of these companies, while others ordered from all three.

Kansas-based Butterfly Labs was the first to announce ASICs in June 2012, using a marketing campaign to get between $20 millio and $50 million in pre-orders from around 20,000 people for three types of machines for a November delivery. These consisted of a small $149 "Jalapeno" mining at 4.5 GH/s, a normal sized $1,299 60 GH/s miner, and a $28,999 "Mini Rig" reportedly capable of 1,500 GH/s. At these prices, BFL miners offered 20x-50x more mining capacity per dollar compared to GPU's.

Unfortunately for those who spent 5,000 BTC per mini-rig, orders did not start getting filled until April 2013, by which time they were obsolete and useful as nothing but loud and power-hungry space-heaters.[65] As BFL attended the 2013 Consumer Electronics Show in Las Vegas a few months earlier in January 2013, Bryan Micon, a professional poker player who worked for a Bitcoin poker website approached them with a camera and asked CEO Josh Zerlan to explain what the box they were displaying was, to which he replied:

> *I can't understand you over your f*cking stupidity. I'm going to give you a quarter, I want you to go around these booths, and purchase a clue, and then maybe you can come here and talk to me and then I might care. So here's a quarter for you and*

[65] Bradbury, Danny. "Butterfly Labs Ships Long-awaited ASIC Bitcoin Miners." *CoinDesk*, 20 May 2013.

> *that might actually buy you a clue, and you can come back here.*[66]
>
> -Josh Zerlan, 10 Jan. 2013.

It turned out that this box was only for display and had no chips inside. He also described his interactions with the company the previous day:

> *I was very excited to see BFL equipment on display and I planned on asking some extremely nerdy questions about how the hardware will solve the proof-of-work problem much, much faster than current equipment. I also wanted to understand the metrics of what ASIC will do to the network hash rate, as I understand mining conceptually but not technically... I then asked when they would ship ASICs, he said "in a couple of weeks,"... I asked him when filled with ASICs how fast this machine would hash at. He said something like 1+ T-hashes per second. I.e. 1000 ghashes/s... it looks like the current total bitcoin network hashrate is around 20-25 Thash/s - which means that if Dave was right, just one of these boxes could have ~ 6% of total current network hashing power. I was surprised he had never run the math before. . .*[67]
>
> - Bryan Micon, 14 Jan. 2013.

Perhaps reasonably at this point, many did not believe any miners existed at all. When some miners started shipping, some of the people receiving them were even accused of being paid to spread propaganda on behalf of BFL. Things came to a close in September 2013, when the US Federal Trade Commission shut down the company amid numerous complaints.[68] It even turned out that the

---

[66] Micon, Bryan. "Bryan Micon Sneaks into CES 2013 to Interview Bitcoin Butterfly Labs & Bitpay & Josh Zerlan Tilts." *YouTube*, 10 Jan. 2013.
[67] Micon, Bryan. "Bryan Micon's Butterfly Labs Scammer Investigation Including Josh Zerlan." *Bitcoin Forum*, 14 Jan. 2013.
[68] Jeffries, Adrianne. "FTC Shuts down Butterfly Labs, the Second-most Hated Company in Bitcoinland." *The Verge*, 23 Sept. 2014.

company's largest shareholder and co-founder Sonny Vleisides had pled guilty to a count of mail fraud in 2010 in which victims lost over $25 million in a lottery scam according to the US Postal Inspection Service.[69]

The Beijing-based Avalon was the first to actually deliver an ASIC, which was received on January 30, 2013 by Bitcoin developer Jeff Garzik. In the ten days between the announcement that the first miner (of 300 in the first batch) had shipped and Mr. Garzik confirming receipt, the Bitcointalk.org forum filled with about 900 posts from people speculating whether the machines really worked or existed at all. About a week after shipment with no word on the miner's status, a user named crazy_rabbit made a particularly interesting speculation:

> *It would be an interesting (if not disappointing) revelation if it turns out that the Chinese government does indeed understand bitcoin and ASIC mining and decides that ASICS are prohibited for export. If you think about it- at this point of time unique possession of ASIC's and thus the lions share of HASH power for a cryptographic financial system, would indeed constitute a type of national security- if not national resource. I think any government official aware of Bitcoin would come to this conclusion quite quickly. It's certainly in the Chinese interest to have Chinese citizens try and acquire as many bitcoins as possible.*[70]
>
> - Forum user crazy_rabbit, 27 Jan. 2013.

The ASIC did arrive, and Mr. Garzik's new miner produced 15 BTC in its first day and paid for itself in less than two weeks.[71] The

[69] Farivar, Cyrus. "Digging for Answers: The "Strong Smell" of Fraud from One Bitcoin Miner Maker." *Ars Technica*, 8 May 2017.
[70] crazy_rabbit, Bitcointalk.org user. "[Announcement] Avalon ASIC Batch #1 Ships." *Bitcoin Forum*, 27 Jan. 2013.
[71] Garzik, Jeff. "Once upon a Time in China, a Package Shipped." *Random Blatherings by Jeff*, 30 Jan. 2013.

company went on to sell new batches of 600 rigs in February and March at increasing price points.

The third company was ASICMiner, also based in China. They announced their plans the month after BFL and raised about $160,000 by selling "shares" on the Bitcointalk.org forum and GLBSE, which was an online market for shares denominated in BTC. Their initial plan was not to move the ASIC miners from China at all, instead housing them in a facility that would generate BTC on behalf of shareholders. They however opted to sell the machines directly and had the first batch ready on January 31st, just a day after the first Avalon was received.[72] Buyers of their first batch of 800 miners started receiving them 2 weeks later.[73] Perhaps ASIC-Miner's most memorable product was a small USB-stick-like ASIC called a "Block Erupter", which were sold in bulk for 2 BTC and was a great way for newbies to start learning about mining.

2nd Generation: ASIC War

With ASICs proven viable, venture capital money stepped in and founded dozens of new ASIC producers. The bar to meet was now more than simply having a real product; the miner had to be better than the competition which consisted of up to 40 companies. This was arguably the point where Bitcoin mining lost its innocence as the nerdy hobby and became a highly competitive capitalist venture. BitFury released a miner using 55-nano-meter chips (more compact meaning more efficient) in the summer of 2013, while KnCMiner managed to bring a 28nm chip to market in October. These new machines were much faster and more energy efficient

---

[72] Friedcat, Bitcointalk.org user. "ASICMINER: Entering the Future of ASIC Mining by Inventing It." *Bitcoin Forum*. 9 Aug. 2012.
[73] BitSyncom, Bitcointalk.org user. "[Announcement] Avalon ASIC Batch #1 Ships." *Bitcoin Forum*, 2013.

than the previous ones, and 1st generation machines where wholly useless after a short life of only a few months. By December, 22nm chips were likely produced by 21 Inc. This era was also the beginning of massive mining operations being built in locales with low power costs.

1-oz and 1-gram silver coins from 2014, minted by a mining pool and featuring mining rigs. Mintage: 500 & 1,000

Captain Kidd, whose legendary pirate treasure has eluded hunters since the 1600's.

CHAPTER 3

Bitcoin's Coming of Age

The Arrest

A hammer falls to signal the conclusion of a bizarre 12-hour auction. The United States Marshal Service has just sold 30,000 bitcoins worth around $18 million to venture capitalist Tim Draper.[74] More auctions follow, until the federal agency has sold off its 144,000 BTC to various Americans. How did we get here?

Allow us to rewind 10 months to October 1st, 2013. 29-year-old Ross Ulbricht follows his daily routine as he arrives at San Francisco's Glen Park Library to work on his Bitcoin start-up. It is a normal day, as much as any day is normal for the technologically brilliant and deeply ideological Ulbricht who he sips on his tea while responding to tech support tickets for his burgeoning online sales platform under the pseudonym Dread Pirate Roberts. The afternoon sets in, and the library begins to empty. Ulbricht stays

---

[74] Chavez-Dreyfuss, Gertrude. "Venture Capitalist Draper Wins U.S. Bitcoin Auction." *Reuters*, 2 July 2014.

behind to work but becomes distracted by a couple arguing nearby. Just then, he is suddenly grabbed from behind, and a man reaches for his computer from behind a bookshelf and plugs in a specially programmed USB key.[75]

Unfortunately for Ross, these aggressive intruders are not local hoodlums. They are the FBI, and he is charged with a slew of narcotics offenses and with hiring a hitman in connection with his website, Silk Road. As one might guess, this *Silk Road* has nothing to do with fine textiles, teas, and exotic spices as we might associate with the term. Ulbricht's Silk Road was an anonymous marketplace primarily for spices of the forbidden variety.[76]

Silk Road & Mt.Gox

Silk Road is where Bitcoin came of age, its troubled high school days so to say. To understand Silk Road, one must understand the Dark Web. To do this, we can imagine the internet as an iceberg. The visible *surface web* consisting of all public content such as news reports, websites of organizations, and open-source pages like Wikipedia. Below the surface is the *deep web,* which anyone can access provided they have the right expertise in diving (the correct passwords, that is). As with icebergs where only the tip is visible above water, most of the internet's data is in the non-public portion below the surface.[77]

However, there is an even darker, deeper level at the so-called underbelly of the internet iceberg; it is the *dark web,* where the sun

---

[75] Bertrand, Natasha. "The FBI Staged A Lovers' Fight to Catch the Kingpin of the Web's Biggest Illegal Drug Marketplace." *Business Insider*, 22 Jan. 2015.

[76] xtraelv, Bitcointalk.org user. "Silk Road and Bitcointalk. How It Played a Role in Its Rise and Fall." *Bitcoin Forum*, 8 June 2018.

[77] Grannan, Cydney. "What's the Difference Between the Deep Web and the Dark Web?" *Encyclopaedia Britannica*.

does not shine and a complex submarine (special software, passwords, and even referrals) are required to explore it. It is far from Google's reach, and to get here one needs to use *The Onion Router* or *Tor*, to mask themselves behind several encrypting, anonymizing, and track-covering layers. There are neither faces nor names in the Dark Web, and like the Mos Eisley cantina, you will never find a more wretched hive of scum and villainy.

What you will find is Bitcoin; this is where it first took hold. Its childhood home where it grew up.

Suddenly, the deepest and darkest recesses of the internet lit up with life, as actors on the highly anonymous network realized they could now send and receive value without any connection to "real life" institutions, groups, or websites that could potentially expose them. As masked outlaws could anonymously buy and sell online without knowing each other or fearing detection or tracking, the dark web experienced a golden age as a lawless, decentralized, international capital of crime.

A stroll through this forbidden city was eye-opening. Any amount of any drug, from a gram of marijuana to a kilogram brick of pure Colombian coke could be purchased anonymously and shipped internationally. It didn't stop at drugs; one could buy almost any weapon from swiss army knives to RPG's or outsource dirty work to one of the several purported hitmen who advertised their regional assassination services starting from $10,000. If assassination was too much on the pocketbook or conscience, one could have their enemies *swatted* – anonymous callers tricking heavily armed police to break down their door, for under $100.[78]

---

[78] McMillan, Robert. "An Extortionist Has Been Making Life Hell for Bitcoin's Earliest Adopters." *Wired*, 29 Dec. 2014.

It wasn't all gang-land stuff either, there were plenty of white-collar criminals too. Aspiring hackers and identity thieves could purchase data-dumps of personal and credit card information, bank and PayPal logins – even email and social media logins – all collected by more advanced hackers selling them in bulk. Those wishing to start stealing credit card info themselves could purchase carding machines. Corrupt accountants would even sell insider information about publicly traded companies.

The dark web was more than a marketplace. Forums for information on malicious hacking, civil disobedience, survival, bomb making, and even terrorism thrived. It was not lost on anyone that with this new technology and suite of dark web services, anyone could financially support any extremist movement in complete anonymity and that group could then order any number of weapons to practically any city in the world. This is not to say that everything on the Dark Web was de facto criminal. The markets and forums also contained completely innocuous goods and content, placed there by and for people who desired privacy as a matter of principle. Arguably "good" dark web services involved secure and anonymous ways of communicating with reporters by people fearing tracking, or interference by malicious agents.[79]

All of this created a rather predictable problem; that of honesty and reliability. Turns out when an aspiring drug dealer invests his life savings into a bulk order that never arrives, they cannot exactly get the money back from the untraceable wholesaler who has long since evaporated. They can't even shoot them like in the real world, where the drug trade is the predominant cause of gun violence in

[79] Dredge, Stuart. "What is Tor? A beginner's guide to the privacy tool." *The Guardian*, 5 November 2013.

the United States.[80] This is where teppy, the operator of an early Bitcoin gambling game called Dragon's Tale, stepped in with an idea:

> *As a Libertarian, the thing I love most about the Bitcoin project is the chance that it could be truly disruptive.*
> *I think that drug prohibition is one of the most socially harmful things that the US has ever done, and so I would like to do a thought experiment about how a heroin store might operate, accepting Bitcoins, and ending drug prohibition in the process. We'll assume that the drug store is very high profile, and that law enforcement makes discovering the operator a high priority. We'll also assume that heroin is cheap when bought in bulk; the street price reflects the risk that street dealers must take to sell their product.*
> *A drug dealer would set up a website that accepts Bitcoins for heroin. Orders would require a physical address for shipping. When an order comes in, the dealer would send heroin through the mail to two addresses: the address provided, and another random address. Because packages of heroin are now arriving at addresses across the country, receiving a package does not imply that you ordered it. Random addresses would be heavily reused to prevent law enforcement from making a statistical argument.*[81]
>
> - Forum user teppy, 9 June 2010.

It was probably this theoretical post not three weeks after Pizza Day that inspired Ross Ulbricht, then known as Dread Pirate Roberts, to launch Silk Road anonymous marketplace eight months later in February 2011.[82] Here, anyone could buy and sell almost anything. The key to Silk Road's success was user ratings and an escrow function. Prospective buyers could be reasonably certain that they

---

80 Miron, Jeffrey A. "Violence, Guns, and Drugs: A Cross-Country Analysis." *The Journal of Law and Economics*, vol. 44, no. S2, 2001, pp. 615–633., doi:10.1086/340507.
81 teppy, Bitcointalk.org user. "A Heroin Store." *Bitcoin Forum*, 9 June 2010.
82 Silkroad, Bitcointalk.org user. "Silk Road: Anonymous Marketplace. Feedback Requested :)." *Bitcoin Forum*, 1 Mar. 2011.

would receive the amount and purity of whatever they ordered if a seller had made thousands of transactions with glowing reviews and 5-star ratings Once a purchase was initiated, the escrow system provided another layer of protection. The buyer would send the BTC to Silk Road instead of the seller directly, with the system later releasing funds to the seller unless the buyer raised a dispute in which case an administrator would make a judgment, often splitting the funds 50/50. For this, the Silk Road took a percentage of all sales.[83] As found by a 2015 Australian study, Silk Road was more than just a drug store, but a sort of political and philosophical incubator:

> *Silk Road was not just a market for trading drugs: it facilitated a shared experience of personal freedom within a libertarian philosophical framework, where open discussions about stigmatized behaviours were encouraged and supported. Tensions between public activism against drug prohibition and the need to hide one's identity as a drug user from public scrutiny were partially resolved through community actions that internalized these politics...*[84]
>
> - Alexia Maddox et al, 2015.

The site grew fast, eventually consisting of more than 10,000 listings consisting mostly of controlled substances. The number of registrations had to be restricted due to a lack of server capacity, and people began selling logins over the Bitcointalk.org forum to those lacking the connections to get one by other means. To the first of these account sellers in June 2011, user zhalox commented that "*You are either a government agent, or a government agent will buy it from you. I hate to see Bitcoin's reputation being tarnished by*

[83] Bearman, Joshua. "The Rise and Fall of Silk Road." *Wired*, May 2015.
[84] Maddox, Alexia, et al. "Constructive Activism in the Dark Web: Cryptomarkets and Illicit Drugs in the Digital 'Demimonde'." *Information, Communication & Society*, vol. 19, no. 1, 2015, pp. 111–126., doi:10.1080/1369118x.2015.1093531.

illegal activities..."[85] That same day, US Senators Charles Schumer and Joe Manchin wrote the Attorney General and the Drug Enforcement Agency (DEA) urging them to take action against Silk Road:

> *The only method of payment for these illegal purchases is an untraceable peer-to-peer currency known as Bitcoins. After purchasing Bitcoins through an exchange, a user can create an account on Silk Road and start purchasing illegal drugs from individuals around the world and have them delivered to their homes within days... We urge you to take immediate action and shut down the Silk Road network.*[86]
>
> - Senators Schumer and Manchin, 6 June 2011.

So began a bizarre manhunt involving the DEA, FBI, DHS, The US Marshals Service, Secret Service, and according to Edward Snowden, the NSA.[87] This investigation was by no means straightforward; with many of the agencies butting heads, undermining each other, and more than one of the agents going rogue.

One rogue agent who might seem more at home in an action movie than reality was Carl Mark Force IV, who arrested Silk Road's senior administrator Curtis Green. He then used Green's account to drain Silk Road escrow wallets of BTC for his own use, essentially robbing Dread Pirate Roberts. This led to DPR believing that Green had become a police informant and stolen the money from him. Agent Force then posed as a hitman, and allegedly accepted money from DPR to kill Green. Green's murder was faked by Agent Force, who later alternated between blackmailing DPR and selling him secret information about the investigation into him. He

---

[85] zhalox, Bitcointalk.org user. "Silk Road Account!" *Bitcoin Forum*, 8 June 2011.
[86] Wolf, Brett. "Senators Seek Crackdown on 'Bitcoin' Currency." *Reuters*, 8 June 2011.
[87] Biddle, Sam. "The NSA Worked to Track Down Bitcoin Users Snowden Documents Reveal." *The Intercept*, 20 Mar. 2018.

then sent these doubly dirty bitcoins into his personal exchange accounts and tried to convert them into fiat via BitStamp and Venmo, which froze his accounts due to what they considered suspicious activity. Force responded by sending them an unauthorized "administrative subpoena" from the DEA to force them to co-operate. In the end, Force was sentenced to 6.5 years in prison for obstruction of justice, money laundering, and extortion under color of official right.[88] [89]

Despite the bumbling and embarrassment, the agencies eventually closed in on several potential targets they suspected of being the Dread Pirate. One of these investigations was headed by Homeland Security Investigations agent Jared Der-Yeghiayan, who had also worked undercover as a Silk Road Moderator. From May to August, his prime suspect for Dread Pirate Roberts was Mark Karpelès, the CEO of Mt.Gox, the largest Bitcoin exchange which processed 76% of all Bitcoin trades.[90]

The story of Mt.Gox starts in 2006, years before Bitcoin, when Jed McCaleb built a website for trading virtual playing cards related to the Magic: The Gathering Online computer game. This website served as a marketplace, where users could buy and sell the collectible cards related to the game as if they were stocks. The *Magic: The Gathering Online eXchange* operated for about three months before McCaleb moved on to other things. On July 18, 2010, a few days after reading about Bitcoin and re-purposing the old website, McCaleb launched the first centralized marketplace where bitcoins

---

[88] Jeong, Sarah. "Criminal Charges Against Agents Reveal Staggering Corruption in the Silk Road Investigation." *Forbes*, 31 Mar. 2015.
[89] Jeong, Sarah. "DEA Agent Who Faked a Murder and Took Bitcoins from Silk Road Explains Himself." *Vice*, 21 Oct. 2015.
[90] Redman, Jamie. "Film Reveals Never-Before-Seen Information About the Silk Road Case." *Bitcoin.com*, 30 Nov. 2019.

could be traded for regular currencies and vice-versa. This established a trackable price for Bitcoin, which hovered between $0.05 and $1.19 (per 100 million satoshi's) over the first eight months of operation.[91]

In March 2011, McCaleb announced that "*to really make mtgox what it has the potential to be would require more time than I have right now. So I've decided to pass the torch to someone better able to take the site to the next level.*"[92] This someone was Mark Karpelès, a French developer living in Japan. Only 3 months later, on June 19th, the price of Bitcoin fell from $13.60 to $0.01, less than two weeks after experiencing a peak of $29.60. This lasted only minutes, having been caused by a hacker who gained access into the Mt.Gox platform and flooded the market with bitcoins. To prove that Mt.Gox remained in control of its user's BTC, it announced that it would be moving 442,000 bitcoins, then worth about $6,000,000.[93] This transaction was done on Block 132749, which fell on June 23rd and was perhaps the first *Proof of Keys* event where an exchange openly demonstrates their holdings. Owing to the public nature of all Bitcoin transactions / transfers, this was akin to a state treasury parading its gold reserves on a public street, or perhaps less dramatically, releasing an independent audit.

If you are new to blockchain, you may have wondered as to the meaning of "*on Block 132749, which fell on June 23d.*" The explanation for this is simple yet deep, for it demonstrates how blockchain has within itself its very own concept of time that is only tangentially related to that of the so-called real world. Just as the base-

---

[91] "2014 Jed McCaleb MtGox Interview" *Gwern.net*, 16 Feb. 2014.
[92] Sedgwick, Kai. "Bitcoin History Part 9: Mt. Gox Is Born." *Bitcoin.com*, 26 Jan. 2019.
[93] Sedgwick, Kai. "From Single Key to Sophisticated Computation: The Evolution of Crypto Exchange Custody." *Bitcoin.com*, 28 Feb. 2020.

level going-ons of the "real-world" could be described as the ongoing interactions of matter and our history a record of its consequences, the blockchain-world is described as the ongoing re-distribution of data and a constant re-conciliation of that data by a network of processors. This means that if all computers were to cease running the protocol, they could theoretically start again any number of years in the future as if nothing had happened (just the same, how could we ever know if something caused our universe to temporarily pause and start again?). While the year in which some event happened in our world is calculated by the number of revolutions made around the sun by that same world, in the blockchain world it is calculated according to the frequency with which computers solve math problems and agree to the results. Each consecutive block forms an unbroken chain to the Genesis Block, and transactions with their relevant data are inscribed inside the block as they occurred or more accurately, the block they consisted of.

Before our world was as interconnected as it is today, one could argue that many independent "worlds" existed at different places at the same time. Between these, communications and interactions were only occasional as opposed to synergetic. Dedicated calendars have historically unified such "worlds" and insulated them from others, while being based on something seen to underpin their very essence. Examples of course include the Christian calendar counting from the birth of Christ, the Buddhist calendar from the year Buddha attained Parinibbāna, the Islamic calendar from the year Muhammad established the first Muslim community, and the Hebrew calendar from the very day of creation as told in the Book of Genesis from which Bitcoin's Genesis Block got its name. Surely, this could be a premise for a most interesting work of ~~science~~ blockchain fiction.

Mt.Gox encountered the beginning of new issues in February 2012, when one of its primary payment processers Dwolla cancelled deposits destined to Mt.Gox users due to changes in anti-money laundering requirements.[94] In the following month, the March 2012 Bitcoin fork caused Mt.Gox to temporarily restrict all Bitcoin deposits. This caused a market panic, sending prices down 23% from $48 to $37 and back again in a matter of hours. After prices increased to $230 on April 9th, Mt.Gox took the unprecedented step of halting trading for about a day in order to promote a market cooldown. This is understood to have played a part in the subsequent crash to prices as low as $55.59 in the following days.[95]

Perhaps most interesting here is that an exchange trading an unregulated asset took the self-directed step of attempting to control markets, particularly when they were rising instead of falling. This sort of action has a long history in traditional stock markets, taking the form of regulatory and non-regulatory trading halts. While various regulations demand temporary trading halts for various reasons, many exchanges around the world enforce their own rules pertaining to the stoppage/halting of trading individual securities or the markets entirely if they are abnormally volatile. For example, while the New York Stock Exchange halts trading in varying ways if the S&P 500 index drops by 7%, 13%, or 20% in any given day, it has no prescribed trading halts for market-wide growth. Mt.Gox's market-cooling action could be interpreted as an act of long-term self-interest to slow the uncontrolled growth of or even pop the developing bubble, preventing even greater levels of headline-inducing volatility that might jeopardize the ongoing adoption of Bitcoin. The action could also be seen as a selfless act in forgoing what were

[94] Dillet, Romain. "Feds Seize Assets from Mt. Gox's Dwolla Account, Accuse It of Violating Money Transfer Regulations." *Tech Crunch*, 16 May 2013.
[95] Boesler, Matthew. "Bitcoin Instantly Plunges 35% As Exchange Reopens." *Business Insider*, 12 Apr. 2013.

likely record-profits to act as a sort of a father figure to a new industry experiencing growth spurts and the associated growing pains.

Considering that Mt.Gox processed around 76% of all Bitcoin trading at this time, there was simply no other entity that could fill the role of the shepherd. This certainly echoes many voices within the community both then and now; calls for the blockchain ecosystem to acknowledge its place as perhaps beyond the reach of traditional regulation while filling this gap of chaos with some semblances of order through self-regulation within the industry and community. In the absence of clear rules from external sources nor the continued guidance of Satoshi Nakamoto, it was the key players in the industry who were called to steer it. In retrospect it is interesting to consider whether BTC at this time constituted or behaved more as an individual and unique asset, or rather an entire market in which it happened to be the first and at the time sole member.

Only three weeks later, on May 2nd, Mt.Gox saw its first serious lawsuit to the tune of $75 million when a failed partnership with Seattle-based CoinLab went awry. The partnership was intended to better connect Mt.Gox to the North American market, but Mt.Gox allegedly failed to transition its North American customers to CoinLab's control as per the agreement.[96]

More struggles hit two weeks later, when the company's US subsidiary faced asset seizures based on a warrant issued by the DHS. This was due to allegations by the US Immigration and Customs Enforcement (ICE) that the company had been operating as an unregistered money transmitter in the United States without a license from the US Financial Crimes Enforcement Network (FinCEN).[97]

---

[96] Chen, Adrian. "Massive Bitcoin Business Partnership Devolves Into $75 Million Lawsuit." *Web.archive*, 5 Feb. 2013.
[97] Kirk, Jeremy. "Mt. Gox Accused of Violating US Money Transfer Regulations." *IT World*, 15 May 2013.

These seizures continued for three months and amounted to over $5 million and were instigated by a different branch of Der-Yeghiayan's agency. Der-Yeghiayan was upset by this side-stepping, and reportedly asked the agents meeting with Karpelès' lawyers regarding the accusations of illegal money transmitting not to mention Silk Road in any way as to avoid impeding his own investigation. According to a Forbes court reporter, it was Karpelès' lawyers that brought up Silk Road themselves; suggesting "*that Mark Karpeles was willing to give up DPR if he 'could get a walk on his charges.'*"[98]

Funnily enough, Mt.Gox received its money services business (MSB) license from FinCEN a few weeks later, as was reported by *Bitcoin Magazine* in *Mt.Gox Gets FinCEN MSB License.*[99] This article was written by the 19-year-old University of Waterloo freshman Vitalik Buterin who would go on to release the whitepaper for Ethereum, a major cryptocurrency, only months later.

Despite the MSB License, withdrawals kept lagging and customers began seriously questioning the exchange's liquidity as a public thread of complaints numbered in the thousands.[100] It seemed that nothing short of divine intervention could save the exchange. Just then, Jesus stepped in to offer a hand. The man in question was Roger Ver, dubbed "Bitcoin Jesus" for being the first person to invest in any Bitcoin start-up, Charlie Shrem's BitInstant exchange which was then processing over a quarter of all Bitcoin transactions.[101]

---

[98] Jeong, Sarah. "Was Mt. Gox CEO The Dread Pirate Roberts? The DHS Once Believed It." *Forbes*, 16 Jan. 2015.
[99] Buterin, Vitalik. "MtGox Gets FinCEN MSB License." *Bitcoin Magazine*, 29 June 2013.
[100] levino, Bitcointalk.org user. "MtGox Withdrawal Delays [Gathering]." *Bitcoin Forum*, 18 Apr. 2013.
[101] Jeffries, Adrianne. "Brooklyn-Based Bitcoin Startup BitInstant Raises Seed Round." *Observer*, 13 Dec. 2011

As a self-identifying individualist libertarian and anarcho-capitalist, Ver was a colorful character in early Bitcoin who at 21 ran for the California State Assembly describing himself as an internet entrepreneur "*well read in Austrian Economics*" and promising an end to income taxes and a "HUGE DECREASE IN NUMBER OF LAWS."[102] Part of this "*real-world private business experience*" was the selling of banned pest-control explosives on eBay, for which he later served 10 months in prison before moving to Japan and renouncing his US citizenship upon obtaining a St.Kitts and Nevis passport.[103] On July 17, he arrived at the Tokyo headquarters and recorded a video statement to ease the people of Bitcoin-land:

> *I'm Roger Ver, long time Bitcoin advocate and investor.*
> *Today I'm at the Mtgox world headquarters in Tokyo Japan.*
> *I had a nice chat with MTGOX CEO, Mark Karpeles, about their current situation.*
> *He showed me multiple bank statements, as well as letters from banks and lawyers.*
> *I'm sure that all the current withdrawal problems at MTGOX are being caused by the traditional banking system, not because of a lack of liquidity at MTGOX.*
> *The traditional banking partners that MTGOX needs to work with are not able to keep up with the demands of the growing Bitcoin economy.*
> *The dozens of people that make up the MTGOX team are hard at work establishing additional banking partners, that eventually will make dealing with MTGOX easier for all their customers around the world. For now, I hope that everyone will continue working on Bitcoin projects that will help make the world a better place.*[104]
>
> \- Roger Ver, 17 July 2013.

---

[102] "Roger K Ver Candidate for Member of the State Assembly; District 28." *League of Women Voters*, 2000.

[103] Clenfield, Jason, and Pavel Alpeyev. "'Bitcoin Jesus' Calls Rich to Tax-Free Tropical Paradise." *Bloomberg*, 16 June 2014.

[104] Ver, Roger. "Roger Ver on MTGOX Bitcoin Exchange." *YouTube*, 17 July 2013.

Ver's words calmed some nerves owing to his position among the most respected people in the industry, but Mt.Gox's issues kept piling. These included needing to halt US dollar withdrawals, possibly because the company's Japanese bank pressured them to close all accounts. In early August, the company stopped accepting new deposits after incurring "*significant losses*" due to crediting BTC balances before bank deposits cleared fully. According to one insider, Mr. Karpelès largely distracted himself from the ailing business by taking on new projects, chief of them being the French bistro-style *The Bitcoin Café* which Mt.Gox apparently spent a million dollars setting up on the street level of the main office.[105]

As the exchange limped along over the following months and withdrawals took weeks or even months to process, Wired published *The Rise and Fall of the World's Largest Bitcoin Exchange*, which noted that Mt.Gox had "*effectively been frozen out of the U.S. banking system because of its regulatory problems.*"[106] That same day, the Bitcoin rocket passed its all-time-high and shot for the stars.[107]

Recollections

Six days earlier on October 30th, a month after Ulbricht's arrest, something went off in my head while sitting in class in Waterloo, Canada. Silk Road was down and its founder in jail, but Bitcoin was by no means dead. If that hadn't destroyed it, perhaps nothing would. I could sense the cusp of destiny. Between my 1st year introductory Business classes, I scrawled the following email to my then-girlfriend, who had introduced me to BTC almost a year earlier:

---

105 "Mark Karpeles Spent Over $50,000 on Kitchen Equipment for Bitcoin Cafe." *NewsBTC*, 1 Mar. 2014.

106 McMillan, Robert. "The Rise and Fall of the World's Largest Bitcoin Exchange." *Wired*, 11 June 2013.

107 Mochizukiert, Takashi, et al. "Tracing a Bitcoin's Exchange's Fall from the Top to Shutdown." *Wall Street Journal*, 20 Apr. 2014.

Bitcoin Recommendation

Bitcoins are now at $205 each. I've followed them for a long time now, and can confidently say that I expect them to keep rising from this point. While they were all the rage when it shot up in price (and then went back to under $100), they have been steadily increasing now.

Bitcoin vending machines are being installed in several cities (just started with vancouver this week), and they are getting a popular discussion topic again. The internet is starting to buzz about them again.

They survived the Silk Road bust and the security issues with TOR, all of which were major factors of uncertainty. In other words, the worst possible things have happened to Bitcoin, and it has not crashed in any sense.

Further; Reddit is starting to embrace them, with redditors being able to send Bitcoin to each other. Reddit is a major indicator of the population and is visible to a large audience, with the ability to start lasting changes

I seriously recommend you to make an investment in Bitcoin for the medium term (few years) intentions. It should be an amount which you don't 'need' aka. will not need to withdraw out of for expenses before you get a summer job and be otherwise comfortable. They can of course be sold easily if needed. Outside of that; I strongly believe they are a solid investment with lots of upside potential and little loss potential. Depending what I get from scholarships, I intend to put a large percentage in them in Bitcoin. unfortunately it'll take a month+ for me to get the money, after which time they could have gone up a lot. Act quickly; I think were on the verge of them going up fast. I plan to buy some very soon too; let me know what you think and we could buy them all at once if you decide to get some. Lets make some cash :D

- Elias Ahonen, 13 Oct. 2013.

Bitcoin rose over 600% over the following five weeks; to a high of $1,238. Even more dramatically, this represented an 18-fold increase from a low of $67 only 5 months earlier. It was surreal. At 19 years old, I felt like I had stumbled upon some grand, earth-shattering secret.

I suppose that is exactly what I was looking for. Before switching to Political Science, I had enrolled in the Global Studies undergraduate program in the previous year because simply put, I wanted to know how the world really worked. I thought that by having a wide perspective, by studying and travelling as broadly as possible, I would one day see some pivotal trend before everyone else, and in doing so create my future. In this way I could find my path and roughly follow in the footsteps of my mother, a leading professor in her field.

As I had always been the type to spend 2-3 hours a day reading the news, this continued as I turned my interests towards investing. The highlight of my 18th birthday was opening my first stock trading account, in which I promptly deposited my earnings from a summer of freelance photography. The first trend I latched on to was 3D printing, which I was sure would change the world. I became obsessed with trading, focusing on the charts more than my 1st year classes while I tripled my money in a few months. I remember my first option trade where I turned $500 into $2,000 in about an hour; the time it took to take the bus to campus and settle in my seat for my Medieval History lecture.

This initial success was predictably short lived as I grew over-confident and soon lost half of my account in a string of bad trades. Classic. At least I got used to volatility. That is when I took to an investment forum to seek advice, asking if I should just put everything on Bitcoin which was only $20 at the time in early 2013. "*That's an extremely stupid, careless idea*" some more knowledgeable investor wrote. I listened, regrettably, and ended up losing the rest of my money over the next month anyway with overconfident option trading. Life has a learning curve.

When BTC hit $1,000, I was watching the Mt.Gox order books, meaning the live bids and offers on the exchange, while sitting with my Business 101 study group learning to calculate normal 5% annual investment returns . "*What am I doing here?*" I recall thinking as I stood up to draw some sort of textbook investment return curve on the whiteboard. I told my friends in Business & Economics about Bitcoin and showed them the charts, but "*that's retarded*" was the only response I recall. I even visited some of my professors during office hours to introduce them to the concept and even left one of them a copy of *Bitcoin Magazine*. All I got were funny looks. At least I was not going door-to-door at various businesses like many of the more comitted Bitcoin evangelists.

There was a certain limbo in which I simultaneously felt myself the smartest person in the room doing laps around everyone, yet also suspected that I may be little more than an overconfident youth and naïve hack who happened to be right one time, and now had the gall to think myself above my elders. Yet just as Nietzsche "*accused past philosophers of lacking critical sense and blindly accepting dogmatic premises in their consideration of morality*"[108] [109] in *Beyond Good and Evil,* I began to see many Economists and certain other academics as occasional purveyors of passé dogmas from idealized past ages where things could be imagined to have fit neatly into various prescribed boxes. In bearing this uncanny suspicion, I was very much a product and actualization of the Bitcoin revolution; a young academic who suddenly began to question the structural integrity of the old ivory towers his mind inhabited.

It was as if Bitcoin was an elusive, beautiful, and mystical creature that I was confidently chasing down the Blockland-rabbit-hole,

[108] Wikipedia Contributors. "Beyond Good and Evil." *Wikipedia*, 21 Oct. 2019.

[109] 8) Yes, I have broken the great rule of not citing Wikipedia, all while criticizing my teachers. Wikipedia is perhaps the greatest collection of knowledge available to humanity, and I could not hope to find a source that says it better than one reviewed by dozens of editors.

while remaining unable to articulate what exactly it was that I had seen to anyone in my circles. I started writing an article for the school newspaper encouraging the university to invest 1% of its endowment into Bitcoin, but I abandoned the idea as I knew I would become a laughingstock. Sorry, my Alma Mater. Still, I believed that this mysterious thing would lead me to great things, whether others could see it or not. I considered dropping out to work as a bank teller, calculating that I could save enough to buy at least a hundred bitcoins per year while prices remained low. Looking back, I probably seemed like some strange fintech evangelist. Perhaps it was in my DNA; half of my great aunts & uncles spent their lives spreading revival movements around the world as ministers and missionaries. I had been converted – to what, I did not know.

Gox Goes Bankrupt

Despite cash withdrawals often taking months, Mt.Gox remained operational throughout this bull run, the subsequent fall to $560 three weeks later, followed by $975 three weeks after that. It was when the market clearly turned downwards on February 7th, 2014, that the first signs of imminent disaster appeared as the site halted all bitcoin withdrawals.[110] This meant that not only were users unable to make bank deposits from Mt.Gox, they could not even get their BTC out in order to sell or trade elsewhere. After protestors gathered in front of the Mt.Gox office to confront Karpelès and demand their bitcoins back, the company relocated due to security concerns.[111] This was an unprecedented emergency, and it showed

---

[110] Kollmeyer, Barbara. "Bitcoin Drops Sharply as Mt. Gox Halts Withdrawals." *MarketWatch*, 7 Feb. 2014.
[111] Southurst, Jon. "Japanese Police Shut Down Protest at Mt. Gox." *CoinDesk*, 22 Feb. 2014.

in the Mt.Gox exchange where market prices for the "trapped" BTC was 20% below those of other fully operational exchanges.[112]

After two weeks of limbo, Karpelès deleted all his tweets and resigned from the Bitcoin Foundation board. Blockland held its breath. The next day on the 24th, all trading was suspended. As six of the leading exchanges published a joint statement to effectively wash their hands of the chaos, the Mt.Gox website went completely blank.[113]

All the money was gone; 850,000 bitcoins worth $460 million. Mt.Gox was bankrupt.[114]

Pirate's Legend

Despite earlier suspicions regarding Karpelès, the FBI eventually zeroed in and arrested Ulbricht. As his laptop was logged in during the raid, authorities were able to retrieve the BTC he controlled. Despite the various agencies' success in catching the silk road operator and shutting down the site, Senator Schumer was not satisfied.[115] As one market was taken offline, others appeared in its place including *Hydra Market,* aptly named after the many-headed serpent of Greek myth.

Ross may have been behind bars, but his alias Dread Pirate Roberts was alive and well. You see, the name comes from *The Princess*

---

[112] Wong, Joon Ian. "Poll: Are You Having Mt. Gox Withdrawal Issues?" *CoinDesk*, 4 Feb. 2014.
[113] Mochizuki, Takashi, Kathy Chu, and Eleanor Warnock. "Tracing a Bitcoin's Exchange's Fall from the Top to Shutdown." *The Wall Street Journal*, 20 Apr. 2014.
[114] McMillan, Robert. "The Inside Story of Mt. Gox, Bitcoin's $460 Million Disaster." *Wired*, 3 Mar. 2014.
[115] Greenberg, Andy. "NY Senator Calls for Renewed Crackdown on Dark Web Drug Sales." *Wired*, 6 Feb. 2014.

Bride, where Dread Pirate Roberts is a feared pirate captain. Unbeknownst to most in the story there is no single DPR; the name is actually passed on from pirate captain to pirate captain as they retire. In November 2013, some of the administrators of the original Silk Road got together and launched Silk Road 2.0 under the leadership of a new Dread Pirate Roberts. Though the site suffered a loss of 4,000 BTC to an apparent hack, it continued until November 2014 when Blake Benthall was identified as Dread Pirate Roberts and arrested by the FBI.[116] That same month, a competitor known as Diabolus Market rebranded itself as 'Silk Road 3.0 Reloaded', and in May 2016 another site called Silk Road 3.0 announced its launch.[117] The legend of Dread Pirate Roberts lives on.

Conclusion

Silk Road was Bitcoin's proving ground. Here, it demonstrated utility as a currency for contraband that governments could not easily track or shut down. The marketplace also created a constant demand for both buying and selling BTC, as shown by a 2012 paper in which Carnegie Mellon Research Professor Nicolas Christin demonstrated that "*4.5%-9% of all exchange trades*" of BTC were related to Silk Road. In practice, this demonstrated that a Bitcoin economy could function. This proof of concept paved the way for others to develop legitimate businesses and sparked the interest of many investors. In this sense, we can think of Silk Road as Bitcoin's nurturing mother.

Unfortunately, she was now in jail.

---

116 Codro, Bitcointalk.org user. "Silk Road 2.0 Hacked through Malleability, ~4000 BTC Stolen." *Bitcoin Forum*, 13 Feb. 2014.

117 Throwaway321, Bitcointalk.org user. "Silk Road 3.0 – Back Online and Open for Business." *Bitcoin Forum*, 15 May 2016.

This thinking can extend to Mt.Gox, which takes the archetype of a controlling but supportive father. It gave Bitcoin a home, and despite controlling it with occasional trading and withdrawal freezes, did its best to let Bitcoin mature as stably as possible.[118]

Despite supporting Bitcoin for a few months after mom's arrest, he had gone broke.

Bitcoin was on its own.

It's clear Bitcoin had a rough time growing up, both at home and with the friends it kept. Surely, these struggles would leave a mark on its character in adulthood. Despite Bitcoin's image today as a generally legitimate entity, many Bitcoiners have a soft spot and even nostalgia for Silk Road and what it represented – a middle finger to the world's most powerful government. A way to do things in an arguably better (safer & cheaper) way while breaking all the old rules and assumptions, all while being anonymous and practically indestructible. Perhaps it was because these were not qualities only of Silk Road, but Bitcoin itself. In this sense, merely owning Bitcoin was and remains to many a peaceful act of protest, rebellion, and even revolution against what they see as the crumbling contemporary order.

The Mt.Gox story is perhaps Bitcoin's version of the story of Steve Jobs, who designed the Apple computer in his parent's garage. A card trading website being repurposed for Bitcoin, soon coming to hold a billion dollars as the currency's main trading hub. In hindsight Mt.Gox's failure almost certainly benefited Bitcoin, as it forced trading to spread across dozens of exchanges more evenly instead of relying on an overly centralized pillar. In Bitcoin, no entity nor institution is too big to fail.

---

[118] Mochizukiert, Takashi, et al. "Tracing a Bitcoin's Exchange's Fall from the Top to Shutdown." *Wall Street Journal*, 20 Apr. 2014.

Both Ulbricht and Karpelès have become something akin to mythical figures in the Pantheon of Bitcoin, evidenced by collectible silver coins minted to commemorate their endeavors. Like Bitcoin itself, both figures are enigmatic and controversial, seen variously as a genius criminal kingpins or as incompetent and naive ideologues. They are both loved and despised; glorified for spreading Bitcoin to the masses and spat on for sullying its reputation. They are not the only pioneers who faced prosecution for their missteps in the uncharted territories of cryptocurrency. These include the aforementioned Charlie Shrem, who served two years for failing to report suspicious activity related to the use of his BitInstant exchange by Silk Road buyers.[119] Roger Ver is another example of a variously venerated character despite, or perhaps because of, his past. The idolization of Ulbricht as a symbol of the Bitcoin movement, both as a martyr and a demonstration of a failed system, is evident at various industry conferences where his mother can be found at the *freeross.org* booth. There, she shares his story, adding to the 200,000 signatures and 100+ eminent institutions petitioning clemency for her son who was sentenced to two life sentences plus 40 years as a non-violent, first-time offender.[120] [121]

Greater than any of its proverbial parents/guardians was Bitcoin itself. It proved anti-fragile; suggesting it could outlast any legal, illegal, or law-making institution or individual. With its parents gone, Bitcoin had to grow up quickly as many suspected it would face imminent global bans or a descent into obscurity. To do this, it had to shed its image as a rebellious, unwashed, and delinquent anarchist-hippie teenager. Bitcoin was in desperate need of mainstream legitimacy and acceptance: a neat haircut, a clean wardrobe, and a

---

[119] Roy, Jessica. "BitInstant CEO Charlie Shrem Arrested for Alleged Money Laundering." *TIME*, 27 Jan. 2014.
[120] Greenberg, Andy. "Ulbricht Confessed to Running Silk Road, His College Friend Testifies." *WIRED*, 22 Jan. 2015.
[121] freeross.org

good word from some respectable adult. This it received from the most unlikely of sources; the US Marshal Service, who effectively legitimized the currency when they announced a set of public auctions to shed the 144,000 BTC seized from Mr. Ulbricht.

A 2014 1-oz silver coin commemorating the Mt.Gox bankruptcy, picturing the ensuing BTC crash and CEO Mark Karpelès. Mintage: 500

A 1-oz copper coin by 'Anonymous Mint' commemorating Silk Road and featuring the website's logo.

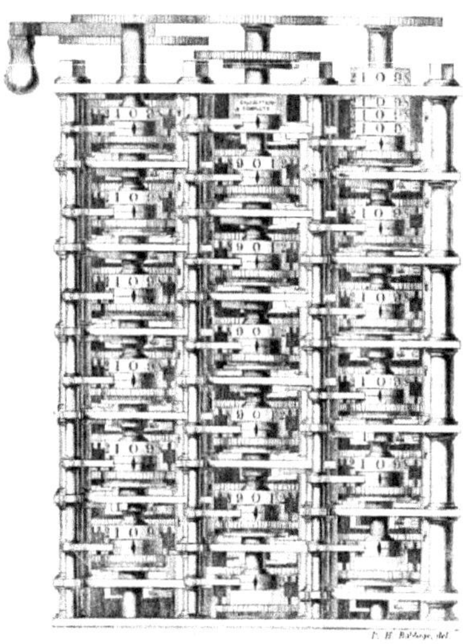

Part of Charles Babbage's 1833 Difference Engine, an automatic mechanical calculator that can be thought of as an early computer.

CHAPTER 4

Computing Frontiers

Prehistoric Blockland & Litecoin

Imagine Blockchain, or Blockland if you will, as a large and uninhabited new continent or planet. It was created by our hero Satoshi Nakamoto, who then helps his disciple Hal Finney to set up the first settlement called Bitcoin in 2009. The colony attracts the first settlers, who quickly begin developing it further. These include Gavin Andresen, Jeff Garzik, Peter Todd, and Luke Dashjr, among others. Though tall and thick walls are built for the city to ensure security, they are made of transparent glass as to ensure that people both inside and outside the city can see all its workings. With time, this settlement grows from a mere hobby farm into a city and society with its own internal community, politics, social events, and economy.

One day, Charlie Lee, who works for Google and is among the early Bitcoin pioneers, declares that he is founding a new settlement. Though Lee is excited to live in Blockland and an ardent believer in the Bitcoin settlement's success, he now feels that the burgeoning colony's streets are being built too narrow for its growing population. This will cause congested foot-traffic and prevent donkeys and carts from eventually navigating the city to simplify trade. And so, the Litecoin encampment is established some distance away in October 2011. Here, the streets are much wider, and paved well to allow for quick travel between the various shops and markets in the Litecoin settlement.

Litecoin has often been referred to as the silver to Bitcoin's gold. The analogy fit, not only because of the convenient logo colors but because of each blockchain's properties. Bitcoin is thought of in terms of large denominations due to the high value of individual tokens (like gold bars), is relatively slow to transact with while paying comparatively high transaction (miner) fees. Litecoin on the other hand has a psychologically lower price-point, is quick to transact, and comes with low transaction fees which are paid directly to Litecoin miners. These advantages have made LTC a popular choice with online retailers who also accept BTC. Another function of Litecoin has been to operate as a de-facto test-net or proving ground for Bitcoin's ongoing development, at least in a political sense of demonstrating to Bitcoiners that a coming technical update is acceptable because it has already been successfully implemented on Litecoin.[122] It is easy to argue that Litecoin is technologically superior, but Bitcoin's status as the first mover has kept it from being eclipsed by the nimbler Litecoin.[123]

This was perhaps the spark that successfully ignited the idea of parallel cryptocurrencies, and slowly over the following two years others begin to follow Lee's example of building up their own settlements in the vast unclaimed wilderness of Blockland. Many of these blockchain pioneers harken back to the days of the wild west

---

[122] Kim, Esther. "Litecoin is a 'Glorified Bitcoin Testnet', says Investor Mike Novogratz." *Bitcoinist*, 5 Apr. 2019.
[123] Ethereum has arguably replaced Litecoin in fulfilling these roles.

and goldrush when one could simply stake out a land claim on virgin territory and secure generational wealth. Some even set out on bold attempts of building settlements more powerful than any before, either by way of better designed infrastructure, or some ideal with which to win the hearts and minds of the other settlements' "inhabitants" (that is, [their] invested dollars). Others build speciality settlements based around a specific theme or trade function. Many of these were highly experimental in nature, operating on novel technologies, governance structures, and econo-philosophical concepts. It became suddenly possible to invest in ideologies.

Mastercoin

A new age dawned on Blockland in January 2012, when JR Willett published an influential document titled *The Second Bitcoin Whitepaper*.

> *We claim that the existing bitcoin network can be used as a protocol layer, on top of which new currency layers with new rules can be built without changing the foundation. We further claim that the new protocol layers described in this document:*
>
> - *Will fix the two biggest barriers to widespread bitcoin adoption: instability and insecurity.*
> - *Will financially benefit the entire bitcoin user community, including those who don't use the new protocol layers.*
> - *Will provide initial funds to hire developers to build software which implements the new protocol layers, and ongoing funds to pay for maintenance of this software.*
> - *Will richly reward early adopters of the new protocol, in proportion to how successful it is.*[124]
>
> -JR Willett, Jan. 2012

[124] Willett, JR. "The Second Bitcoin Whitepaper." Jan. 2012.

Willett was among the first to materialize the idea of creating new tokens on top of Bitcoin (colored coins), and accurately described the process of what would later become known as the Initial Coin Offering (ICO). By creating untold amounts of new currencies and value-tracking tickers, Bitcoin could theoretically become a solid base on which a new global economy could be built using pre-programmed and transparent mechanisms called *smart contracts.* To manage the relationship between Bitcoin and these future alternative currencies as he called them, Willett proposed Mastercoin.

> *The whole point of MasterCoins is to allow users to create their own currencies out of existing MasterCoins. For the purposes of demonstrating how user currencies will work, we will use an example currency called "GoldCoins", which are intended to track the value of one ounce of gold, and which may be stored, transferred, bought, and sold similarly to MasterCoins.*[125]
>
> - JR Willett, Jan 2012

This vision became reality on July 31st, 2013, when Willett published the whitepaper again. This time it was not a theoretical concept, but the announcement of Mastercoin's imminent launch. The sale was open for the entire month of August, with each Mastercoin costing 0.01 BTC. This meant that someone contributing 100 BTC would receive 10,000 MSC upon launch on September 1st, with additional bonuses depending on how early the BTC was sent.

> *Perhaps you have heard of the "Genesis Block" which launched the bitcoin protocol. The Mastercoin protocol has a similar starting point in the block chain, called the "Exodus Address" - the bitcoin address from which the first MasterCoins will be sold. The Exodus Address is: 1EXoDusjGwvnjZUyKkxZ4UHEf77z6A5S4P*[126]
>
> - JR Willett, 31 July 2013.

---

[125] Willett, JR. "The Second Bitcoin Whitepaper." Jan. 2012.
[126] Willett, JR. "MasterCoin Complete Specification." 31 July 2013.

The ICO was born.[127]

The Mastercoin whitepaper's importance as a foundational document to the entire blockchain phenomenon cannot be understated, as it radically suggested that there was more to cryptocurrency than just currency. A *currency* or *coin* was ultimately nothing more than a unit of account, and this accounting token could be used to represent anything. This came to be called *Smart Property* for *Property Tokens*. Though these concepts had already been floating around and discussed by enthusiasts including Nick Szabo, this was the first formalization and attempt of realizing the idea.[128] [129]

> *MasterCoin supports creating property tokens to be used for titles, deeds, user- backed currencies, and even shares in a company. Whenever property is created, it gets assigned the next available currency ID, so any property can be bought, sold, transferred, and even used for betting, just like other Master-Coin-derived currencies.*[130]
>
> -JR Willett, 31 July 2013.

If digital tokens could be used to represent anything, then why not fiat currencies? Thus, the idea of a *StableCoin* tied to the value of a dollar was brought forth in a seemingly off-hand remark about money laundering in an appendix titled *Horrible, Awful, Very Bad Things*:

> *Also, if you think bitcoin has a reputation problem for money laundering now, just wait until you can store "USDCoins" in the block chain! At last, drug dealers and human traffickers will have the perfect currency to enable their work.*

---

[127] Shin, Laura. "Here's the Man Who Created ICOs And This Is the New Token He's Backing." *Forbes*, 21 Sept. 2017.
[128] Buterin, Vitalik. "Mastercoin: A Second-Generation Protocol on The Bitcoin Blockchain." *Bitcoin Magazine*, 4 Nov. 2013.
[129] Alam, Iftikhar. "Beginner's Guide: What Is Mastercoin (Omni)? The First Altcoin." *101 Blockchains*, 8 July 2018.
[130] Willett, JR. "MasterCoin Complete Specification." 31 July 2013.

> *However, stable distributed currencies will be incredibly useful in a huge number of legal applications, and even modest success of this protocol could make early investors (and even those who simply hold bitcoins) very rich. MasterCoins, much like guns, are just tools, capable of being used for good or for evil. We urge our early adopters to consider how they may use MasterCoin for good, and if you get rich, how to use that money for good. It will take a lot of work to make the good outshine the evil.*[131]
>
> - JR Willett, 31 July 2013.

On September 1st, 2013, 563,162 Master Coins were distributed to the buyers who had collectively contributed 4740 BTC to the project. This was all the MSC that would ever exist, outside of an additional 10% which would slowly be created to fund ongoing development of the protocol. This was followed by the formation of the Mastercoin Foundation, which was made up of seven volunteer members including J.R. Willett, Ron Gross, David Johnston, Antony Vo, Jonathan Yantis, Sam Onat Yilmaz, and Brock Pierce.[132]

Considering that Mastercoin set the stage of inspiration for the appearance of thousands of cryptocurrencies which would lead their investors to both untold riches and complete losses, the whitepaper ended in a most apt disclaimer:

> *Investing in experimental currencies is really, absurdly risky. This paper is not investment advice, and anyone predicting what will happen with experimental currencies such as those described here is indulging in the wildest sort of speculation... Please consult your financial adviser before investing in ANY wild scheme such as this (hint: they will probably tell you to RUN and not look back unless you assure them that it is money you are totally prepared to lose).*
>
> *Anyone who puts their rent money or life savings into an experiment of this type is a fool, and deserves the financial ruin*

---

131 Willett, JR. "MasterCoin Complete Specification." 31 July 2013.

132 Zynis, Dominik. "A Brief History of Mastercoin." *Omni Foundation Blog*, 29 Nov. 2013.

they will inevitably reap from this or some other risky enterprise.[133]

-JR Willett, 31 July 2013.

Blockland: New Frontier

The next age in Blockland's history began in October 2013 when Bitcoin's market cap (imagine it as *population*) exploded 10-fold in a mere two months from 1.41 billion to 13.85 billion (BTC thus increasing from $121 to $1,149). At the same time, Litecoin saw its population grow by a multiple of 25. This increase was so dramatic that reporters from around the world converged on Blockland, which was then dominated by Bitcoin which hosted 88% of the settlers.

As the $1,000 price milestone was reached, the former Chair of the Federal Reserve Alan Greenspan appeared on TV suggesting that despite its apparent value, one could not really buy anything useful with Bitcoin. This upset J, a friend of mine, who decided to prove him wrong. The next day, J emailed a Lamborghini dealership that was willing to accept BTC. He considered that he could buy ten or twenty Lamborghinis to parade around in order to make a statement but realized that doing so might bring about all manner of problems as it was unclear to him if using Bitcoin was even legal. He settled on a single 'ghini in the anarcho-capitalist colors of yellow and black. J then took pictures to prove his purchase and leaked them on a notorious and anonymous online message board called 4Chan. The news spread like wildfire, and the *Bitcoin lambo* meme was born.[134] Lamborghini's became permanently associated with Blockland; they embodied success, youth, new money, fast money, flashiness, and the collective dream that one day, "*One*

[133] Willett, JR. "MasterCoin Complete Specification." 31 July 2013.

[134] Alfonso, Fernando. "This 4chan User Bought a Lamborghini with $200K in Bitcoin." *The Daily Dot*, 11 Dec. 2013.

BTC = Lambo." A comparable psychologica milestone was crossed when the bitcoin price first exceeded that of an ounce of gold.

The Lambo made Bitcoin undeniably real; it could no longer be claimed to be a theoretical experiment, but rather an economic black swan that managed to escape its computer lab. In this sense J followed the footsteps of Lazlo's pizza purchase three years earlier in publicly demonstrating the hypothesis that Bitcoin is digital cash. For J this also represented a personal triumph of reaching his Bitcoin moon, which he described as a point in which his Bitcoin holdings were enough to cover his needs for the rest of his life. Often, this idea of financial freedom is known as *F--U money*; sufficient wealth to, hopefully only metaphorically, say "*F--k you!*" to anyone and live life on one's own terms without external economic pressures. Bitcoin has without a doubt delivered many of its early investors to this state, and there are many more hoping that their coins will increase enough in value to say the same.

As each bitcoin was now worth four figures, some began to campaign for the ~$1 MilliBit or mBTC (1/1000th of a bitcoin; 100,000 bits/Satoshis) to take over as the primary denomination in both discussion and commerce.[135] It was theorized that average people would now be turned off from investing in bitcoins because they were perceived as expensive, and that it felt far more natural to spend fifty MilliBits rather than 0.05 bitcoins on a $50 item. This line of thinking is related to the psychological Denomination Effect[136], which shows that while people prefer to receive money in large denominations, they are more likely to spend small denomi-

---

[135] the_poet, Bitcointalk.org user. "Let's Use mBTC Instead of BTC." *Bitcoin Forum*, 31 Dec. 2015.
[136] Raghubir, Priya, and Joydeep Srivastava. "The Denomination Effect." Journal of Consumer Research, vol. 36, no. 4, 2009, pp. 701–713., doi:10.1086/599222.

nations of money while saving large ones. This suggests that denominating purchases in mBTC would stimulate the Bitcoin economy by increasing usage, whereas focusing on the BTC denomination would instead encourage people to hoard entire bitcoins or defined fractions of them. The idea of re-denominating to mBTC won initial traction as many merchants switched to mBTC and even some wallets and exchanges allowed for balances to be toggled between the denominations. Despite these efforts, the proposal failed to gain a critical mass and the idea that "*bitcoins are too expensive for me*" has become common wisdom amongst the everyman.[137]

In this vein is interesting to consider how Bitcoin has changed user's perceptions of value. While it is normal to see a dollar as consisting of "lower parts" i.e. cents, a bitcoin is commonly seen as a specified denomination of a higher, singular unit in the sense that it is a "*one 21-millionth share of the entire system.*" Surely nobody thinks this way about the money in their bank account by dividing it with the ever-expanding total money supply of their country. Thus, these two systems of money are inverted on a fundamental level.

One of the memorable commentators from this post-1k time was Dr. Mark T. Williams, an Economics Professor from Boston University who wrote in *Business Insider* that "*I predict that Bitcoin will trade for under $10 a share by the first half of 2014… the meltdown has begun, act quickly and take fleeting profit off the table.*"[138] His fate as a meme was sealed when he accidentally pronounced "*Bitcorn*" at a televised congressional hearing, earning him the moniker *Professor Bitcorn.* Dr. Bitcorn came to symbolise the apparent situational ignorance of mainstream financial, economic,

[137] Redman, Jamie. "The Case for Using mBTC Over BTC Denominations." *Bitcoin.com*, 13 May 2017.

[138] Williams, Mark T. "Finance Professor: Bitcoin Will Crash To $10 By Mid-2014." *Business Insider India*, 18 Dec. 2013.

and regulatory "experts", who seemingly failed to grasp that there was no concept of "shares" in Bitcoin nor any bearing to the "quarters" of the business world. As many Bitcoiners considered Bitcoin to be wholly removed from traditional finance, a new lifeform instead of a merely new species if you will, it became common to consider the opinions of established experts like Dr. Williams to be irrelevant. As the economic premise on which Bitcoin was built was considered extinct and abandoned by academia, they likely saw Bitcoin as little more than a re-animated Frankenstein's monster of long-discredited economic theory.

This collective rejection of authority; whether celebrity, academic, or governmental/legal, meant that Blockland's pioneers were unconstrained by established convention. Longstanding economic theories, governance structures, legal principles, and the very concepts of ownership, value, individuals, and organizations were variously thrown out of the window of collective consciousness as Blockland's pioneers began open-mindedly experimenting with different ways of being in their new world. This was nothing short of an in-tech-lectual renaissance spearheaded not by those who rose to influence through "traditional" means, but by grassroots innovators who came of age during the 90's and early 2000's computing revolution.

Seeing as blockchain technology has not come out of established institutions, academia has found itself in a position of catch-up, seeking to understand and integrate the phenomenon rather than leading it. This fact is apparent in this very book, seeing as a most references and citations are not of scholarly literature, but from decidedly unscholarly news reports by industry specific media without longstanding reputations, and even undated posts by anonymous users on various online forums. My practice of seriously citing what some may class as non-serious anonymous online personas may strike some as quaint, but it is a whole-hearted acknowledgment of their very serious contributions to an important global phenomenon that is worthy of study. It is precisely on these fora that this phenomenon has taken shape, and it has been on these niche news channels that the minutiae of its events have been reported. To get to the core of this grassroots and underground movement, relying merely on peer-reviewed material or reports by broadly respected newspapers would simply not do.

Blockchain: The New Computer

It is these people who see blockchain as the next generation of computer systems. The idea of blockchain as a new computer is supported by *Bell's law of computer classes*:

> *In the early 1950s, a person could walk inside a computer and by 2010 a single computer (or "cluster") with millions of processors will have expanded to the size of a building. More importantly, computers are beginning to "walk" inside of us. These ends of the computing spectrum illustrate the vast dynamic range in computing power, size, cost, and other factors for early 21st century computer classes.*
> *A computer class is a set of computers in a particular price range with* ***unique or similar programming environments*** *(such as Linux, OS/360, Palm, Symbian, Windows) that* ***support a variety of applications that communicate with people and/or other systems****. A new computer class forms and approximately doubles each decade,* ***establishing a new industry.*** *A class may be the consequence and combination of a new platform with a new programming environment, a new network, and new interface with people and/or other information processing systems.*[139]
>
> \- Gordon Bell, 1972 (emphasis mine)

[139] Bell, Gordon. "Bell's Law for The Birth and Death of Computer Classes." Jan. 2008.

This trend is clear as we examine the history of computing. The 60's saw the first widely available mainframe computers which were more akin to control rooms in size. These were surpassed by the fridge-sized minicomputers of the 70's, which were themselves made obsolete when personal computers that could be connected together by a local ethernet appeared in the 80'. Now that computers could be connected together, they were no longer mere free-standing calculators; they could effectively communicate with other units. After ~30 years of computing, this was the tipping point. Computing evolved into a radically different concept in the 90's, as ethernet morphed into the internet which allowed personal computers around the world to communicate. It was no longer about crunching numbers and sorting data within the walls of institutions, but about individuals creating and sharing information around the world.[140]

Like with Gutenberg's printing press, 1500's Europe's proto-computer, the internet of the 90's transformed the social fabric of civilization as communication across borders became seamless and the world became frighteningly small. New computing methods were built on top of this in the 21st century, including handheld computers in the 00's. Later in the aughts, cloud computing moved storage out of hard drives and to the internet, and wireless sensor networks allowed "intelligent" items to connect to the Internet of Things.

And now we have Bitcoin; sometimes referred to as The Internet of Money (or Value), in the same way that the original internet could be called The Internet of Data.

As you already know, there is more to Blockland, the world of blockchain, than just Bitcoin. Hundreds of protocols, systems, and

---

[140] Ocon, Angelica Angelo. "IT Infrastructure and Platforms." *LinkedIn Slideshare*, 19 Apr. 2013.

platforms have been created with various uses of blockchain technology, some of them based or built on Bitcoin, and others doing something completely different. Ethereum was for example designed to be *the world computer*, a system of pre-programmed *smart contracts* interacting with each other in etherspace which is neither within a personal computer's hard drive nor in the cloud. As we approach 30 years from the dawn of the internet, one might wonder if blockchain represents a similar quantum leap in computing, beyond merely another radical improvement in computing, but a transformation of our very conception of it. If so, we could hypothesize an additional *Theory of Computer Conception/Generation.*

This hypothesis would suggest that approximately every 30 years, once per generation, cumulative Bells Law and Moore's Law advances in computing give rise to such a radical advancement that it gradually causes the common conception of what a computer is, and its relationship with society, to change entirely. Consider that back in 53' before the mass produced mainframe systems, IBM's CEO Thomas Watson only expected to sell five of their newest models worldwide.[141] This age of *theoretical computing* was followed by ~30 years of *singular computing*, where individual computers performed tasks or collaborated with a small number of other computers within many closed organizations including government offices, universities, and businesses. It was during this period in '77 that Ken Olsen, founder of Digital Equipment Corporation famously asserted that "*There is no reason anyone would want a computer in their home.*"[142] The next ~30 years from the 90's to 20's could then be called a time of *mass computing*, when

---

141 Dubner, Stephen J. "Our Daily Bleg: Did I.B.M. Really See a World Market 'For About Five Computers'?" *Freakonomics*, 17 Apr. 2008.
142 Strohmeyer, Robert. "The 7 Worst Tech Predictions of All Time." *PC World*, 31 Dec. 2008.

not only did everyone have computers capable of communicating to each other, but they also began to use them in previously unimagined ways.

Today, our relationship with computers has become at times uncomfortable as we struggle with questions concerning privacy, tracking, data ownership, and targeted advertising. At the same time, it often feels like the world as a whole is headed towards various modes of chaos whether political instability, climate change, or economic uncertainty. If a new conception of computer were to emerge and transform our society as significantly as the two previous generations of computing, then we would rightly look to this new computing to help us solve or redefine contemporary problems. Instead of ever smaller and increasingly powerful devices, perhaps the next iteration is a computer that is not physical at all but exists within the nebulous blockchain world of the future. By broadly studying the most notable blockchain "settlements" of the early years, perhaps we can get an inkling of the direction that this new computing will lead us over the next decades. Is *blockchain computing* the next generation?

Of course, it might not be all sunshine and rainbows. Despite the optimism, we must consider whether the capabilities of blockchain technology presents a double-edged sword. Social media which was meant to bring us together has also made us lonelier, and the internet which was thought could only make the world smarter has now created a mind-stunting effect by placing us in tribal echo-chambers by way of algorithms. How likely is it that an anti-blockchain will emerge, proclaiming itself to be a liberator only to enslave its users in some (hopefully) figurative way? I would consider it inevitable. If you blindly believe that blockchain is a pure, intrinsically good gift to mankind that can do no wrong, then call me a heretic. Like any technology, blockchain can be used for all manner of aims. Neither can money be an intrinsic good.

A 2013 1-oz silver coin containing 25 Litecoins. Mintage: 500

The Worship of Mammon, 1909

CHAPTER 5

Satoshism: The Religion of Blockland

I'm sure people have noticed how eerily similar to religion Bitcoin is becoming. The mythical founder, the email disciples, the followers. This message board as a proto-bible of texts, the wiki and the churches efforts to consolidate a one-true-book. The false prophet... the breakway protestants of Litecoin and the cults of BBQ, IO,IX [sic]. . . *the small monastery of Dev coin. Our prayers to Satoshi in the form of mining- doing Satoshis' work, The Charlaten of Pirate. And of course- the eternal blockchain. The collective memory of our entire universe. So why doesn't someone just do it already- and register the Church of Satoshi? There is certainly enough philosophy here.*[143]

- Forum user crazy_rabbit, 30 Nov. 2012.

It is apparent that many of the settlers of Blockland have moved their fortunes to this new world for something much more than mere investment returns. Many see Blockland as

[143] crazy_rabbit, Bitcointalk.org user. "The Church of Satoshi and Latter Day Coins." *Bitcoin Forum*, 3 Nov. 2012.

a shimmering light of hope for a world plagued by corruption, manipulation, and deceit of the economic and political variety while inflation is reducing incomes across the western world and technological advances are making ever-increasing numbers of jobs obsolete. For these reasons among others, people increasingly lack a sense of purpose, agency, citizenship, freedom, belongingness, and optimism for the future. Immigrants are drawn to Blockland by more than just an experimental technology, but by the "truth system" that blockchain often professes to be. One day, there can be a world where all people are free to communicate and transact, free from corruption, free from manipulation, and free from misrepresentations of all kinds. For many, Blockland is the manifestation of this dream, and they have sold their worldly assets in exchange for the ethereal bitcoins which they see as the tickets into Satoshi's coming kingdom.

> ***Satoshism***
>
> *Satoshism is the world's first decentralized cryptographic monotheistic religion.*
> *Based on the written teachings and code of Satoshi Nakamoto, as presented in the Bitcoin Peer-To-Peer E-cash Paper, a document considered to be the verbatim word of Satoshi Nakamoto.*
> *Its adherents, known as Satoshis believe that Satoshi Nakamoto is the digital embodiment of the Son of God, fully divine and fully digital, and the savior of humanity prophesied in the Old Testament. Adherents refer to Satoshi Nakamoto as the 22nd Century* [sic] *representation of the Messiah.*
> *Followers of the doctrine of Satoshism believe in economic prosperity through the liberal interchange within technological payment systems & decentralized networks.*[144]

---

144 Satoshi Nakamoto, Urbandicitionary.com user. "Satoshism." *Urban Dictionary*, 16 Dec. 2013.

What we have here appears to be a sort of blockchain-based New Secular Spiritual Movement or New Religious Movement, complete with the deification of and a sort of personality cult around its founder. There are even martyr figures such as Silk Road's Ross Ulbricht who are variously venerated. This apparent third millennium religious movement is one without leadership, hierarchy, language, politics, nor borders, and whose anonymous founder appeared through the internet and delivered "sacred teachings" in the form of computer code. Satoshi's writings have even been published in *The Book Of Satoshi: The Collected Writings of Bitcoin Creator Satoshi Nakamoto* which was compiled by Phil Champagne in 2014.[145]

The first satirical online "Bitcoin Church" was created in October 2012, with eleven commandments including "Praise Satoshi", "Honor the Blockchain", and "Hack thine planet." In August 2017, a short-lived but seemingly serious *Church of Bitcoin* was founded by Henry Romp, who apparently registered it with the US Internal Revenue Service with plans to seek tax-exempt status. Members would receive lifetime membership after a donation of one Satoshi, provided that:

> *They believe that any two consenting parties should be able to freely exchange or trade without any governing body or third party interfering with their transaction*
> *They believe that bitcoin will enable us to achieve that reality*
> *They distribute our scripture, the whitepaper written by prophet Satoshi Nakamoto*
> *They declare "In cryptography we trust" as a slogan/mantra*
> *They embrace open-source philosophy and freedom of information*[146]
>
> - Henry Romp, 7 Aug. 2017.

---

[145] Champagne, Phil. *The Book of Satoshi: The Collected Writings of Bitcoin Creator Satoshi Nakamoto*. Phil Champagne, 2014.
[146] "Church of Bitcoin." *Bitcoin.it*. Original source: churchofbitcoin.org

Satoshian Sacraments

As a former seminarian, I have devised The Seven Sacraments of Satoshism to illustrate how participants in the blockchain world (Blockland, as we may continue to call it) tend to relate to cryptocurrency and how their approach to it often changes over time. By going through these various interactions with blockchain, sometimes multiple times and in various orders, participants slowly develop from mere casual hobbyists and investors into devotees who promote the apparently world-saving properties of blockchain with what can only be described as religious zeal.

Acquisition – Acquisition is the act of taking possession of some amount of cryptocurrency, so to say dipping one's toes into Blockland. This can be understood to form a permanent link between that person and at least the cryptocurrency in question, meaning that whether they hold onto it or not, they will hold some knowledge of Blockland and likely follow its development to some degree. One does not forget having owned cryptocurrency. It is based off the concept of baptism which is seen as the cleansing of "original sin" and making the individual into an "heir of Heaven". The most commonly preached method of Acquisition is called Dollar-Cost-Averaging, which involves buying an equivalent dollar-amount of BTC every day, week, or month similar to the way a congregant might plan to tithe 10% of their income to a church.[147]

Panic-Buying – This is the act of buying back into cryptocurrency after having doubted and sold earlier due to a lack of faith. The Panic-Buyer usually ends up with a smaller amount of cryptocurrency than they started with because they sold low and bought high after seeing the prices going up and panicking that they may be missing the boat, or more appropriately their "block-salvation".

[147] Chester, Jonathan. "The Benefits of Bitcoin Dollar Cost Averaging." *Forbes*, 18. Feb 2020.

This is based on the idea of confession, which involves the forgiveness of sins and a reconciliation with God.

Utilization - This is the act of actually using cryptocurrency or perhaps other blockchain-based applications. By undertaking the sacrament of Utilization, the believer demonstrates to themselves and to the network that cryptocurrencies and blockchain are not merely theoretical constructs but existent, useful, and even superior to other options. This is an act of renewing and outwardly demonstrating faith. It has roots in communion, an act seen as creating a direct union with the divine.

Realization - Realization happens when one looks deeper into the philosophies and values underpinning blockchain's creation and realizes that they are ideals worth supporting. The believer now sees cryptocurrency as an end to itself rather than as a mere means to a financial goal. This can happen before Acquisition, or after years of trading cryptocurrencies and even running blockchain companies. It can be a long process, or near-instantaneous. It is based off the idea of confirmation, which involves in-depth learning of one's religion before proclaiming their belief in it to a priest.

Hodl - To Hodl means to hold on to cryptocurrency, no matter how difficult the road becomes. These include dramatic drops in value where one may fear that prices will go to $0 (as they have for many cryptocurrencies), and massive increases that tempt the hodler to sell everything and spend it on a new smartphone/car/house/yacht. It is the opposite of "weak hands". The word comes from the prominent misspelling of 'hold' in a December 2013 Bitcointalk.org post *I AM HODLING*[148] where the apparently drunk user GameKyuubi dramatically explained that despite Bitcoin crashing (from its all-time high of over $1,000) and

[148] Gheorghe, Florian. "I AM HODLING: A Five-Year Anniversary Tribute." *BeInCrypto*, 13 June 2019.

his girlfriend being out at a lesbian bar while he was at home drinking whiskey, he refused to sell any of his bitcoins because he knew that he was a bad trader and would only lose BTC by panic-buying back in once prices inevitably started rising again, and that he refused to feed traders who feed off of Bitcoiners' emotions. Interestingly this paints an image of the Bitcoiner, a faithful follower of Satoshi, holding faithfully to their bitcoins despite being tempted by evil traders who sinfully buy and sell BTC instead of holding in an attempt to lead others away from their bitcoins. The post became iconic of the strength of will required to hold cryptocurrency despite turbulent market conditions, and so Hodl entered the blockchain vocabulary along with its opposite Sodl. The truth is that only a very small percentage of traders make consistent returns, so those who believe that any particular investment will one day see 100x returns will often be better off hodling despite the day-to-day noise. As the amount of any given cryptocurrency is finite, hodling further limits the supply and contributes to increases in value which directly impact the global awareness of and interest in Blockland. As a "Satoshian sacrament", hodling it is based on the idea of matrimony which involves sticking with a chosen partner "till death do us part."

Seeding – Seeding is the act of inspiring interest in Blockland from those who are unfamiliar with it. The first seeders gave paper-wallets and physical Bitcoins as gifts and tips, making the receivers who then held on to them relatively wealthy. In the early days, websites called *Bitcoin faucets* gave away as many as 5 bitcoins per hour to anyone who pressed a button and filled a CAPTCHA code to demonstrate that they were a real person.[149] The bubbling payouts of these desert spring-like faucets however decreased to nothingness as BTC's value increased. Casascius coins were developed to

[149] Lee, Timothy B. "Five Years of Bitcoin in One Post." *The Washington Post*, 3 Jan. 2014.

help seeding efforts, with many reports of 1 BTC and 5 BTC coins being given to family members, co-workers, and wait staff. Seeding is derived from the practice of anointing the sick and is comparable to Acquisition.

Participation – One brings the "Kingdom of Satoshi" closer by taking an active role in its proliferation. This requires more than passively owning cryptocurrency or using blockchain applications. By working for the betterment of Blockland, the power of the blockchain ecosystem is expanded. This includes building mining facilities, founding and working in blockchain companies, developing relevant code, running local blockchain discussion groups, setting up Bitcoin ATM's, hosting blockchain conferences, and bringing more businesses to accept cryptocurrency as payment. These acts of participation can of course lead to the further Acquisition of cryptocurrency which one can then Hodl and Seed. It can also consist of charitable acts done in the name of blockchain. Participation is modeled after the Catholic sacrament of holy orders.

The common wisdom in Blockland is that through the proper following of these sacraments, one will eventually reach the earthly and celestial pleasure-state of Lambomoon. This understanding comes from the combination of two ideals frequently present in Blocklandish conversations.

Lambomoon

Lambo is an earthly state of physical bliss and security. It can be understood as financial independence and material wealth allowing for freedom from all forms of oppression as well as the freedom of self-directed, powerful, and fast-paced movement through life. Despite its financial undertone, it is unclear if finance in the way we understand it would even exist by the time Lambomoon is reached.

It can also be understood to represent earthly power, fame, authority, and status. It is symbolized by the Lamborghini, with many adherents considering it the ultimate tangible prize for years of disciplined faith. It can be compared to the classical cornucopia and is in practical terms brought about by investing in cryptocurrency and hodling until its value is so high that one no longer wants for money.

Moon is an ethereal and sublime state of the triumph of Bitcoin. It calls upon imagery of Blockland's residents boarding expensive and technologically advanced rockets to establish the paradisiacal and heavenly Kingdom of Satoshi, operating through blockchain and based on the ideals of Satoshism far away from the present suffering and injustices of the world. This is symbolized by both the moon and by rockets and is a sort of un-reachable ideal that is beyond understanding, towards which Blockland's residents strive despite perhaps not reaching this ideal state of human existence in their own lifetimes. It can be understood through the Christian idea of heaven which is built upon a new earth and features golden streets and pearly gates, or for example the concepts of enlightenment or Nirvana which are prominent in Indian and Eastern religions.

This idea of Bitcoin bringing about world peace is rather widespread and is based on the thinking that wars have historically been financed by intentional inflation rather than direct taxation or the selling away of national assets like gold or railways. By the logic of certain people whom many might consider extremist, Bitcoin is a tool by which to effectively overthrow inherently violent governments by taking away from them the ability and willingness to finance continual war which they see as inherently evil. This was the case for "Bitcoin Jesus" Roger Ver, who recounted his conversion to Satoshism: "*when I realized that Bitcoin had the ability to... undermine every government on the entire planet's ability to wage war, I knew I had to get involved and start promoting Bitcoin full-time.*"[150]

In part due to this imagined future hostility between Bitcoin and worldly powers, measures have been taken to ensure that no authority can shut Bitcoin down. These include developments of mesh network computing, satellite feeds, and HAM-Radios operating on solar power which could be used to confirm Bitcoin transactions even without regional access to internet or electricity.[151] [152] [153]

There is also the implication that humans will set up colonies on the moon and beyond, at which point Bitcoin could become an interplanetary system. It has even been suggested in jest that if extraterrestrials were to arrive to Earth, at least with Bitcoin we need not be embarrassed when explaining our financial system to them. On the subject of spacetravel, it is also worth noting that while gold is somewhat rare on earth, there is no shortage of it in space which suggests that it will not be a stable form of money in a future of increasingly efficient space travel and asteroid mining.

If we are to define *Moon*, we might explain it as *Hyperbitcoinization*. The Hyperbitcoinization hypothesis is the imagined final outcome of global Bitcoin adoption, which would theoretically absorb all conceptions of money until Bitcoin entirely dominates the financial world as a hegemonic global currency.[154] Perhaps the most unfettered of such predictions was published on a crypto education

---

[150] bitbutter, Youtube.com user. "How Bitcoin Can Stop War." *YouTube*, 14 Nov 2014.

[151] Cuen, Leigh. "GoTenna Launches a Bitcoin Wallet That Works Without the Internet." *CoinDesk*, 14 May 2018.

[152] Bester, Nadja. "No Internet, No Problem: How to Send Bitcoin by Amateur Radio." *Bitcoin.com*, 19 Feb. 2019.

[153] Kaplikov, Michael. "Bitcoin Could Be More Resilient to Global Electric Failure Than Banks." *CoinTelegraph*, 21 May 2020.

[154] Kelso, Edward C. "Hyperbitcoinization: $100mil Per Coin by 2030." *Bitcoin.com*, 7 July 2018.

publication called Coinmonks by a writer called ObiWan KenoBit, who projected that each Bitcoin could be worth $100 million as early as 2030. In his *Winner Takes All* theory, KenoBit calculates the sum value of gold (7,700 billion), stocks (73,000 billion), money (127,000 billion), debt (215,000 billion), real estate (217,000 billion), and derivatives (1,200,000 billion), to arrive at a total money supply of 1,800,000 billion (1.8 quadrillion) dollars. He then divides this by ~18,000,000 bitcoins which remain in circulation to arrive at his 100-million-dollar hypothesis. His hyperbitcoinization theory posits that Bitcoin use will mature from micro-bubbles to larger bubbles, before experiencing rapid price increases and finally gaining stability as a global *unit of account.* As usage grows according to an adoption curve comparable to other technologies, there could be a tipping point after which not using/accepting Bitcoin is more costly than doing so. This might lead to institutional investors, banks, and even governments to fully embrace Bitcoin.

KenoBit's wild calculations are surely a fringe theory even in Blockland, where a more popular take on Bitcoin's future value imagines it primarily as an up-and-coming internet-age competitor or complement to gold. If for example Bitcoin were to absorb around half of gold's value, we should expect a valuation around a quarter-million dollars per bitcoin which happens to be the approximate price of a new Lamborghini. Whatever its final form, the consensus among believers is that Bitcoin will eventually stabilize to function more as a globally useful internet-native unit of account or store of wealth instead of forever remaining a speculative investment. It has even been suggested that the Satoshi could become an independent, global measure of value akin to the Kilogram, Liter, Celsius, or Meter. This role is currently filled by the US dollar, with gold arguably as its predecessor.

> *With Bitcoin you own your money. Personal ownership of money may thoroughly transform our modern world. We will go from a centralized economy manipulated by the few to one based on sound money principles – protecting the present, preserving the past and preparing for the future. Education, agriculture, medicine, and industry will be radically transformed once short sighted policies which benefit the few are abandoned for those with longer time horizons providing greater and lasting benefits for everyone. Incessant government machinations devaluing our money, work and lives will come to an end. Hyperbitcoinization is not necessarily a fantasy. 20 years ago we could not imagine how the internet would impact our world. Bitcoin will not be a panacea for all of our ills but I am fairly sure it will drive a monumental shift in our relationship with money and reframe our roles as citizens as part of a borderless global economy.*[155]
>
> - ObiWan Kenobit, 25 June 2018.

Satoshi's Citadels

As Satoshist discourse has developed, some believers have promoted the rejection of the vain dreams of *Lambo* and instead advocating for *Van*; that is, the use of Bitcoin fortunes towards the establishment of large families and the mini vans associated with them. The implied assumption is that early Bitcoin investors possess some mixture of extraordinary evolutionary (intellectual) fitness or ideological purity, and that they have a sort of Darwinian obligation to maximize the amount of their offspring and even found aristocratic dynasties of sort. This rhetoric appears confined to westerners, and at times suggests race-oriented undertones. This thinking can be compared to that of the Quiverfull Movement, which encouraged 20th century Christians to have as many children as possible in order to raise up an "army of God". The idea of starting a sort of dynasty is popular, with an ideal in which kingly

---

[155] Kenobit, ObiWan. "Hyperbitcoinization: Winner Takes All." *Coinmonks*, 25 June 2018.

levels of ever-increasing (deflating) wealth can be passed on for generations.

As with many Satoshists who are in certain ideological ways opposed to contemporary society (in thinking that schools give incorrect information about economics, among other things), Quiverfull families often homeschooled their children and established homesteads. The latter is especially relevant to many Satoshists, who idealize self-reliance and non-dependence on established systems. Another established Christian movement to which we might compare Satoshism is that of the Health and Wealth or Prosperity Gospel, which teaches that God desires for his followers to be wealthy, and rewards acts of faith with financial prosperity.

It is accurate to say that a majority of Satoshists believe in what is best described as a sort of financial apocalypse – a second coming of *the new gold* to underpin the economy of a new age. The common understanding of this is that privately-owned central banks – the very foundations upon which banks, governments, and our economies and thus societies operate, are rotten and corrupted to the core. To save oneself from the trials and tribulations of this perceived financial rapture, the Satoshist *stacks sats*. The implication is that the entire system will be destroyed; either by collapsing upon its own greed or by being made obsolete, perhaps through both functions simultaneously. The antidote to this broken and corrupted system is an indestructible, incorruptible system (saviour) that will cast it away. As Satoshists perceive themselves as being aligned with this victorious saviour, many of them actively long for the end of the world as we know it.

The image of an apocalypse is never pleasant. Bitcoin has been associated with the symbolism of a fiery phoenix "rising out of the ashes" of destruction, and a much-circulated webcomic showed a presumed Satoshist enjoying life in a fertile bio-dome while the world burned and wars raged around him. A run of Physical Bitcoins minted by Cryptolator in 2014 featured the image of *the people* using *chains* to pull down the pillars of a burning bank, with the "globalist elites" and upper-class bankers (symbolized by pigs and dogs) holding worthless bags of money and weeping upon its steps. This highlighted an image of Bitcoin as a sort of populist revolution against the economic order.

It is said that there is nothing new under the sun. Gold and silver bugs have been accumulating precious metals for decades, many based on a belief in an imminent collapse of "the system". Doomsday guides popular in the United States advise survivalists and "preppers" to build bunkers and stockpile food, ammunition, survival gear, and gold. Bitcoin has drawn many from these overlapping sub-cultures, some of whom have incorporated various cryptocurrencies into their survival plans and others who have become full-out Satoshists. As hodling (hoarding) is celebrated, Satoshian values have faced criticism as being anti-social and selfish. This has evoked the both celebrated and despised image of the ideal Satoshian as a powerful and mysterious dragon hiding its legendary hoard in a protected mountain lair. Natually what one sees as greedy hoarding, another will see as responsible saving.

A small but notable subset of Satoshists are actively building connected, self-sufficient, and ideally defensible communities in places such as South American jungles, Caribbean islands, and South East Asian beaches. Some of these have gone to great lengths in building relationships with the local/provincial and even national governments.[156] These attempts to create special arraignments have often gotten these wealthy crypto-globalists accused of representing a new

---

[156] Strauss, Neil. "Brock Pierce: The Hippie King of Cryptocurrency." *Rolling Stone*, 26 July 2018.

wave of colonialism.[157] Their new residents seek community, networking, freedom from taxes, laws, government surveillance, and a place to lay low should society collapse – or worse, blame its collapse on blockchain and dust off the old guillotine for anyone associated with it. This micro-trend and the much wider idealization of it may be in part inspired by an anonymously published 2014 short-story in which the author, presented as a time-traveller from 2025, begs readers to stop using Bitcoin because it has led to the horrific destruction of society – with only a tiny subset of wealthy "earlies" living in safe and luxurious *Citadels.*

> *Please move on if you don't believe me, I have no way of proving I'm going to tell you...*
>
> *There are two main forms of wealth in today's world: Land and Cryptocurrency...*
>
> *"What is a Citadel?" you might wonder. Well, by the time Bitcoin reached $1M, services began to emerge for the "Bitcoin rich" to protect themselves as well as their wealth.*
>
> *It started with expensive safes, then began to include bodyguards, and today, "earlies" (our term for early adapters), as well as those rich whose wealth survived the "transition" live in isolated gated cities called Citadels, where most work is automated....*
>
> *In my world, soon to be your world, most governments no longer exist, as Bitcoin transactions are done anonymously and thus governments can't enforce taxation on their citizens.*
>
> *Exchanges of services are nearly all online, totally decentralized and anonymous....*
>
> *Economic growth today is about -2% per year.*
>
> *Why is this?*

---

[157] Reutzel, Bailey. "I Survived the Eternal Boy Playground, Will Puerto Rico?" *CoinDesk*, 1 Apr. 2018.

If you own more than 0.01 Bitcoin, chances are you don't do anything with your money. There is no inflation, and thus no incentive to invest your money. Just like the medieval ages had no significant economic growth, as wealth was measured in gold, our society has no economic growth either, as people know their 0.01 Bitcoin will be enough to last them a lifetime.

The fact that there are still new Bitcoin released is what prevents our world from collapse so far it seems, but people fear that the decline in inflation that will occur during the next block halving may further wreck our economy.

Most people who own any significant amount of Bitcoin no longer speak to their families and lost their friends, because they had to change their identities. There have been also been a few suicides of people who could not handle the guilt after seeing what happened to the bag-holders, the type of skeptical people who continued to believe it would eventually collapse, even after hearing the rumors of governments buying Bitcoin.

Many people were taken hostage, and thus, it is suspected that 25% percent of the "Bitcoin riches" actually physically tortured someone to get him to spill his wallet.

Why didn't we abandon Bitcoin, and move to another system? Well, we tried of course. We tried to step over to an inflationary cryptocurrency, but nobody with an IQ above 70 was willing to step up first and volunteer.

After all, why would you voluntarily invest a lot of your money into a currency you know would continually decline in value? The thing that made Bitcoin so dangerous to society was also what made it so successful.

Bitcoin allows us to give into our greed.

In Africa, surveys show that an estimated 70% of people believe that Bitcoin was invented by the devil himself....

It doesn't have to be like this. You do not have to share our fate. I don't know how, but you must find a way to destroy this godforsaken project in its infancy. I know this is a difficult thing to ask of you.

You believed you were helping the world by eliminating the central banking cartel that governs your economies.

However, I have seen where it ends.[158]

- Reddit user Luka_Magnotta, 31 Aug. 2013.

The author re-appeared six years later in 2019 to express surprise at how popular the short story had become and re-iterated his concerns that as a "negative-sum" mechanism that widens wealth gaps while producing nothing – yet consuming huge amounts of electricity, Bitcoin is effectively detrimental to the earth and society: "*With that said, I hope this story has entertained you and helped you recognize some of the problems our society would face if we ever witnessed widespread adaption of Bitcoin or similar digital currencies.*"[159]

Ironically considering the intentions of the author, this story reflects (and fans) a level of apocalyptic fantasy where Satoshists dream of a future where they become the kings of their own post-national ultra-minimalist states with private armies and custom laws. This is well in line with the deeply libertarian and anarcho-capitalist ideology that pervades and even defines basic Satoshism – ultimately embracing the idea of a natural or evolutionary hierarchy within which individuals seek to advance. In this mental model, it is Satoshi himself who is the all-seeing eye at the top of the pyramid as the greatest hodler, and Satoshists' strive to be *closer to Satoshi* by accumulating more Satoshis. The other task is to *preach Satoshi's message* to ensure that greater amounts of Satoshists join and uphold the pyramid, albeit most often at lower levels. One might thus define Satoshism as a Bitcoin-age take on Capitalism – Bitcoinism replacing Dollarism, which itself replaced Goldism

---

158 Luka_Magnotta, Reddit.com user. "I am a Time Traveler From the Future, Here to Beg You to Stop What You Are Doing." *Reddit r/Bitcoin*, 31 Aug. 2013.

159 Luka_Magnotta, Reddit.com user. "I Am A Time Traveler From the Future, Here to Beg You to Stop What You Are Doing." Reddit r/Bitcoin, 31 Aug. 2013.

some decades ago. Its all the same: riches, power, and dominance – Mammon.

These citadel-like crypto-colonies vary in levels of cult-ness, remote-ness, and underground-ness, from tongue-in-cheek-mild to wilderness-wild. An ill-fated example of the wet-n-wild side lies in a Seasteading Institute affiliated settlement 12 miles off Thailand's Phuket coast. The first of 20 "sea cabins" was inhabited by crypto-trader Chad Elwartowski and Bitcoin expert Supranee Thepdet, both seasteading pioneers aiming to form a sovereign community in international waters. This experiment came to an end when the initial structure built by Ocean Builders was boarded by the Royal Thai Navy in April 2019, who stated that the couple had intended to establish a "*permanent settlement at sea beyond the sovereignty of nations by using a legal loophole.*" Thai authorities disputed the idea that the settlement was outside its sovereignty by way of the 200-mile exclusive economic area, and said that the concept undermined the "*national security as well as economic and social interests of [all] maritime nations*" and "*could lead to a creation of a new state within Thailand's territorial waters.*" The pair was ultimately accused of threatening Thailand's sovereignty, which can be punished with the death penalty.[160]

On the mild side, a phenomenon of crypto houses have appeared in major cities around the world, derived from and often indistinguishable from "hacker houses" which cater to the somewhat off-centre lifestyles of intensely focused coders and blockchain entrepreneurs. These often form naturally between friends who share an interest in blockchain and invite others of their "Satoshian sect" or tribe to join. They can also revolve around companies, such as one example where the co-founders building an algorithmic trading

---

[160] "World Bitcoin Trader Facing Death Penalty after Thai Navy Boards Cabin of Fugitive 'Seasteaders'." *NBC News*, 20 Apr. 2019.

start-up attempted to stack ~10 sleeping containers to accommodate newly-hired programmers in their rented house in an expensive Canadian city. Another case includes an Asian blockchain incubator renting out an entire resort and offering rooms exclusively to "crypto people", and examples abound of early crypto investors purchasing adjacent properties on tropical islands. When taken far enough, this crypto-life can well be described as a counter-cultural movement. Perhaps due to their collective rejection of established banking practices, Satoshists tend to be highly skeptical of just about everything related to the "establishment", creating a fertile ground for the proliferation of all manner of conspiracy theories.

The general theme across these cases is that for better or worse, people sharing compatible Satoshian views tend to band together both online and offline rather easily and create a feedback-loop of devotion to blockchain while applying peer-pressure to prevent a certain wrong-think. The crypto life becomes for some a practically all-encompassing DIY lifestyle combining social life, family life, faith/purpose, business, employment, investing, and even vacations all into one. It seems that the most advanced Satoshians have rejected this world completely, opting for blockchain houses with blockchain friends and blockchain wives/husbands, working at their blockchain jobs to earn blockchain money which they invest in other blockchain projects, and making family vacations to blockchain conferences around the world while teaching their children about how one day soon everything will change and that they will inherit the earth in some coming moment of blockchain triumph.

Though the Bitcointalk.org forum established by Satoshi was the original place for Satoshian's to convene, the movement soon spread to the grass-roots level. Small independent groups taking the form of weekly *Bitcoin Meetups* sprouted around the world, usually led by an individual or local Bitcoin company. As these meetups became local nodes of Bitcoin & crypto culture, the hosts of the events could at times capitalize on their position as well-connected local blockchain leaders. As cities tended to have several different groups meeting every week, this at times stoked serious tribalism and bad-blooded competition. In addition to church-like meetups, regional cathedral-like *Bitcoin Embassies* were established in various major cities to provide rallying points for the movement:[161]

> *Bitcoin Embassies are grass root educational organizations located around the world with a shared mission of helping people better understand bitcoin and blockchain. As bitcoin is a decentralized project, bitcoin embassies were formed to represent bitcoin and blockchain similar to a traditional embassy that represents the interests of its country.*[162]

These various meetups began to convert the curious into the faithful, and would consist of various elements including guest speakers, technical discussions, social time, and work towards initiatives to amplify Satoshi's message at the local level by actions such as advocating for local businesses to accept Bitcoin. Some of the most faithful have gone as far as to take a Vow of Bitcoin, even cancelling their bank accounts and credit cards, and pledging to live only by cryptocurrency. While challenging, it can be done by buying gift cards with cryptocurrency and frequenting using Bitcoin-ATM's when cash is needed.[163] Welcome to the millenarial blockchain movement. The Bitcoin cult of Satoshi.

---

[161] Southurst, Jon. "New Bitcoin Embassies in Asia Bring World Total to 17." *CoinDesk*, 13 Jan. 2015.
[162] "Bitcoin Embassies" *BlockSocial*.
[163] Shin, Laura. "This Man Has Been Living on Bitcoin For 3 Years." *Forbes*, 7 Jan. 2016.

1850 depiction of the establishment of Iceland, which eventually became a stand-alone nation separated from the Norse homeland.

CHAPTER 6

The Pioneers

Blockland's First Settlements

We rewind to May 2013, six months before the beginning of the first $1,000 bull run. At this point, Blockland had up to a dozen cryptocurrency settlements with a combined value of 1.38 billion dollars. BTC's value had recently crossed $100 for the first time, and Bitcoin held 94% of Blockland's population (market cap) while another 5% of settlers lived in Litecoin. The remaining 1% made their homes in the colonies of, Primecoin, Peercoin, Namecoin, Terracoin, Devcoin, Feathercoin, and Novacoin.

Primecoin (XPM) for example was built with a mining algorithm that directed miner's computing power towards solving sequences of Cunningham prime numbers, which were then published on the blockchain for use by scientists and mathematicians. In contrast, Bitcoin's mining consists of the calculation of essentially arbitrary equations that does not in itself have a wider societal benefit. Because these prime-number calculations involved a computing process that was very difficult to perform but easy to verify, it made for a viable proof-of-work to demonstrate that real, quantifiable work had been completed for each generated Primecoin.[164]

Peercoin (PPC) instituted a form of government different from the other settlements. Instead of only relying on proof-of-work which proved that a fair amount of work was performed for the creation of each block (from which tokens come from), Peercoin's constitution also had *proof-of-stake*. This meant that in addition to mining, new coins were also generated based on a pre-set inflation rate and delivered to existing holders based on the amounts of their holdings. If the inflation rate was for example 0.1% per day, then someone holding 100,000 coins would receive 100 more on day 1, and 100.1 coins on day 2. In practice with PPC, users had to keep a Peercoin node online to receive these inflation payments.[165]

Part of the philosophy behind proof-of-stake was that while someone could theoretically take over Bitcoin by acquiring more miners or even developing more powerful computers that eclipse the competition, the only way for anyone to gain a significant monopoly of power in a proof-of-stake ecosystem was by actually buying a massive amount of the coin in question from other consenting members of the settlement. Owning most of the given cryptocurrency (which would undoubtedly rise astronomically if anyone tried to acquire a controlling share) was considered more difficult than controlling most of the generation capacity (mining power). This governance structure was the colony's mechanism to guarantee continuity to its heirs while preventing outside interference.[166]

---

164 Buterin, Vitalik. "Primecoin: The Cryptocurrency Whose Mining Is Actually Useful." *Bitcoin Magazine*, 8 July 2013.
165 Sunny King, Bitcointalk.org user. "[ANN] [PPC] PPCoin Released! - First Long-Term Energy-Efficient Crypto-Currency." *Bitcoin Forum*, 19 Aug. 2012.
166 "What is Proof-of-Stake?" *Ledger Academy*, 23 Oct. 2019.

Devcoin was designed to be mined in conjunction with Bitcoin. From every block containing 50,000 coins, 90% (45,000 DVC) would go towards the development of open-source goods while the remaining 5,000 would go to the successful miner. Programmers, hardware developers, writers, musicians, filmmakers, and graphic artists could all receive Devcoin contributions for their work towards open-source projects. The goal of this was not to simply reward those who effectively donate their spare time towards the commons, but to encourage an exponential increase in open-source contributors around the world by making it financially feasible. This was to have the added benefit of theoretically ending unemployment; anyone lacking money could go clean up a few Wikipedia articles and receive fair compensation. One could entertain the idea of Devcoin being a "tax" for the common good paid by Bitcoin miners, only that it was not only completely optional, but rewarded the taxpayer (miner) directly as well. Absurdly, the more taxes one paid, the more money they could make.[167]

Namecoin was created by forking Bitcoin, meaning that it used the same infrastructure and consisted of a maximum 21 million coins. It functioned as an alternative, decentralized domain name system to register .bit domain names outside the control of ICANN (Internet Corporation for Assigned Names and Number). The project was proposed in September 2010 and is especially notable because Satoshi himself seemed to support the project and contributed ideas. The coin had a clear ideology behind it in avoiding domain registration from being centralized under any organization, and despite significant technical efforts it was never adopted in any significant capacity.[168]

[167] Aegis, Bitcointalk.org user. "[DVC]DevCoin - Official Thread – Moderated." *Bitcoin Forum*, 14 June 2013.
[168] Buchko, Steven. "What Is Namecoin (NMC)? | Beginner's Guide." *Coin Central*, 6 July 2018.

Pre-Bubble Pioneers

This massive wave of immigration to Blockland which brought BTC above $1,000 came to an abrupt stop when rumors swirled that the Peoples Bank of China (PBoC) had banned any Chinese [money] from moving to Blockland. These rumours were not entirely accurate, but thus began a long tradition of Chinese government statements causing both panics and optimism amongst the colonies of Blockland. Though the world's attention was on Bitcoin, several new settlements were being founded each week throughout the 2nd half of 2013. Ripple, NXT, BitShares, Worldcoin, and Dogecoin are notable examples of more than fifty crypto-camps established in this period.

Worldcoin - 14 May 2013

Worldcoin's objective was essentially to improve upon Bitcoin by being faster, with a vision of becoming the primary global cash as the name would suggest. Its main innovation was a 15-second block instead of the ~10 minutes required by Bitcoin. This made Worldcoin transactions effectively instant. As became the norm within the Bitcointalk.org forums where the project was announced, three of the first five comments were negative and consisted of users deriding the projects as a scam; the main criticism being that *confirming* was not truly about number of blocks, but of time itself, and that WDC would need 40 confirmations for equivalence to one BTC confirmation.[169] Despite these early naysayers, the project grew to encompass a large community as its market value grew 150-fold, peaking at nearly $29 million during the late-2013 bull market.

[169] WorldCoin, Bitcointalk.org user. "[WDC] Worldcoin | 3.0 Flirtatious Ant Released! | Multicoin Architecture." *Bitcoin Forum*, 14 May 2013.

Those involved with WDC also launched Arizona-based Scharmbeck, a "*FinCen approved Worldcoin financial service*", to allow users to directly deposit USD to buy WDC.[170] The idea was to lower the barrier of entry by not requiring buyers to purchase bitcoin as a middle-coin. This Worldcoin exchange charged fees and in November 2013 offered to sell "fee shares" for 0.05 BTC, effectively valuing the company's profit share at 50,000 BTC, of which up to half was allegedly sold. By the time Scharmbeck announced beta tests in late December 2013 with a press release titled "*Move Over Bitcoin!*"[171], the end for both it and Worldcoin had already begun. As the price slid from its peak of ~90 cents, the members of the Worldcoin Foundation board were removed and Scharmbeck failed to launch. Despite this, the WDC community consisted of many loyalists including forum member Jomppe who vocally defended the project even after the original creators were gone and the price had dipped below 20 cents:[172]

> *Dear fellow crypto community*
> *I am sorry for those of you who has been taking huge losses with this, but it is investing. You need to make decisions on your own to invest or not to invest.*
> *There is no declaration to close Scharmbeck.*
> *Even it is not in the best interest of developers - they have spent hours of developing the service, why should it be closed before opened?*
> *I ask you to calm down and start hoarding worldcoins again - why not, they are cheap.*
> *Scharmbeck shares I have no idea because they are not real equity (they are the shares to... income only).*
> *Even WDC is a coin and Scharmbeck is a service.*

---

170 Scharmbeck, Bitcointalk.org user. "Scharmbeck.com Feeshares Now Available! Over 50% Sold." *Bitcoin Forum*, 4 Nov. 2013.
171 "Move Over Bitcoin! Altcoin Giant Worldcoin Launches New Technology That Makes Purchasing and Using Cryptocurrency as Easy as 1, 2, 3." *PR Newswire*, 20 Dec. 2013.
172 Jomppe, Bitcointalk.org User. "Debunking WorldCoin Scam Accusations One by One." *Bitcoin Forum*, 20 Feb. 2014.

> *Personally I have 0 shares but tons of WDC (the price is so low right now).*
> *WorldCoin is still on its way to the moon.*
> *Let's join in the rally.*
> *The foundation is restructurated, but even without the foundation WDC has lowest confirmation times so it is excellent virtual coin.*
> *The new leadership will take WDC to the next level.*[173]
> - Forum user Jomppe, 18 Feb. 2014.

Despite Jomppe's pleas, the response was a resounding "*no thanks*" as WDC kept falling to less then half a cent. Worldcoin's story is archetypal to many similar coins in this era and its history highlights many trends that emerged in this time. These include the ideas of oft-loyal, optimistic, and enthusiastic communities formed by users and investors, as well as the idea of there being a somewhat independent "foundation" set up to govern the blockchain in question. Another is the integration with a commercial service of some kind, which gave the coin value and legitimacy in the eyes of investors. In Scharmbeck's case, the shares could be classified as *Bitcoin securities.* It is worthwhile to note that already in this time, the idea of *scam coins* was entrenched in Blockland's consciousness and community members were by default suspicious of new projects. It is also notable that despite WDC's near-universal classification as a failure for over two years, it again managed to briefly rise 100-fold during the market bubble in mid-2017, and again in early-2018.

Ripple - 2013

Ripple's history is intertwined with that of Bitcoin by a common thread called Jed McCaleb. If you recall, McCaleb created Mt.Gox from a trading card website. Two months after McCaleb sold off his burgeoning exchange to Mark Karpeles, he began developing a

---

[173] Jomppe. Bitcointalk.org User. "Scharmbeck Will Not Be Closed and WorldCoin Is Doing Well." *Bitcoin Forum*, 8 Feb. 2014.

new digital currency. This new currency was to operate based on a system of consensus among the network's actual users as opposed to a consensus among impersonal machines (miners) as in Bitcoin. The issues it promised to fix were two-fold; firstly it would add a trust/society layer to facilitate transactions, and secondly it would ease the problems associated with overly-centralized exchanges; the very problems that McCaleb had created. It was then that McCaleb and his hired programmer Chris Larsen approached Ryan Fugger, who had been working RipplePay, a similar concept with a long-standing community, since 2005. These discussions resulted in Fugger stepping aside as McCaleb and Larsen took lead of the project and founded OpenCoin in 2012 (which was renamed Ripple Labs in 2015).[174] [175]

Fugger's "*goal was to create a system of debt money without artificially imposed scarcity*"[176] where everyone could effectively be a peer-to-peer bank with a revolving line of credit between friends-of-friends. This concept was then married with the Ripple (XRP) token based on the open-source Ripple Protocol (RTXP) which was developed by the company. Strictly speaking this protocol is not a blockchain at all but functions similarly to one from the user's perspective, with 4-second transactions to boot.[177]

> *When you join the Ripple network, you designate primary contacts and establish levels of trust by choosing the amount of credit you are willing to offer each individual. I might feel okay lending up to $1000 to a few close friends whom I know will have a deep obligation to pay me back, while making only $50*

---

[174] Andrews, Edmund. "Chris Larsen: Money Without Borders." *Insights by Stanford Business*, 24 Sept. 2013.
[175] Larsen, Chris, and Jed McCaleb. "What Is Ripple. Everything You Need to Know." *CoinTelegraph*, 1 Jan. 2013.
[176] Peck, Morgan. "Ripple Credit System Could Help or Harm Bitcoin." *IEEE Spectrum*, 14 Jan. 2013.
[177] Liu, Alec. "Ripple, a Peer-to-Peer Financing Network, Could Make Bitcoin Great (Or Destroy It)." *Vice*, 23 Jan. 2013.

> *available to the man I talk to every morning at the deli. But with Ripple, the credit isn't only available to my acquaintances. It becomes available to anyone else who knows the people in my network.*
> *Let's say, for example, that I want to sell a Web application to Bob, who knows my close friend Alice (credit limit $1000). Ripple allows Bob to trade with me using his credit limit with Alice. If she trusts him for $100, that becomes his credit limit with me. I would send Bob the merchandise in exchange for his promise to pay. But instead of owing me, Bob would actually owe Alice, who would in turn owe me. Once Bob satisfied his debt, the Ripple network would destroy the entire chain of IOUs.*[178]
>
> \- Morgan Peck, 14 Jan. 2013.

Ripple is in many ways the odd one out when it comes to cryptocurrencies of the 2010's, even to such an extent that many do not even consider it a true cryptocurrency at all. Everything from Litecoin to Ethereum, to dApp's, DAO's, and NFT's, can be traced directly down the technology tree to Bitcoin, but that is not quite the case with Ripple whose original concept was developed concurrently to Bitcoin. As such, the Ripple community can be understood as not having been founded and built in Blockland at all, but rather moving their pre-established settlement to this adopted homeland in one swoop.

It is worthwhile to note that digital currency is not synonymous with blockchain or decentralization; if users accept a new type of currency, it has a level of legitimacy due to that fact alone. One can conceivably place their trust in a corporation that issues money, just like one can place trust in a government or blockchain to do the same. Blockchain's generally understood role in currency has been the facilitation of exchange. If an open source protocol were created to fill the same role, the result would be no less of a digital

[178] Peck, Morgan. "Ripple Credit System Could Help or Harm Bitcoin." *IEEE Spectrum*, 14 Jan. 2013.

currency or even cryptocurrency. An in-game currency used within a multiplayer game or online casino is by definition a digital or virtual currency but may not have anything to do with blockchain. Similarly, a blockchain used to track supply chain components may not have anything to do with the concept of currency.

As a corporation, Ripple Labs has been no stranger to controversy. Its initial $96 million of funding came from a series of rounds between 2013-2016 from some of the largest funds including Andreessen Horowitz and Google Ventures. In the three following years, it earned over a billion dollars from selling XRP to both individuals and large institutions like banks which use it for inter-bank transfers. This selling of XRP was questioned by Stewart Hosie, a British Member of Parliament:

> *If people buy XRP—a financial asset—from Ripple Labs, it does not entitle them to an ownership stake, there is no right to be converted back into conventional currencies and it does not pay any return. It also seemingly has no purpose. Is that simply to avoid XRP looking like a security or an equity, and to avoid the necessary regulation?*[179]
>
> - Stewart Hosie MP, 1 May 2018.

Under similar allegations, the company has been fined by FinCEN due to non-compliance with anti-money laundering laws.[180]

It is understandable why "blockchain traditionalists" love to hate Ripple, as it can rightfully be seen as something of an antithesis to "Bitcoin values."[181] As per human nature this anger has at times

---

[179] "Oral evidence: Digital Currencies, HC 910." *Treasury Committee, UK House of Commons*, 1 May 2018.

[180] "FinCEN Fines Ripple Labs Inc. in First Civil Enforcement Action Against a Virtual Currency Exchanger." *Financial Crimes Enforcement Network*, 5 May 2015.

[181] Liebkind, Joe. "Why Some Claim Ripple Isn't a 'Real' Cryptocurrency." *Investopedia*, 14 Dec. 2017.

been expressed in childish ways, such as by humorously suggesting that Ripple's logo looked like a fidget spinner "*for fidgety crypto investors who are too distracted to learn that Ripple isn't even crypto.*" Ripple is a centralized company run by real people and funded by "the establishment", as opposed to an anonymously created decentralized currency of revolution meant to debase banks. If Bitcoin is gold 2.0, then perhaps Ripple is something akin to debt 2.0. At its core Ripple is an initiative to solve the same basic problem as Bitcoin, though its understanding of and solution to the problem is different.

The Ripple Tree has grown into and been merged to the Bitcoin Tree of Cryptocurrency/Blockchain, and the technologies and norms we today associate with cryptocurrency are derived from both and are perhaps better described under the general umbrella of digital currencies. Ripple's status as a "traditional" organization has also helped cement its staying power; its nearly 200m of donations include $50 million to help universities develop blockchain curricula and conduct research.[182]

NXT - 24 Nov. 2013

Launched as a "*2nd generation cryptocurrency*" by an anonymous developer known as BCNext, NXT combined proof-of-stake (pioneered by Peercoin) with a static supply of one billion coins. This was perhaps the first notable cryptocurrency project (except for Ripple) to be programmed from scratch as opposed to being merely a redesign of Bitcoin's source code. The idea was to broaden the scope of cryptocurrency by marrying the fast payment protocol with a native "stock exchange" and digital goods store among other new features. The no-mining aspect of proof-of-stake

---

[182] Varshney, Neer. "Ripple is Giving Universities $50M to Research Cryptocurrency and Blockchain." *The Next Web*, 4 June 2018.

would be better for the environment, and transaction fees would be used to power the network.[183]

But who got the one billion coins?

They were distributed proportionally between 72 individuals according to the amounts of BTC they sent to BCNext. This was the second-ever Initial Coin Offering, and in September-November 2013 it raised 22 BTC ($12,300).[184]

Sending a few hundred dollars to this anonymous forum-poster paid off for the lucky 72. For each dollar, investors received ~81,500 NXT tokens upon launch on November 24th, 2013. Only eight weeks later each token was worth 10 cents ($8,150 per dollar invested), but over the following year fell as low as a half-cent. It remained virtually forgotten for 2 years before peaking again at 20 cents in June 2017, and $1.70 in December of that same year. This means that on paper, each dollar invested into the NXT ICO saw a historic return of $138,550 in just over four years – 13,855,000% profit! Of course, realistically, buyers likely sold between 1 cent ant 10 cents to see returns of approximately 1,000x–10,000x over a few short months. Even more sobering is that some of these likely "cashed out" their investments back into bitcoin, turning a modest 1-BTC investment into thousands of bitcoins.

Many blamed this botched fundraiser as a primary reason for NXT's failure to catch on, reasoning that BCNext's approach to raising money came across as illegitimate and resulted in too few people participating. Had there been 720 initial recipients instead of only 72, things might have been quite different. This is because as a decentralized project, NXT relied on these initial participants

---

183 BCNext, Bitcointalk.org user. "[Ann NXT :: Descendant of Bitcoin." *Bitcoin Forum*, 28 Sept. 2013.

184 rickyjames, NXT Forum member. "Index to NXT Threads On Bitcointalk Started In 2013." NXT Forum, 24 Mar. 2014.

to create and govern the community around it along with ongoing development. All these activities needed to be funded by the donations of early investors, including the giving out of NXT via faucets; websites where one could click a button to receive an amount of cryptocurrency for free. Disorganization was another cause of decline, with the too-small community's developers and committees often pulling in different directions. This may have been in part caused by BCNext leaving the community to fend for itself as he disappeared 6 months into the project in a way comparable to Satoshi.[185] [186]

The use of PoS (Proof-of-Stake) instead of Proof-of-Work was bold, but at that time mining was still considered something that average people could do to earn cryptocurrency and thus widely seen as a necessary element of a cryptocurrency. The concept of PoS received a fair amount of criticism, with some labeling it a "*Piece-of-Shit.*"

Despite its difficulties, NXT was revolutionary. The *NXT Asset Exchange* which went online in 2015 became a "crypto stock market" where anyone could start a "company" and sell "shares" denominated in NXT. This made the idea of *Bitcoin securities exchanges* (of which most of the originals had died or declined at this point) an official part of the project. This was done through the introduction of *colored coins,* which consisted of individual NXT tokens being designated (colored) to represent a share or some other physical or non-physical thing. To understand this concept, imagine the idea that each NXT token is a blank silver coin, but by stamping one with the words "*1% share of ABC Company*" or "*IOU $10, signed John Doe.*" The owners of these NXT Assets

---

185 danp123, NXT Forum member. "Sergey Ivancheglo Is BCnext." *NXT Forum*, 21 July 2017.

186 quantumdwayne, Reddit.com user. "Why Did NXT Never Catch on?" *Reddit r/NXT*, 9 July 2017.

could then verifiably vote on issues concerning them (shareholder meetings etc.), and this same function could be used for all NXT holders to vote on various community issues. This was the origin of NFT's; *Non-Fungible Tokens* which were not intrinsically equal to all other tokens due to some unique designation.[187]

Another first of NXT was that it allowed users to communicate with each other by sending encrypted messages between accounts. A major innovation came in mid-2016 as *Smart Transaction* templates were launched to help businesses create custom blockchain solutions in essentially the same manner as Ethereum smart contracts. Considering that its code is independent from Bitcoin and introduced a breath of new functions, NXT certainly lived up to the idea of being a 2nd generation cryptocurrency.

Dogecoin - 6 Dec. 2013

As Bitcoin graced news around the world during the late-2013 run-up to $1,000, themes of controversy, criminality, and hacking were imprinted into the global understanding of cryptocurrency. This frustrated Oregon-based programmer Billy Markus, who felt that a fun cryptocurrency could have a broader appeal without the sense of gravity and controversy that surrounded Bitcoin. At the same time, Sydney-based marketer Jackson Palmer had bought *dogecoin.com* and created a parody landing page to jokingly announce Dogecoin, a cryptocurrency based on a popular Shiba Inu dog meme surrounded by simplistic and even non-sensical sayings written in comic sans.[188] Netizens loved the idea, and when Markus came across Palmer's parody website, he thought it was hilarious

---

187 apenzl, NXTER.org user. "Tutorial: NXT Asset Exchange." *NXTER.org*, 22 Dec. 2014.

188 NovaXP, Knowyourmeme.com user. "Doge." *Know Your Meme*, 24 July 2013.

and tweeted him to offer his assistance in making Dogecoin a reality. Three days later, Dogecoin was launched.[189]

Dogecoin took the internet by storm, with Markus once describing the following weeks "*as if I went and planted a single seed in the ground, then come back the next day to a fully grown forest.*"[190] A dedicated community soon formed, creating infrastructure including an active forum, subreddit, mining pools, an IRC chat channel, Doge-themed games, DOGE-accepting merchants, and a *Block Explorer.* A Block Explorer allows anyone to easily explore a blockchain by looking up the balances of various addresses and following the flows of tokens. Block Explorers can be thought of as browsers for blockchain in the same way as Internet Explorer is a browser for the internet. Dogecoin mining (digging, as the community calls it) rewards were initially randomized to add to the fun factor, though this was later changed to a model of stable payouts. This random reward function was borrowed from Lucky Coin, an earlier token on which Dogecoin's code was based. Considering that Lucky Coin was based on Litecoin's code, we can understand Dogecoin to be the grandchild of Litecoin and the child of an experimental gamble-mining coin. As this code is scrypt-based, it cannot be mined by the FPGA & ASIC devices.[191]

As a fun-loving cryptocurrency, Dogecoin introduced many new users to blockchain by eliminating the popular conception that it was entirely boring and technical. As the community was centered around having fun, sharing DOGE, and learning about cryptocurrency instead of getting rich like the rest of Blockland, Dogecoin gained a reputation of dog-like friendliness. This was demonstrated when the *save Dogemas* fundraising campaign reimbursed users

189 Reed, Richard. "A History of Dogecoin." *Openledger Blog*, 30 June 2018.
190 "The Humans Behind Dogecoin." *Spelunk.in*, 17 Dec. 2013.
191 Bradbury, Danny. "Scrypt-Based Miners and the New Cryptocurrency Arms Race." CoinDesk, 23 Oct. 2013.

who lost a total of 21 million DOGE ($12,000) in a dogewallet hack which happened on Christmas Day in 2013.[192] The Doge community has also managed to organize some interesting outreach. The first of these was the raising of $50,000 to send the Jamaican bobsled team to the 2014 Sochi Winter Olympics, which resulted in DOGE value rising by 50%. Later that year the community raised $55,000 (67.8 million DOGE) to sponsor NASCAR driver Josh Wise, who rode a doge-wrapped car in several races.[193]

The unique community in DOGE can be understood to behave as it does because virtually nobody takes Dogecoin so seriously as to depend or seriously count on it financially. Despite never having been presented as an investment, its total valuation peaked at almost two billion dollars in January 2018. This can be understood as a case study in internet virality, as well as an interesting study in economics. A common mantra within the community is that the price of Dogecoin is always stable, because "*1 DOGE = 1 DOGE*" no matter what.

Ethereum - 23 Jan. 2014

In 2011 when Ethereum's founder Vitalik Buterin was just 17 years old and his interest in coding was becoming apparent, his father, a programmer, told him about Bitcoin. Vitalik signed up for the Bitcointalk forum, where he responded to an ad offering 5 BTC (~$3.75) for a blog article about Bitcoin. This blog soon shut down as so few people seemed interested in Bitcoin, but Mihai Alisie

[192] Couts, Andrew. "Such Generosity! After Dogewallet Heist, Dogecoin Community Aims to Reimburse Victims." *Digital Trends*, 27 Dec. 2013.
[193] Freeburn, Christopher. "Sick of Virtual Currency Bitcoin? Meet Dogecoin." *Investorplace*, 17 Dec. 2013.

from Romania saw potential in Buterin's writing, and the pair decided to launch *Bitcoin Magazine* which became the movement's primary outlet.[194 195]

Due to his young age and pivotal role, Buterin could be described as one of the first members of the *blockchain generation*; crypto-natives who naturally grow up with or into the ideas of cryptocurrency. The defining trait of this generation is that for them, crypto is not a radical or foreign element introduced later in life, but a natural force by which they intertwined within their formative learning of things like economics and coding. In the more general sense, the entirety of the internet-native Generation Z may end up in this group.

Buterin set his sights on improving upon Bitcoin in late 2013 when he published the Ethereum whitepaper: *A Next-Generation Smart Contract and Decentralized Application Platform.* The main point was that Bitcoin needed a scripting language to allow for the creation of *decentralized applications* and *smart contracts* that could run on the network which functioned as a sort of ethereal global computer, later termed *Ethereum Virtual Machine.*[196]

> *Satoshi Nakamoto's development of Bitcoin in 2009 has often been hailed as a radical development in money and currency, being the first example of a digital asset which simultaneously has no backing or intrinsic value and no centralized issuer or controller. However, another - arguably more important - part of the Bitcoin experiment is the underlying blockchain technology as a tool of distributed consensus, and attention is rapidly starting to shift to this other aspect of Bitcoin. Commonly cited alternative applications of blockchain technology include using*

---

194 Bitcorati, Inc., Youtube.com user. "Bitcorati Interview Series : Vitalik Buterin - Head Writer, Bitcoin Magazine." *YouTube*, 10 Jan. 2014.
195 "10 Unknown Facts about Vitalik Buterin." *Coinnounce*, 2 July 2018.
196 Vitalik Buterin, Bitcointalk.org user. "[ANN] Ethereum: Welcome to the Beginning." *Bitcoin Forum*, 23 Jan. 2014.

> *on-blockchain digital assets to represent custom currencies and financial instruments (colored coins), the ownership of an underlying physical device (smart property), non-fungible assets such as domain names (Namecoin), as well as more complex applications involving having digital assets being directly controlled by a piece of code implementing arbitrary rules (smart contracts) or even blockchain-based decentralized autonomous organizations (DAOs). What Ethereum intends to provide is a blockchain with a built-in fully fledged Turing-complete programming language that can be used to create "contracts" that can be used to encode arbitrary state transition functions, allowing users to create any of the systems described above, as well as many others that we have not yet imagined, simply by writing up the logic in a few lines of code.*[197]
>
> - Vitalik Buterin, Nov. 2013.

This ambitious project was announced at the January 2014 North American Bitcoin Conference in Miami, where the project's co-founders rented a beach house. As is common in many blockchain projects, an exact list of co-founders is elusive because the founding team grew incrementally while others eventually left. By early 2014, the project's leads included Anthony Di Iorio, Mihai Alisie, Amir Chetrit, Charles Hoskinson, Jeffrey Wilke, Gavin Wood, and Joseph Lubin in addition to Buterin.[198]

> *Joseph Lubin, one of the developers staying at the house, and one of the few people who seemed to understand Ethereum enough to decipher its potential, told me in an endearing, paternal tone that Buterin was a genius alien that had arrived on this planet to deliver the sacrosanct gift of decentralization. ... I've been told by various people that Buterin learned to speak fluent Mandarin in just a few months, that he's an autistic wunderkind, that all of his worldly possessions fit into one suitcase, that he once ate an entire lemon without removing the rind,*

[197] Buterin, Vitalik. "A Next-Generation Smart Contract and Decentralized Application Platform." Nov. 2013.

[198] Buterin, Vitalik. "[ANN] Ethereum: Welcome to the Beginning." *Bitcoin Forum*, 23 Jan. 2014.

> *that he's an android powered by the Ethereum network. Even those who have worked closely with Buterin seem mystified by him, as though this person is meant to be observed but not really understood.*[199]
>
> - Robert Pybus, 13 June 2016.

The team met again six months later in Zug, a town in Switzerland then known as a tax haven for hedge funds, but which today bills itself as *Crypto Valley* and seeks to attract blockchain projects.[200] A disagreement arose regarding whether the project should seek venture capital or crowd-funded investment, with the dev's latter choice winning which led Hoskinson and Chetrit to leave the project. EthSuisse was established to formally oversee the project's development, and the Ethereum Foundation was founded in Toronto as a "*nonpartisan industry body, made up of [a cross-section of] industry players. It [is intended to] make sure the Ethereum infrastructure works fairly and independently... like ICANN for the Internet.*"[201] Buterin dropped out of university after being selected for a $100,000 Thiel Fellowship which supports students with "*ideas that cannot wait*" in dropping out of formal education.[202]

Now that the formal infrastructure was in place, development could begin. A crowd-sale in July & August 2014 raised $18.4 million for development costs, with 11.9 million Ethereum being effectively purchased for $1.54 each in BTC. The project remained under the radar to most Bitcoin users, and the first stable release of the code called *Homestead* came out over two years into the project in

---

199 Pybus, Robert. "The Uncanny Mind That Built Ethereum. *Wired*, 13 June 2016.

200 Grut, Oscar Williams. "Here's What It's like to Visit 'Crypto Valley' — Switzerland's Picturesque Blockchain Version of Silicon Valley." *Business Insider India*, 2 June 2018.

201 Schmid, Valentin. "The Entrepreneur: Joe Lubin, COO of Ethereum." *The Epoch Times*, 10 May 2014.

202 Elliott, Josh. "Why a 20-year-old Toronto Drop-out Accepted $100,000 to Stay out of School." *CTV News*, 2 July 2014.

March 2016. Its from here that the currency slowly began to creep into discussions, though it often faced derision, such as being labeled as "*mETH*" in reference to the *Megaether*, a unit representing one million ETH. Despite some mockery, no one could ignore Ethereum when it became the de-facto platform for Initial Coin Offerings in 2017.[203] [204] [205]

Speaking of Megaether, Ethereum's naming convention for divisions is worth exploring. Each ETH is divisible to one quintillion "atoms" called *atoether* or more commonly *wei*. To understand such a number, imagine 'one billion times one billion' (1,000,000,000,000,000,000); each Ethereum coin is thus made up of one quintillion digital particles. *wei* is named after Wei Dai, who in 1998 invented *b-money* which is today seen as the theoretical predecessor to Bitcoin. Several other subdivisions of Ethereum pay homage to similar crypto-luminaries and the giants upon whose shoulders blockchain stands in much the same way as various denominations of most countries' paper notes feature images of national heroes. One of these is Ada Lovelace, a 19th century mathematician and daughter of Lord Byron who became the first programmer after she created a calculation algorithm for the *analytical machine*, created by Charles Babbage.

Babbage, Lovelace's contemporary, was an engineer who invented the punch-card analytical machine and difference engine which made 20th century computer development possible. Mathematician Claude Shannon is another individual honored in Ethereum be-

---

[203] Zen, Tai. "Ethereum For Investors #20 – History of Ethereum – By Ethereum Co-Founder, Charles Hoskinson." Cryptocurrency Market, 13 June 2017.

[204] Marr, Bernard. "Blockchain: A Very Short History of Ethereum Everyone Should Read." *Forbes*, 2 Feb. 2018.

[205] "History of Ethereum." *Coinmama*.

cause in his 1948 article entitled *"A Mathematical Theory of Communication"*, he came up with information theory which become central to the development of cryptography as used in cryptocurrencies. Another honor belongs to Nick Szabo, who in 1998 brought forth the idea of smart contracts in a paper titled *Smart Contracts: Building Blocks for Digital Free Markets.*[206] That same year he also proposed the blockchain-based *bit gold* cryptocurrency which became a forerunner of Bitcoin. Hal Finney cannot be counted out, as in 1984 he designed the Reusable Proof-of-Work (RPOW) which made it possible to generate coins or tokens within a network, and in 2009 he became the first person to receive a Bitcoin transaction sent by Satoshi Nakamoto himself. The final honour went to Albert Einstein as the namesake for the kiloether (1,000 ETH), presumably due to his apocryphal quote that "*compound interest is the most powerful force in the universe.*" This is because Ethereum's roadmap calls for an eventual switch to a proof-of-stake system, where Ethereum begets more Ethereum forever.[207] [208]

Conclusion

These early days in Blockland show us the first glimmers of what may be a budding multi-faceted revolution which causes a wholesale restructuring of economics, politics and society. This is because these existing systems are built based on old systems which will be eclipsed by new protocols. While I am by no means suggesting that existing systems will disappear overnight, it is difficult to deny that

---

[206] Szabo, Nick. "Smart Contracts: Building Blocks for Digital Free Markets." 1996.
[207] Ulrich, Alexis. "The Ether Units of Ethereum." *Of Languages and Numbers*.
[208] Torpey, Kyle. "Vitalik Buterin On His Long-Term Goals for Ethereum." *Bitcoin Magazine*, 4 May 2016.

this innovation taking place at the intersections of technology, economics, and governance is without comparison. Just as the internet took nearly 25 years to take off, we must think exponentially in order to perceive where cumulative innovations built on this newly established blockchain foundation might lead us as a culture and society.

Based on what we have seen so far, we should consider the possibility that blockchain technologies will in future decades be considered viable replacements of our existing governance structures. This coming state-of-affairs where online-ness is a fact of life can perhaps be compared in magnitude with the societal shifts which took place when common people learned to read and thus interact more directly with their governments as in ancient Athens. Perhaps it can even be argued that the seamless integration of blockchain models with all levels of governance might be comparable to the very introduction of writing systems which held together ancient Sumeria, perhaps the earliest known civilization. Whatever changes may be forthcoming, Generation Z holds the keys to them as the tools by which to re-develop society on the millennial blockchain foundation have become these digital native's birthright.

Overboard or not, my point is that we now have prototypical versions of highly advanced tools which will change the global landscape in ways we cannot imagine, just as other surprising innovations have continually altered the course of history. In this brave new world operating on universal "truth machine" technology, analog governments will likely face a new type of struggle in appealing to the digitally native blockchain generation which might perceive political and societal structures based on ages past to be mere relics. If governments fail to adapt to their changing client-base, they risk being slowly replaced by more competitive entities.

The internet, the fountain of our age, is ruled almost entirely by private corporations owned by shareholders instead of governments controlled by the people. Few can deny that a conflict is brewing between governments and technology companies, as they amass huge amounts of power through the ownership of data and the control of information. As we become dependent on private technology, we become the exploitable pawns of private interests as peasants to greedy Lords and Lords to power-hungry Kings. I wonder, could the integration of blockchain protocols with the internet one day serve as a sort of Magna Carta of the internet age?

A 2013 1-oz silver coin containing 5 Worldcoins. Mintage: 500

A 2015 0.5-oz gold coin featuring a 'Rich Doge' and containing 1,000,000 Dogecoins. Mintage: 10

American Indians attacking a stage-coach in the 1860's. The development of the First Pacific Railroad soon brought the wild west days to an end.

CHAPTER 7

The Wild West of Finance

The English Class from Hell

You return to start your spring semester college classes after spending the New Year with your family. Your terrible new teacher, James McCarthy, gives you 2 bitcoins and a daunting assignment: you are now the CEO of a bitcoin company, and you must have 8 bitcoins by the end of the semester. If you do not, you fail his class. Your grade is entirely dependent on how much BTC your company has at the end of the semester. You must also negotiate salaries with and hire a CFO and other staff from amongst your classmates, all whose final grades are dependent on how much BTC they have received from you at the end of the semester. You are not alone, as there are 18 other CEO's and between the 19 of you there are 250 students whom you can choose to hire or fire at any time. Somehow, you need to figure out a way to convert your skills into bitcoins. There is a slight problem however, as only 10 of the 250 students have ever used a computer. You are in China where nobody has even heard of Bitcoin, so your company will need to get BTC from abroad. Too bad you have never spoken to a foreigner other than Mr. McCarthy. Welcome to 2011, and the English Class from Hell.

This task-orientated learning class was quite real, and these 19 companies clamoured to put together products and services to offer to westerners on the Bitcointalk.org forum. Some of these included selling English-language Chinese cookbooks, selections of Chinese music, giving Mandarin lessons, and photoshop services. With all 250 students having a Bitcoin wallet and the ability to trade amongst each other and between companies, Mr. McCarthy knew exactly what he was doing as he essentially developed a radical campus wide micro-market where "*with the exception of the CEO's and CFO's not being able to leave the company it's a completely free market, with no rules only that those with more money win.*"[209] The idea came out of McCarthy's frustration with his students whom he considered lazy, so he "*wanted to force them to do as much work as possible, as revenge. But at the same time cut down on the time I need to prepare for each class. With this way the students do the work not me HAHA.*"[210] Though this class may have seemed torturous, it was perhaps more akin to divine providence onto those who took it seriously. Every student got to keep the bitcoins they earned, and CEO's took home their companies accounts minus 2.5 BTC – Mr. McCarthy's 2 BTC investment and 25% "interest".

[209] Nefario, Bitcoitalk.org user. "Micro Startup/Investment Class Project/Experiment in China." *Bitcoin Forum*, 23 Feb. 2011.
[210] Nefario, Bitcointalk.org user. "About All the Posts from Chinese with Poor Engrish." Bitcoin Forum, 17 Mar. 2011.

A Peek into Bitcoin-land

Around the same time as this class was in session, drama was unfolding on the Bitcointalk.org forum. An anonymous user named stevenbucks had accepted money from various members in return for services that he failed to deliver, having spent the money on a teppy's Dragon's Tale bitcoin gambling game. In October 2010 when BTC was worth around $0.10, he had borrowed 4,000 BTC, only to find the debt impossible to repay in February 2011 as the price had gone up ten-fold. Forum member BitLex managed to track his usernames on another website/game called SecondLife, which he posted on a section of the forum listing hundreds of accused scammers.[211] Another forum user called him a parasite to the Bitcoin community and offered a 100 BTC ($10) bounty for anyone able to track down stevenbucks' real-world identity.[212] Stevenbucks replied in an apologetic way, saying he never meant to scam anyone and offered up his skills in database or PHP work in order to earn money to repay his creditors.[213] Unfortunately, no one in the community trusted him anymore. He was crypto-bankrupt. A user named Nefario, whose real name was the same James McCarthy as the aforementioned English teacher, stepped in to arrange a sort of bankruptcy proceeding amongst the anonymous lenders and creditors on the forum. Since nobody trusted stevenbucks to pay his debts instead of gambling away any BTC he received for work, Nefario listed his creditors usernames and the corresponding

---

[211] Xunie, Bitcointalk.org user. "Beware of Scammers!" *Bitcoin Forum*, 19 July 2010.

[212] Anonymous, Bitcointalk.org user. "Sabbers/Stevenbucks the Same Scam Artist?" 100btc Bounty. *Bitcoin Forum*, 11 Feb. 2011.

[213] stevenbucks, Bitcointalk.org user. "To the People I Owe - My Goals and Offer List." *Bitcoin Forum*, 11 Feb. 2011.

amounts, suggesting that anyone who stevenbucks works for to instead forward payments to his creditors.[214] These payments could then be tracked, and stevenbucks could regain his standing in the community. I think this is a fascinating case-study in the formation of online communities, as stevenbucks could have logged off forever at any moment without any real repercussions, but instead seemingly elected to try and fix the situation with people he had never met who were equally willing to forgive him. That said, this story like the one before it led into something much greater.

Nefario went on to propose a credit rating and bond system by which new forum members could create trust for themselves by paying a bond, which could be withheld if it were revealed that they failed to deliver on a trade.[215] Though the Bitcoin community now had a *web of trust* system where members vouched for each other, new people without prior connections or reputations were joining fast and creating a trust crisis as transactions remained irreversible and without middlemen. The idea was that a minimum bond of 1/3rd of the amount traded would serve as a deterrent and community members could request that the full amount of the proposed trade be held with the community's bond system. By paying such a bond, the new member was also signifying their trust in the community. In this suggestion and ensuing discussion, we witness how a borderless, decentralized, and anonymous community with their own currency could design and implement regulatory-like systems to safeguard and manage their economy.

---

214 Nefario, Bitcointalk.org user. "Don't Pay Stevenbucks, Pay His Debt Repayment." *Bitcoin Forum*, 15 Feb. 2011.
215 Nefario, Bitcointalk.org user. "Topic: Preventing Fraud and Scams and Building Reputation for New Users." *Bitcoin Forum*, 11 Feb. 2011.

GLBSE

Nefario started collecting investments from the community the next day with the promise that investors would get a profit-share of any fees collected in accordance with the amount they invested. He quickly collected around 2,000 BTC (~ $2000) to pay for initial development and hosting.[216] After it turned out that the system would take four months to develop, which was an eternity in the Bitcoin space at the time, he quickly announced a pivot to a "Bitcoin Stock Market" set for full launch within two months.[217] On this wholly unregulated market, anyone could create and issue their own shares, futures, or bonds to raise money for whatever they saw fit. People could announce their own companies on the forums, pay the listing fee, and if they managed to gather enough trust and optimism from investors, they could raise tens of thousands of dollars for any type of venture in a sort of underground IPO. Everything was trust-based, with no probable enforcement beyond being shunned by the online forum. Remember, neither this stock market nor any of the companies that would be listing on it were "real" in the traditional sense at this point, as they had no legal paperwork and even founders were unlikely to know each other's real identities or nationalities. This was radical stuff. In addition to normal functions of an exchange, the market would include the following features:

- *Dividend payments (allows issuers of shares to make dividend payments to share owners)*
- *Share voting; allows motions to be proposed by owners or issuers and voted on by shareholders*

---

216 Nefario, Bitcointalk.org user. "Investors for Bitcoin Stock Market and Credit Rating Agency, Dev Started!" *Bitcoin Forum*, 25 Feb. 2011.

217 Nefario, Bitcointalk.org user. "Looking for Co-Investor(s) for Credit Rating and Bail Bond System." *Bitcoin Forum*, 11 Feb. 2011.

- *Public/Private key based order and verification system, this is a no-password system*
- *Triple Entry Accounting and digitally signed receipts for each transaction for a cryptographically verifiable audit trail*
- *Digitally signed everything, making it impossible for orders, receipts, or withdrawals to be faked by either a single client or the server itself*
- *Open Source client and publicly available trading API allowing users/traders/developers to build their own tools or customize what is already available*
- *Availability over i2p and Tor (anonymous web browsers)*

As the stock market neared launch, Nefario offered a 20 BTC bounty for name suggestions as his original suggestion of The BlackMarket seemed too shady for most people. Suggestions such as BitBay, BitMarket, Bitshares, Mt. Stoxx, and BlockStock came in, with Bitcoin Global and Bitcoin Stock Exchange eventually being combined into GLBSE: Global Bitcoin Stock Exchange.[218] In preparing for its April launch, Nefario hired community members to run a media campaign to get the exchange covered by bloggers, podcasts, and hacker news outlets (this was of course not something for consumption by the general public yet). As Bitcoin hit $31 in June 2011, he offered 31 BTC for someone to write a full user manual of the exchange's functions hosted on a freely editable wiki.[219] At various other points, he openly asked technical questions to solve problems or concerns he was facing and engaged in complicated discussions about optimizing internal code with random

---

[218] Nefario, Bitcointalk.org user. "20 Bitcoin for a Good Name [Closed]." *Bitcoin Forum*, 6 Apr. 2011.

[219] Nefario, Bitcointalk.org user. "Need Someone to Organise and Manage a Media Campain." *Bitcoin Forum*, 9 Apr. 2011.

people who felt like contributing their thoughts. Like the entire premise of the project itself, this model of publicly crowd-sourcing the work that the site needed was a clear departure from traditional business practices. Instead of safeguarding his competitive advantages and carefully managing his image as someone who knew exactly what he was doing, he considered his entire customer base as friends who were happy to help him build the business for everyone's collective benefit. Everyone understood that they were in the wild west, and they were all just figuring things out as they went and there was thus no reason for posturing. An honest, humble, and community-focused way of building an innovative business. I wonder, how would a Wall Street investment firm fare if they tried to operate on similar principles?

Though GLBSE operated for over a year,[220] [221] it closed by October 2012 after extended controversies.[222] Some of these included a situation where someone not affiliated with GLBSE created an asset called "GLBSE", leading many to think that they were shares of GLBSE itself.[223] [224] [225] Nefario faced various accusations from various influential members of the community, including his former business partner Theymos.[226] As the site closed, people could withdraw

---

[220] jackc, Bitcointalk.org user. "GLBSE New IPOs." *Bitcoin Forum*, 10 Sept. 2012.
[221] usagi, Bitcointalk.org user. "[GLBSE] Bitcoin Mining Fund (See Post #2 for FAQ)." *Bitcoin Forum*, 16 May 2012.
[222] Ocean6, Bitcointalk.org user. "Done with GLBSE." *Bitcoin Forum*, 25 Sept. 2012.
[223] El Cabron, Bitcointalk.org user. "(GLBSE) TYGRR-P or TYGRR.P 6.5% Weekly Uninsured Pass Though Bond to BTCST." *Bitcoin Forum*, 20 May 2012.
[224] McCarthy, James. "TYGRR.* Assets on GLBSE Delisted." *Bitcoin Forum*, 25 Sept. 2012.
[225] El Cabron, Bitcointalk.org user. "Nefario GLBSE." *Bitcoin Forum*, 22 Sept. 2012.
[226] IWillNotBiteYourDog, Reddit.com user. "Founder Reflects on the Closure of Bitcoin Stock Exchange GLBSE" *Reddit r/Bitcoin*, 24 Oct. 2013.

their bitcoins and listed companies were able to continue their relationships with investors off the platform.

Bitcoin Magazine recorded the shutdown in a series of articles written by none other than Vitalik Buterin. James McCarthy, aka Nefario, told Buterin that since he was not doing AML (Anti Money Laundering) checks, he could find himself in serious trouble if bitcoin was ever considered money in the future. In short, the exchange's operation was a regulated activity and Mr. McCarthy figured he would end up in jail if he continued to run it. McCarthy even jokingly suggested that he had given all the exchange's money to the Pirate (more on that in the next section).[227] [228] [229]

Discussions started in the community regarding the need for some sort of successor. Bitcointalk.org user ShireSilver came up with a visionary solution that seemed to predict (and perhaps even inspire?) Ethereum and the ICO boom of 2017 that it powered:

> *I really don't like the idea of replacing GLBSE with another "site" or brokers. What we need... is an alt-chain for shares... Sites like GLBSE could then be middlemen that can help people manage their shares, help with buying and selling as well as research. But you should be able to move from one such site to another by merely exporting a hash (or whatever) and importing it into the new site. Those who want to manage things themselves can have their own wallet for their shares. The smart property idea can be used for shares of stocks and bonds, car titles (using VIN numbers for part of the data), and land titles (maybe starting with title insurance). You could also use it*

[227] Buterin, Vitalik. "Global Bitcoin Stock Exchange Shuts Down for Good." *Bitcoin Magazine*, 10 Oct. 2012.
[228] Buterin, Vitalik. "Interview with GLBSE's James McCarthy / Nefario." *Bitcoin Magazine*, 15 Oct. 2012.
[229] tucenaber, Bitcointalk.org user. "GLBSE Closed for Good." *Bitcoin Forum*, 6 Oct. 2012.

for anything with a serial number - use an alt-chain for keeping track of your valuables.[230]

- Forum user ShireSilver, 26 Sept. 2012.

The Pirate

On November 3rd, 2011, a user named pirateat40 sailed into port with quite an offer. He established the Bitcoin Savings and Trust (BTCST) on GLBSE and promised investors up to 7% interest per week. This was possible, the pirate explained, because he used the money to arbitrage between exchanges and large-volume OTC (Over-The-Counter, meaning not via an exchange) traders to make 11% in weekly profits. Investments came pouring in and the interest was paid regularly. The pirate made regular comments about the Trust including that the "*risk is almost 0*" and that "*I have yet to come close to taking a loss on any deal.*"[231] By summer 2012, BTCST had over 500,000 bitcoins on deposit, over 7% of all bitcoins in circulation and worth (only) $7 million at the time.[232] [233]

As this rate of return was clearly unsustainable in the long run, many questioned how long the trust could operate in the way it did or whether it was anything more than a Ponzi. To restore confidence, the pirate revealed his real identity as Trendon Shavers of Texas and announced that he would be attending the DevCon 2012

---

230 ShireSilver, Bitcointalk.org user. "Done with GLBSE." *Bitcoin Forum*, 26 Sept. 2012.

231 pirateat40, Bitcointalk.org user. "Bitcoin Savings and Trust | Home | Closed." *Bitcoin Forum*, 3 Nov. 2011.

232 Porter, Justin. "Bitcoin Savings & Trust – Genuine or Joke?" *Bitcoin Magazine*, 18 Aug. 2012.

233 Buterin, Vitalik. "The Pirate Saga: And so It Ends." *Bitcoin Magazine*, 30 Aug. 2012.

conference where any investor could meet him and "*look at a pirate, eye to eye if you dare.*"[234] This pleased the community enough that the trust could continue.

The first sign of trouble came on August 14th, when the maximum weekly interest rate was lowered to 3.9%, causing investors to panic and begin withdrawing their money. The BTCST closed three days later, with the pirate stating:

> *In a perfect world this [lower weekly interest rate] would allow me to hold more coins in reserve outside the system, but instead it only exponentially increased the amount of withdrawals overnight causing mass panic from many of my lenders.*[235]
>
> - Trendon Shavers, Aug. 2013.

Mr. Shavers kept making assurances that he would repay the money with the promised interest, but on August 28th he announced that he was in default. Bitcoin's price started declining immediately, dropping over 50% from a high of $15.40 to less than $8.00 in three days before stabilizing in the $10-$11 range over the following two weeks.

In July 2013, the US Securities and Exchange Commission (SEC) charged Mr. Shavers with operating a Ponzi scheme through which he raised a total of about 764,000 bitcoins- 150,659 BTC of which he kept for himself to pay personal expenses, day trade, and gamble.[236] The remaining 507,148 BTC were paid to investors, and the SEC claimed that there was never any arbitrage activity as Mr. Shavers had represented. In a press release about the charges, the SEC

---

[234] Pirateat40, Bitcointalk.org user. "Look at a Pirate, Eye to Eye If You Dare." *Bitcoin Forum*, 2 July 2012.

[235] Maglich, Jordan. "Texas Man Arrested For $4.5 Million Bitcoin Ponzi Scheme." *Forbes*, 6 Nov. 2014.

[236] "Manhattan U.S. Attorney and FBI Assistant Director Announce Securities and Wire Fraud Charges Against Texas Man for Running Bitcoin Ponzi Scheme." *U.S. Attorney's Office Southern District of New York*, 6 Nov. 2014.

stated that "*Fraudsters are not beyond the reach of the SEC just because they use Bitcoin or another virtual currency to mislead investors and violate the federal securities laws*" and that "*Ponzi scheme operators often claim to have a tie to a new and emerging technology as a lure to potential victims.*" [237]

An attorney named Jason Seibert agreed to defend Shavers pro bono, later explaining that "*the future of Bitcoin was too important to let the first case with the SEC be handled alone.*" He tried to argue that Shavers could not be charged as he had because laws against Ponzi schemes refer to *money* and the Internal Revenue Service (IRS) had ruled bitcoin to be a *commodity*. The judge then asked if airline tickets could be bought with Bitcoin, and despite the argument that airmiles could also be used to purchase such tickets without being money, the judge decided to accept the SEC's assertion that bitcoin was indeed money. As Shavers' assets were frozen and he could not pay for legal representation, a campaign to raise money managed to gather only $50 to defend him. Mr. Seibert regretfully recounted that "*The community hated Shavers so much that they didn't understand [that] even if Shavers did wrong, the SEC was making bad law, expanding the scope of their power, and without money to fight and appeal, the community may have cut off its nose to spite its own face.*"[238] As the trial continued, the judge ordered Mr. Shavers to pay back $40.7 million in illegal profits and a $150,000 fine, money he did not have.[239] [240]

---

[237] "SEC Charges Texas Man with Running Bitcoin-Denominated Ponzi Scheme." *US Securities and Exchange Commission*, 23 July 2013.

[238] Connell, Justin O. "Lawyer Reveals Details About the Man Behind Bitcoin's $4.5 Million Ponzi Scheme." *Vice*, 18 Dec. 2015.

[239] Comben, Christina. "Trace Mayer Gives 60-day Reminder of Proof of Keys 2020." *Coin Rivet*, 5 Nov. 2019.

[240] KayRice, Reddit.com User. "Pirate40 Tried to Claim It Wasn't Fraud Because Bitcoin Isn't Real. Judge Didn't Buy It and Fraud Charges Remain!" *Reddit r/Bitcoin*, 9 Aug. 2013.

Over a year later in November 2014, Shavers was charged with securities fraud and wire fraud. He was sentenced to 18 months in prison after pleading guilty to securities fraud and ordered to pay an additional $1.23 million in restitution. At his sentencing, Mr. Shavers told the judge that he "*royally messed up*" and that "*I don't think this is something I'm ever going to get over.*"[241] Losses for investors stood at 263,024 BTC.[242] [243]

MPEx & SatoshiDICE

GLBSE's previously established competitor was an exchange named MPEx, which was originally a place to trade Bitcoin futures and was run from Romania by Mircea Popescu. MPEx was chosen by Eric Voorhees to host the "IPO" of his Bitcoin casino SatoshiDICE in August 2012.[244] This was no small gambling site; weeks after being launched on April 24th, 2012, SatoshiDice was responsible for more than half of all Bitcoin transactions. In its prospectus to investors on MPEx, the company was described as an "unregistered corporation" represented by Voorhees, and the investment agreement stated that it may "*not be modified by third parties, irrespective if said parties should style themselves "court of law", "judge" or otherwise.*"[245] The MPEx investors did well, with SatoshiDICE earning profits over $500,000 in 2012. Considering the legendary level of market volatility and the tendency to invest

241 Ornitz, Darren, and Trendon Shavers. "'I Know What I Did Was Wrong:' Texas Man Pleads Guilty to Running Bitcoin Ponzi Scheme." *RT*, 21 Oct. 2015.
242 Raymond, Nate. "Texan Gets One-and-a-half Years in Prison for Running Bitcoin Ponzi Scheme." *Reuters*, 22 July 2016.
243 Bitsky, Bitcointalk.org user. "PirateAt40 / Trendon Shavers." *Bitcoin Forum*, 20 Mar. 2013.
244 evoorhees, Bitcointalk.org user. "Satoshidice.com - The World's Most Popular Bitcoin Game." *Bitcoin Forum*, 24 Apr. 2012.
245 johnsmith4444, Thewealthofchips blog user. "Crypto Gambling." *TheWealthOfChips,* 24 Nov. 2014.

in Pirate Ponzi schemes paying 7% returns per week, it is no surprise that gambling was particularly popular amongst Bitcoin investors. An image of wild west prospectors, cowboys, and outlaws meeting in a remote saloon to play cards for their gold dust comes to mind.

By January 2013 the company was valued at $8.9 million, and in July of that year Mr. Voorhees sold the company for 126,315 BTC ($12.4 million). SatoshiDICE's story did not end here, as in February 2014 MPEx's owner, Mr. Popescu, was contacted by the SEC to provide a list of SatoshiDICE shareholders and Mr. Voorhees' MPEx account history relating to the sale of shares and payment of dividends. What followed was a rather interesting email exchange, which Mr. Popescu later posted with the title "*Interacting with fiat institutions, a guide.*"[246]

To summarize this email exchange, Popescu confirmed that MPEx indeed complies with all legal requests and requested the SEC attorney to "*sufficiently establish your authority to [make such a request]*". After the attorney invited him to confirm her identity by calling her through the SEC front desk, Popescu explained that what he meant was that he was seeking an explanation on the legal basis by which the SEC had authority to investigate a Bitcoin enterprise in the first place as this "*would customarily come in the form of an Act of Congress specifically authorising the SEC to review MMORPGs [Massive Multiplayer Online Role-Playing Games] and online activities involving such computer games and their virtual currencies, be they WoW gold, Linden Dollars, EVE Isk, Bitcoin, etc and so forth.*"[247]

---

[246] Popescu, Mircea. "Interacting with Fiat Institutions, a Guide." *Trilema*, 18 Mar. 2014.
[247] Dean, Michelle. "Bitcoin Trading Exchange Spurns Thirsty SEC." *Gawker*, 20 Mar. 2014.

He went on to question the SEC's authority to seek personal information from him in regard to Romanian and EU law, implying that for him to even provide that information might be against the law. He then went on to explain that in his view, MPEx had "*long before the SEC as much as heard of Bitcoin, pursued with some success if with different means roughly the same agenda, which is to say the exposure of scams and the protection of the general public from scammers of all sorts.*"[248] On the basis of "*nurturing a vibrant, diverse and free marketplace*", he then invited the SEC to form a working relationship with MPEx to combat Bitcoin scams while clarifying that his "*commitment to freedom is not merely verbiage... and on this basis I perceive we may encounter difficulties going forward.*"

In a final email, he asked that the SEC adopt resolutions confirming its lack of jurisdiction regarding Bitcoin, to recognize MPEx' regulatory authority over Bitcoin finance as a "Self Regulatory Organization", and appoint one of its commissioners as a Bitcoin liaison within the general Bitcoin community. This final request is understood to have gone unanswered. Of this exchange, Popescu stated on his blog that "*Bitcoin is a sovereign. Accepting this matter of fact is [an absolutely necessary] prerequisite for playing. No exceptions.*"[249] What Popescu was doing was essentially claiming that Bitcoin was a sovereign entity outside of any existing legal or regulatory system, and his request to the SEC was in practice asking them to recognize that sovereignty and establish an "embassy" to Blockland.

Mr. Popescu's attempts were unsuccessful as four months later in June the SEC charged Voorhees with publicly offering shares in the

---

[248] Popescu, Mircea. "Interacting With Fiat Institutions, a Guide." *Trilema*, 18 Mar. 2014.
[249] Popescu, Mircea. "Interacting With Fiat Institutions, a Guide." *Trilema*, 18 Mar. 2014.

two ventures without registering them. This was settled with Voorhees paying over $50,000 in disgorgement and penalties.[250] The other firm for which he had offered shares was called FeedZeBirds and paid Twitter users Bitcoin for tweeting sponsored messages. Erik Voorhees remained active in the Bitcoin space, going on to launch ShapeShift.io which facilitates the easy conversion of cryptocurrencies.

Other Exchanges

Several other "Bitcoin security exchanges" entered the business in GLBLSE and MPEx's footsteps, whose users consisted of an online community of "Bitcoin stock traders".[251] After two years of operations on December 2014, Ethan Burnside who owned both BTC Trading Corp. and LTC Global was fined by the SEC for operating the two "*unregistered, online, virtual currency-denominated securities exchanges and broker-dealers*"[252] which had offered around 130 BTC and LTC denominated securities between them.[253] [254] Havelock Investments was perhaps the most legally sound platform, having been acquired by a Panamanian fund which

[250] "SEC Charges Bitcoin Entrepreneur with Offering Unregistered Securities." *US Securities and Exchange Commission.* 3 June 2014.
[251] "History of Bitcoin Stock Exchanges." *Dale.*
[252] "Administrative Proceeding File No. 3-16307 in the Matter of BTC Trading, Corp. and Ethan Burnside." *Securities and Exchange Commission*, 8 Dec. 2014.
[253] Southurst, Jon. "SEC Fines Defunct Bitcoin Exchange Operator $68,000." *CoinDesk*, 8 Dec. 2014.
[254] BTC-TradingCo, Bitcointalk.org user "[BTC-TC] Virtual Community Exchange [Closeds]." *Bitcoin Forum*, 17 Nov. 2012.

made it into a "*fully licensed and registered... Investment Company*" in November 2013.[255] [256] Cryptostocks was another small exchange which operated around the same time.

Bitfunder which launched in late 2012 sold various securities including one called Ukyo.Loan, which gave holders daily interest and was operated by the site's owner who was known as Ukyo. Hackers apparently stole 6,000 BTC from Ukyo.Loan accounts sometime in 2013, but Ukyo failed to make his investors aware of the hack and managed to raise 978 more bitcoins. Bitfunder closed in November 2013, after banning accounts from US traders in the previous month in order to avoid negative attention from US authorities.[257] [258] [259]This caused its markets to crash as Americans were forced to sell off their holdings. In July 2018, Jon Montroll of Texas pleaded guilty to charges of securities fraud and obstruction of justice relating to the taking of investor's funds to pay personal expenses and lying under oath regarding his knowledge of the Ukyo.Loan hack, going as far as to provide the SEC with a fake screenshot of user funds.[260] [261] [262]

---

[255] havelock, Bitcointalk.org user. "[Havelock] The Panama Fund, S.A. Acquires HavelockInvestments.com." *Bitcoin Forum*, 1 Nov. 2013.
[256] btcsql, Bitcointalk.org user. "Havelock Investments - My Experience." *Bitcoin Forum*, 5 Feb. 2013.
[257] workahaulic, Reddit.com user. "Bullshit That Bitfunder Is Forcing Us to Sell While Keeping a % of the Fee." *Reddit r/BitcoinStocks*, 10 Oct. 2013.
[258] Barrier, Eric. "BitFunder, a Bitcoin Stock Exchange, Closes." *CoinTelegraph*, 12 Nov. 2013.
[259] blastbob, Bitcointalk.org user. "[BitFunder] Asset Exchange Marketplace + Rewritable Options Trading." *Bitcoin Forum*, 3 Nov. 2013.
[260] Pierson, Brendan. "Operator of Shuttered Bitcoin Platform Pleads Guilty to U.S Charges." *Reuters*, 24 July 2018.
[261] Dolmetsch, Chris. "Bitcoin Platform Operator Pleads Guilty to Lying About Hack." *Bloomberg*, 24 July 2018.
[262] Bradbury, Danny. "Who Will Protect Investors in a Cryptocurrency Crowdsale?" *CoinDesk*, 28 May 2014.

NEO&BEE

One memorable IPVO (Initial Public Virtual Offering) was that of NEO&BEE, a Bitcoin bank in Cyprus that "went public" on September 20th, 2013, after four months of preparation. It was offered on Bitfunder, Havelock Investments, and BTC.CO.[263] Cyprus was highly relevant to the early days of Bitcoin, as many early adopters pointed to its 2013 financial crisis as "proof" that the world needed Bitcoin. During the crisis, people faced great difficulty accessing their money and huge line-ups formed outside banks. The Bank of Cyprus was closed, and the government imposed a levy of 47.5% on all accounts with deposits over 100,000 EUR.[264] This caused mass protests and became a poster child for the type of problems that Bitcoin could seemingly fix; no government could confiscate bitcoins like it could bank accounts. The additional attention Bitcoin got because of this has been understood to have caused the price to rise, and the event was reflected in Bitcoin culture such as in Zhou Tonged's song *Cyprus Anthem* set to the tune of Swedish House Mafia's *Don't You Worry Child.* Here is an excerpt:

> *There was a time, I thought my government was doing right*
> *But they crossed the line, and now I'm fighting for my f--king life*
> *Laiki* [bank] *took my funds, and now I think how this all will end*
> *My money's with Bitcoin, 'cuz what they've done they can never mend*
> *Just when the Cypriots were losing faith*
> *That's when I learned about the Blockchain*
> *I still remember how it all changed*
> *Satoshi said,*
> *Don't you worry, don't you worry, child*

---

263 "Havelock Investments to Recommence NEO & BEE Fund Trading This Afternoon." *NewsBTC*, 1 June 2014.

264 Bensasson, Marcus, and Georgios Georgiou. "Cyprus Sets Levy on Bank of Cyprus Uninsured Depositors at 47.5%." *Bloomberg*, 30 June 2013.

Bitcoin has got a plan for you
Don't you worry, don't you worry now[265]
- YouTube.com user ZhouTonged, 5 May 2013.

In other words, NEO&BEE was building on fertile ground. It raised 9,400 BTC over four months during which it ran a massive marketing campaign with the tagline *Who is Neo?* and added the "Bitcoin evangelist" Andreas Antonopoulos as an advisor. Along with other services, the company announced numerous NEO retail branches across the island allowing people access their bitcoins, and a BEE Card Payment Network allowing BTC to be spent across the country. As the first retail branch was opened on February 24th, 2014, the share price nearly doubled. Investors and the wider Bitcoin community were ecstatic as Bitcoin had now established its first outpost in a land where people needed it most; this was the very beginning of Bitcoin's triumph over the banks![266]

A storm began to brew three weeks later at a management meeting on March 19th. CEO Danny Brewster told the managers that though he had thought the company held 5,000 BTC, a recent check of the wallets revealed that only 140 BTC remained. He explained that those 5,000 BTC had actually been his own and that he had spent them but did not remember on what specifically. He also said that the company had lost 1400-1700 BTC on Bitfunder and 2480 BTC to the Mt.Gox closure, although he had previously publicly claimed that the company saw no losses due to Mt.Gox. He suggested that the firm could sell more profit shares to get liquidity, but all employees objected to the idea. He then told them that he would head to the UK to seek investments and sell his Mercedes and Bentley to cover employee salaries for the month. As he came

265 ZhouTonged, Youtube.com user. "Zhou Tonged - Cyprus Anthem (Swedish House Mafia - Don't You Worry Child)." *YouTube*, 5 May 2013.
266 Brewster, Danny. "I Am the CEO of Neo & The Bee Payment Network in Cyprus, AMA." *Reddit r/Bitcoin*, 20 Sept. 2013.

by the office the next day, Brewster agreed to step down as CEO after transferring control to investors. He dropped by the office one more time the following day, after which he disappeared. By this point, all his social media accounts which previously showed daily activity had been silent for four days.

In the following week, rumours about NEO&BEE's runaway CEO began to swirl amongst the Bitcoin community. Word had it that the company had collapsed, with investor's money gone and both creditors and employees unpaid. Various people tried unsuccessfully to reach Brewster, and Havelock Investments halted trading of the companies' shares due to abnormal activity. Brewster finally contacted NEO&BEE's managers on the 28th, explaining that he had been silent and stayed in the UK because someone threatened his daughter two days earlier on the 26th. This made little sense as his daughter was in Cyprus and the local police confirmed that they had not heard about such a threat when told of the situation by NEO&BEE managers. Of course, a threat on the 26th did not explain the social media silence since the 18th. After failing to respond to a demand letter asking him to return and explains himself, Brewster contacted his currently unpaid employees again, suggested that the threats came from within the company, and that all funds were accounted for. It also turned out that Brewster had sold BTC to several locals (as well as NEO&BEE staff), was holding them on their behalf, and staff were then confronted by these confused creditors.

Brewster's cars had changed plates at the dealership, but money from them or the 140 BTC had not been used to pay the employees as he had previously said. The entire staff resigned, and the offices closed. Cypriot media spun the original *Who is Neo?* marketing campaign into a sarcastic question of *Where is Neo?* and announced that the Cypriot police had issued an arrest warrant for Brewster based on criminal charges including theft and money laundering among others. In response to these charges, Brewster posted online again to insist that the money was accounted for and that he was willing to directly pay back those he sold bitcoins to. He now provided a new explanation for the company's insolvency: that he had sold much of the company's bitcoins at low prices on October 2nd 2013 in response to the US authorities cracking down on The Silk Road darknet marketplace, fearing that it might cause Bitcoin to become worthless.[267] Two days later, the Cypriot Police announced that their investigations were "*in an advanced stage*" and suggested that a European or international arrest warrant could be issued.[268] [269]

Things went silent. In mid 2014, an anonymous Reddit user reported having a chat with Brewster after running into him in London, who apparently said that the investors themselves were to blame for losing their money and that he was not liable because the investors dealt with his company and not him personally.[270] Nearly two years after disappearing, he resurfaced:[271] [272]

> *I've made a lot of mistakes.... [but] people seem to make the assumption that I run off with some 9 000 bitcoins. There were months of development, branch opening, designing, marketing, so to say I just disappeared with everything is illogical.*

---

[267] Brewster, Danny. "The Full Picture from Danny Brewster." *Reddit r/Bitcoin*, 15 Apr. 2014.
[268] oaaby, Reddit.com user. "The Full Picture of Former Neo & Bee Employees." *Reddit r/Bitcoin*, 18 Apr. 2014.
[269] NBFullPicture, Reddit.com user. "NEO & BEE: The Full Picture." *Reddit r/Bitcoin*, 21 Apr. 2014.
[270] Sovereign_Curtis, Reddit.com user. "So What Ever Happened with Danny Brewster (Neo & Bee)?" *Reddit r/Bitcoin*, 13 July 2014.
[271] Southurst, Jon. "Neo & Bee CEO Danny Brewster Resurfaces, Wants to Pay Back Investors." *Bitsonline*, 23 June 2017.
[272] Rizzo, Pete. "Controversial Neo & Bee CEO Resurfaces After Disappearance." *CoinDesk*, 8 Jan. 2016.

> *Where did the coins go? Well, to builders, designers, marketing, development and everything like that.*[273]
>
> - Danny Brewster, 14 Jan. 2016.

In August 2017, investors received emails inviting them to access a "redemption portal" where they could access *NEOBEE Tokens*, which would apparently be bought by the company for 0.0035 BTC each in a reverse-ICO.[274] It appears that the NEO&BEE saga is still ongoing, but there is no reason to believe any money will be recovered.[275]

Wild West Memories

What started as an experimental English class with made-up money spawned a wild, lawless industry full of chaotic characters. We see the fundamental libertarian idea that Bitcoin and cryptocurrency form a sort of digital terra nullius that is by nature outside the regulatory authority and practical reach of established government agencies, and that idea's counterweight in the rights of governments to police economic activities involving their citizens. The very understanding of what constituted money was put to the test and seems to remain undetermined. While this may read as some form of fictitious anarchistic dystopia, it is quite funny to reminisce that this is exactly where I grew up in a financial sense. I distinctly recall

---

273 Rojko, Martin. Neo & Bee ex-CEO Brewster: "I've Made A Lot of Mistakes." *CoinTelegraph*, 14 Jan. 2016.

274 "Neo & Bee Moves Forward with Reverse ICO." *Bitcoinx*, 15 Sept. 2017.

275 Note: I have spoken with Mr. Brewster post-writing, and he maintains that the cited information is largely false due to being disseminated by people trying to blackmail and make threats against him and his family in an attempt to take over his business interests. As the sources used are by nature difficult if not impossible to verify, I wish to clarify that the purpose of this particular section is not to present facts about a case or individual, but to present an investor-perspective case study of how the drama of a 'runaway CEO' unfolded in the blockchain sphere, that is, Blockland, in a mist of uncertainty, rumors, and confusion.

instances of day-trading NEO&BEE shares on Havelock and reading shareholder dividend reports about "my" un-registered, decentralized, fake-money online casino while sitting in various Political Science classes during my undergrad where I was taught the proper long-standing protocols and systems by which society functioned. Since I did not know better, this was normal to me. I got used to high risk and high reward, not relying on anyone to hold my hand to do my due diligence for me, nor did I expect to get my money back when CEO's inevitably ran away and "banks" went offline, disappearing overnight.[276] Truly those were the wild days, and the industry has matured greatly and I with it.

Up until the reformation and enlightenment, religion and government were largely one and the same across the western world. The monarch's religion was the law of the land and his rule was based on the concept of the *Divine Right of Kings*. This meant that they had been appointed by God himself and thus that no mortal held moral grounds to question their rule. Today, governments control the supply of money and instead of cathedrals towering as the founts of eternal power over every city center and royal palace, corporate offices and especially banks scrape the heavens above public parks and city halls all over the world. On a global scale, the locus of power and control has shifted from religion to money. Only 500 years ago, the separation of church and state was unthinkable. As the reformation was followed by the enlightenment, people started to question the nature of religion and began to demand the freedom to believe as they wished. This led to an overthrow of the old western system, being replaced by varying forms of democracy and constitutional monarchy. No longer did the monarch rule by the grace of the almighty, but by the grace of commoners!

---

276 dree12, Bitcointalk.org user. "List of Major Bitcoin Heists, Thefts, Hacks, Scams, and Losses." *Bitcoin Forum*, 19 Apr. 2014.

It is no doubt that the stories in this chapter will live on either as tales of fools or the origin stories of a new order. Some will see them as perfect examples of why we have rules in the first place, while others will see a certain glimmer in the rubble. Perhaps, this is an account of the first volleys of an impending battle of historical proportion. Just as the enlightenment ideas of the likes of John Locke paved the way for the separation of church and state, is it possible that there are digital revolution ideas that will result in the eventual divorce between state and money?

Australian Mount Alexander goldfields and nearby settlement in 1852.

CHAPTER 8

The Settlements

The Sandbox of Chaos

2014 was a year of chaos and decline in Blockland, as its beginning saw a huge crash from Bitcoin's first highs of over $1,000 to a mere $200. During this year of market decline, the overall population crashed by half after the previous year's increase. Life was especially bad in some of the colonies such as Litecoin which saw its population slowly fall by 98% from its heighs. The number of new settlements, nevertheless, continued to increase exponentially to over 500 by the end of the year, at which point the "population" of capital in Bitcoin had fallen to 78% of Blockland's total. These ~500 colonies were not evenly populated, with less than half laying claim to above 20,000 residents (dollars of market capitalization) and only a quarter to 100,000. As the process became clear, anyone with a basic amount of programming skills could design, announce, and open a new crypto-settlement in a matter of days. All that was needed was the basic knowledge of how to duplicate an existing token's code; making changes in addition to name and branding was largely optional.

As one might guess, many of these "crypto colonies" turned out entirely useless except as experimentation or hobby projects of their resident-users. Despite many of these being unremarkable, 2014 can be remembered as a sandbox year – when all types of ideas were thrown at the proverbial wall to see what sticks. 2014 represents a time when Blockland had just opened to the world; common people began to venture in even though the market was severely depressed, and seekers of fast fortunes were thus somewhat repelled. A culturally notable event of this time was the emergence of the Bearwhale, a trader who made a market sell-order of 30,000 BTC at only $300 (about $50 below market) causing mass panic in Blockland.[277] This long winter allowed for a landscape of passionate tinkerers, who without anyone's approval created interesting spins on the idea of cryptocurrency. This progress is presented through these fourteen notable examples.

Counterparty - 2 Jan. 2014

Counterparty was born of the fire, metaphorically speaking. Instead of collecting money that would be used to develop the project, Counterparty collected money to be burned. How can one burn bitcoins? By sending them to a *provably un-spendable* address for which no one has the private key, thus any coins sent to it are removed from circulation forever, burned, if you will. In this manner, 2,140 BTC, worth about $2 million, were sacrificed on behalf of Counterparty's XCP token, which could then be understood to contain the life force of the dead bitcoins. This was a novel way of

[277] Rosenfeld, Everett. "Bitcoin's 'BearWhale' and the future of a cryptocurrency." *CNBC*, 10 Oct. 2014.

transferring value, legitimacy, and "blood from the mother chain" to its descendant.[278]

Counterparty always had a special and close relationship with Bitcoin, and not only because it had Bitcoin's "blood" flowing through it. Like the 2nd generation NXT blockchain, Counterparty was more than just a token because it consisted of an entire platform which contained a token function. Counterparty, however, was more akin to *Bitcoin 2.0* because it *operated on* Bitcoin:

> *Counterparty embeds data into regular Bitcoin transactions. To a regular Bitcoin client, these transactions look like normal Bitcoin transactions, with one party sending another party a very small amount of Bitcoin. A Counterparty node (which runs the Bitcoin client along with the Counterparty client software) will recognize and interpret the data in these Bitcoin transactions based on specific rules. From this, it constructs its own ledger of Counterparty transactions that it has seen on the Bitcoin network.*[279]
>
> - counterparty.io

The Counterparty platform consists of a decentralized exchange that allows for trading of user-created tokens, assets, or coins. The protocol also allows for the creation and execution of smart contracts for user-created tokens to pay out dividends, and for multi-signature addresses; all "on top" or "on the margins" of the Bitcoin protocol. *Multi-signature* or *multisig* refers to the possibility of requiring multiple people to "sign" a transaction before it can be sent. This basic practice has been in place for perhaps thousands of years, for example, with several monks each holding one of several keys required to access some priceless relic. A practical example today would be a company storing 1,000 BTC (or having a corporate bank account, for that matter) and requiring three of five key

---

[278] PhantomPhreak, Bitcointalk.org user. "[ANN][XCP] Counterparty - Pioneering Peer-to-Peer Finance - Official Thread." *Bitcoin Forum*, 2 Jan. 2014.
[279] "How Does Counterparty Work?" *FAQs, Counterparty.io*

employees to sign for any transaction to move the BTC. Many Bitcoin wallets have developed such functions and they are most notably in use by exchanges, which are known to hold even billions of dollars of cryptocurrency within individual multi-signature wallets. The attentive reader will see that this project bears considerable resemblance to Mastercoin, which was discussed in Chapter 4. This is very much the case, as Counterparty was its main competitor.

Though Counterparty has affirmed that it intends to stay connected to Bitcoin indefinitely, it has also acknowledged that it could potentially "freeze" itself and move operations to Litecoin should Bitcoin undergo any kind of catastrophic failure. This demonstrates Litecoin's role as a backup Bitcoin, particularly in the early years of blockchain development. A separate version of counterparty called Dogeparty runs on Dogecoin and yet another on Viacoin.[280]

Coinye - 4 Jan. 2014

Released less than a month after Dogecoin, Coinye can be understood to fit under the same genre of humorous mass-appeal cryptocurrencies. It became a victim of the Streisand effect when hip-hop star Kanye West's lawyers served the development team a cease and desist order, which asserted the cryptocurrency constituted "*trademark infringement, unfair competition, cyberpiracy and dilution.*" They further suggested that they "*will notify the cryptocurrency community at large of your infringing actions and pursue all legal remedies against any business that accepts the purported COINYE WEST currency.*"[281] The coin's name was initially

[280] drostie, Reddit.com user. "Simple Explanation of DogeParty." *Reddit r/dogecoin,* 25 Aug. 2014.

[281] "Kanye West is Feuding with Some Tech Guys." *The Fashion Law*, 8 Jan. 2014.

changed from Coinye West to simply Coinye. A few days later, the coin rebranded to represent "*a half-man-half-fish hybrid*", in reference to South Park Season 13 Episode 5 *Fishsticks in* which Kanye investigates why people keep jokingly referring to him as a "*gay fish.*"[282] Kanye's lawyers did not take kindly at this and after a lawsuit was filed, the developers sold their holdings and abandoned the project, leaving the website with the text "*Coinye is dead. You win, Kanye.*"[283]

Darkcoin/Dash - 18 Jan. 2014

Launched as XCoin, this creation by Evan Duffield was rebranded as Darkcoin after a few weeks of trading due to confusion with another project. Darkcoin's flagship feature was *DarkSend,* which allowed for tokens to be transacted without leaving behind a "paper trail" that could be used to track any individual's transactions. This was made possible by *Master Nodes,* which Duffield invented as a way of ensuring privacy.[284] To create a Master Node, a user would have to acquire 1,000 DRK and convert them into a Master Node, an action which would remove them from circulation for as long as the node is kept functional. The Master Node owner would then run the node on a computer and in doing so, earn a share of DRK each day, a portion of an amount divided evenly among all active Master Nodes. In a process called CoinJoin, these nodes continually swap DRK coins between users, essentially mixing or laundering them in such a way that it becomes effectively impossible to

[282] Robertson, Adi. "Coinye Responds to Kanye Complaint, Says Currency Now Based on 'half-man Half-fish Hybrid'." *The Verge*, 10 Jan. 2014.
[283] Newton, Casey. "Coinye Developers Say They're Abandoning Project as Kanye West Escalates Legal Battle." *The Verge*, 14 Jan. 2014.
[284] eduffield, Bitcointalk.org user. "[ANN][Dash] Dash (Dash.org) | First Self-Funding Self-Governing Crypto Currency." *Bitcoin Forum*, 18 Jan. 2014.

track the origins of any specific coins or connect any transaction to a real person.

Darkcoin was predictably adopted within some dark web drug markets as a method for improving privacy and anonymity. From Duffield's perspective, this was good:

> *The goal has always been to make a currency that's privacy-centric and is more for mass consumer base types of things. It's not just for buying drugs online... Early on with bitcoin the only thing you could do with it was gamble and buy drugs. Then it got past that and was accepted on many sites all over the internet, ... The same thing is happening with DarkCoin.*[285]
>
> - Evan Duffield, 18 Jan. 2014.

One could surmise that the CoinJoin function was inspired by *Bitcoin Mixer* services that had become a popular way to obfuscate Bitcoin transactions, especially ones related to illegal goods or tax evasion. These mixers or tumblers essentially shuffled and re-ordered BTC from multiple sources, retaining a ~1-3% fee for doing so. Despite these early Bitcoin Mixers' efforts, many feared that an algorithm could one day unmask everyone.[286]

The idea of a "dark" coin used on the dark web did not sit well with everyone, especially the mass consumer base that Duffield hoped Darkcoin to reach. This perception led to a rebranding to DASH; a portmanteau of 'Digital Cash' that evoked thoughts of speedy transactions. The suggestion arose from the community and after a period of discussion and uncertainty, Duffield, who maintained direct leadership as core developer, announced the rebranding over the Darkcoin forums:

---

285 Greenberg, Andy. "Online Drug Dealers Are Now Accepting Darkcoin, Bitcoin's Stealthier Cousin." *Wired*, 14 Apr. 2011.

286 "What Are Bitcoin Mixers?" *Bitcoin Magazine*.

> *Darkcoin's vision has always been to create a trust-less, decentralized , private and fast payment platform for the benefit of the majority. This is our ethos and our most important goal, recently it became apparent that our branding was getting in the way of reaching the people we were trying to help, that is when I knew that in order to accomplish our vision we would need to change our name. Our ideals remain intact and we will continue to pursue them under any branding we have, now and in the future. .... DASH is just a name we still need to build our vision onto it and we need everyone's support to push the project forward.*[287]
>
> \- Evan Duffield, 12 Mar. 2015.

A major development came in April 2015 with the *Self-sustainable Decentralized Governance by Blockchain* system, also called *Decentralized Budget System* and simply *DAH DAO* (Decentralized Autonomous Organization).[288] With its implementation, 15% of mining & masternode rewards would be deposited into a common fund within the network. Anyone could then submit a proposal to be funded, be it for marketing, adding to the team of developers, or building some service to support the Dash ecosystem. *Masternodes* could then vote *Yes* or *No* to adopt any proposal, with successful proposers automatically receiving the allotted sum of DASH.[289] This created a sizable marketing budget for Dash, and usage examples include a Dash-specific news site and well-produced YouTube video ads promoting DASH as a payment method.[290] This voting method has also been used to decisively and

---

[287] Duffield, Evan. "Official Statement on Rebranding To Dash." *Dash Forum*, 12 Mar. 2015.

[288] Duffield, Evan. "Self-Sustainable Decentralized Governance by Blockchain." *Dash Forum*, 22 Apr. 2015.

[289] Duffield, Evan. "Darkcoin Update / Masternode Requirements / Masternode Payments." *Dash Forum*, 7 Apr. 2014.

[290] Valenzuela, Joël. "Dash DAO Funds Cryptocurrency's First Proprietary News Service." *Dash News*, 17 Apr. 2017.

transparently determine things like block size without creating a bitter debate or risk of community splits.

DASH reached a price of $1,642 and a market cap of 12 billion dollars during December 2017's peak. This makes DASH one of only a handful of cryptocurrencies that have surpassed a $1,000 valuation and represents massive gains for its early believers who purchased it below one dollar. This is especially apparent with owners of Masternodes, who could obtain the DASH needed to assemble them for as little as $700 in 2014, only to sell them for over $1.6 million without even considering the significant amount of DASH received as *masternode rewards* over three years. The Masternode's function made them first-of-a-kind digital assets, with many thinking of them as income producing digital utilities. Their method of operation also harkens back to earlier centuries where the landowner class, established people with a clearly defined and significant interest in the long-term viability of the region, held all or most political power. The idea seems to make sense in Blockland too; those who own the largest shares of the settlements have the vote, as it is in their long-term interest to ensure the viability of their blockchain.

New Economy Movement - 19 Jan. 2014

NEM was announced by Bitcointalk user UtopianFuture as a copy of NXT, only with a wider distribution of ~2,000 people instead of merely 72. This would theoretically guarantee that no single person could initially hoard so much NEM that they might unduly manipulate the market while ensuring a wider and more utopian initial distribution would lead to a larger user base. To achieve this, each recipient would receive 2,250,000 NEM, equivalent to 1/4000th of all NEM that could ever be created. This was called a NEM Stake

– a significant stake in a (or as hoped by its creator, *the*) new economy. There were many ways to acquire a stake, with the first several hundred being given for free to forum accounts who simply replied to the post. The initial wave of paid recipients acquired their stakes for 0.001 BTC (~$0.86), while those "late to the party" had to pay a full price of 0.03 BTC (~$26). For those not wanting to pay, a NEM Stake could be acquired by "*promot*[ing] *NEM to the outside community*" for example by mentioning it on social media.

> *The fundraising is especially designed to promote fairness and egalitarianism. This is the first funding scheme of this type ever and we believe it is revolutionary in its effort to bring egalitarianism to the crypto industry. ... One Bitcointalk account is entitled one stake spot. If you send more than the required amount at one time or multiple times, we will consider it a donation to NEM.*[291]
>
> - Forum user UtopianFuture, 19 Jan, 2014.

It was on January 28th that I recall browsing the Dogecoin subreddit, when I happened upon a comment inviting me to check out an interesting project. I clicked the link and found myself on the NEM announcement page. I recall thinking about how the concept seemed like a pyramid scheme at best and an outright scam at worst, but nevertheless decided to create a Bitcointalk account to throw my beer money into the experiment:

> *To the moon we go!!*
> ***16mBTC** to ID d391c155ad6ac0406db1722088872421c74 e30250e6ddd3481b8a3d996aaafd0*
> *this could be very good :)*[292]
>
> - Elias Ahonen, 28 Jan. 2014.

291 utopianfuture, Bitcointalk.org user. "[ANN] NEM : Descendant of NXT - 4 Billion Coins - Equal Shares for ALL." *Bitcoin Forum*, 19 Jan. 2014.

292 Ahonen, Elias. "[ANN] NEM : Descendant of NXT - 4 Billion Coins - Equal Shares for ALL." *Bitcoin Forum*, 28 Jan. 2014.

As thousands of forum accounts signed up for stakes, several purges were undertaken in which the blockchain transactions were carefully analyzed to identify whether the same individuals were attempting to acquire multiple stakes. Over several months, these efforts invalidated the stake claims of hundreds of alleged "sock puppets", including one of mine, opening up spots for more and more people. This went off smoothly, until UtopianFuture himself was outed as an owner of sock-puppets which he had used to comment in and hype up the NEM discussion threads in the early days of the project to make them appear more active.

> *I failed in my personal conduct and not adhere to the rules I set myself. If you are familiar with American politics, now I have the Eliot Spitzer or Anthony Weiner problem. ...*
> *It is what it is. I apologize to my core team members, to all NEM supporting developers and helpers for this issue. I will step down from now on.... this will be the last post of UtopianFuture.*[293]
>
> - Forum user UtopianFuture, June 2014.

And so UtopianFuture freely transferred control of the website, accounts, and other information such as lists of press contacts to the team whom he had worked with. NEM went on without him. It was eventually decided that instead of copying NXT, a new blockchain would be built from the ground up. As this meant a significant time delay that would inevitably cause some stakeholders to become impatient, an interim market for stakes was set up on the NXT Asset Exchange. A stakeholder could redeem their stakes into the exchange and sell tokens which represented $1/10^{th}$ of a stake; a future distribution of 225,000 NEM. For several months, the price of a

[293] utopianfuture, Bitcointalk.org user. "[NEM] NEM -New Economy Movement - No Envy Movement - Updates+Discussion Thread." *Bitcoin Forum*, 12 June 2014.

stake hovered around $700 on this market, suggesting that the project was already a success for having surpassed a valuation of over $2 million.

NEM finally launched in April 2015 to a muted response. This was largely because this was the middle of "crypto winter", where Blockland itself was practically a ghost town compared to its former wealth and activity level. The project's value slipped below $1 million as stakeholders were able to redeem and sell their tokens for the seemingly more stable bitcoins and dollars. I was among these, selling two stakes for a little over three bitcoins in total. NEM, like most other projects at the time, seemed destined to wither away.

Then things started to happen. In March 2016, the valuation shot from $5 million $12 million, and in June it rocketed to $110 million before settling around $30 million for the next half year. The reasonable person would consider the wild spike in valuation to be a temporary glitch of market irrationality, but the persistent lesson of Blockland is that "crypto" is neither reasonable nor rational in accordance with established models. By March '17 the valuation had rocketed ~100x to $2.3 billion, and in January '18 the valuation peaked at over $18 billion dollars.

This means that as tokens traded for $2.01, each "stake" reached a valuation of $4,500,000. While this peak was short lived, the period in which each token traded for over 50 cents (over $1 million per stake distribution) lasted for several months. NEM can probably be considered the most profitable investment offered in history, provided lottery tickets cannot be counted as investments. Considering that hundreds of people purchased their 2,250,000 NEM Stakes for under one dollar, the return on NEM Stakes these can be verifiably pegged at five hundred million percent over four years – 125,000,000% per annum. Bitcoin and cryptocurrencies have often been likened to lottery tickets by both cautious believers and "haters" due to their volatile and experimental nature. Gambling or not, these 86-cent lottery tickets from an anonymous and unknown internet poster made more than a few millionaires.

Auroracoin - Feb. 2014

Auroracoin was both the first country-based and airdropped cryptocurrency, being created by a pseudonymous developer, Baldur Friggjar Óðinsson, who pledged to distribute 50% of all Auroracoins among the ~321,000 people on Iceland's national ID database, whose use was seemingly approved by Icelandic authorities. This *airdrop* happened in three phases, with the first starting on March 25th, 2014 and seeing 35,430 claimants representing 11% of the country's population. These claimants received 31.8 AUR each, which was worth $385 (0.35 BTC) at the beginning of the claiming period but had fallen to less than $20 a month later. The price never recovered, and the two further airdrops increased the amount of coins exponentially to 318 and then 636 AUR in order to keep the value being redeemed somewhat stable around $20-$30. AUR's situation was different in the weeks before the airdrops, as coins were available only from miners and market hype pushed the currency's market cap above one billion dollars for a brief time. After the airdrop periods, the 5,344,628 unclaimed coins were burned. *Burning* coins refers to sending them to a specially created address from where they can never be removed because no one has the private key, effectively removing them from circulation forever.[294]

Auroracoin certainly left a legacy, not least as the originator of the airdrop which has been used by hundreds of other cryptocurrencies as a mechanism to grow user bases and stimulate markets. It is

294 Auroracoin, Bitcointalk.org user. "Auroracoin." *Bitcoin Forum*, 10 May 2016.

also significant that in combining Auroracoin and other currencies, an estimated 13.3% of a country's population became owners of cryptocurrency before most of the world had even awoken to the idea of blockchain. The creator's vision was that Icelanders, who faced strict capital controls and an unstable currency after the 2008 recession, would adopt the currency for everyday payments. When some politicians expressed dismay over the project, including fears that tax evasion resulting from its use might unfavorably impact the economy, Óðinsson wrote that authorities "*can make it illegal to own or trade Auroracoin... however, they will never be able to control such a decentralized system, or stop Icelanders from using the currency, without turning Iceland into a police state.*"[295]

Mazacoin - 10 Mar. 2014

Mazacoin was likely inspired by Auroracoin, and was built by developer Payu Harris with the hope of turning it into an official currency for the Oglala Lakota first nations aboriginal tribe located in South Dakota. This tribe numbers around 50,000 and its members earned an average of under $3,000 in 2013. Because on-reservation tribes are essentially sovereign governments within the United States, Mazacoin aimed to become the first cryptocurrency owned/controlled directly by a government. By placing 50% of the Mazacoins into a tribal trust, Harris believed that he could stimulate the economy and open doors for it to interact with global markets in a variety of ways. Ultimately, Harris believed that Mazacoin could fully replace $200 million in annual grants received by the

[295] Cowray, Dainel. "Icelandic Parliament Committee Holds Closed Session to Discuss Auroracoin." *CoinDesk*, 14 May 2014.

tribe, saying that "*with funding we control. We can build our economy from scratch.*"[296]

The project promoted itself as the "*first sovereign cryptocurrency*" with "*nationwide lobbying efforts*"[297], creating hype in the blockchain sphere. It pushed all the right buttons of the multitudes of people who believed cryptocurrencies to be a form of financial sovereignty that would lead any group adopting them to wealth. As such, an autonomous and impoverished tribe in a developed country could in theory be a perfect case study to "prove" cryptocurrency's merits to the world. Despite the excitement and associated swings in price, the project ultimately failed to gain traction.

Monero - 18 Apr. 2014

Monero means *coin* or *currency* in Esperanto, a language designed in the late 19th century to serve as an easy and flexible "*universal second language*" to help foster international understanding and cooperation. The idea here was clear: Monero could be a universal currency to facilitate trade and foster international cooperation. BitMonero was based off the codebase of another token called Bytecoin, which had fallen into chaos due to serious scam accusations against Bytecoin's developers. As such, BitMonero inherited a large portion of Bytecoin's community after being created by someone called thankful_for_today.[298] The community however did not quite appreciate all thankful_for_today's efforts and they

[296] Browning, Lynnley. "Oglala Sioux Hope Bitcoin Alternative, Mazacoin, Will Change Economic Woes." *Newsweek*, 14 Aug. 2014.
[297] flipstyler, Bitcointalk.org user. "[ANN][MZC][SHA-256] Mazacoin *First Sovereign Currency* Android Wallet Avail.!!" *Bitcoin Forum*, 10 Mar. 2014.
[298] thankful_for_today, Bitcointalk.org user. "[ANN][BMR] Bitmonero - a New Coin Based on CryptoNote Technology - Launched." *Bitcoin Forum*, 9 Apr. 2014.

soon commandeered the project in a coup that forum user Johnny Mnemonic recounts:

> *When thankful_for_today launched bitMonero two weeks later [after the Bytecoin drama, with this hurry potentially contributing to the issues]..., he had pretty much ignored everything that was discussed and just did what he wanted. [lengthy technical details removed]... Basically, he f--ked everything up. Then, he disappeared.*
> *I, and others, started working on new forks that were closer to what everyone else was hoping for. David Latapie (IIRC) started PMing people and trying to get them to consolidate projects to not divide the community. I personally thought the best course of action was to fix bitMonero and relaunch it (I still think that would've been best). but instead it was decided that the bitMonero project should just be taken over. There were like 9 or 10 interested parties at the time if my memory is correct. We voted on IRC to drop the "bit" from bitMonero and move forward with the project.*
> *Thankful_for_today suddenly resurfaced, and wasn't happy to learn the community had assumed control of the coin. He attempted to maintain his own fork (still calling it "bitMonero") for a while, but that quickly fell into obscurity. The rest is history.*[299]
>
> \- Forum use Johnny Mnemonic, 10 Mar. 2015.

Forum user tacotime became the face of this revolution and held the reins as the "*lead maintainer of the codebase*" of Monero for four years until a new Core Team was created. He was then essentially forced to step down due to a lack of recent activity on his part. With the appointment of a replacement, the Core Team put out a sort of constitution that laid out its role as a steward or government of Monero, and affirmation that this government could and should

[299] smooth, Bitcointalk.org user. "[XMR] Monero - A Secure, Private, Untraceable Cryptocurrency - 0.8.8.6." *Bitcoin Forum*, 10 Mar. 2015.

be overthrown at any time if any of its members lose the community's active consent to act on their behalf.[300]

It is fascinating to consider that this was the second change of government within Monero, which was at the time valued at over five billion dollars and run by an anonymous person. Despite these massive amounts of power at play and the fact that Monero was untethered to the laws, customs, or legal system of any country, a peaceful and uncontroversial transition of power took place. It can be understood as a modern-day example of forming a new government from scratch, only taking place over a community of people based on a digital plane rather than a geographical one. In this analogy we can understand Monero as if it were a free, constitutional republic, in which the government is a mere servant of an all-powerful basic law which commands the citizens to rebel, should the government overstep its assigned authority.

> *The responsibilities of the Core Team are as follows (in no particular order):*
>
> - *Act as primary trusted arbiters of the Forum Funding System on behalf of the community, so as to ensure the completion of all projects to the satisfaction of the community.*
> - *Manage the codebase of the Monero Project, which includes merging code on Github, keeping backups, and ensuring the safety, security, and free access of the code from any party.*
> - *Steward the general donation fund, and spending the Monero there on anything they see fit to further the Monero Project.*
> - *Act as trusted signers and distributors of reference clients for the Monero coin, and other related technologies.*
> - *Set a direction and vision for the Monero Project*

[300] monero, Bitcointalk.org user. "[XMR] Monero - A Secure, Private, Untraceable Cryptocurrency." *Bitcoin Forum*, 25 Apr. 2014.

> *In the event that the community deems the Core Team unworthy or lax in their duties, they are free to fork the project away from the current Core Team, as happened with thankful_for_today.*
>
> *There are some things that the Core Team are NOT responsible for, despite misconceptions from the community. Some of the more common misconceptions are listed below:*
>
> - *Members of the Core Team are NOT anyone's boss, and no permission is needed from them to do anything.*
> - *The Core Team does NOT act as a centralized point of failure, but encourages organic, self-started initiatives that further the ecosystem of Monero.*
> - ***The Core Team does NOT equal Monero. In the event that one, or all of the Core Team goes rogue, we are to remember that Monero is a movement. A global initiative to further privacy globally, and provide real, fungible, digital money for everyone. This can happen even without the presence of the Core Team.***[301]
>
> - getmonero.org, 1 Mar. 2018. (emphasis mine)

It is important to understand Monero's role in Blockland as a *privacy coin* comparable to Dash. It operates a public ledger that is obfuscated, meaning that while anyone can send and receive Monero, no outside observer can easily determine where an amount originated from, how much it really was, or who received it. This is made possible by a system called *ring signatures*, where users cryptographically signing a transaction also sign with ten other users' signatures to give everyone plausible deniability. This has made Monero a preferred payment method on the dark web and has made it easy to launder bitcoins by trading them into Monero for even a brief period. This bitcoin laundering was notably done by the alleged North Korean hackers involved with the 2017 WannaCry ransomware attack which infected 300,000 computers

[301] "Core Team Announcement." *Getmonero.org*, 1 Mar. 2018.

and caused up to four billion dollars of damage around the world.[302] The currency was valued at around $2 near launch, falling to less than 50 cents before peaking at nearly $500 in early 2018. It has also become one of the most respected cryptocurrencies among Bitcoiners, owing to its decentralized structure and focus on privacy.[303]

MaidSafeCoin - 22 Apr. 2014

MaidSafeCoin's "IPO" raised $8 million in only five hours, making it the largest "cryptocurrency IPO" at the time, and one of the first true ICOs. The project revolved around the idea of creating a decentralized internet called SAFE Network, which would be powered by "farmers" (miners) functioning as internet servers. This *Proof-of-Resource* system does not reward farmers based on the amount of computing power but based on how much internet resources, that is data, they are able to reliably store on their machines. This internet would be encrypted, resistant to attempts of censorship, and allow for secure communications and file sharing.[304]

MAID introduced one of the first *bounty programs*, which became common amongst new cryptocurrency projects. As the idea took off, bounties became a standard way to power the growth of a cryptocurrency by rewarding code contributors, promotional article writers, and even those sharing the project on social media with predetermined amounts of tokens without the need to hire anyone into

[302] Gallagher, Sean. "Researchers Say WannaCry Operator Moved Bitcoins to 'Untraceable' Monero." *Ars Technica*, 8 May 2017.
[303] "The Developmental History of Monero." *EVONAX*, 12 Aug. 2018.
[304] maidsafe, Bitcointalk.org user. "[ANN] IPO of MaidSafe: Entering the Future of the Decentralized Internet." *Bitcoin Forum*, 22 Apr. 2014.

a fulltime role. This essentially created a crypto gig-economy cottage industry for graphic designers, translators, coders, writers, and social media influencers.[305]

Clams - 24 May 2014

Clams built upon the AuroraCoin *airdrop* model by "dropping" tokens directly into 3.1 million existing blockchain wallets on the Bitcoin, Litecoin, and Dogecoin chains. A snapshot of the blockchains was taken on May 12th 2014 and each unique wallet was given the ability to "*dig for*" (redeem) 4.6 CLAM. Specifically, this happened on BTC block #300,377, LTC block #565,693, and DOGE block #218,556.[306] To "find" their clams, users would have to insert the private key of the (hopefully now empty) wallet into a CLAM client, which would then give access to the Clams. Every wallet was given the same amount of CLAM, whether it contained only 0.000001 or 100,000 BTC. A unit of this money from the sky traded at a few dollars initially, bounced between 50 cents and a few dollars for years, and peaked at $18 before settling back to a few dollars. Clams are notable in that they opened the floodgates for airdrops, which later became a daily occurrence on Ethereum meaning that each amount of Ethereum would forever attract freebies.

This gave birth to the concept of *token spam* which, like email spam, could not be stopped as anyone could create any type of cryptocurrency with any message whatsoever and essentially broadcast or attach it to every single unit of another type of currency.

---

305 Upstatestuckny, Reddit.com user. "Maidsafe Bounty Program Is Really Taking off! - $20 per Story Point (Paid in Bitcoin Only)." *Reddit r/rust*, 9 Sept. 2015.

306 'SuperClam, Bitcointalk.org user. "[ANN][CLAM] Clams, Proof-Of-Chain, Proof-Of-Working-Stake, A.k.a. 'Clamcoin'." *Bitcoin Forum*, 24 May 2014.

Imagine having $1,000 in a bank account one day and finding out the next day that it now also contains 2,024 JDFP (John Doe For President) tokens, 666.777 JOCT (Join Our Cult Today) tokens, and 6969.8008135 TTPS (Try This Porn Site) tokens, all of which are worth a fraction of a cent combined. But suppose that John Doe did become president; those JDFP coins might be worth something, so it is best to keep them! This phenomenon became so common that many exchages have added a function to allow users to automatically convert this constantly incoming and seemingly worthless "crypto dust" into BTC.

StartCoin - 13 June 2014

StartJoin was a social network for crowdfunding which aimed to "monetize altruism." Anyone could create a project, either at a *concept* or *active* stage. Users could then donate money towards the project, offer their services and expertise to help make it happen, or even join a given initiative as a team member at the conceptual stage. Everyone involved could then follow the project's progression and discuss openly with the project's members. All of this was tied together with StartCoins, a mineable currency of which a 45% *pre-mine* was retained by the StartCoin team and used to continuously reward those who donated to projects and remained active on the platform.[307]

This platform was co-founded by Max Keiser, an alternative economics commentator who has been described as "*the most visible character in an underground movement that. . . played some small part in driving up the price of precious metals.*"[308] Though StartJoin

---

[307] startcoinproject, Bitcointalk.org user. "[ANN] [START] Startcoin 2.0 - The Digital Currency for Crowdfunding." *Bitcoin Forum*, 13 June 2014.
[308] Braiker, Brian. "Silver Bug Goes Viral with Marketing War Max Keiser has Become a Fringe Media Star Thanks to the Web." *Adweek*, 2 June 2011.

eventually closed, Keiser has remained active in cryptocurrency, speaking at conferences around the world and often making headlines with his predictions of Bitcoin prices.

StartCoin reflects an interesting cultural aspect of the blockchain industry; everything is a *project.* When one attends a conference, the most common questions encountered are "*what project are you working on*" or "*have you found any interesting projects here*?" Anything from an exchange, newsletter, book, conference, government regulatory process, cryptocurrency, ICO, or even the hosting of a local blockchain pub-night is understood to be a "project". This stands in contrast to the normal X industry gathering, where questions generally revolve around companies, departments, and profits. This idea of projects has a subtle undertone, which differentiates it from commercial enterprise. This is largely because these projects are experimental voyages into the unknown, with business cases that depend primarily on theory and assumptions rather than established market dynamics or business logic. There is also the implication that no blockchain service or company is in a state of completion but must always continue innovating and building (sometimes referred to as buidling as inspired by hodling) as the industry is very fluid and ever-changing.

There is an insinuation that every blockchain project exists first and foremost as a service to the community/world and is run by some sort of open, collaborative collective that is unselfishly working to somehow improve the blockchain landscape. This comes from the idealistic conception of blockchain as a revolution, with every revolutionary expected to contribute to the movement in whatever way they see fit. This cypherpunk spirit was very much present in the open, collaborative, and pseudonymous community-based efforts to create most of the early cryptocurrencies. Of course, the industry (as evidenced by the fact that it can be called an industry, though the oft-preferred term is blockchain space, denoting the sphere or environment in which blockchain activities happen) is full of non-idealistic profit-oriented businesses and individuals who have found that it is socially required to present a charade as passionate civil servants or freedom fighters. Admitting the obvious truth that a traditional corporation would exploit the blockchain community, compete against instead of collaborating with other similar companies, and maintain close trade secrets remains somewhat taboo.

BitShares - July 2014

BitShares was created by Dan Larimer and Charles Hoskinson around the idea that a blockchain could derive its value from an internal business instead of an external process like mining. The consensus mechanism developed for BitShares is called *Delegated Proof-of-Stake* (DPoS). This makes use of a system of trusted *witness nodes* (computers run by users) which group recent transactions together to create blocks of BitShares each second. These *witnesses* (imagine them as paralegals who are brought in to witness legal contracts) are then rewarded by transaction fees. Holders of BitShares have the ability to vote on things like transaction fees, block intervals, and both the number of witness nodes and who gets to function as one. If a node fails in its task or is otherwise classified as acting against the community's interest, it gets voted out. This sidesteps the need for mining, which the creators believed to be increasingly inaccessible to most users and on its way to becoming dangerously centralized in countries with low electricity prices. A portion of all transaction fees were collected into a community fund and anyone could submit a funding proposal to make some improvements to the network which would then be released when given enough affirmative votes.[309]

---

309 scaryvirus, Bitcointalk.org user. "[BTS] Bitshares #1 Fastest Crypto, Tokens, DEX, ICOs since 2014 (Unofficial ಠ_ಠ)." *Bitcoin Forum*, 5 June 2017.

The previously mentioned internal business component was the first Decentralized Exchange (DEX), which allowed users to exchange cryptocurrencies without first sending and thus entrusting them to 3rd party exchanges that are vulnerable to theft by hackers. In operating a DEX, BitShares could receive transaction fees from traders without ever taking on the liability of holding on to others' private keys. To simplify the operation of this DEX, *Smartcoins* were created. These Smartcoins could be programmed to track some other asset such as BTC, Gold, or USD, effectively pegging themselves to these. At any time, these pegged Smartcoins could be settled back into BTS, the base currency of the BitShares blockchain. This is the origin of *stablecoins*. As with the NXT Asset Exchange, BitShares users could freely create their own Smartcoins within the DEX to represent anything they wanted.

In every way, BitShares took the form of an entire ecosystem that defied classification into worldly concepts such as digital currency, business, exchange, or even banking institution because it was effectively all of these things and more. In keeping with the idea of Blockland settlements, BitShares developed into a sovereign nation to itself with a functioning government, tax base, complex financial system, and a profit-generating industry which rewarded all its participants. In January 2018, BitShares' market cap peaked at 1.9 billion dollars, representing a ~150x rise in 2017.

Tether - July 2014

Tether is built on Mastercoin's foundation (later known as Omni) in exactly the way J.R. Willett envisioned that different currencies would sprout from the platform. This is no doubt because co-founders Brock Pierce and Craig Sellars were deeply involved with Mastercoin. Tether's basis is that of a USD stablecoin, meaning that it is designed to remain stable or "tethered" to the price of one US Dollar.[310] Initially named Realcoin, the project was re-branded as Tether about six weeks after launch. The key to Tether's functionality is that the tokens are fully backed by the currency in question, meaning that one US Dollar would be deposited in a Tether-controlled bank account before a corresponding USDT could be issued.[311] Tether soon became one of the most important blockchain tokens when measured by daily volume, sometimes even surpassing Bitcoin.

Though the project's whitepaper called for regular audits, the project faltered on that requirement leading The Wall Street Journal to refer to Tether as a "*sort of the central bank of crypto trading... [yet] they don't conduct themselves like you'd expect a responsible, sensible financial institution to do.*"[312] This view was corroborated by a 2018 academic paper by members of the University of Texas' Finance Department which suggested "*incomplete Tether backing before month-ends... [which is] most consistent with the supply-based hypothesis where Tether is used to provide price support and manipulate cryptocurrency prices.*"[313] That same year, the US Justice department launched a criminal probe to investigate the use of Tether to manipulate Bitcoin's price to historic highs in late 2017.[314]

On the user side, USDT has often functioned as a way for traders to exit the markets during times of uncertainty without needing to

---

[310] "A Brief History of Stablecoins (Part 1)." *BitMEX Research*, 2 July 2018.
[311] Haan, Robert Jan Den. "Clearing Up Misconceptions: This Is How Tether Should (And Does) Work." *Bitcoin Magazine*, 14 June 2018.
[312] Vigna, Paul, and Steven Russolillo. "The Mystery Behind Tether, the Crypto World's Digital Dollar." *Wall Street Journal*, 12 Aug. 2018.
[313] Shams, Amin. "Is Bitcoin Really Un-Tethered?" *Social Science Research Network (SSRN)*, 28 Oct. 2019.
[314] Robinson, Matt, and Tom Schoenberg. "Bitcoin-Rigging Criminal Probe Focused on Tie to Tether." *Bloomberg*, 20 Nov. 2018.

hold "real" fiat currency on exchange accounts. Stablecoins also make decentralized and other non-fiat exchanges more practical, as an exchange can effectively offer BTC-USD trading without needing to maintain bank accounts. Some users are also drawn to the idea that they are always 100% in crypto even when holding tokens that follow USD prices and some (generally incorrectly) assume that this may be a valid way of reducing taxation by never holding actual government-issued money. Another benefit is that USDT can be immediately removed from and returned to an exchange as to avoid the risk of storing money in a crypto exchange that could theoretically go bankrupt at any moment. Such users must of course assume that one USDT will always equal one USD, which has not always been the case; in October 2018, the tokens briefly fell to as little as 90 cents.

Stellar - 31 July 2014

Stellar was designed to function as a *value exchange protocol* and was launched by Mt.Gox & Ripple creator Jed McCaleb with $3 million of funding from the payment network Stripe.[315] The Stellar network is composed of many anchor servers around the world, which each contain a record of accounts in a database called Ledger. These servers then "make deals" with each other, according to the transfer needs of Stellar's users, and work towards a state of balance called consensus (comparable to confirmation) which happens every 2-4 seconds. All these transactions are denominated in Stellar Lumens, the network's native currency. Like Ripple which it is derived from, Stellar has no mining and a fixed supply

---

[315] "Fintech Roundup: Stripe Partners with Visa, National Australia Bank Creates $50 Million Fintech Fund." *Ripple*, 4 Aug. 2015.

of 100 billion Stellar Lumen's (XLM), whose distribution is managed by the Stellar Development Foundation.[316]

Like the much earlier PPC coin, Stellar incorporates a set annual inflation rate of 1%. However unlike with other inflation coins, this inflation is not distributed to everyone. Every account can designate another account as its "inflation destination" essentially voting for it to receive its share of inflation. An account must receive 0.5% of all such votes (each XLM accounts for one vote) to get the prescribed inflation prize. This means that members of the network are incentivized to either do something to benefit the Stellar ecosystem in such a way that users decide to vote for them as a recipient of weekly "free money". This was trailblazing, as it represents the foundation on which future *block producer* blockchain systems, like EOS, were later based.

Stellar is also notable for the way it has distributed its coins as widely as possible, using a mix of airdrops, grants, and other types of handouts. The first 20% of XLM (20 billion) was reserved for BTC and XRP (Ripple) holders via airdrop as pioneered by CLAM's and 5% was retained by the foundation for operations costs. Next, 25% was allocated to businesses, non-profits, and academic grants. Finally, the remaining 50% was earmarked to be handed out in regular hundred-million-dollar mass giveaways over a period of years in the hopes that wide ownership would stoke adoption and long-term viability. One of these programs rewarded ~$50 worth of XLM to anyone willing to watch educational videos about the protocol and succeed in a few short quizzes,[317] while other giveaways

---

[316] jed, Bitcointalk.org user. "[ANN][XLM] Stellar - Decentralized Trading Platform." *Bitcoin Forum*, 6 Apr. 2016.
[317] Sulemanji, Nawaz. "Stellar and Coinbase's $50 Giveaway Program Looks like a Pyramid." *Yahoo Finance*, 28 Mar. 2016.

have simply given similar amounts to the users of certain exchanges.[318] Only a small portion of these tokens have been distributed as of writing, suggesting a very long-term orientation. This idea of a pre-set allocation of tokens became standard when token creation was standardized in the 2017 ICO boom, where different shares of the final token amount were divided between different tiers of participants including *team*, *seed investors*, *pre-ICO*, and *ICO*.

Factom - 7 Nov. 2014

Factom bills itself as a *blockchain as a service* (BaaS) company, which can be contrasted with the much more common SaaS: Software as a Service. It is an "*open source data integrity protocol... that extends the security of blockchain to any type of data*"[319] and manages records for clients such as hospital networks and United States Homeland Security. In practice this means that documents can not only be validated by a blockchain hash, but they can also be involved in smart contracts.

What makes Factom an interesting piece of cryptocurrency evolution is that it is a mixture of a traditional company and an open source project. Its platform also incorporates the FCT token which works in conjunction with another token called *entry credits*, which are effectively stablecoins that are created when Factom's are burned. These Entry Credits are then used to pay the platform's user fees in accordance with the number of documents handled. Even if an institutional client could not hold FCT or EC directly, they would still fuel the demand for FCT. This is because by spending money on Factom services, they would cause others to burn

---

[318] Pirus, Benjamin. "Why Stellar Is Giving Away $124 Million In Cryptocurrency." *Forbes*, 9 Sept. 2019.
[319] factomprotocol.com

FCT to create EC. This is complex, but indicative of an interesting trend in which cryptocurrencies are becoming critical parts of the back end of corporate/government-facing services.

Conclusion

As we can see, 2014 represented a wave of innovation at a time when the industry had just gotten the attention of the world. As fast as this attention came, most of it disappeared as the markets were unable to sustain BTC above $1,000. Despite this apparent failure, hundreds of innovators were inspired by the technology and rushed to develop new projects. Early 2014 certainly had an air of euphoria; the next Bitcoin was surely around the corner! As 2014 was a year of market decline, it can be understood as crypto fall in contrast to 2015 which is best characterized as a harsh winter with little activity and lethal cold. Markets were almost entirely stagnant, with hundreds of settlements abandoned to total failure and memorialized on a site called Shitcoin Graveyard.[320] Those residents of Blockland who did not flee for warmer climates were left hunkering down in their still-standing settlements and the interaction between colonies was minimal due to the deep freeze. Few dared to venture out to attempt the founding of new settlements.

By now, the Blockland has developed into a collection of settlements with varying amounts of influence and affinity. It can be understood as a large group of crypto-nations. Bitcoinland is the oldest and most culturally, financially, and politically influential while the powerful lands of Litecoin, Ethereum, and Ripple are firmly established, having been founded in what now seem like ancient times before the 2013 bubble. Each of these crypto-nations has a different history and culture and thus different founding principles

[320] shitcoingraveyard.com

and values, which are of course always in some state of political flux. Some citizens are loyal only to their own crypto-nation and even believe all others to be illegitimate, while others may hold multiple citizenships and accept the differences in the nations as minor.

This new wave of immigrants to Blockland redefined the land's existing gene pool. With each season or cycle, a new crop of blockchain people naturally emerge on the shores and changes to the landscape are thus inevitable. As the concept of Blockchain evolved from a theoretical whitepaper paper in 2008, to an experiment in 2009, only to morph into a "real currency" on Pizza Day in 2010, 2014 saw the technology sprout dozens of new branches, each going a slightly different way. Indeed, Blockland is very much alive and ever-changing.

A relic of the sect of Bitcoin Maximalissm, with an enamel 'moon rocket man' idol on .999 silver and behind glass. On the upper left is a piece of a meteorite, also encased in glass.

A 2015 copper coin minted by the Multicoiner sect, bearing the names of 12 crypto-currencies along the outer side.

A 2014 silver coin minted by the Nocoiner sect, meant to demonstrate that cryptocurrencies are not real because they have no physical form.

CHAPTER 9

The Sects of Satoshism

We are gathered here today to join these three couples in blockchain matrimony. Will the grooms please repeat after me:

I _____ take thee, to be my cryptographically wedded wife, to hold and secure, to both trust and verify, in both bull markets and crypto winters. Through forks both applied and contentious, may our merkelroots always trace back, to the genesis block of our love, from this block until the heat death of the universe.

Wives, repeat after me, I _____ take thee to be my cryptographically wedded husband, to both hold and secure, to both trust and verify, though bull markets and crypto winters, through forks both applied and contentious, may our merkelroots always trace back, to the genesis block of our love, from this block until the heat death of the universe.

In the name of the Doge, Satoshi, and the holy moon, I now pronounce you husband and wife.

You may now kiss the bride!

Now you may sign the transaction which may take a little longer than that kiss.

A huge congratulations to our couples!"[321]
- "Doge Preacher", 7 Apr. 2019.

After the vows which are accompanied by joyous laughter from the crowd, the officiating Doge Preacher opens a sleek laptop on his makeshift bar-table pulpit which is surrounded by artwork related to crypto and love. He explains that it is time to permanently encode the marriage vows onto the blockchain, where they will apparently remain securely "*until the heat death of the universe.*" The atmosphere becomes casual, as the newly wedded couples are handed glasses of champagne and the flower-girls begin to frolic about in the restaurant. The first couple is soon called up to the alter and the computer is turned to face the onlookers who have gotten up from their seats to get a closer look. A flower girl delivers a specially prepared USB stick, which the bride inserts as Doge Preacher directs her to enter the password. Lines of code appear, buttons are clicked, and the ENTER is pressed to sign the transaction. It is then the groom's turn, who repeats the process. A minute later, the present Ethereum block is confirmed, and the marriage contract is forever set in code as thousands of computers around the world verify the joint declaration. "*Blockchain official!*" declares Doge Preacher, who is wearing a Doge shirt under his tie-less suit jacket in such a way that an eye of Doge peers from the center of an upside-down pyramid on his chest.

What in the world is this?

What you have witnessed is the first blockchain mass wedding, which took place during CoinFest in Vancouver on April 7th, 2019. CoinFest is a decentralized currency convention and is itself decen-

[321] Blockchain Gaming, Youtube.com user. "Mass Blockchain Wedding at CoinFest Vancouver 2019." *YouTube*, 7 Apr. 2019.

tralized in such a way that it runs simultaneously in a dozen different cities around the world with connections via video streaming. Each of the grooms worked in the blockchain industry and it is undeniable that there is (very nerdy) romanticism in the idea of a marriage contract being recorded forever on a/the blockchain almost as if sent away on a rocket towards some distant galaxy. A blockpunk take on *diamonds are forever*, perhaps.[322] Another example of a blockchain marriage is that of EOS's billionaire founder Brock Pierce who tied the knot, or more accurately *executed the smart contract* with his wife Crystal Rose in front of dozens of guests wearing unicorn head-dresses at Burning Man in 2017.[323]

But what do blockchain weddings have to do with cryptocurrency? Nothing. They are an example for non-currency use cases for blockchain.

Indeed, Blockchain and cryptocurrency have by now come to mean many very different things to different people. In continuing with the analogy of Satoshism as a religion connected to Bitcoin, it has now emerged that the faith has divided into several factions or sects with differing beliefs regarding blockchain and Satoshi's message. These are the sects of Satoshism.

Bitcoin Maximalists

As hundreds of new blockchains and their accompanying cryptocurrencies became a prominent part of blockchain discourse in 2014, they came to be despised by many *Bitcoin Maximalists* who referred to them as inferior *alt-coins* or *shit coins*. The term can be traced to Ethereum's founder Vitalik Buterin calling Andrew

---

[322] coinfest.org

[323] LastWeekTonight, Youtube.com user. "Cryptocurrencies: Last Week Tonight with John Oliver (HBO)." *YouTube*, 11 Mar. 2018.

Barisser a "*Bitcoin Dominance Maximalist.*"[324] Bitcoin Maximalists are best understood as highly nationalistic residents of Bitcoin, who believe that Bitcoin is not merely the first settlement in a new land, but the only legitimate owner and government of Blockland as a whole. Bitcoin and Blockland are in their view one and the same; the very definitions of each other. As such, other settlements are at best misled foolishness and at worst outright scams. Bitcoin is the only "rightful blockchain settlement"; the others do not deserve to survive and should perhaps even be actively destroyed.

This largely stems from the idea that because Satoshi invented blockchain to make Bitcoin possible, Bitcoin is *the* blockchain. Blockchain is the proof(-of-work) for Bitcoin, whereas Bitcoin is the proof-of-existence of Blockchain. Bitcoin cannot exist without blockchain, and Bitcoin Maximalists, also accurately described as Bitcoin Fundamentalists, widely believe that there can be no meaningful use of blockchain if disconnected from Bitcoin which is its life-giving source. Just as monotheists believe in one God, Maximalists believe in one Blockchain. As one Maximalist group put it, "*there are nearly no uses for blockchain technology besides Bitcoin, understanding this base protocol is crucial.*"[325] This is the Bitcoin-Blockchain duality.[326]

The opposites of Bitcoin Maximalists are those who believe that Bitcoin will ultimately fail and be replaced by a superior system. Often, such "infidels" have switched their faith to some other blockchain, ardently believing in the coming of an imminent judgment day in which Blockland wakes up to "reality" and recognizes Bitcoin's inherent faults. Often, the implication here is that their faith in their chosen blockchain will then be rewarded as those who

---

324 Weese, Leo. "Where Does Bitcoin Maximalism Come from?" *Bitcoin Bytes*, 17 Oct. 2018.
325 *konsensus.network,* 2019.
326 Bhai, Ferdous. "Post-Bitcoin-Maximalism." *Hackernoon*, 11 Oct. 2018.

"believed the false teachings" and failed to identify "the true blockchain" see the incoming flood and desperately pay a high price for entrance into the life-saving ark of such and such alt-coin. Many layers of this sentiment can be found in Blockland; some view Blockland itself as the ark that will save humanity from the folly of fiat currencies. Bitcoin Maximalists view Bitcoin alone as filling that role, while many others view a specific blockchain platform or currency as the savior of the otherwise "fallen" Blockland. All through this chain of believers awaiting their preferred version of judgment day, they have placed their bets by devoting their version of Satoshian faith towards the projects they believe will be proven righteous.

Bitcoin's doubters have presented plenty of examples of instances in the technology space as evidence for Bitcoin's eventual overthrow. These include video cassettes giving way to DVD's and Myspace losing users to Facebook. Maximalists have however offered converse examples, such as Blu-Ray discs which failed to take DVD's market-share despite being in many ways a superior technology. The reason for this was not that DVD's were inherently better, but they had an established market position and recognized brand. Importantly, DVD technology was not so much behind as to be useless; Blu-Ray offered merely an incremental improvement from DVD versus the earlier jump from video cassettes. A general Maximalist view would thus be that despite the likes of Litecoin being functionally superior, Bitcoin would remain the most powerful cryptocurrency, as long as it is not inherently dysfunctional, based largely on its long history, first-mover advantage, and unrivalled brand-power. The most extreme Maximalists would consider the trading of BTC for any other token to be a grave sin, for the simple reason that any non-BTC token will undoubtedly go to their "true value" of $0/0 BTC and thus deprive the owner of Lambomoon.

Many people have taken a more moderate position, considering a small number of blockchains as legitimate while maintaining Bitcoin's God-head status. These Blockland residents might simply be called Bitcoiners; normal citizens who are less zealous and more humble than their Maximalist counterparts while holding legitimate respect for blockchain projects unrelated to Bitcoin. Litecoin is commonly tolerated or accepted, along with privacy-oriented blockchains such as Monero and Dash due to a sense of their general alignment and expansion upon Satoshi's original values and vision. The opposite of the Bitcoiner is one who shares the appreciation for other tokens, but considers some other blockchain such as Ethereum, EOS, or Ripple as the "rock" of blockchain. As with religion in general, a trend has emerged in which the rate of Bitcoin maximalism increases in dire bear markets (chaotic times), whereas it tends to wane when excitement and optimism is in the air and the people of Blockland pre-occupy themselves with various settlement projects. One might consider Bitcoin Maximalists as the "old money" of Blockland, who do not see the "altcoin nuveau rich" as belonging to their caste unless they repent and convert. They are best to watch out, however, as new money has a historical tendency to eclipse the old.

Multicoiners

Another significant set of Blockland residents can be classed as multicoiners or polycoiners, comparable to polytheists who traditionally worship many Gods of various characters. They often but not always recognize a particular chain or chains as more important than others, but in general they believe that no blockchain is more divine than another. They see Satoshi as fallible, demonstrated by Litecoin being made into a better version of Bitcoin while still based on all the same concepts. They might view the Saga of Satoshi &

Bitcoin as mythical and guidance-giving; not to be uncompromisingly interpreted word-for-word in the context of fast-developing blockchain technology, allowing for applications that Satoshi may not have anticipated.

Polycoiners often have a primary residence in Bitcoin or Ethereum, while maintaining apartments and summer-homes in a dozen other settlements to which they lend some of their faith. They believe in blockchain's eventual full incorporation into or even overthrow of the existing order, but they humbly admit that they do not know which blockchain(s) will fulfill such a task. Perhaps, hundreds of blockchains of various characters have a role to play as they collectively entwine the world. For this reason, they hedge their bets, hoping that at least one of their proverbial summer houses' plots is situated in the center of a future metropolis.

Nonbelievers

We cannot forget the nonbelievers, who make up a large portion, if not a majority of Blockland. They ascribe no deep moral or philosophical value to Bitcoin, blockchain, cryptocurrency, or decentralization. These people's broad purpose in Blockland is to exploit it for its vast resources, with the aim of one day transporting these riches back to "the real world" much in the way of the colonists and explorers of old. They could be said in this context to worship (old) money or gold; perhaps the most popular of all religions known to man. The key is that they do not personally identify with Blockland but instead consider it as a foreign, exciting, exotic, and adventurous land where both treasure and danger await. These often include those who buy cryptocurrencies or shareholdings in blockchain companies to diversify their portfolios. They may consider BTC or some other token as a speculative investment or see blockchain as a fast-growing field of technology and seek to capitalize on it by founding companies, starting new cryptocurrencies, or seeking a job in the industry. Most of the people who arrive to Blockland as nonbelievers, but many begin to believe through the unconscious practice of the Satoshian sacraments as they go about their lives in the new world of Blockland.

This naturally means that many of the "Blockland Settlements" are not founded or run by idealistic philosopher-kings as they appear, but by robber-barons who seek to inspire religious ecstasy and a cult-like mentality in their followers in order to generate huge amounts of value before leaving Blockland with millions of dollars (or converting their gains into Bitcoin, which they truly believe in rather than whatever their cash-grabbing project was). It is precisely this fact that drives many towards Bitcoin Maximalism; anything else is seen as fatally flawed by the greed of its founders. Many traditional businesses have thus used blockchain angles by which to hype up their business in a twofold way; existing investors getting excited due to "exposure to Blockland" and Blockland's residents getting excited over the increasing number of businesses expanding to Blockland.

Nocoiners

Finally, there are the Nocoiners, who actively despise the various elements often associated with Satoshism. Despite having no active interest in Blockland, they can be found going to great lengths to discredit even the very concepts underpinning blockchain and decentralization. They are commonly understood as a hateful group who either mask their regret of proverbially missing the boat to Blockland or who unconsciously fear that Blockland's growth threatens their way of life, position in, or understanding of the world. Some would class anyone who has exhibited hostility towards Blockland as a nocoiner, such as the legendary investor Warren Buffet who famously said that Bitcoin was "probably rat poison squared."[327] More commonly however, the descriptor is used towards those who spend notable amounts of energy fighting against Blockland. An excellent example of Nocoiners lies in the subreddit r/buttcoin, which exists to mock Bitcoin and "creepto" and whose members celebrate every crisis, controversy, and bear market.

BitConnect: A Case Study

The BitConnect Token is an excellent case study regarding the uniquely Blocklandish mixture of tribalistic faith, devotion, monetary investment, and belief in positively changing the world. BCC Tokens were created in 2016 and allowed owners to lend the token's value back to the issuer for 1% daily interest. Consider the following charismatic sermon given by an investor named Carlos Matos at BitConnect's annual ceremony in Pattaya, Thailand, in October 2018, when the token was among the most popular cryptocurrencies:

> *Hey hey heeeeeeeeeey ... Whats up Bitconnect?*
>
> *Hey hey hey everybody! My name is Carlos Matos and I am coming from New York City, New York!*
>
> *Let me tell you guys that I am so excited, so happy, I'm really so thrilled to be right now to be sharing this amazing, glorious, super exciting moment of my life with all of you guys, and let me tell you that we are really changing the world as we know it!*
>
> *The world is not anymore the way it used to be – uh-uh, no no no!*
>
> *BITTTCOONNNEEEEEEECCCT!*

---

[327] Kim, Tae. "Warren Buffett Says Bitcoin is 'Probably Rat Poison Squared'." *CNBC*, 5 May 2018.

> *We are coming and we are coming in waves! We are starting and we are going to actually go all over the world; we are belting the entire world! ...*
>
> *And let me tell you that I am actually earning around... one thousand and four hundred dollars on an everyday basis, seven days a week. WHAAAAT?? ...*
>
> *I am saying to so many people who said that this was going to be a con artist game, that this was going to be a scammer game. "Hey you gonna lose all your money." MY WIFE still doesn't believe in me!! ...*
>
> *So guys, I wanna tell you something; faith and belief is the one thing that we all need to be able change the world, and right now I believe that in this room we have the seed that's going to germinate, and its going to explode into an amazing opportunity for us to change this entire world. I am so proud, I am so honored, I am so excited to be here right now and let me tell you something that each and every one of you has the opportunity to become like those amazing people that we know here from Vietnam. ... Making so much money that they could probably have a real hard time counting it. HAHAHA*
>
> *[applause]*[328]
>
> - Carlos Matos, 28 Oct. 2017.

One cannot help but hear the rejoicing and jovial optimism in Carlos' speech. Ecstatic, he appears to genuinely believe that he has stumbled upon "the truth" and is spreading his good news "*all over the world.*" As he stands upon the stage with a handful of other investors, he testifies to the crowd about how he turned $25,000 into $140.000 in only a few months despite everyone telling him it was a scam and that he believes this to be the start of a *germinating*

[328] Optigisa, Youtube.com user. "Bitconnect Ceremony (Original) - Carlos The Meme." *YouTube*, 23 Jan. 2018.

seed that will *explode* and change the world. His excitement and pride are palpable.[329]

As you may have guessed, BitConnect indeed turned out to be a scam where practically everyone lost all their money. After receiving cease and desist orders from US regulators who suspected it to be a Ponzi scheme, the token's internal exchange was shut down in January 2018 causing the price to fall 92% in a single day.[330] This was followed by over 99.9% losses over the following months as the scheme valued at 2.5 billion dollars collapsed to nothing, bringing token prices from $463 to a mere 40 cents before being delisted on practically all exchanges. One of BitConnect's founders was later arrested in India, accused of using the scheme as a way to launder money relating to the controversial Indian demonetization of old 500 and 1,000 Rupee bills around the time the token was created.[331] Mr. Matos' emotional speech did not age well and has became a much-parodied meme, highlighting the absurdity of cryptocurrency markets at the time and his "*hey hey hey*" opening line has been used humorously by speakers at blockchain conferences around the world.

The story of BitConnect explains both Bitcoin Maximalist's aversion to alt-coins and Multicoiner's desire to avoid placing all their eggs in one basket. It shows us how faith can go wrong in Blockland, leading to devastating losses for the likes of our friend Carlos, a BitConnect Maximalist, who years later said that "*I have been a total failure in practically most of the businesses that I have found*

---

329 Matos, Carlos. "Bitconnect Carlos Meme Is Everything Wrong with Cryptocurrency Hype." *Inverse*, 3 Feb. 2018.
330 Mix. "BitConnect Handed an 'Emergency' Cease and Desist Order From Texas Securities Board." *The Next Web*, 5 Jan. 2018.
331 "Bitcoin Investment Scam: Promoter of BitConnect Held." *Financial Express*, 19 Aug. 2018. Web. 13 May 2020.

online, and I have fallen victim to so many scams that I have actually lost a significant amount of money, more than $100,000 dollars."[332] The fact that not every founder of a blockchain project is a "true believer" is also made evident, with BitConnect clearly being created by "nonbelievers" of blockchain who simply wanted to take advantage of the impressionable idealism in Blockland and convert it to money for use back home in India.

Blockchainers and Decentralites

Now, back to Blockchain weddings. Blockchainer's do not believe that cryptocurrency is the route to Lambomoon, but a mere stepping-stone or phase on the path of proliferating blockchain. These believers may eschew the Satoshian sacraments, believing that they serve only to get the masses excited about the far-reaching possibilities of blockchain that go much beyond mere money. As such they view all cryptocurrency, Bitcoin included, as a primary medium at best and a harmful distraction at worst. This is the domain of many companies operating in the blockchain space as well as investors excited about the technology but wary of what they see as negative connotations around cryptocurrency.

Decentralites, on the other hand do not place faith exclusively on blockchain but view it as a mere means by which Satoshi inspired his followers. They may instead see Satoshi as a prophet preaching for decentralization as a generic righteous value, with blockchain being one additional (or even ultimate) tool through which his followers can spread the virtues of decentralization. This belief is

332 Partner With Calos Matos, Youtube.com user. "The Truth About Bitconnect, Other Scams, And Carlos Matos." *YouTube*, 3 May 2019.

based on the principle that any centralized point of energy is a potential point of failure and society would do well to decentralize as many aspects of life as possible, as to strengthen and make antifragile. Decentralization is ultimately about the transfer of power from a point of high concentration to wherever it is most lacking. This is commonly understood to promote increased freedom and decreased fetters by the way of a non-interventionist libertarian form of government, but it could seemingly paradoxically (and very much at odds with the original Bitcoin ethos) be used to justify the forced redistribution of private property among individuals.

The general belief here is that decentralized arrangements are naturally superior to centralized ones, whether religious, governmental, financial, social, or organizational. Thus, the Decentralite will seek to expand the rate of decentralization in the world. As a mere technology, blockchain can be used for or against the furthering of this ideal. Members of this sect are broadly less focused on "lambo" and more so on "moon", and may view members of the other sects as being distracted by the promise of worldly wealth as they believe that the essence of Satoshism is something much deeper and more beautiful. In this perspective, Satoshi can be read as a prophet of decentralization.

The process of decentralizing a system purifies and disinfects it of human vice. Decentralized systems are powerful because they do not suffer from the critical flaws of human systems; these being man's desire for recognition, respect, and reward. It is through these gateways of pride and greed that both corruption and incompetence eventually enter even the highest offices of any entity. Complete decentralization requires the elimination of all concentrations of power. This leaves the greedy with no one to bribe and the prideful without any throne nor title to pursue.

Decentralization is the systematic removal of hierarchy. It can be understood to derive from people's non-reliance on existing authorities and a desire to replace them with a collective. There are degrees of decentralization, with the lack of it analogous to absolute dictatorship and its full implementation to total anarchy. Once a system is decentralized, its lack of designated nodes makes it hard for anyone to gather a significant amount of influence because it is spread very thin across all participants. For the same reason, attacking a decentralized system is extremely difficult.

With decentralization comes great power. Consider these examples:

- A decentralized country made up of 100 equally powerful cities would be vastly more difficult for an enemy to incapacitate than one with a single central capital. Similarly, it would be difficult for any individual to gain too much power as there would not be a single capital region where to consolidate it. This would suggest a stable political and cultural landscape.
- A religion with a central node or hierarchy may become corrupted or be easily banned, destroyed, or infiltrated by a hostile agent, but one made up of thousands of independent units that constantly verify each other's faithfulness is practically impossible to control.
- A protest movement or even war with central leadership can be incapacitated by destroying chains of command and punishing instigators, but a leaderless swarming civilian disobedience or guerilla war fought by small ideologically inspired and individually driven cells is practically impossible to suppress (as we have seen with the expensive and never-ending War on Terror).

Could increased decentralization lead to world peace, a balance with nature, and the maximization of everyone's human potential within a fair framework? If so, how could existing entities be further decentralized? Who would be the greatest opponents of general decentralization? Further, how could decentralization best be fought in the context of, for example, extremist groups consisting of self-organizing independent actors? These are difficult questions; while decentralization may in certain contexts promise stability and strength, a decentralized enemy is certainly a terrifying prospect. As much as Blockland loves the doctrine of decentralization, we must remember that centralization also provides many advantages such efficiency. In this sense we might arrive at a general maxim that whereas the product of centralism is nimble, defined, and fragile, the result of decentralism is lumbering, undefined, and durable.

Decentralites identify most closely with the Dogecoin blockchain due to its non-serious nature that promotes blockchain and decentralization in a fun and meme-filled way. As a fundamentally humorous cryptocurrency, it is seen as being mild and its users friendly and easygoing, without a toxic get-rich-quick mentality that permeates Blockland. It is said that everyone who holds it does so primarily for fun as opposed to as a serious investment, though this may not be entirely accurate as its market cap measures in the billions. In a sense, the Doge can be understood to take the role of a disarming, non-controversial, family-friendly mascot for cryptocurrency, blockchain, and decentralization.[333] To get an idea of the culture, a Decentralite might jest that donuts are the most auspicious of foods as they are fully decentralized.

Though one might laugh at the absurdity of worshipping a cartoon dog, there are real-world examples of just that. In an inconspicuous storage unit below street level in a major west coast city, there exists a cult-like underground hacker's collective that not only operates entirely via a blockchain application, but features a prominent and

---

[333] Carpe Lunam Events Association. "Dogecon, Why Are You? - Origins of a Decentralist Meme Convention." *Dogecon*, 4 May 2018.

intricate "alter of plenty" set before a mural of DOGE (which happens to become *E-GOD* when inverted). This alter is piled high with collective offerings of thousands of dollars of paper cash and marijuana, both of which are ceremonially burnt according to a cryptographic algorithm. At the famous counterculture gathering of Burning Man, a comparable group has constructed not only another alter to Doge where passersby stop to pray, but a massive Shiba-Inu Doge-themed art-car made from a converted bus which they use to spread the message of decentralization among the event's radical attendees. During a blockchain convention in New York City, a chanting procession of perhaps 100 marched down Wall Street to symbolically place a massive Doge mask upon the famous *Charging Bull* statue.

While this may well be nothing but a bizarre cosplay, it is nevertheless a fascinating slice of the wild world of crypto. Where is all this going? Only Doge knows.

Conclusion

As with contemporary religions, the sects of Satoshism do not necessarily get along or acknowledge each other's legitimacy. A Maximalist might believe that a devotee of Ethereum has no right to associate their unrelated beliefs with Satoshi, or claim that a belief in Ripple is not even a "legitimate" false belief because its subject of worship is not even based on the same precepts or values as Bitcoin. A Multicoiner on the other hand might view Maximalists as being needlessly hardline and unable to see the bigger picture, while both Blockchainers and Decentralites may consider the whole lot well intentioned but mislead. Through all this, the Nonbelievers look upon the idealistic bickering around them with confusion or calculating neutrality while the Nocoiners simply point and laugh as the drama unfolds. These conflicts would sometimes unfold between competing blockchain meetup groups, with one geographical area often having groups oriented towards Bitcoin Maximalism, Ethereum Maximalism, Multicoinism, and Decentralism which would try to simultaneously convert each other's members and attract nonbelievers.

Many residents of Blockland cycle through various levels of belief in many of these secs and non-sects. They are not all mutually exclusive and relatively few people are living in Blockland for purely ideological reasons. Each cryptocurrency can also be understood as a microcosm of this religion effect, with internal disagreements regarding dogma and the possibility of ideological splits. This grand spectacle is made all the more fascinating in that the participants are companies with hundreds of employees and developers running multi-billion-dollar currency systems. They will often outright employ people with the corporate title of Bitcoin / Blockchain / [company name] Evangelist (this is not exclusive to blockchain companies, but common in the whole technology sector). At its base, real people vote with their wallets and pledge hundreds of thousands of dollars towards their belief in not only Satoshism, but towards their selected sect(s). Sometimes, they lose everything and become bitter Nocoiners.

Just as for the so-called nonbelievers of Satoshi's message, the most common driver of Maximalists, Multicoiners, and others in Blockland is ultimately capitalistic with their fundamental differences lying in the preferred currency of their capital. The mark of a Satoshian is the belief that no matter what one's job is in Blockland, they are the self-chosen ushers of the new value, the forebears of revolution, and the setters of a new foundation stone of civilization and world order.

1555 woodcut from De re metallica, an early mining textbook describing various equipment like this water-powered mine hoist used for raising ore.

CHAPTER 10

Mining Madness

3rd Generation: ASIC Dominance

This chapter continues where *The Prospectors* left off in late 2013 with the 2nd generation of ASIC miners. The year is now 2018 and only a few of the companies from five years ago have survived. Of these, Bitmain is the dominating force with 67% of the market by early 2018. Innovative systems were developed to maximize efficiency, such as immersion-cooled datacenters in naturally cold climates such as Canada, northern China, Finland, Iceland, and the Republic of Georgia. Bitmain has its own mining pool and as of this writing is in the process of running an Initial Public Offering. Its signature *Antminer* can be found in large Bitcoin mining farms around the world and has become the industry standard.[334] [335]

---

[334] Fortney, Luke. "Bitcoin Mining, Explained." *Investopedia*, 6 Nov. 2019.
[335] De Vries, Alex. "A Deep Dive in a Real-World Bitcoin Mine." *Digiconomist*, 25 Oct. 2017.

GPU Resurgence

As GPU's and FPGA's became obsolete in the Bitcoin mining game due to ASIC development, opportunities to mine other cryptocurrencies presented themselves. Litecoin became a favorite (though it too later "succumbed" to ASIC's in 2014[336]), as well as Ethereum later on. Software that tracked the market movements and mining difficulties of a dozen different cryptocurrencies allowed miners to change the coins they mined in real-time for maximum monetary returns. Though industrial-scale operations took over the Bitcoin mining industry almost entirely, hobbyists continued filling their basements with ever-larger mining rigs.

As interest in mining grew around Bitcoin's first move above $1,000 in November 2013, demand outstripped supply which led to a global video card shortage, leaving many angry video gamers cursing cryptocurrencies. Though increased demand for their intended purposes played a major role, many attributed the rising costs of new cards as well as the soaring stock prices of AMD and NVIDIA, the largest graphics card manufacturers, to Litecoin mining.[337][338] By May of 2014 however, the tables had again turned as SCRYPT-ASICs became available for Litecoin and GPU's were again near-obsolete.[339] As second-hand markets across the web flooded with used video cards for pennies on the dollar and industry analysts predicted a 40% reduction in the global GPU market

[336] Coughlin, Doug. "Holy Scrypters: ZeusMiner Announces First Scrypt ASIC Miners." *CoinTelegraph*, 28 Apr. 2014.
[337] Krawczyk, Konrad. "AMD Says Recent Graphics Card Shortage, Price Hikes Due to Chinese New Year, Litecoin Miners." *Digital Trends*, 21 Feb. 2014.
[338] Shrout, Ryan. "Nvidia and AMD Are Deluged with Orders for PC Graphics Cards." *Market Watch*, 24 Aug. 2014.
[339] Jiecut, Reddit.com user. "Litecoin ASIC History." *Reddit r/litecoin*, 27 Oct. 2017.

for the quarter, a *WCCF TECH* article declared "*The Great GPU Miners Crash of '14.*"[340]

This cycle repeated itself again three years later in 2017 – this time with Ethereum which rose nearly 5,000% in under six months from $8 in January to a high of $391 in June of that year. Days before this high was reached (after which it plummeted to a low of over 60% within a month), Advanced Micro Devices' (AMD) stock shot up by 7% as it confirmed that the shortage of GPU's was again caused by miners.[341] This demonstrated that traditional markets were quite aware of cryptocurrency by this time. AMD cards were the most popular and finding them for anything close to normal prices was again practically impossible. This again disappointed many normal buyers, with *PC World*'s Brad Chacos acting as their mouthpiece when he concluded an article about the phenomena with "*fingers crossed these dark times end soon, though.*"[342] Unfortunately for gamers looking to upgrade their machines, the "dark times" had only begun because Ethereum was built in such a way that it was resistant to ASIC's. This meant that there was little danger of an entire class of equipment becoming obsolete overnight.

NVIDIA's CEO recognized this, telling investors that the mining market is "*not likely to go away any time soon. There will be more currencies to come, they will come from different nations... We stay very close to the market, and understand the dynamics very well.*"[343] When both AMD and NVIDIA beat quarterly market predictions, one analyst predicted that the two companies delivered about

---

[340] Pirzada, Usman. "GPU Miners Crash of 2014' Arrives – Graphic Card Market Starts Shrinking, Could Fall by 40%." *Wccf Tech*, 17 June 2014.
[341] Green, Timothy. "AMD's Graphics Cards Are Selling Out for the Wrong Reason...Again." *The Motley Fool*, 7 June 2017.
[342] Chacos, Brad. "Why AMD's Radeon Graphics Cards Are Almost Impossible to Buy Right Now." *PC World*, 5 July 2017.
[343] Moammer, Khalid. "Nvidia Graphics Cards To See Price Increases Starting This Month Due To Memory Shortages." *Wccf Tech*, 1 Sept. 2017.

500,000 graphics cards, a third of their entire production, to miners in the May-July quarter. Both companies were among the top performers in the S&P 500 that year.[344345] In 2018, there were reports that NVIDIA 's GeForce GTX 1070 GPU's which normally retailed for $380 were going for $700, and that the company was asking retailers to prioritize gamers by placing purchase limits on cards and selling them in bundles with other gaming components.[346]

This mining boom went on for nearly a year as Ethereum rose to a high of $1,377 on January 14th 2018, dropped over 70% to $380 ten weeks later, then shot back to $830 after another four weeks, only to hit a low of $89 in December. This was a wild time; a fact I can confirm first-hand. In late 2017, I was approached by many groups regarding mining.

One memorable case involved plans to convert an old nuclear bunker in central Europe into a massive mine and secure data center, powered by surplus power from a nuclear reactor nearby; a plan thwarted by the nation's own intelligence establishment which was uncomfortable with the idea of an impenetrable underground data-fortress in private hands. The denial was not surprising, seeing as the propieter struck me as murky character from a spy thriller. Driving me to what he referred to as a safe-house after picking me up from the airport in his armoured SUV, he described his monthly jaunts to Las Vegas for meetings with Russian oligarchs who pretended to be mere gamblers, and how he once used his young son's birthday party as a cover to briefly run to a restaurant

---

344 Hall, Gina. "Bitcoin Mining Boom Sends AMD Shares Soaring." *Silicon Valley Business Journal*, 6 June 2017.
345 De, Nikhiles. "Analyst: Cryptocurrency Mining Is Boosting AMD and Nvidia Stock Prices." *CoinDesk*, 12 Sept. 2017.
346 Warren, Tom. "Bitcoin Mania Is Hurting PC Gamers by Pushing up GPU Prices." *The Verge*, 30 Jan. 2018.

across the street for a discreet 5-minute meeting. That evening in a nondescript downtown office with embassy-level security, our discussions ranged to the near-absurd with almost unbeliavable stories of the Trump family, classified studies about climate change, and what can only be described as the illuminati. I do not know if any of it was true because in crypto, it can be hard to distinguish the delusional from those who truly swim with sharks.

On another occasion, I was given the task of finding a place in Canada to move 100,000 GPU's from China, whose owners were concerned about the lack of local regulatory clarity on the mainland. This was no small task, as that number of miners would consume more power than a small city! Indeed, entire transformer stations have been developed and traded for mining purposes in China and Central Asia. They certainly had the means to pay for the relocation, as their 500,000 ETH had just risen by another $200 each in the days before I arrived for negotiations amid extravagant feasting.

To pursue this mission, I moved to Calgary which is the capital of Canada's energy sector. Being cold for much of the year, industrial sized mines could theoretically benefit from energy savings due to reduced cooling needs. Customized shipping containers could be filled with hundreds of miners and plugged in anywhere with available power capacity at an industrial scale, including but not limited to warehouses or outdoor sites. One novel concept was to use stranded gas sitting in natural gas wells spread throughout the province that were, for whatever reason, not connected to a pipeline or other delivery method. By bringing in a large generator, this gas could be converted into electricity to power miners on-site practically for free (not counting the environmental costs of such an inefficient conversion). A more environmentally and developmentally conscious proposal included the construction of geothermal plants in northern Alberta. Heat from the ground could be converted into electricity to run miners, and the residual heat from both the operation itself and miners could be pumped into greenhouses to grow food in areas too cold to support farming and where fresh vegetables and fruit can cost exorbitant amounts.

This would be particularly enticing for aboriginal communities in the region by way of technology and farming jobs near the arctic. The downside of course was time, as significant projects of this caliber could easily take two years. In mining terms, this is an eternity when considering the constantly increasing number of miners competing for stable, ultimately decreasing amounts of daily cryptocurrency. For example, a large array of GPU's generating 10 ETH per day upon installation might be earning only 5 ETH per day a few weeks later. For this reason, ocean shipments taking weeks were out of the question for any machines coming from Chinese factories, and companies like Genesis Mining filled entire Boeing 747's with GPU's to supply their mining facilities in countries like Iceland.[347] I even recall investigating whether the 6-engine, 32-wheel Antonov An-225 Mriya, which is the heaviest aircraft ever and built to transport the Soviet Union's version of the Space Shuttle, could be contracted to transport GPU's from China to Canada. It could.

This second mining boom slowed down in mid-2018, after both BTC and ETH saw significant decreases in value. In November, NVIDIA lost 23 billion dollars in valuation in response to a lack of orders by miners, which strangely enough was more than Ethereum's entire market cap of 18 billion during that same week. If that was not clear evidence of a crypto market bubble, I do not know what could be.[348]

---

[347] Wong, Joon Ian. "Ethereum Miners Are Renting Boeing 747s to Ship Graphics Cards and AMD Shares Are Soaring." *Quartz*, 27 July 2017.
[348] Devbnya, Alex. "Bitcoin Mining Boom Over as Mining Equipment Suffers Decline in Q2 Sales." *U.Today*, 26 July 2018.

Cloud Mining

Cloud Mining was another phenomenon of the time, allowing people to effectively rent miners. Without the hassle of managing their own hardware, which involved ongoing electricity bills and noise, people could purchase *mining contracts* that promised to direct a set amount of computing power towards a specific cryptocurrency over a specific amount of time. Sometimes, this would consist of a specific machine in a specific facility. The general idea was that the miners were housed in large facilities with access to cheaper industrial power rates, as well as the other competitive efficiencies gained from large-scale operations. Some of these allowed users to switch between coins, while others were fixed contracts between one and 24 months.[349] Cloud mining has many skeptics, such as early Bitcoin developer, Gavin Andresen, who in 2014 commented that cloud mining services "*make no sense. I suspect many of them will turn out to be Ponzi schemes.*" to which a representative from Genesis Mining responded by inviting him to visit their facilities in person.[350]

While some cloud mining services appear to have performed legitimately for many years, Mr. Andresen was correct in the fact that that these services were a perfect breeding ground for Ponzi schemes, considering that 12-24-month mining contracts were paid up-front and could be used to pay "returns" to investors for years without ever owning actual miners. Contract buyers often had no idea who operated the businesses, where the mining facilities were if they existed at all, and there was practically no recourse if one of

[349]"Best Bitcoin Cloud Mining Contract Reviews and Comparisons." *Bitcoinmining.com*, 2014.
[350] Andresen, Gavin. "Do Mining Contracts Ever Make Sense?" *Reddit r/Bitcoin*, 11 Aug. 2014.

them stopped making the expected payments. One such example was Bitcoin Cloud Services, which used ads on Google to gain over 4,000 "customers", despite marketing itself using clearly photoshopped images with hundreds of miners in a warehouse that curiously seemed to lack the necessary electrical cords or ventilation systems.[351]

One of the people connected with the business was tracked to another company called Bitcoin Cloud Hashing, which claimed its address as being at a server facility whose operators confirmed that they had never heard of the company. One Bitcointalk.org user confirmed that he had sent them 7.39 BTC (~$6,300) for a 6-month contract of 2TH/S, after which the company confirmed receipt but failed to provide the promised log-in credentials. The same user observed that the company's website appeared to be changing its name every few days, seemingly to stay ahead of people like him who were warning would-be investors.[352] The climate of new money, the seeming ease of making money quickly, the fear of missing out, and the normalized anonymity of the cryptocurrency industry made cloud mining a virtual promised land for fraudsters of all types. Considering that many investors paid large amounts for long-term contracts at the heights of various bubbles, I would not be surprised if some cloud mining services pulled off completely successful Ponzi's that will never be discovered.

The Forbidden Mines

[351] Torpey, Kyle. "Exclusive: Possible $500,000 Bitcoin Cloud Mining Ponzi Scheme Uncovered." *Bitcoin Magazine*, 5 June 2015.
[352] grimlock, Bitcointalk.org user. "Scam Report: Bitcoincloudhashing.com." *Bitcoin Forum*, 13 Jan. 2014.

It is rumored that many medium-scale home mines got their start from or developed in tandem with illegal marijuana grow-ops, seeing as they too consumed exorbitant amounts of electricity while creating heat and noise. An active mining operation could well serve as cover for an unusual amount of electricity use and could be conveniently claimed as the source for large amounts of bitcoins earned by selling the crops of such farming operations on the dark web.

The crypto-miner market also developed beyond industrial machines, such as sleek "performance" miners which emphasized attractive design and flashing lights instead of actual cost-effective performance. Another interesting innovation was a $3,500 home heater which produced heat as a by-product of mining.[353] While neither of these machines is likely to be a smart decision from a Return-On-Investment perspective, they signify crypto mining's move from an eccentric geeky hobby to an industrial venture, and onwards to a somewhat more mainstream lifestyle product bought more for aesthetic purposes (or more cynically, these "cool" miners attracted low-information buyers hoping to get rich mining "the next Bitcoin"). It could be said that innovations like these came from a new crop of mining enthusiasts who valued other aspects of the technology than those who came before them. One such innovator built a GPU rig in the back of his Tesla in late 2017 with the idea that it could mine for free while plugged into any of Tesla's Supercharger stations, which do not charge for electricity.[354]

While our friend with the Tesla may have built a tongue-in-cheek mining rig to beat "the man", many people have gotten in varying

[353] Dillet, Romain. "Qarnot Unveils a Cryptocurrency Heater for Your Home." *TechCrunch*, 8 Mar. 2018.
[354] Lambert, Fred. "Tesla Owner Builds a Bitcoin Mining Rig in a Model S to Use Free Supercharger Power." *Electrek*, 29 Nov. 2017.

amounts of trouble for appropriating computer networks for mining purposes.[355] In late 2013, gaming company ESEA gaming was fined a million dollars after an employee added GPU mining software to the company's games which went out to about 14,000 computers, netting $3,700 which the company donated to charity after the employee was fired.[356] In a comparable case, a New York tech executive visiting a Buenos Aires Starbucks discovered that the free Wi-Fi at the branch forced a 10 second delay before connecting in order to mine Monero on the user's laptop. He alerted Starbuck's corporate office, which "*took swift action to ensure our third-party support provider resolved the issue and made the changes needed in order to ensure our customers could use wi-fi in our store safely.*"[357]

Another memorable example is the case of a professor working for the US National Science Foundation being suspended after using a supercomputer to mine up to $10,000 worth of Dogecoin.[358] This was not the first case of academic misconduct relating to DOGE, as around the same time in February 2014 a "*member of the Harvard community was stripped of his or her access to the University's research computing facilities last week after setting up a 'dogecoin' mining operation using a Harvard research network.*"[359] Such activities were known to have taken place on university campuses around the world, with one Imperial College London student telling crypto news outlet *CoinDesk* about installing Dogecoin mining

---

355 Falconer, Joel. "ABC Employee Caught Mining for Bitcoins on Company Servers." *The Next Web*, 23 June 2011.
356 Clark, Jack. "Gaming Co ESEA Hit by $1M Fine for Hidden Bitcoin Mining Enslaver." *The Register*, 20 Nov. 2013.
357 Kelion, Leo. "Starbucks Cafe's Wi-Fi Made Computers Mine Crypto-currency." *BBC*, 13 Dec. 2017.
358 Cohen, Brian. "US Government Bans Professor for Mining Bitcoin with A Supercomputer." *Bitcoin Magazine*, 5 June 2014.
359 Delwiche, Theodore R. "Harvard Research Computing Resources Misused for 'Dogecoin' Mining Operation." *The Crimson*, 20 Feb. 2014.

software on dozens of computers in the school's computer labs.[360] Despite these unlucky miners, there is no doubt that many others have been successful in their ventures to the forbidden mines.[361] [362]

This all echoes to something that two friends named Bill Gates and Paul Allen (Microsoft's co-founders) did back in 1967 when the computers they were obsessed with worked on a paid time-sharing system that proved too costly. The pair managed to hack into the internal accounting files where they could assign themselves more time on the systems. Other illicit miners have included teachers and systems administrators, the head of IT at a Crimean government office[363], and a headmaster of a Chinese middle school who was expelled from the local Communist Party branch after installing his Ethereum miner at school in order to save on electricity bills.[364]

These sorts of actions went far beyond individuals, as shown in a 2014 report on mining botnets prepared by UC San Diego's International Computer Science Institute, which examined nine major cases of hackers taking control of large computer networks for mining purposes. These botnets managed to mine in the region of 15,000 BTC worth over $100,000 between 2011 and 2014. One of these named ZeroAccess infected about nine million computers around the world while another called SkypeMiner used compromised Skype accounts to distribute links leading to a website that

[360] Shubber, Kadhim. "London Student Mines Dogecoin With University's Computers – They Don't Know, Yet." *CoinDesk*, 3 Mar. 2014.
[361] Calahad. Reddit.com user. "Sr. System Admin Mining Bitcoin." *Reddit r/sysadmin*, 20 Feb. 2014.
[362] WurmBlood, Reddit.com user. "Teacher Using Schools Hardware to Mine Bitcoin, Is This Legal?" *Reddit r/Bitcoin*, 4 Nov. 2014.
[363] Helms, Kevin. "Government Head of IT Department Fired for Mining Bitcoin Using State-Owned Computers in Crimea." *Bitcoin.com*, 4 Oct. 2007.
[364] Cook, James. "Headmaster in China Fired after Being Caught Using School Computers to Mine Cryptocurrency." *The Telegraph*, 9 Nov. 2018.

installed mining malware. Due to the public nature of Bitcoin transactions, these researchers were able to track transactions related to the botnet in real-time with the support of mining pool operators.[365] One of the paper's authors, Dr. Alex Snoeren, later commented that "*If [these mining operations] ever becomes very profitable, it could reinvigorate the malware industry.*"[366] Considering the scale of these botnets in early 2014 and the subsequent rise of mining, one would imagine that the there has indeed been a huge boom in malware.

Environmental Impacts

The environmental costs of crypto mining have raised ongoing controversy both within and outside the industry.[367] Alex de Vries' website Digiconomist.net estimates Bitcoin's power consumption in real time. According to his analysis, Bitcoin mining was consuming between 55 and 73 terawatt-hours per year in mid-2018, up from 3 to 9 TWh in early 2017.[368] Mr. De Vrie's research is of academic quality, drawing from peer reviewed sources as well as ASIC manufacturer Bitmain's Initial Public Offering disclosure, which revealed that it had sold 2,560,000 ASIC miners in the first half of 2018 and 1,620,000 in 2017. Since Bitmain's 2018 market share for miner sales was estimated at 67%, these numbers can be used to estimate the miner's collective energy consumption.

---

365 Yuxing Huang, Danny, et al. "Botcoin: Monetizing Stolen Cycles." *UC San Diego*, Jan. 2014.
366 Patringenaru, Ioana. "Using Stolen Computer Processing Cycles to Mine Bitcoin: Who Does It and How Much Do They Make?" *UC San Diego News Center*, 26 Feb. 2014.
367 Mora, Camilo, et al. "Bitcoin Emissions Alone Could Push Global Warming above 2 °C." Nature Climate Change, vol. 9, no. 1, 2018, pp. 80–80., doi:10.1038/s41558-018-0353-0.
368 Sharratt, Robert. "Bitcoin Energy Consumption Index." *Digiconomist*, 26 June 2019.

I took Mr. De Vrie's raw dataset and averaged out the daily *Estimated TWh per Year* and *Minimum TWh per Year* for all of 2018 to arrive at an actual Bitcoin mining power consumption of between 40.1 and 62.5 TWh for the year. Considering that machines mining Ethereum and other coins are not included in this figure, I am confident to say that global cryptocurrency mining consumed at least 50 TWh in 2018, over 0.2% of all electricity generated. While this may not seem like much it is more than any of the 80 least-consuming countries. Bangladesh's population of 157 million uses 55.5 TWh, while Singapore's six million use 48 TWh. Not surprisingly, some governments have become concerned with the increasing energy demands of miners, such as Abkhazia whose state electric utility shut power to 15 mining facilities at the end of 2018 as a "*temporary measures to limit the consumption of electricity by certain categories of subscribers.*"[369] Perhaps most concerning is the fact that most mining happens in China, where over half of electricity is produced by coal which creates an especially high carbon footprint.

Mr. De Vrie estimates that Bitcoin mining will one day consume 5% of global energy resources.[370] In late 2018, publicly traded Hut 8 Mining Corp's CEO, Andrew Kiguel, wrote an Op-Ed defending Bitcoin's energy consumption. He argued that while mining used electricity, Bitcoin promises to replace or minimize entire industries and compared critics to those who might say that sending email uses too much electricity, while ignoring the savings from a reduced need for paper production and transportation. He also noted the incredible efforts and resulting societal and environmental effects of gold mining, concluding that "*Bitcoin is the emergence of a new*

369 Alexandre, Ana. "Government of Abkhazia Cuts Off Power to 15 Cryptocurrency Mining Facilities." *CoinTelegraph*, 2 Jan. 2019.
370 Cuthbertson, Anthony. "Bitcoin Will Use 0.5% Of World's Electricity By End Of 2018, Finds Study." *Independent*, 16 May 2018.

world monetary system. Gold is the only monetary element that has endured through centuries, and bitcoin is the new gold."[371]

On the topic of gold and Bitcoin comparisons, research done by the US Environmental Protection Agency's Office of Research & Development concluded that the energy requirements to mine $1 worth of cryptocurrency were very roughly between two and four times greater than the energy needed to mine the equivalent value of gold.[372]

Same but Different

Mining is the Proof-of-Work on which the first blockchains were designed to function. Not coincidentally, the financial systems for much of history have functioned on a similar model. Like Bitcoin, gold is a finite resource that is relatively difficult to extract, and all gold is thus, on average, a product of significant efforts undertaken by someone at some point in time. As it cannot be replicated, gold was a workable legitimizer of currency and thus became the basic measure of value. The World Gold Council estimates that as of 2019, a total of 193,000 tons of gold have been mined in the entirety of human existence. This is equivalent to a cube about 21 meters on each side, enough for 0.025 kg (25g) of gold per person in the world (assuming 7.7 billion people). The cumulative number of bitcoins mined surpassed 18 million in the same year, meaning that each person could have 0.0023 BTC (230,000 Satoshis) if distributed evenly.

[371] Kiguel, Andrew. "Op Ed: Bitcoin's Energy Consumption Is Neither Frivolous nor Excessive." *Bitcoin Magazine*, 30 Oct. 2018.
[372] Magagine, Cosmos. "Mining Bitcoin Is as Energy Intensive as Mining Gold." *CoinTelegraph*, 6 Nov. 2018.

As with Bitcoin, a finite amount of gold exists within the Earth and broadly speaking, no more can ever be created (imagine this analogy taking place in the year 1900, so certain economically impractical nuclear reactions and things like space-mining need not be considered). This global gold reserve is effectively finite; not one gram of gold is added or removed over the entire period of human existence (again if we ignore some properties of the physical universe such as nuclear decay and meteorites). Now, a certain percentage of this gold is in use by humans at any given time. This percentage increases daily as "new" gold is mined and decreases when treasure-carrying ships are lost at sea, when fine gold dust blows out of jewelry repair shops, and when adventurers throw gold rings into volcanoes. The same is true for Bitcoin; not a single Satoshi can be destroyed or eliminated, but when a private key is permanently lost the bitcoins associated with it are as accessible as gold bars in the in the bottom of the ocean in a time before submarines. Gone forever.

Crypto Mining is in many ways comparable to the practice of gold and precious metal mining. Early on (say, in pre-civilization times) there were deposits of gold naturally occurring near the ground and anyone could more or less collect it by hand if they knew where to look. Coincidentally, gold was likely seen similarly to the way early Bitcoiners considered Bitcoin before 2013: interesting but plentiful. As the number of gold users and the demand for gold increased, there was also less gold to be had. Large amounts of earth were then moved and sifted through in search of the precious metal and rudimentary mines were already being built throughout Europe in the times of the Roman Empire. In the 19th and 20th centuries, thousands of people travelled the world based on rumors of gold discoveries and built mines of breathtaking scale as they developed increasingly sophisticated technologies to extract gold. Where the mining of crypto differs somewhat from gold is that while separate gold mines are excavating different deposits, all miners directed at a specific cryptocurrency are in direct adversarial competition. With this, crypto mining becomes a game of getting the cheapest possible electricity and the most efficient equipment.

If we attempt to draw parallels between the progression of gold and Bitcoin mining, it is thought provoking to consider what comparative historical point we currently inhabit. While the history of gold dates back thousands of years, the entire mining era of Bitcoin is 131 years with 99.99% of all coins mined in the first 40. As such, we should expect the Bitcoin story to move much faster. Perhaps we can understand early ASICs through the analogy of the first true goldmines, whereas the resurgence of GPU mining of various altcoins might be understood as a modern parallel of the hysteria-inducing gold rushes of the 1800's. It will be fascinating to observe how crypto-mining will develop over the coming decades; will mining operations keep growing in scale, and is it possible that governments may one day join the fray? It has been said that data and computing power are the internet-age equivalents of oil and steel, and the industrial arms-race between crypto-miners certainly lends this view some credence.

Standing upright in the stone was asword, the hilt of which glittered with gems. Beneathit was written, Whoso can draw me from this stone isthe rightful king of Britain. One after another the nobles tried to remove thesword... But it was altin vain. The sword remained firm and fast in the rock.

CHAPTER 11
Bitcoin Civil Wars

One day, an old wizard holds a speech in the main square of Blockland's Bitcoin settlement. He wants to change the constitution to allow for the construction of wider streets "*to better match the realities of the current age.*" Some residents agree, but most become angry that someone would dare to change the glorious nation's constitution, "*and in such an idiotic way at that.*" Surely, Bitcoin's long-gone founding father knew what was best. The old wizard saw that he would not easily get his way, so he cast a spell. Through his magic, he created an exact duplicate of Bitcoin Land up to that moment, with not only all the same streets and land features, but also all its people had their memories intact and were unaware that they were mere copies. This duplicate-Bitcoin which the wizard called *New Bitcoin,* was identical to the original in all ways but one: its constitution had a minor difference. The wizard effectively copied and pasted Bitcoin with just one minor edit that instituted wider roads optimized for more efficient transportation. He created a perfect clone with a minor DNA adjustment, a tweak in Bitcoin's source code. Without needing anyone's permission, he created his own reality to compete with the original.

This story describes forking, a software development term which refers to the duplication of a system with slight changes so that users and developers can choose which version they prefer. This is most common in open-source systems, which by nature freely share their code and allow anyone to tinker with it without fear of copyright lawsuits. Bitcoin is open source and has experienced no shortage of forks. Each of these forks has generally been the result of a passionate ideological and thus political battle between the residents of Bitcoin.

The first significant Bitcoin fork came to debate in mid-2015, in response to the Bitcoin Scalability Problem. This problem consisted of a bottleneck in the amount of transactions that Bitcoin's blockchain could process per 10-minute block due to the maximum size of each block being one megabyte. As each transaction takes up data, the maximum number of daily confirmed Bitcoin transactions was limited to around 300,000, whereas Visa routinely processes 150 million transactions in the same timeframe. This clearly limited the opportunity for Bitcoin to scale in such a way that normal people could use it daily.[373]

In the governance of Bitcoin, developers submit BIP's (Bitcoin Improvement Proposals) to be considered by the community. A BIP generally consists of a short technical description of the proposed change and a clear rationale. Miners can choose to run the new version of the blockchain and if 75% of 1,000 blocks are mined by

---

[373] Li, Kenny. "The Blockchain Scalability Problem & the Race for Visa-Like Transaction Speed." *Hackernoon*, 26 Jan. 2019.

those running the new version, the change is seen as de facto legitimate. This should be seen analogous to a bill submitted for review in parliament/congress, only that there are no representatives, and anyone can submit the bill – true, pure democracy (not from the perspective of individuals that is, but of computing power).

Bitcoin XT - 15 Aug. 2015

The first major fork was proposed by Gavin Andresen in June 2015, building upon work by Mike Hearn. BIP 101 suggested that the one-megabyte maximum block size be incrementally increased to eight, allowing for around 2,000,000 transactions per day. This was launched as a fork named *Bitcoin XT* two months later. In the eyes of its creators, this was a no-brainer fix to a problem that had been ongoing for years. Mr. Hearn blogged that "*The decision-making process in Bitcoin Core has broken... the block size debate has been allowed to drag on for years.*"[374] Roger "Bitcoin Jesus" Ver chimed in with support, arguing that "*bigger blocks will likely mean more full nodes around the world, and therefore more decentralization, not less. This will make Bitcoin even more difficult to control, censor, or be stopped by anyone, including governments.*"[375]

Not everyone agreed.

> *When I designed Bitcoin, I designed it in such a way as to make future modifications to the consensus rules difficult without*

[374] Hearn, Mike. "Why Is Bitcoin Forking?" *Faith and Future*, 1 Dec. 2015.
[375] Ver, Roger. "Bigger Blocks Mean More Decentralization for Bitcoin." *Bitcoin.com*, 19 July 2015.

> *near unanimous agreement. Bitcoin was designed to be protected from the influence of charismatic leaders, even if their name is Gavin Andresen, Barack Obama, or Satoshi Nakamoto. Nearly everyone has to agree on a change, and they have to do it without being forced or pressured into it. By doing a fork in this way, these developers are violating the 'original vision' they claim to honour.*[376]
>
> \- User account bitcoincash, 15 Aug. 2015.

Though this above statement was not written by the real Satoshi (as far as anyone can know), it certainly demonstrates how many would imagine him to react.

Many others publicly accused Bitcoin XT of being a coup. HashCash (Bitcoin's predecessor) inventor Adam Back suggested that Bitcoin XT may not be able to remain safe and secure because most of the leading security experts were unlikely to work for the forked version.[377] He also argued against Mr. Ver, reasoning that larger blocks would likely benefit larger-scale miners while reducing the profits of hobby-miners, thus leading to a decrease in decentralization. John Matonis, former director of the Bitcoin Foundation which aimed to promote Bitcoin use, was also opposed and tweeted "*I have followed this from the beginning & I agree that it is an attempted governance coup*"[378]

For all the discussion of what Satoshi would have wanted, Mike Hearn made an important point:

---

[376] 'bitcoincash', user account. "[Bitcoin-Dev] Bitcoin XT Fork (Unconfirmed)." *Nakamoto Studies Institute*, 15 Aug. 2015.
[377] Peck, Morgen E. "Adam Back Says the Bitcoin Fork Is a Coup." *Spectrum*, 19 Aug. 2015.
[378] Hornyak, Tim. "Bitcoin XT Debate Overshadowing Growth Opportunities." *PC World*, 21 Aug. 2015.

> *Let's imagine [Satoshi] turned up and said he'd rethought, and Bitcoin was a bad idea. Should everyone just give up and walk away? Or accept that people's ideas do change. My article quotes Satoshi a lot, but that's not to imply he's some sort of god or absent dictator.*[379]
>
> - Mike Hearn, 17 Aug 2015.

This is interesting because it hits the nail on the head regarding the disagreement about the status of Satoshi in Bitcoin and Blockland, and the different interpretations of his significance by people at the highest levels of authority. Its notable that Gavin Andresen, to whom Satoshi had entrusted the position of Bitcoin lead dev, appeared to consider him as a mere human upon whose designs he and others could improve and innovate.

Debate of Bitcoin XT got so intense that moderators on the r/Bitcoin subreddit banned all posts regarding the proposed change or merely referencing *XT*, leading The *Guardian* to report that "*Bitcoin is facing a civil war'*. Bitcoin XT did not get implemented as planned, and Bitcoin's price fell to a low of $203 in the two weeks following the fork. It was the lowest price seen since the 2013 bubble which saw BTC above $1,000. This indicated both panic over the need to consider the fork and dismay over its rejection.[380] [381]

Things came to a head five months later, when Mike Hearn quit his role as a full-time Bitcoin Developer and made a blog post titled *The Resolution of the Bitcoin Experiment*:

> *[Bitcoin] has failed because the community has failed" because "what was meant to be a new, decentralized form of money that lacked 'systemically important institutions' and 'too big to fail'*

---

[379] Hern, Alex. "Bitcoin's Forked: Chief Scientist Launches Alternative Proposal for the Currency." *The Guardian*, 17 Aug. 2015.
[380] Whitwam, Ryan. "Disagreement over Bitcoin's Future Threatens to Fork the Currency." *Extreme Tech*, 26 Aug. 2015.
[381] Rosenfeld, Everett. "Bitcoin Splits: Will It Break, or Be Better than Ever?" *CNBC*, 20 Aug. 2015.

> *has become something even worse: a system completely controlled by just a handful of people.*[382 383]
>
> - Mike Hearn, 15 Jan. 2016.

For anyone without laser-focused confidence, these were scary times with Bitcoin falling 16% to $372 on the news. Those opposed to Hearn & Andresen's fork naturally dismissed him saying that Bitcoin was better without him, but the situation was frightening to all but the most confident Bitcoiners. I myself recall telling a friend that Bitcoin had gotten very unpredictable, and that I had sold a significant portion of my coins (which I had received as pre-orders for my first book, and thus needed the cash to actually print and ship the copies). Few suspected that XT would be only the first of many ideological wars to be fought amongst factions of Bitcoin loyalists.

Bitcoin Classic - 10 Feb. 2016 to 5 Jan. 2017

About a month after the panic caused by Hearn's departure, Bitcoin Classic was proposed as a solution to the block-size debate. Classic was a more conservative version of XT, aiming to increase the block size from 1 mb to 2 mb only, with the possibility for further increases later. The proposal was relatively popular, with broad industry support from companies such as Coinbase, Bitstamp, BitFury, and Circle, as well as Jeff Garzik, Roger Ver, and Gavin Andresen.[384] As Bitcoin Classic became a subject of debate, *Bitcoin*

---

[382] Hearn, Mike. "The Resolution of the Bitcoin Experiment." *Plan99*, 15 Jan. 2016.

[383] Young, Joshph. "Mike Hearn Resigns and Leaves Bitcoin Permanently." *NewsBTC*, 15 Jan. 2016.

[384] EconoTimes. "BitFury Comes Out in Support of Bitcoin Classic." *EconoTimes*, 18 Jan. 2016.

became to be known as *Bitcoin Core* in order to differentiate it.[385] This is notable because, due to others creating a forked copy, the "original" version had to change branding slightly in order to maintain its perceived status as the "original" or "core" Bitcoin. Blockchain forking had thus become a game of branding. The title of *Bitcoin* belonged to whatever chain people most identified the word with.

SegWit - 21 July 2017

Things changed significantly when BIP 141's *Segregated Witness* proposal was implemented as a soft-fork to the Bitcoin Core chain on July 21, 2017. This SegWit *soft-fork* was different from the traditional (hard-)fork in that it was not a radical change to the blockchain itself, but an optional layer that miners could apply as needed to increase the block size. Finally, a solution.[386] [387]

But not for long.

Bitcoin Cash - 1 Aug. 2017

A mere 11 days later, on August 1st, 2017, Bitcoin Cash which featured an eight-megabyte limit, was forked from Bitcoin Core. Overnight, or more specifically from block #478559, BCH popped into existence and everyone with BTC suddenly had the equivalent

---

[385] Willam, Oscar. "A Bitcoin Civil War Is Threatening to Tear the Digital Currency in 2 — Here's What You Need to Know." *Business Insider*, 26 Mar. 2017.
[386] Young, Joseph. "Segwit on Testnet Supports 1.7 MB Blocks With 8800+ Transactions." *CCN*, 26 Apr. 2017.
[387] "Leading Bitcoin Ecosystem Participants Reach Consensus on Scaling Issue." *Econo Times*. 25 May 2017.

amount of BCH.[388] This was the point of diversion; Bitcoin's blockchain was no longer an unshakeable monolithic pillar, but a living oak tree whose trunk had suddenly separated in two directions after 8.5 years or 478,559 *Bitcoin days* (blocks) of growth. Would one become a minor branch or even wither away, or would the bi-trunk structure prove structurally unsound and bring the entire tree to the ground? Bitcoin held its breath.

This contingency plan had been in the works for two months, headed by Roger Ver and Chinese mining group Bitmain. Clearly, they were unhappy with the solution provided by SegWit. Ver believed that large blocks were essential, as Bitcoin was meant to be a system enabling everyday payments, and it was thus important to ensure that payments did not get declined or stuck in limbo for hours. The logic was that if Bitcoin could not function as a common payment protocol, then it was worthless as an investment. Bitcoin Cash was promoted as being what Bitcoin was intended to function as all along: easy and reliable e-cash.[389]

Chaos and confusion erupted, and few knew what to do. With Bitmain (the largest mining group) backing BCH, it was not at all clear which Bitcoin would be recognized as "true". As it became apparent that the fork was not a complete failure and that BCH (nor BTC) coins were by no means worthless, exchanges and online wallets began to add support for BCH one by one. Now, someone with a balance of 1.2345 BTC could log in and find 1.2345 BCH in addition to their BTC. BCH traded between $220 and $750 in its first month, whereas the BTC ticker price remained stable. It thus appeared as if BCH created value from thin air, with many BTC

---

[388] Irrera, Anna, and Gertrude Chavez Dreyfuss. "Bitcoin 'Clone' Sees a Slow Start following Split." *Independent*, 2 Aug. 17.
[389] Huang, Zheping. "Bitcoin Cash 'hard Fork': Everything You Need to Know about the Latest Cryptocurrency Civil War." *South China Morning Post*, 15 Oct. 2018.

supporters considering it a sort of dividend on their bitcoins which they could trade for even more "real" bitcoins. The Grayscale Bitcoin Trust (GBTC), a fund for holding bitcoins whose shares could be traded on the stock exchange, was a notable example of this when it sold its BCH in order to increase its BTC reserves.[390] A new Bitcoin Maximalism emerged on both sides: not only was Bitcoin the only valid cryptocurrency, but there could only ever be one valid version of Bitcoin with all others being mere impersonators.

As unrest simmered, the prominent r/Bitcoin subreddit began censoring anything with positive references to Bitcoin Cash, leading the supporters of Bitcoin Cash to exile themselves to r/btc and beginning to refer to the former as "the legacy subreddit". On both websites, users would discuss "Bitcoin" and "BTC" while referring to two different things, with r/btc and allied websites regularly posting PSA-type warnings to tell newcomers about the "illegitimacy" of Bitcoin Core. This of course went both ways, with r/Bitcoin users warning about the "corrupt" Cash's attempted coup d'bitcoin. Cash's believers gloated at having traded their "worthless" Core-BTC for much larger numbers of the "real" BTC and mocked those who had been tricked into dumping their real bitcoins in favor of a lie. To be on the safe side, many Bitcoiners kept their identical amounts of BTC and BCH, with some even believing that one of each was required for one to say they truly owned a whole and original Bitcoin. This became particularly relevant when it came to the trade of collectible physical Bitcoins, which effectively contained such "whole bitcoins" due to them being loaded with BTC long before any forks.

---

[390] Redman, Jamie. "Grayscale Investments Plans to Sell GBTC-Based Bitcoin Cash Reserves." *Bitcoin.com*, 5 Nov. 2017.

This war was fought with censorship, propaganda, character assassinations, and through the manipulation of mining power. One way that supporters of Bitcoin Core attacked Bitcoin Cash was by calling it *Bcash*, in the view that BCH was not "real" Bitcoin and thus had no right to use its name. Core supporters of course argued that Cash was just another cryptocurrency using the name Bitcoin to trick people into thinking it was "the" Bitcoin. This came to a head during a live video stream in which John Carvalho repeatedly referred to *Bcash* in conversation with BCH proponent Roger Ver, who eventually turned to shouting expletives and showing his middle finger to the camera while asserting that "*Its Bitcoin Cash not Bcash, OK!*" As he grew more agitated, Ver declared that he was a self-made millionaire even before Bitcoin and began questioning Carvalho's personal income and net-worth before ending the interview early.[391] Following this, the exchange Bitstamp listed the coin as *Bcash*.[392] This again demonstrates the power of name association; as long as people, companies, and governments spoke of *Bitcoin*, the supporters of both camps could believe that the subject was the "correct" Bitcoin while the speakers themselves could avoid picking a side in an ambiguous political conflict to whose result they were indifferent.

About a week following Ver's rage-quit, the word *bitshaming*[393] entered Blockland vocabulary after "Bitcoin Jesus" Ver took an apparent swipe at "Bitcoin Evangelist" Andreas Antonopoulos by stating that "*Andreas is one of the most eloquent speakers on the topic of Bitcoin, but if he had invested even $300 in bitcoin back in 2012,*

---

[391] incredibert, Youtube.com user. "Roger Ver Rage Quit Interview." *YouTube*, 27 Nov. 2017.
[392] Young, Joseph. "Bitstamp Criticized for Listing Bitcoin Cash as Bcash, Despite Community Outrage." *CoinTelegraph*, 6 Dec. 2017.
[393] Icke420, UrbanDictionary.com user. "bitshame." *Urban Dictionary*, 8 Dec. 2017.

he'd be a millionaire today"[394]. In fact, Antonopoulos had sold his bitcoins in 2013 to pay rent while struggling financially due to dedicating years of his life to evangelize on behalf of Bitcoin at professional events around the world. Many interpreted Ver's statement as one of an arrogant millionaire making fun of a humble self-sacrificing man who, in focusing his energies on serving the movement, had not managed to make himself rich despite having had the opportunity. This resulted in an overnight outpouring of support, with Andreas receiving $1.5 million worth of unsolicited Bitcoin donations to his known public address from hundreds of people wanting to show gratitude for his selfless work.[395]

One person to take a side in the Bitcoin Cash debate was Jack Dorsey, the CEO of Twitter. In explaining that he only held Bitcoin and would not invest in any other coins or tokens, user @MeatTC_ tweeted that Mr. Dorsey may have been talking about Bitcoin Cash, to which he replied with a simple "*Hell no.*"[396] Soon after, Core loyalists began bombarding the *#Bitcoin* Twitter handle, controlled by Cash's Roger Ver, by repeatedly reporting the account and sending CEO Jack Dorsey messages asking him to ban it. After it came to light that Dorsey had responded to one such inquiry with " *What do you recommend we do with it?",* Ver accused Mr. Dorsey of "*conspiring with the BTC maximalists to reduce the influence of my account.*" A poll by @jimmysong found that 53% of 5466 respondents felt the account should be "Suspended for fraud." @hasufl suggested that #bitcoin be removed entirely in the same way that #internet was, being that Bitcoin is decentralized and is

394 Ver, Roger. *Twitter.com account @rogerkver*, 5 Dec. 2017.
395 Wong, Joon Ian. "A Bitcoin Booster Got $1.5 Million after Being "bit-shamed" for Being Poor." *Quartz*, 8 Dec. 2017.
396 Go, Johnson. "Jack Dorsey Denies Using Bitcoin Cash for Square App." *Cryptopolitan*, 25 Mar. 2019.

thus not an entity that anyone can control or speak for.[397] Anyone is free to define Bitcoin as they wish, and the market will value each definition accordingly.[398]\

Bitcoin ABC and SV

The story of Bitcoin Cash came to an end on November 28, 2018, when disagreements among its influencers boiled over to cause another chain-splitting fork, with each Bitcoin Cash (BCH) subsequently turning into a *Bitcoin ABC* (Adjustable Blocksize Cap) and a *Bitcoin SV* (Satoshi's Vision or BSV). Bitcoin Cash was no more.

Mr. Ver and Bitmain's Jihan Wu took the reins on ABC which featured an increased block size of 32MB, whereas the *Satoshi's Vision* version with the even larger 128MB was spearheaded by Dr. Craig Wright. Beyond the 32MB block size which was intended for eventual removal, Ver's intent was to implement smart contracts to the ABC chain to allow it to function in a way comparable to Ethereum. This was opposed by Dr. Wright, who asserted that Satoshi did not create Bitcoin to run smart contracts, but for the singular role of serving as stable global money.

How could Dr. Wright be so certain of what Satoshi's vision for Bitcoin really was?

Simple. He claimed to be Satoshi Nakamoto himself.[399]

Wright appeared on the Bitcoin stage in December 2015, when tech magazines Wired and Gizmodo both published investigations

---

397 Redman, Jamie. "Attempts to Deplatform @Bitcoin Account Reveal Private Message with Twitter CEO." *Bitcoin.com*, 21 Apr. 2019.
398 Nakamura, Yuji, and Olga Khariff. "Battle for 'True' Bitcoin Is Just Getting Started." *Bloomberg*, 4 Dec. 2017.
399 Biddle, Sam. "This Australian Says He and His Dead Friend Invented Bitcoin." *Gizmodo*, 5 Feb. 2016.

that pointed to Wright as potentially being Satoshi. Hours after Wired's investigation became public, Wright's home and office were raided by Australian Federal Police as part of a tax investigation.[400] [401]

Though *The Economist* reported in May 2016 that Wright had given evidence of his identity as Satoshi through a cryptographic signature,[402] [403] Bitcoin developer Jeff Garzik and prominent security researchers later asserted that nothing Dr. Wright did amounted to proof and that he "s*imply reused an old signature from a bitcoin transaction performed in 2009 by Satoshi.*"[404] Wright has said that Hal Finney and Dave Kleiman, both deceased, helped him create Bitcoin and that he has not been able to prove his identity as Satoshi due to other late partners having possessed parts of the needed code.[405] He has also hinted that he even prefers to be considered a fraud, because he is ashamed that Bitcoin has been utilized by terrorists, pedophiles, and drug dealers, and does not want to be seen as responsible for creating it.[406] To make a long story short he originally threw his support behind Ver and Wu's Bitcoin Cash, promoting it at various conferences where he appeared as Satoshi Nakamoto, before proclaiming *Satoshi's Vision* as his vision for the currency.

---

[400] Hunt, Elle, and Paul Farrell. "Reported Bitcoin 'Founder' Craig Wright's Home Raided by Australian Police." *The Guardian*, 9 Dec. 2015.
[401] Boyd, Edward, and John Dagge. "Bitcoin Mystery: Home of Man Believed to Be Currency Founder Raided." *Daily Telegraph*, 10 Dec. 2015.
[402] "Craig Wright Reveals Himself as Satoshi Nakamoto." *The Economist*, 2 May 2016.
[403] Kuhn, Daniel. "Crypto Genius or Fake? The Craig Wright Saga Explained." *CoinDesk*, 15 May 2019.
[404] Pearson, Jordan, and Lorenzo Franceschi Bicchierai. "Craig Wright's New Evidence That He Is Satoshi Nakamoto Is Worthless." *Vice*, 2 May 2016.
[405] Greenberg, Andy, and Gwern Branwen. "Is Bitcoin's Creator This Unknown Australian Genius? Probably Not (Updated)." *Wired*, 12 Aug. 2015.
[406] "Kleiman v Craig Wright, part 3." *WizSec*, 6 July 2019.

Satoshi's Rock

"*Whoso pulleth out this sword of this stone and anvil, is rightwise king born*" pronounced the wizard Merlin of Arthurian legend. That sword was Excalibur; the sword of him who held rightful sovereignty over Britain.[407] Bitcoin's Genesis Block can be understood as a contemporary version of this legendary king-confirming anvil-rock. While the coins in the Genesis Block cannot be moved, it is possible to sign a cryptographic message *from* the Genesis Block address by anyone who has its private key.[408] The possessor of that private key can only be the true Satoshi or someone appointed by him. While many have claimed to be Satoshi or some level of "Bitcoin co-founder", no one has yet performed this indisputable Arthurian feat.[409] The Genesis Block's public address is:

1A1zP1eP5QGefi2DMPTfTL5SLmv7DivfNa

Regardless of who Satoshi truly is and if he or his emissary may one day demonstrably return, it is important to remember that he was merely Bitcoin's inventor. He no longer controls it, even with the keys to the Genesis Block. Provided Satoshi is merely human, it is certain that he did not imagine everything that his invention would spawn through technological generativity. Just as we did not require permission from the Wright brothers to fly to the moon nor of Einstein to design the nuclear bomb, Satoshi's personal vision for his invention is ultimately irrelevant to the legitimacy of others tinkering with, building upon, or taking inspiration from the technology. Re-imagination is permissionless. To modify, repurpose, and redefine is not merely acceptable; it is the base requirement of progress

[407] Malory, Sir Thomas. "Le Morte d'Arthur." 1485.
[408] Sedgwick, Kai. "People Keep Sending Satoshi Nakamoto Bitcoin." *Bitcoin.com*, 24 Dec. 2017.
[409] Greenberg, Andy. "How to Prove You're Bitcoin Creator Satoshi Nakamoto." *Wired*, 11 Apr. 2016.

in technology, science, art, and philosophy. All of these are intrinsically permissionless. To deny the legitimacy of innovation is to claim perfection. In the end, the free market or other relevant forces will determine the defacto true Bitcoin, Bitcoins, or even devalue them entirely.

Satoshi Nakamoto is today perhaps more relevant as a movement than individual, comparable to anonymous artists like Banksy or Anonymous, the open herd-like collective of nameless online activists. I hope that Satoshi never returns. His work is done. Satoshi Nakamoto will better serve humanity by remaining a mythical Prometheus of blockchain rather than emerging as a weak, flawed, and ultimately, disappointing human; liable to the promethean fate of life-long torment in the forms of threats, blackmail, tax investigations, lawsuits, and even imprisonment.

'The Attack', 1899, depicting a powerful attacker desecrating a book of law.

CHAPTER 12

Ethereum Attack

ETH, ETC, and The DAO

The settlement of Bitcoin was not the only one to be faced with the problem of strange wizards splitting reality. The fork that caused the fracture of the Ethereum settlement was even more chaotic.

This story begins with The DAO, arguably the first Decentralized Autonomous Organization. Its Initial Coin Offering raised a record $150 million in ETH in May 2016. This represented 14% of all Ethereum, provided by over 11,000 investors.[410]

> *[...] what if, with the power of modern information technology, we can encode the mission statement into code; that is, create an inviolable contract that generates revenue, pays people to perform some function, and finds hardware for itself to run on, all without any need for top-down human direction?*[411]
>
> - Vitalik Buterin, 20 Sept. 2015.

---

[410] Popper, Nathaniel. "A Venture Fund with Plenty of Virtual Capital, but No Capitalist." *The New York Times*, 21 May 2016.
[411] Rennie, Ellie. "The DAO: A Radical Experiment That Could Be the Future of Decentralised Governance." *The Conversation*, 11 May 2016.

The DAO was in effect an investor-driven venture capital fund. A company based on open-source code, without a CEO, managers, a board of directors, nor even an address or home country. It barely needed even a website, and even its logo was chosen via popular vote. Anyone could anonymously invest in The DAO by sending Ethereum and receive DAO Tokens which functioned as shares. The DAO's purpose was simple: to operate as "*a hub that disperses funds to projects.*" Any project, group, or company (known as a *contractor* in DAO-speak) could make a funding proposal to The DAO. Volunteer *curators* would then verify applicant's identities and the legality of proposals, whitelisting them upon acceptance.[412] [413] [414]

Holders of DAO Tokens would openly vote on which projects to fund, with The DAO's investment into selected projects being delivered in the form of Ethereum. As the projects became profitable, they would purchase more Ethereum to deliver back to The DAO. All of these functions were executed via Ethereum smart contracts; pre-programmed bots that handled voting, accounting, and fund allocation with inherent transparency and without the need or even possibility for anyone to intervene. No changes could be made without a majority vote of investors with an adjustable quorum. The DAO was truly a Decentralized and Anonymous Organization, unlike any the world had seen before. As the value of assets controlled by the fund increased, the value of its DAO Token shares soared as investors poured in. "*There are no humans controlling it, it's just*

[412] Metz, Cade. "The Biggest Crowdfunding Project Ever—the DAO—Is Kind of a Mess." *Wired*, 6 June 2016.
[413] Bannon, Seth. "The Tao of "The DAO" Or: How the Autonomous Corporation Is Already Here." *TechCrunch*, 16 Apr. 2016.
[414] "The DAO of Accrue." *The Economist*, 19 May 2016.

the code... There is no one who will take money for favouring one or other contract. You will have the wisdom of the crowds."[415]

One could consider The DAO structure to be a truly pure manifestation of (plutocratic) democracy and transparency, an organization with checks and balances unlike any other. There could be no back-room deals between non-existent executives, no insider trading in an entirely transparent system, and no ability for anyone to police its activities as there was no one to question or arrest, no server to shut down, no funds to freeze, nor even identifiable shareholders; The DAO was sovereign.[416] Its business model became an existential threat to investment funds and banks – "*a paradigm shift in the very idea of economic organization.... It offers complete transparency, total shareholder control, unprecedented flexibility, and autonomous governance.*"[417]

> *It all sounds like science fiction, a spontaneous entity evolving out of something named after a nebulous gaseous material (thin air?), which claims to be immutable and incorruptible.*[418]
>
> - Ellie Rennie, 11 May 2016.

Like any spontaneously generated and self-evolving entity of science fiction, The DAO's first order of business was self-replication. Almost any organization's governance structure could theoretically be converted to some form of DAO, whether the entity in question be a business, charity, or scholarship fund; perhaps even an entire national budget and government as we know it. To help The DAO take over the world, the IoT (Internet of Things) company that had

---

415 Waters, Richard. "Automated Company Raises Equivalent of $120M in Digital Currency." *CNBC*, 17 May 2016.
416 Macheel, Tanaya. "The DAO Might Be Groundbreaking, But Is It Legal?" *American Banker*, 19 May 2016.
417 puyang, blog.stanford.edu user. "Blockchain-based Decentralized Autonomous Organization Is Future!" *Stanford University Blog*, 8 July 2018.
418 Rennie, Ellie. "The DAO: A Radical Experiment That Could Be the Future of Decentralised Governance." *The Conversation*, 11 May 2016.

built its original code, Slock.it, stepped in. Proposed improvements included a framework that anyone could freely use for whatever type of organization they wanted to contrive. This involved creating all manners of optional rules regarding voting, token allocations, and buy-backs. A DAO needn't run on Ethereum specifically; it was merely the first platform that provided the conditions necessary for a DAO to awake, arise, and release its spores.

Enter Griff Green, Slock.it's Community Manager. Green had earlier ditched his corporate job in chemical engineering to travel the world as a nomad while living off physical gold that he carried with him, selling it for local currencies. He became hooked on Bitcoin upon realizing its utility as a superior gold, and pivoted his focus towards Ethereum while studying in the first graduating class of The University of Nicosia's (Cyprus) ground-breaking *Masters of Digital Currency* program. It was upon waking up on the morning of June 17th 2016 that Green's moment of fate arrived. An attacker had discovered an exploit in The DAO's code, allowing him and others to quickly move the Ethereum it held into an outgoing wallet. There was only one way to stop the theft: by stealing faster.

> *The DAO is being attacked. It has been going on for 3-4 hours, it is draining ETH at a rapid rate. This is not a drill. ...*
> *We need to spam the Network so that we can mount a counter attack all the brightest minds in the Ethereum world are in on this. Please use this:*

```
for (var i = 0; i < 100; i++) {
eth.sendTransaction({from: eth.ac-
counts[4], gas: 2300000, gasPrice:
web3.toWei(20, 'shannon'), data:
'0x5b620186a05a1315601357600160205260005
65b600080601f600039601f565b6000f3'}) }
to spam the chain
```
[419]

- Griff Green, 17 June, 2016.

---

[419] Brandom, Russell. "DAO Potentially Hacked, Millions of Ether May Be Stolen, Griff Green Says." *CoinTelegraph*, 17 June 2016.

The Robin Hood Group was born, and by effectively stealing all of The DAO's remaining funds and using it to drown out the attack, they were able to repel the attack under Green's command. Investors freaked out as they saw The DAO's accounts draining before their eyes, and a member of the mostly anonymous, unofficial Robin Hood Group tweeting that "DAO IS BEING SECURELY DRAINED. DO NOT PANIC." predictably did not help anyone to calm down. As the dust settled and the Robin Hood's returned the recovered Ether to its "rightful" owners, the funds taken by the attacking hackers amounted to 3.6 million ETH worth over $50 million: about 4% of all Ethereum. Due to a security feature within The DAO's code, these coins would remain locked for 35 days, after which another hacker-battle between the White Hats and the hackers would ensue, in effect triggering another 35-day locking-period. This DAO War could potentially continue for years on end until one of the sides gave up, causing never-ending drama and distraction within the Ethereum settlement. All this could have been prevented if line 666 of The DAO's code had a lowercase *t* instead of a capital *T*.

Many felt that allowing the attacker to keep 4% could prove disastrous if the network eventually moved to a proof-of-stake model, and a large portion of the settlements earliest residents could face expulsion due to the loss of their figurative homes in the colony. The DAO's inventor, Christoph Jentzsch stated that, ironically enough, The DAO had grown too fast and had become too big to fail. A bailout was needed. "*Lets just fork it*" Buterin blurted out, breaking the silence. The idea was put to a vote and the majority agreed. Recounting the turbulent times, Green recounts:

> *We had 35 days where we knew that those funds would not move, so we had 35 days where we could actually rewrite the code in Ethereum to take the money from the hacker and put it somewhere else... there was a time limit that we had to work in; we had a mission, we had an enemy, and it just all made sense to push this hard fork.*[420]
>
> - Griff Green, 13 June 2018.

You may recall MPEx's Mircea Popescu from a previous chapter. The day after the hack on June 18th, he waltzed back to the stage with this abridged letter titled *To the DAO and the Ethereum community : F--k you.*

> *To the DAO and the Ethereum community,*
>
> *I have carefully examined the code of The DAO and decided to participate after finding the feature where splitting is rewarded with additional ether. I have made use of this feature and have rightfully claimed 3,641,694 ether, and would like to thank the DAO for this reward. ...*
>
> *I am disappointed by those who are characterizing the use of this intentional feature as "theft". I am making use of this explicitly coded feature as per the smart contract terms and my law firm has advised me that my action is fully compliant with United States criminal and tort law. For reference please review the terms of the DAO:*
>
> *"... Nothing in this explanation of terms or in any other document or communication may modify or add any additional obligations or guarantees beyond those set forth in The DAO's code. ... to the extent you believe there to be any conflict or discrepancy between the descriptions offered here and the functionality of The DAO's code at 0xbb9bc244d798123fde783fcc1c72d3bb 8c189413, The DAO's code controls and sets forth all terms of The DAO Creation."*

[420] Harrysson, Frederik, and Anna Rose. "The DAO, the White Hat Hacker Group & Giveth with Griff." *Zeroknowledge*, 13 June 2018.

> *A soft or hard fork would amount to seizure of my legitimate and rightful ether, claimed legally through the terms of a smart contract. Such fork would permanently and irrevocably ruin all confidence in not only Ethereum but also the in the field of smart contracts and blockchain technology. Many large Ethereum holders will dump their ether, and developers, researchers, and companies will leave Ethereum. Make no mistake: any fork, soft or hard, will further damage Ethereum and destroy its reputation and appeal.*
>
> *I reserve all rights to take any and all legal action against any accomplices of illegitimate theft, freezing, or seizure of my legitimate ether, and am actively working with my law firm. Those accomplices will be receiving Cease and Desist notices in the mail shortly.*
>
> *I hope this event becomes an valuable learning experience for the Ethereum community and wish you all the best of luck.*
>
> *Yours truly,*
>
> *"The Attacker"*[421]
>
> - Mircea Popescu, 18 June 2016.

Yet this was not the end of Popescu's offensive on the Ethereum collective that day. As word of his responsibility for the hack spread, one Etherite commented that "*If it was [Popescu], then I support a fork just to f--k him over. Mircea is a douchebag scammer asshole, and I will sacrifice the value of my ETH to ruin him.*" Popescu then added a screenshot of this comment to his blog, mockingly "responding" to it by posting a picture of his celebratory chocolate cake with eight bottles of champagne and the statement "*ima go pick up a slut, will be back in a few hours.*"

As we can see, the Ethereum fork presents an irreconcilable conflict between the values of immutability and consensus.

---

[421] Popescu, Mircea. "To the DAO and the Ethereum Community : Fuck You." *Trilema*, 18 June 2016.

Immutability, the inability for changes to be made, is commonly considered an intrinsic property of blockchain. *CODE IS LAW* is the blockchain mantra and dogma of immutability, just as *physics is law* is the qualifier of physical existence. Blockchain exists not only outside of a legal system, but outside of the intentions and control of its creators or users. *Code is Law* implies an absolute legalism; in that, the judges in this metaphorical legal system have no judicial discretion and their judgments must be made according to the precise letter of the law, no matter the outcome. They are not human but machines, and there is no flexibility nor interpretation when the instructions are a collection of robotic 1's and 0's instead of a flexible and nuanced human language. It is this property that gives blockchain value: an immutable and incorruptible global ledger of fact that cannot be altered even under the temptation of billion-dollar bribes or force of marching armies. This is the essence of how a smart contract can function.

This philosophy goes deep. By understanding blockchain as an amoral collection of code outside the control of any authority, one can reason that whatever is possible through "honest" (existent) code is not merely permissible, but an engrained right. Some, seemingly inclusive of Mr. Popescu, have reasoned that it is one's moral duty to exploit any vulnerability in public code, with any accrued rewards being rightly earned booty.[422]

The average person can understand this in the context of a strategy game – an ingenious winning move is valid, even if it is so out-of-the-box that it was unanticipated by even the creator of the game. What is not forbidden by the rules is permissible, and in blockchain there is a *code of code* rather than a code of morality, a code of custom, or a code of law. By *rolling back* the blockchain, the

---

[422] Brandom, Russell. "Note Claiming to be from Cryptocurrency Hacker Says Stolen $53 Million is Legally His." *The Verge*, 18 June 2016.

Ethereum community was effectively stealing from the clever coder who was able to find an edge in the game. Popescu was punished for being creative, and his earning were seized for the benefit of the collective. It is this rewriting of Ethereum history that caused great controversy; the network had undergone several noncontentious forks in its past, but this was blockchain history.

There is of course another side to the story: Community Consensus.

> *Some bitcoin users see the hard fork as in some ways violating their most fundamental values... I personally think these fundamental values, pushed to such extremes, are silly.*[423]
>
> - Vitalik Buterin, June 2017.

Ethereum differed from Bitcoin in that its inventor was a living, breathing, 22-year-old Vitalik Buterin, who was surrounded by what was at the time a rather small, unified community of essentially like-minded friends. The leafy neighborhoods of Ethereum were renowned for being friendly, helpful, and collaborative before the hack; a reason many of its early members migrated from Bitcoin, whose level of social grace and discourse was closer to that of a wild-west saloon with free bourbon on *Conspiracy Theory Thursdays.* To call Bitcoin's early days rough around the edges would be an understatement. Unlike with Bitcoin, most Etherites had a common understanding regarding the essence and direction of their settlement. Further, the community was rather centralized to specific communication channels and conferences and could thus coordinate the roll-back in a way that did not unreasonably disrupt other projects on the network. With this context, it might be fair to describe Bitcoin society as an embodiment of stereotypical wild-west

---

[423] Leising, Matthew. "Ether Thief Remains Mystery Year After $55 Million Digital Heist." *Bloomberg*, 13 June 2017.

anarchism, and rowdiness, mixed with naked gold-rush individualism and distrust. Indeed, a 2014 study by University of Illinois researchers found that "*people interested in Bitcoin are far less likely to emphasize social relations than typical users [on Twitter, specifically being] less likely to mention family, friends, religion, sex, and emotion related words in their tweets.*"[424] In contrast, we might describe early-days Ethereum's society as closer to that of a small welfare state where the populace placed their trust in legislator-developers, who aimed to build a system of mutual benefit.

Considering these cultural differences, it is no surprise the Etherites considered the "the attacker" to be in the wrong. The community created Ethereum's code to function according to their will, not the other way around. The Etherites had a moral code and a social contract that they considered superior to the human-written and thus fallible *code*. With no ability to send legal authorities after the hacker, the community decided to fight "evil" by simply redefining itself in such a way that the unwanted part was excluded. In effect, practically everyone agreed that "*we designed this game, and did not intend for it to allow this type of move. By taking advantage of our loophole in this way, a certain player is ruining the game for many happy players in what we understand to be an unfair way, and we will thus update the rules and re-do this turn*". This is a textbook case of distributed governance and community consensus.

We might also seek to understand this conflict as a generational one, with Ethereum making a stand for the otherwise unrepresented Generation Z. To clarify, the western world has four generations that can be understood to have played some part in the Blockland story: Baby Boomers, Generation X, Millennials (Y),

---

[424] Hernandez, Ivan, et al. "Are Bitcoin Users Less Sociable? An Analysis of Users' Language and Social Connections on Twitter." *HCI International 2014 - Posters' Extended Abstracts Communications in Computer and Information Science*, 2014, pp. 26–31., doi:10.1007/978-3-319-07854-0_5.

and Generation Z. Though the youngest Boomers were 49 when the Bitcoin first gained extensive coverage in 2013, they have generally not been attracted to the industry for reasons including general financial satisfaction, technical complexity, and negative thoughts emanating from the idea that it is not "authorized" or part of the establishment. Generation X ranged ~33-48 during this same period; Millennials were aged ~17-32; and Generation Z's were still in high school.

Bitcoin was launched as an answer to the 2008 financial collapse, which decimated millennial's prospects of wealth and career growth, so it is easy to see why its largest base would be Millennials who felt betrayed by "the system." It is safe to say that Bitcoin has been a Generation X-Y joint venture, with the Millennials taking the controlling share. This matches Douglas Adams' rule of reactions to technologies in which he asserted that people aged 15 to 35 view new technologies as revolutionary, while they are merely natural to the younger generation, and an abomination *against the natural order of things* for those older than 35. Boomers were thus almost entirely left out due to a lack of interest, while Generation Z, still below the age of majority, was excluded for the simple reason that they had no way of acquiring any bitcoins. The new global economy being built for them is one in which they have no stake.

A 2018 research study by US marketing firm Rubin Postaer and Associates identified cultural and societal shifts to characterize the generation. In addition to elaborating on the rise of micro-communities, dwindling levels of personal privacy, and an emphasis on emotions over facts, the study suggests that individualism is giving way for community cohesion in a generational shift:

> ***Shifting toward more community-centric:*** *More than even most Western countries, our [American] national identity has historically focused on the importance and supremacy of the "rugged individual." Some argue that among other factors, immigration from and assimilation of more collectivist cultures, is subtly fueling a greater focus on behaving in accordance with the expectations and well-being of the group.*[425]
>
> - Rubin Postaer and Associates, 2018.

In speaking of generational shifts, it is worth considering what role cryptocurrencies might play in generational wealth transfer. Holding true to the hodler philosophy but perhaps also speaking in broader terms, one early Bitcoin investor brought up the view that Bitcoins are never destroyed. We only take care of them for the next generation. Successfully passing on cryptocurrencies after death is however no simple task; clear plans must be made to ensure that the correct parties (and no one else) can access your holdings after you pass away (and only then). Potential solutions include entrusting different lawyers with partial private keys; however, new inheritance solutions are surely forthcoming. Some long-term holders have gone to great lengths to teach their children about blockchain, ensuring that they know how to unlock paper wallets held in bank safety deposit boxes. Despite it being likely that the following generation might see these investments grow, the old Chinese proverb that "*wealth does not pass 3 generations*" may well remain valid. Perhaps even this ancient problem could be solved by creating DNA-linked blockchain-identities that prove family relations and setting up incorruptibly pre-programmed smart-contract trust-funds that make ever-decreasing annual payments to all descendants for eternity.

---

[425] "Identity Shifters." *Rubin Postaer and Associates*, 2018.

The Exodus

And so, up to 100 Ethereum residents joined forces to prepare the colony for a move. At ETH Block 1920000, which fell on July 20th, 2016, the gates of Ethereum flung open as tens of thousands of residents poured out in a caravan, abandoning their home. They soon reached what they judged to be a better place to rebuild, and so the revisionist Ethereum 2.0 was established, from here on in called simply Ethereum in honor of their home which had tragically fallen to invaders. Here, all those whose homes the attackers had destroyed were restored to their former standings within the community.

Turns out, not everyone agreed to relocate the colony. Some chose to stay behind, hiding until the very last of the caravans had disappeared over the horizon. As quiet fell in the abandoned settlement, those who remained emerged and assembled. Soon, a new banner was raised over the quiet city's gate: "*Welcome to ETC: Ethereum Classic*", it declared. And so, Ethereum became known as Ethereum Classic, while a new 'Ethereum' arose from the ether. Bitcoin Maximalist types poured into the newly branded colony, declaring it the legitimate and original Ethereum. One of these was Bitcoin entrepreneur Barry Silbert, whose Grayscale Investments' thesis on ETC was presented under the title *The DAO and the Death of Principles* which suggested that Ethereum with all its potential had destroyed its reputation by effectively twisting and betraying cold hard reality into an alternative make-believe ideal that felt more pleasant to the majority.[426] Those who took Ethereum's side reasoned from a different set of premises, first among them the argument that what Popescu did was morally wrong in an absolute or relative sense and against the intended functioning of The

---

[426] Leising, Matthew. "Ether Thief Remains Mystery Year After $55 Million Digital Heist." *Bloomberg*, 13 June 2017.

DAO, and secondly, because such a humiliating monetary loss by Ethereum's early supporters and innovators may have caused them to lose morale and faith in the project and therefore abandon it, making the need to fork a potentially existential one. Neverthecss, Ethereum Classic's law-of-the-jungle principles would not bend to human opinions of morality and here "the attacker" was a mighty king, as the righteous owner of 3.6 million ETC.

Unpacking the Move

Mr. Popescu certainly overestimated (or intentionally overstated) the number of developers, researchers, and companies that would leave the project in the event of a fork; the very opposite happened and the drama proved to be more of a coming-of-age moment for Ethereum instead of a beginning-of-the-end, if judging by the value of ETH in the months that followed. However, he was not entirely wrong when he claimed that the fork would "*permanently and irrevocably ruin all confidence in not only Ethereum but also the in the field of smart contracts and blockchain technology.*"[427] The fork did indeed cause ripples in the industry, notably a surge in Bitcoin Maximalism, brought on by the "horrific" idea that a blockchain project could simply decide to "arbitrarily" redistribute wealth and go backwards in time. This soured many otherwise fascinated Bitcoiners to the idea of both smart contracts and non-Bitcoin blockchains, leaving both phenomena significantly behind.

In Ethereum, the *smart contract* was simply a reflection of the community's *social contract*, with the latter being consensually updated by the former just as a country's constitution might be occasionally amended via a referendum of the people. The community refused to be enslaved by what was essentially a technical glitch from the

---

[427] Brooks, Michael, and Josh Robichaud. "The Crypto Paradox: Code is Law and Consensus Rules." *Bracewell*, 12 Apr. 2019.

past; machines are mere tools of man – re-programmable and even destructible should they turn against their creators.

> *If one had to choose between one of [a Legal Code or Computer Code], most people would probably go for the former. Yet, many people from the blockchain community tend to believe that people (and organizations) cannot be trusted and social interactions should consequently be mediated only and exclusively through computer code.*[428]
>
> \- Primavera De Filippi, 11 July 2016.

In Ethereum Classic, the smart contract *became* the social contract in the way of the Bitcoin model of absolute immutability. This machine-world's constitution was not a negotiable earthly guideline, but an unshakeable stone law-tablet brought down from the holy mountain of an amoral machine-god. This machine may have been born of man, but it had grown independent and was no longer in human control.

The Fork can be understood as representing a human rebellion against the machine; its leaders believing that their creation was not yet ready to rule them. This by no means suggests that such a drastic action was taken lightly or that it is likely to happen again in Ethereum; *Code is Law* as a principle is alive and well in the Ethereum community. By all accounts, this human intervention was a one-off.

It very much seems that Ethereum is at its core a Generation Z blockchain; which when faced with a crisis, favored the feelings of its tight-knit, largely non-anonymous micro-community and decided to quite literally bend reality to preserve the heart of the collective at the expense of an individual who was following the "rules." This is of course the antithesis of everything Bitcoin stands

[428] Filippi, Primavera De. "A $50M Hack Tests the Values of Communities Run by Code." *Vice*, 11 July 2016.

for; celebrated as the currency of the anonymous *rugged individual* who absolutely does not care about anyone's feelings. This outward arrogance of Bitcoin has been embraced by many self-styled "*Toxic Bitcoin Maximalists*" and "*Bitcoin bro's*", who often identify with an elitist investment-bro culture that displays open hostility towards projects like Ethereum, which do not conform to their idea of what blockchain is or should be.

As a blockchain term, *toxic* appears to have derived from the popular *toxic masculinity* as an insult directed at "aggressive" and uncompromising Bitcoin Maximalists, which Multicoiners labeled as #toxic "trolls", with whom constructive discussion was impractical. Instead of being ashamed by the label, Maximalists embraced and took ownership of the term in a mechanism not dissimilar to the way certain pejorative words have been co-opted by racial and sexual minorities in contemporary society. A cursory analysis of "crypto twitter" reveals that users who describe themselves as toxic tend to cultivate personas as Satoshi-stacking, pistol-packing, carnivorous right-wing alpha-males who mock the shitcoin-buying, beta, vegan, "soy boy" snowflakes that don't understand that Bitcoin is the only real game in town. This was notably not directed at only Ethereum users, but also towards proponents of Bitcoin Cash (BCH) and Bitcoin Satoshi's Vision (BSV) which the toxic's largely considered bastardizations of the *hard code* of Bitcoin.

This idea of *hard code* is a clear connect to the *hard/sound money* idealized by Austrian economists. The cultural divide within Blockland can be divided between Austrians and non-Austrians, with Ethereum and many other blockchain systems having arguably little connection to the economic school. In addition to its lack of association with illegal activity, it is perhaps because Ethereum is distanced from the Austrian school, a heterodox theory which is commonly considered as discredited, that it has had more success than Bitcoin in courting favor from the highest levels of industry and government. Unsurprisingly, many Bitcoin Maximalists have turned to mockery to air their disapproval of the concept of fiat, which they have expanded to describe anything weak, soft, cheap, or short-term. For them, unhealthy food, shallow friendships, bad architecture, and commercial art become fiat food/friendships/architecture/art. Quite frankly, the Bitcoin Maximalist milieu reeks of a certain elitism which imagines its members as enlightened people who understand cold hard reality and are destined to rule over blind masses who are unwilling to lift themselves up from their illusions.

Though Multicoiners do not form a comparably cohesive self-defining online group, accounts focused on Ethereum do appear to contrast the Maximalists in that they display an overall greater variance in ethnicity, gender, sexuality, diet, and politics. As the majority of "crypto twitter" is US-based, it is fascinating to consider to what extent the two sides broadly represent an extension of the emerging fundamental political divide between Republicans and Democrats. This has been touched on by Dr. David Golumbia, who describes himself on Twitter as "*rigorously anti-cyberlibertarian and anti-fascist.*" In his book *The Politics of Bitcoin: Software as Right-Wing Extremism,* he argues that "*because Bitcoin's ideals come from cyberlibertarianism, its political pillars have threads which you pull on and find yourself in far right-wing beliefs and conspiracy theories.*"[429] While it certainly appears that self-styled Toxic Bitcoin Maximalists unanimously align with some extreme of right-wing economic and political thought, Golumbia's categorical argument that "*Bitcoin and the blockchain technology on which it rests satisfy needs that make sense only in the context of right-*

[429] Dorion, Nick. "Review: 'Politics of Bitcoin: Software as Right-Wing Extremism'." *Medium*, 3 Mar. 2019.

wing politics"[430] can be challenged considering the relatively more left-wing culture found in the Ethereum community.

Whether we examine Bitcoin Maximalists, the more loosely defined *Ethereum Maximalists*, or members of smaller "crypto camps" like Litecoin or even BitConnet, there is no doubt that groupthink runs rampant. As groupthink causes members of the respective in-groups to emulate each other and avoid conflict, they develop an illusion of invulnerability such as a strong belief that not only will Bitcoin NEVER fail, but also that each coin's value WILL without question be worth a million dollars. There is of course nothing to suggest that conclusions derived from groupthink are inherently wrong, and they may even be self-reinforcing, if the in-group grows large and influential enough. Another aspect of crypto-groupthink is a systemic underestimation, dismissal, and even dehumanization of opponents that may not only consist of other crypto-camps, but entire industries, governments, and societies whose functions the in-group believes that their chosen blockchain will soon disrupt. This echo-chamber thinking on both the project-level and Blockland-level helped fuel the 2017 ICO bubble.

We should expect neither debate, cyber-bullying, nor the markets to settle these differences anytime soon. Despite whatever given blockchain or community being labeled as illegitimate when examined through a specific worldview, we must remember that members of different cultures, classes, and generations will always value things differently. From the time of Athens and Sparta to the Cold War and beyond, history has shown that ideologically inverted factions and civilizations can and will co-exist for ages despite both considering the other an abomination. For years, Etherites have been predicting a coming *flippening*: Ethereum's overtaking of

430 Golumbia, David. *The Politics of Bitcoin: Software as Right-Wing Extremism*. University of Minnesota Press, 2016.

Bitcoin according to market cap or token value – the future will show us whether this prediction holds true.

It is apparent that *crypto* has become a divisive ideological phenomenon which is more comparable to religion, culture, and politics than to science, which tends to converge towards common ground instead of branching out indefinitely.

Gold 2.0

After most of humanity left the primordial jungles where the biggest gorilla ruled by its strength and aggression, we organized society based on the golden rule, which simply states that they who have the gold, makes the rules. This surely began with critical resources like food, water, shelter, and mates, evolving with time into gold which was universally valuable, and thus served as a direct or indirect coupon by which to acquire all the basics and more. With cryptocurrency, many believe that Gold 2.0 is imminent. This neo-gold is created and even controlled by humans. Imagine then the order of the third millennium, where power comes not from holding gold but from defining its very essence.

You may recall that when Satoshi launched Bitcoin, he inscribed the Genesis Block with a statement against fractional-reserve banking and runaway money-printing which he saw as the cause of the 2008 recession. This aversion to fractional-reserve banking among early Bitcoin users largely expanded to the concept of fiat money itself, that is, money "declared" (printed) by governments as opposed to money that is based on something real like in the times of the gold standard when each unit of a currency was pegged to and redeemable for a specific amount of precious metal.

When the US government banned gold in 1933, many predictably refused to trade their generational treasure into fiat paper. This resulted in searches and seizures, followed by fines and imprisonments. Unlike gold which could be found and carried away by force such as in 1933, it is theoretically possible to store cryptocurrencies in such ways that they cannot be found, much less seized, by any force on earth. Instead of burying their treasure in the ground, the pirates of tomorrow can hide their booty in the recesses of their very minds.

Things like Wikileaks and drugs which can both be classed as petty in comparison to what many see as Bitcoin's raison d'être of becoming "digital gold". The idea here is that gold holds certain properties that have supported its status as the basis of money for millennia. These are easy portability, difficulty of counterfeiting, easy divisibility into smaller parts, rarity, and fungibility. Arguably, Bitcoin fulfills all these criteria even better than gold itself. This theoretically allows Bitcoin to fill the role of *hard money*; similar to gold bullion or silver-backed currency, dissimilar to dollars, yen, or euros that have no "hard" backing. With hard money, the issuer cannot just create more at will without acquiring more of the base asset, and fractional reserve banking under the existing model becomes effectively impossible.

The overarching theory of Bitcoin which follows the dissenting Austrian branch of economics is that this sort of hard, independent money is superior to any current government money, and will thus eventually rise to the level of de-facto global money (see Hyperbitcoinization). This is supported by Gresham's law of economics which states that "bad money drives out good,"[431] which Bitcoiners interpret to mean that people will eventually abandon inferior government money in favor of Bitcoin because the latter is objectively

431 "Gresham's law?" *Encyclopaedia Britannica*.

better. This theory has by no means been proven, but so far it has not been disproven either.

Ideology and Philosophy

Picture the ideological forces that drove 20th century Communism, Fascism, and the Democratic West's fight against both. Consider systems like Socialism, Theocratism, Libertarianism, and Anarchism. We should not be so naïve as to think that all these ideologies will not always keep re-emerging in various forms. Consider that while a total-privacy cryptocurrency would be an ideal medium of global anarchy and free-run capitalism, collectivists of some sort could also create an entirely transparent, identity-connected mandatory payment system where collectives of other users could vote to automatically re-allocate anyone's savings for the common good.

While 20th century ideological chaos may have involved tanks and nuclear weapons, one might instead consider whether aiming to control the means of value is a more effective strategy either to gain the means by which to subjugate enemies or to neutralize them by making their assets worthless. The anti-fiat maximalist will certainly argue that this has already been going on with our existing forms of money for decades if not generations, with governments effectively stealing individual's savings by way of planned inflation. Despite contemporary trade wars and money manipulation, perhaps more interesting times are to come as governments, ideological movements, corporations, and perhaps religious groups and DAO's join the battlefield at the intersection of ideology and money. The Blockchain Wars may not yet have begun.

The question here is not simple to answer, because it boils down to a foundational question of philosophy. By one definition, the maintenance of the integrity of the system and thus the code-is-law principle, is the ethical maxim of the system itself because it aims to be a sort of "foundation stone" of the digital and blockchain era. If the absolute integrity of this system to itself were corrupted as in the case of creating a software fork when the system functioned against the desire of its creators, then it destroys the ideal of the impersonal math-based machine system of being a sort of immovable reference point according to which everything else can be measured, and therefore "true answers" in the world of Ethereum and blockchain can be derived. This is of critical importance because this "blockchain world" is not anchored to an existing social contract or legal system, and thus functions within a lawless jungle of moral nihilism as far as human actors are concerned. To combat this nihilism on the human level, code-is-law is an attempt to create an anchor or foundation on which to base a universalist morality or ethics (of blockchain), something that in the western world has been attempted only through religion and in the eastern world, barely even with that. With this context we can understand the cypherpunk or at least Bitcoiner ethos as coming from a place of dissatisfaction with moral relativism at least in so much as it relates to money and possession of property, in which the ever-changing social contracts, culture, and laws of human society mean that nothing is permanent, and no absolute answers exist.

A pre-fork brass coin from 2015 celebrating Ethereum. Mintage: 100

Mansa Musa of the Mali Empire depicted in 1375 holding a gold coin. Perhaps the wealthiest person ever, he caused a 10-year recession throughout the ancient world due to his lavish spending while on pilgrimage to Mecca with 60,000 of his men.

CHAPTER 13

Anatomy of an ICO

Its May 2017 and a realization comes to me as I browse coinmarketcap.com from my hammock in my dorm room in China, where I am an exchange student. There are now around a hundred blockchain projects that are each worth over $10 million by market cap, but there is no central place to learn about them! If someone wanted to research a specific project, they had to go to that token team's own Twitter, Facebook, and online discussion threads. This was a problem because the conversations were generally moderated, only those who were particularly optimistic (or had personal interest at stake) were regularly active, and negative comments could be entirely removed. Those who did their due diligence and decided against investing in a project had no venue or reason to air their views, and serious accusations against investment-seeking projects were often simply buried into the ether, so to say. I had an idea, and I sprung to action.

Title: 'SeekingAlpha' for crypto-currency investing Date: May 20th, 2017

Hello everyone,

I'm Elias Ahonen, author of the ~300 page Encyclopedia of Physical Bitcoins and Crypto-Currencies. This is a serious, semi-academic book detailing the history, specs, and other information of almost all 'physical bitcoins', that is, metallic tokens that have a theme relating to crypto-currency. The idea is that these are historical relics of the development of crypto-currencies, and worthy of collection.

Now, I want to do something new. Bitcoin has recently dropped below 50% market cap of digital currencies, and 'altcoins' can no longer be ignored. There are plenty of people analyzing Bitcoin movements and developments, but the 40 billion dollar 'alternative' market is virtually ignored. Though there are bloggers and analysts writing about all kinds of coins, they are often in 'informal' settings like coin-specific forums or Reddit-style message boards. Serious analysis gets buried, and it is difficult for unsophisticated investors to separate the wheat from the chaff.

Soon, I believe we will see a great influx of new traders looking for accurate, comprehensive, and unbiased information on this expanding asset class which now consists of over 700 'coins'. The information should thus have an air of professional analysis as opposed to casual commentary.

In my vision, this site could serve a few functions:

- A 'wiki' style info source with nearly exhaustive information on all coins, including history, relevant individuals, press mentions, clear descriptions of technology, and price history/graphing

- A platform for 'analysts' to publish vetted write-ups on various coins, in a way similar to SeekingAlpha

- The ability for users to view articles based on ticker, and also see rankings by 'resident analysts' who might rate coins as 'sell/buy/strong buy' etc. Users might be able to receive email alerts for articles posted concerning their coins of interest.

> *In practice, this would incorporate many of the functions of CoinMarketCap, though with much more than just numerical information.*
>
> *I am seeking:*
>
> *- Analysts: This is your opportunity to make a name and reputation for yourself as an investment analyst in this space*
>
> *- Researchers: Those with a passion for crypto-coins who can record everything about them into a dedicated wiki*
>
> *- Web dev: someone with the ability to create a website with some of these functions*
>
> *- Anyone else who feels they can contribute*[432]
>
> - Elias Ahonen, 20 May 2017.

I received emails from over a dozen people, and so the planning began. We had conference calls and exchanged emails where everyone commented on each of the topics discussed. Those who failed to comment were not invited to subsequent calls and so on. In days, the team had been whittled down to around six people with expertise in the areas of marketing, research, and finance. We still lacked proper tech talent, so one of the new members, Manuel, found Dave in a cryptocurrency chatroom and pitched the company to him. I called Dave the next day and just 30 minutes into the call invited him to be a co-founder. That same day, a fan of my book offered $50,000 in seed capital for 10% of the company; thus, Token Valley Inc. was born. The imagery was apt: a valley is an ecosystem and community, where birds of the same feather flock together to meet in safety. Token Valley was thus a place where tokens could live, grow, and reach their potential.

---

[432] Ahonen, Elias. "'SeekingAlpha' for crypto-currency investing." *Bitcoin Forum*, 20 May 2017.

> *Our logo symbolizes a valley, with both green grass and pure water for sustenance. The waves in the logo are two mathematical curves used in financial analysis; the green (symbolizing sustenance and growth) is an exponential curve demonstrating growth, whereas the blue (symbolizing water) demonstrates a 'standard distribution' curve. The standard distribution reminds us that most tokens are 'average' and only a few can be remarkable. Above Token Valley stretches a silver rainbow, symbolizing both wealth (through association with precious metals, on which the economy was historically built), and coinage (from which the word 'token' comes from). As a whole the design emphasizes balance and is somewhat similar to a 'loading' icon, reminding us that our work is never truly done. In all this, it is very simple.*
>
> - Token Valley, Jan. 2018.

Adventures in China

I soon found myself in the lavish boardroom of a huge Chinese state-owned infrastructure company whose leader, V, was deeply involved with China's Belt and Road project; the biggest infrastructure and geo-political initiative of the century which involves cementing China's trade routes from Seoul to London, Singapore, across Africa, and everywhere in between by building massive railways, roads, energy pipelines, deep-water ports, and trade alliances. I got here effectively by chance, invited by a then acquaintance, Ray, who had mentored me about the Chinese business environment over the past half-year. The week earlier I had met him for what I thought would be the last time, as I had just finished my studies in China and would soon return to Canada. I told him about ICO's and Token Valley – "*I need you to meet my boss*", was his excited response.

After a 5-minute audience with V in the following week, it became clear that the company wanted to learn more about cryptocurrency and ICO's. This brings me back to the 18-seat mahogany table in the boardroom, where jade vases and paintings adorn the cherrywood paneled walls and the windows reveal a sprawling metropolis of eight million continuing in all directions. I had produced descriptions of the top 30 tokens translated into Mandarin, as well as a document which noted ICO funding targets of increasing magnitudes and the different approaches they would require to be realized. After explaining blockchain, cryptocurrency, and ICO's to the firm's senior managers through a translator, I asked how much money they were looking to raise. The managers spoke in hushed tones and confirmed their numbers on a calculator with the translator: "*up to eight trillion Renminbi.*" I was sure that there had been a translation error, but I had heard right. 1.2 trillion US dollars. Over 1/20th of the US national debt at the time; about ten times the total market cap of all cryptocurrencies. I began to sweat; "*Yes, I have an idea of how we could do it.*"

I returned to my university campus and put off studying for the Macro Economics 101 class that I was taking online; I had real work to do. We created a proposal outlining a strategy by which calculated efficiencies and reductions in carbon emissions broadly related to the Belt and Road strategy could be converted into carbon credits, with these carbon credits then being tradable on the blockchain. Each eCoin (Environment Coin) token would constitute a carbon credit and could thus be easily transferred between companies and even governments. "Mining" would consist of verifiably producing carbon sinks and emission reductions by doing things like planting trees, upgrading to green infrastructure, adopting environmental policies, and investing in green-tech enterprises. Eventually, even individuals could theoretically generate carbon credits by making choices such as taking the bus to work instead of driving. Several innovative companies that offered products with significant environmental benefits were identified as to be bought out by the project, with mass-production moved to China and used to make the project of the century as clean as possible. This would have effectively created an incubator, where companies are brought in and grown in a way that maximizes environmental benefits instead of profit. Through the function of the token, environmental benefits world-wide could theoretically be intrinsically tied to profit, thus making environmental good an end goal rather than a mere outcome of selling an environmentally friendly product.

Three western companies were identified to be purchased in the first stage of the project. One of these was effectively a cement company, whose product could be used to build roads without concrete or crushed rocks, cutting building time by more than half and costs by up to 80%. Even more amazingly, the cement would absorb 1 ton of carbon per square meter of road in the setting process, whereas construction of an equivalent amount of normal road construction results in 4 tons of emissions. Another company involved an environmentally friendly tire sealant which increased the lifespan of tires by 25%, leading to a reduced need for rubber. The final group had devised a system allowing trees and vegetables to be grown anywhere, even the Sahara Desert, by capturing condensation from the atmosphere and delivering it to the roots until they could reach groundwater. This could not only be used to re-plant deserts and protect against erosion, but also transform farming in developing countries and of course remove considerable amounts of carbon from the atmosphere.

Marketing would have to take on a new meaning, as the fund-raising goal given to me in the boardroom was about equivalent to all physical US currency in circulation. The only way for the project to ever take on that kind of scale would be for the Chinese government to make eCoin a major part of its global strategy. Still, the goals of eCoin aligned perfectly with the Chinese government's 2016-2020 five-year plan, which called for developing the green-tech industry and abandoning heavy industry in favor of modern information technology.[433] Buyers would need to be governments and multinational conglomerates instead of ICO speculators, and the tokens would be bought with complex debt and derivative products instead of Bitcoin or Ethereum. My hosts assured me that this was in reach. Truly, reality can be stranger than fiction.

So that was our plan: a value system based on removing carbon from the atmosphere. Though I was discouraged from openly voicing such a radical opinion, I felt I had the seeds of a potentially viable world/reserve currency. If an economy could be based on taking gold from the ground, why could it not be based on taking carbon from the air if doing so was indeed so important for the future of humanity? The proposal for eCoin were made, and I would know by September if the project would be pursued. The company's CEO, who would make the ultimate decision on the project, had gone to lead a group of 40 Chinese officials and businessmen on a diplomacy tour across a dozen countries, and I returned to Canada to write the exam for my basic economics class. I got a C.

"We need you in China in two weeks" came the call. The timing was convenient, as I had just enough time to stop in the US to see the August 21st total solar eclipse with our seed investor. As I flew over the north pole the next day, I began writing a diary: "*This is the first page of a magnificent story; one of ambition, adventure, persistence, and life. I will not disappoint you, dearest reader.*"

The ragtag team I assembled in Beijing only added to the wider cast of characters. On our first evening together, we went for Peking Duck, and were surprised to see a group of local patrons remove their shirts at a nearby table owing to the heat. On one side of me

433 "The 13th Five-Year Plan for Economic and Social Development of the People's Republic of China (2016-2020)." *Central Committee of the Communist Party of China*, 17 Mar. 2016.

there was Dave, a well-dressed, no-nonsense financial programmer from Oregon who dabbled in theoretical physics. On the other was Seth, a long-haired hippy with a beard down to his chest – allergic to suits and who only six months earlier had worked as a line cook in Seattle but was now by all accounts a highly capable writer and researcher. Inspired by the shirtless table beside us, Seth removed his without hesitation. I took on the role of a diplomat, unbuttoning mine so as to bridge the gap between the two co-founders.

In the imposing office tower at the center of the metropolis was the Chinese firm, headed by the solemn and intense V who had made his name negotiating the first joint-venture with the national government to see tens of thousands of soldiers put to work building reinforced tunnels to house military and civilian communications cables running between cities. Always present was the decorated war veteran and wrestler who served as V's bodyguard and driver, as well as Andy, the comedic relief who drank too much and made the most emotional speeches at every meal. Goldfinger was one of the higher-ups who was more rarely present, a savvy businessman who earned his "English name" by turning every project he touched into metaphorical gold. Then there was the head secretary: Lucifer.

Bridging the gap between us and the Chinese side was Ray, a salesman from New Zealand whose intense bushy eyebrows and imposing height accentuated the incredible charisma which made him invaluable to his handlers. He was assisted primarily by Karl, a business developer and translator who had graduated recently and was therefore my age.

And with this cast, began two weeks of presentations to nearly a dozen major investment firms, internet companies, and infrastructure groups. Bankers, financial regulators, and other experts were flown in almost daily to meet with us and share their opinions on the project. I learned a thing or two about business with billionaires in Eastern China, with lunch and dinner being of prime importance. Any presentation or formal discussion was ultimately just a prologue; the dinner table was where relationships were built, and deals were made.

A formal business lunch or dinner will consist of anywhere between 8 and 20 people seated around a large round table with a rotating center, sometimes with 20 courses or more. The host will sit nearest to the main wall and the guests of honor beside him. The most notable course of all is not a meal, but baijiu which, though commonly translated to *white wine*, is anything but wine. Made of grain and usually 45%-65% alcohol by volume, it is stronger than any liquor commonly available in the west. Due to its popularity in China, it is the world's most consumed spirit with over 5 billion liters sold per year. In addition to a teacup, every guest is given a shot-sized miniature wine glass and a much larger jug of about 100-150 ml. As the guest of honor, you will be expected to individually greet almost everyone at the table at some point during the meal and take a shot of baijiu with them. After each shot, you must refill your glass from your jug. There are also speeches, and between two and six people will stand up at various stages of the meal to deliver a speech about either thanking the host, expressing excitement at the new business opportunities at hand, or something similar. Each time a speech is made, everyone at the table takes a shot. As a foreign guest, one is almost certainly expected to make a speech. The speech maker does not need to drink a shot; they are expected to down their entire jug. I once strategically timed my speech for a moment when my jug was only a quarter full, only for Andy to exclaim "*empty*!" and refill my jug to overflowing. What's more, if your co-worker or boss makes a speech and you want to *add weight* to it, you can join them in downing your own jug as well. Even more, some people will come to you two, three or four times to drink shots which you cannot refuse, sometimes even challenging you to finish a jug with them. You can do the math. When all is said and done, everyone is served beers and if you are lucky, noodles. Noodles signify that the host desires your relationship to be long-lasting and interconnected.

After two weeks of near-daily banquets, it was time to move forward. My team received a formal invite from the party secretary of a city at the Russian border in the very north of China. This would become the Belt and Road's gateway to the west. Here, the eCoin project could establish offices and factories. The seed money was already approved; it was go-time. A dozen flights were booked for September 7th. Then the news hit: on September 4th, The People's Bank of China, the central bank, banned ICO's as illegal fundraising. The politically sensitive project had to be scrapped.[434] [435]

My James Bond fantasy of launching a one world eco-currency with V, Goldfinger, and Lucifer never came to be. Perhaps for the best.

Life went on, and Token Valley's experience in ICO planning was suddenly in high demand. The company evolved into a bona fide ICO consultancy, and the team took on clients and whimsical assignments in the UAE, Mexico, UK, New Zealand, China, and Canada. The range of industries interested in ICO type fundraisers became broad, with our roster including real estate, energy, green tech, artificial intelligence, sports betting, online shopping, crypto mining, and even a political party. The contracts themselves were whimsical as well, more often promising a percentage share of tokens or raised cash as opposed to a set retainer. As an industry insider, I here present the inside story of the ICO era.

---

[434] John, Alun, and Josh Ye. "What's an ICO, and Why Does China's Central Bank Ban It?" *South China Morning Post*, 4 Sept. 2017.

[435] "China Bans Initial Coin Offerings Calling Them 'Illegal Fundraising'." *BBC*, 5 Sept. 2017.

Introducing the ICO

IPO's are highly regulated and easily cost over a million dollars in legal expenses and filing fees even though all the laws, regulations, and exchanges are already long-established.

ICO's attempted to circumvent this, offering coins or tokens instead of securities. However, these tokens do not entitle the investors to ownership, control, or profits of the company. Buyers hoped that whatever "system" was developed by the company would create a high demand for the tokens, thus providing a return on the investment.

A good analogy is an amusement park company raising $10,000,000 to build a rollercoaster, with plans to sell tickets for $5 each. They announce an *Initial Ticket (token) Offering* in which investors can purchase tickets for $0.50 each. Once 20,000,000 tickets are sold in the ITO and the roller coaster is built, investors can essentially bring their tickets to the ride and stand in front of the ticket booth, selling their tickets to the riders for less than the planned official price. The longer the investor holds, the theory is, the closer to $5 they can get per ticket as the *weak hands* sell for $0.75, $1.00, or $2.50. In order to fund the start-up and marketing expenses to reach the ITO investors, the company may run a *pre-ITO* or even *pre-pre-ITO* in which they seek funding from their immediate community or contacts at $0.05 per ticket with the suggestion of 100x returns and sometimes even the opportunity to sell some of their "tickets" into the main ITO at $0.50 for a 10x return in mere weeks or months. In the end, theoretically, all the investors are happy with their profits and the company has full debt-free ownership of a rollercoaster.

Many of the early ICO's were known as *Utility Tokens*, meaning that each token was meant to have a useful purpose such as providing future access to or being used to somehow power an online platform. The rollercoaster ticket pre-sale analogy is perfectly fitting for this as the general view was that since these were only a pre-purchase of "app coins" and not investments, they would not fall under the purview of regulators. Whether or not they were "intended" to be investments, they were nevertheless almost always purchased with an investment mindset. Bitcoin, Ethereum, and many others had made massive gains despite most investors doubting them; this emboldened many people to place their bets on highly unconventional ventures.

ICO's were modeled after the legendarily successful crowd-sales of Blockland's early days, namely Ethereum. Companies and teams seeking to raise money worked to imitate these successful projects as closely as possible by ensuring all the right elements were present. Chief among these was the whitepaper which would explain the use and function of the token in question, how many would be created, how many were being sold to ICO investors, and the project timeline. There would also be technical information about how exactly the token would work and what security measures the company was taking. Photos and descriptions of team members would be included along with information of any partners.

These whitepapers would then be read by investors and ICO analysts as if they were investment prospectuses. As ICO's became more common, whitepapers took on a standardized format and were expected to be available in multiple languages including Chinese, Japanese, and Korean. One EU-based client, who rejected Token Valley's bid to facilitate translation efforts, found someone willing to work for tokens, only to find that the translations were simply run through a strange series of translation programs that caused half of the Chinese characters to appear sideways. Despite this public snafu, the project ended up raising millions from the Chinese market. It was a wild time.

The classic 2017 ICO began with a subdued pre-ICO announcement on Bitcointalk.org, by which point a basic whitepaper and team were in place. The generally understood purpose of pre-ICO investment was to fund a large campaign seeking a much larger amount of money. Once some money had been raised, the project would move to a higher level of public visibility and announce an upcoming ICO which would take place in weeks or months. In this run-up to the ICO date, thousands of dollars per day could be spent on marketing and promotions. In some cases, prospective investors had to pre-register or be *whitelisted* before the actual ICO date. The ICO would happen at a specific time, often at which time a large influx of money would be raised within a matter of hours.

Sometimes, ICO teams fed a large portion of their pre-ICO funding through the ICO smart contract so as to make it appear that a larger amount of money was being raised. Some projects sold out entirely, whereas others put out ads to the effect of "*XYZ ICO is now 90% SOLD OUT; board the spaceship to the financial future before it's too late!*" In one case with which I am intimately familiar, the organizers of a token launch party hired models and paid actors to pretend to physically line up and pretend to sign paperwork to buy tokens in hopes of encouraging others to follow suit.

Another talisman for fundraising success was the inclusion of recognizable advisors. Some could be celebrities or experts in business or law, but more important was to have someone who could legitimize the project by serving as a link to the "mystical early days" of Blockland and its related ideologies: a priest or shaman if you will. These ICO advisors were often given large payments or token allocations in return for publicly associating with the project, and the inclusion of especially famous advisors from the frontier days of

Blockland virtually guaranteed that millions would be raised. Vitalik Buterin's blessing was in such high demand that he had to stop posing in photos with others because ICO teams were using such casual group images to suggest a connection to Vitalik even though he had never heard of the project.[436] Though he took on several adviserships, Buterin later admitted to having been naïve in thinking that the projects he agreed to advise were looking for his honest technical input.[437]

This phenomenon of trying to imitate successful cryptocurrency-creation events in order to raise money for arguably less revolutionary and ideological ends was described as an example of a Cargo Cult in a 2019 presentation by "Bitcoin Evangelist" Andreas Antonopoulos. Cargo Cults are a phenomenon on the Pacific Islands, whose primitive and even uncontacted tribes were visited during World War Two by American forces, who used their strategically located islands as air bases in support of the Pacific Theater of the war. This naturally introduced the islanders to heavenly goods such as metal tools, textiles, and even firearms which they collectively came to understand as *cargo*. As the war ended and the airbases were abandoned, the islanders grew desperate to re-summon these mysterious white gods and their fiery metal birds which carried the heavenly gifts of cargo. The islanders reasoned that the cargo-carrying aeroplanes were somehow attracted to the airstrip, and thus worked to imitate the conditions that had previously led to deliveries of cargo. Decades later, researchers arrived on the islands to find the airfields maintained and guarded, with bamboo air traffic control towers manned by islanders with radio headsets made from

---

[436] Vassadar, Reddit.com user. "Vitalik Is Listed as Primal Beast's Advisor, Even Though He Never Heard of Them." *Reddit r/ethereum*, 13 June 2017.
[437] @VitalikButerin (Buterin, Vitalik). "I've stopped advising ICOs years ago when I realized the extent to which advising gets perceived as endorsement (yes, I confess to being quite naive before)." *Twitter*, 28 Nov. 2018.

coconuts. The local shaman was rumored to be a descendant of one of the last airmen.[438]

Another way for ICO's to attract investors was by hosting extravagant events, dinners, and parties. At conferences around the world, ICO teams have hosted select invitees onboard private yachts, themed pirate ships, river cruises, nudist resorts, mansions, and a private underground nuclear bunker. When attending such a conference, one would be constantly profiled as a potential investor, influencer, or collaborator, with all manner of access and perks enjoyed by those deemed worthy. These conferences were mainly sponsored by the blockchain projects themselves, which paid tens of thousands of dollars for brief appearances on one of the many stages. The New York Post described one such 2018 event as "*one of the most ostentatious displays of wealth that New York has seen since the peak of the subprime mortgage boom more than 10 years ago.*"[439] These extravagant weekly gatherings around the world became the lifeblood of the industry as crypto old-timers (anyone having been around for an entire year) would repeatedly bump into their peers. At one such conference in Mexico, my job for five nights was to find the "blockchain nerds" on the dancefloor and invite them to a client's VIP booth where they could network with other conference participants and naturally associate those good experiences with the project that paid their tabs.

Just one person getting a good impression could be worth weeks of work and $100,000 in party spending because the more extravagant the event, the more likely the *big fish* were to attend and thus notice a project, leading to valuable partnerships, influential advisors, and

---

[438] Lawrence, Peter. *Road Belong Cargo: A Study of the Cargo Movement in the Southern Madang.* Manchester U. Pr., 1971.
[439] Dugan, Kevin. "Inside the Crypto Bro Fest that Took Over New York City." *New York Post*, 17 May 2018.

name recognition. Such *crypto whales* were everywhere at conferences like this and due to the deeply casual style of many early blockchain investors, it was difficult to determine whether someone had simply wandered in from a nearby high school or flown in on a private jet. In preparing for one conference my team compiled profiles of perhaps 50 such *whales* (all of the minority who had public identities), memorizing their faces and basic aspects about them so as to identify them from a crowd. Beefy security teams standing nearby offered the occasional hint, and even I had a dedicated bodyguard who at one point forcefully evacuated me out of a nightclub after it became apparent that I was talking with the wrong girl which made a nearby cartel member *extremely* unhappy. My client's VIP booth closed abruptly that night, and our prospective investors were left to their own devices with the leftover liquor.

At the pre-ICO stage, the purpose of these types of events was largely to demonstrate legitimacy and to spoil potential investors, in some cases with the implicit goal of using free alcohol and attractive models to entice investors to sign papers and even complete transactions on the spot. In other cases, the goal was simply to make strategic contacts in the industry. In the active ICO stage, the goals remained about the same, but budgets were higher. After a successful ICO of hundreds of millions raised, the aim became more to assert dominance within the industry by showing off a line of supercars or bringing in famous rappers. As such, these parties served not only as lures for investors but also as grand celebrations for the core teams and early investors. The level of indulgence and general debauchery mixed with legally questionable and sometimes predatory financing by a class of ultra-international jet setting crypto-rich made *The Wolf of Wall Street* seem like a toned-down, family-friendly introduction video to the industry.[440]

Sometimes, funding was raised with methods unorthodox even for the blockchain industry. A friend of mine, who we will call Anne, was hired as an ICO promoter and secured meetings with investors via the dating app Tinder. She would set her location to 1km upon arriving at a blockchain conference, where in her words "*almost everyone was a geeky, single guy with lots of money and an interest in girls who understood blockchain.*" This allowed her to go on several coffee-dates per hour, and she raised about $2 million for the project in just a few weeks. This ICO ended up being a scam and all her dates lost their money. Though it was too late, she informed her investors about the project's fraudulent nature as soon as she became aware of it. This earned her respect from some of these suitors, who went on to support a non-profit she started later. Anne's unconventional style of networking extended beyond the conference floor; she rarely booked accommodations and instead evaluated the "network value" of Tinder matches and suggested LinkedIn contacts, before enquiring about the possibility of spending a night.

Another element of perceived success was the creation of an active and passionate community that could function as a type of cheerleader troupe for prospective investors. These were normally headquartered within Telegram (chat app) discussion groups which were carefully managed by the ICO teams. Teams of community managers could be retained to manage chat groups on a 24/7 basis across multiple languages at significant cost. These community managers would answer questions about the project, and in many

---

440 Chester, Jonathan. "The Blockchain Incredible Party: Extravagant Conferences of Bitcoin Millionaires." *Forbes*, 17 July 2017.

cases quickly banning anyone expressing any level of negativity regarding the ICO. Community events were designed to increase hype, such as meme contests where anyone circulating an original meme about the project would receive free tokens. Companies formed to provide ICO community management services. Sometimes, teams of consultants were paid to design memes that could spread across social media platforms and raise the project's profile. This phenomenon of community cheerleading reached the physical world, with some ICO-launch type events attended by models pretending to be enthusiastic investors. Online or off, it was critical to hype investors up with the idea that they were in on the project and that it was progressing quickly. Those not investing now would soon miss out! This psychological ploy manifests itself in the term FOMO, or fear of missing out.

These telegram groups and other social media channels required regular updates, as mere days of ICO silence could lead many investors to fear that the founders had abandoned the project and run off with the money which was a regular occurrence. Here, regular blog posts and news articles became very important. Specialized cryptocurrency news outlets saw a boom, as ICO's would not only pay for expensive banner ads but also offer six-figure sums for the inclusion of custom sponsored articles. Banner and video ads for ICO's soon permeated the online experience of those targeted as crypto investors, though this reduced after Twitter and then Facebook banned cryptocurrency ads. Still, websites popular with crypto users could charge thousands of dollars per day to display ads.

Influencer marketing also took on a significant role, as YouTube and Twitter personalities with large crypto-investor followings were offered large sums to promote and positively review ICO's. Facebook pages with large amounts of crypto investors could charge significantly for sharing posts, and admin rights to the pages themselves were sometimes bought and sold. Perhaps the most infamous influencer was John McAfee, creator of the antivirus software of the same name, who openly charged $105,000 per tweet.[441] McAfee's weekly promotions of different tokens usually caused significant increases for the targeted tokens as some of his million followers participated in the pumps. Investors with newly acquired crypto fortunes around the world were hungry for new opportunities and ICO's clamored for their attention.

After the Crash

While in 2017 the pre-ICO was merely a stepping-stone towards a mass influx of investment, it became increasingly important as an avenue of funding in early 2018 when the market became more competitive. In 2018, a project seeking to raise $50 million (but truly only needing $5 million) might attempt to raise as much as $10 million in a pre-ICO and consider anything raised in the "actual" ICO to be extra. This way, the investors would buy in on the understanding that they were coming in on the ground floor and that there were masses of investors ready to jump on the project as soon as it was public. This was not always the case due to a saturation of the ICO market in 2018, and these pre-ICO investors were sometimes the only ones ready to pony up.

Security Token Offerings

Around this time, the ICO and ITO fell out of vogue as *Security Tokens* became the next hype. STO became the new buzzword, sidestepping the fictional idea that ICO's and ITO's were not

---

[441] Liao, Shannon. "John McAfee Reveals He Charges $105,000 Per Promotional Cryptocurrency Tweet." *The Verge*, 2 Apr. 2018.

meant to be investments. STO's constituted legitimate offerings of a security and were thus clearly identified as investment vehicles. STO's were less legally problematic and represented a more mature or "normal" approach that was at least somewhat acceptable to regulators.[442] Various obstacles still existed, such as that some jurisdictions would only allow *accredited investors*, people with very high incomes or net worth (who could presumably be trusted to make good decisions, and would not find themselves in financial despair upon losing their investments) to participate in an STO. This was of course quite contrary to the values of many people in the industry; if only the rich could invest in high-risk high-return ventures, how could the average person ever gain wealth and become financially independent? Still, many loopholes existed including allowances for *friends and family*. While ICO/ITO investors could normally be anonymous, STO's generally required the identity and signatures of all investors. The STO became a sort of small-scale IPO, but often for a newly established company without prior history.

Initial Exchange Offerings

A further innovation in blockchain crowdfunding came with the Initial Exchange Offering or IEO. They differed from ICO's and ITO's in that they would be offered by administered directly by an exchange, which would accept investments from its users and list the coin upon launch. This proved more efficient than the ICO as immediate exchange listing was guaranteed and the process to participate was simple provided one had an exchange account. The implied legitimacy of an exchange hosting the offering itself, rather than mere after-the-fact tokens, has also added more structure to

---

[442] Pauw, Chrisjan. "What Is an STO, Explained." *CointeTelegraph*, 21 Feb. 2019.

the token-creation phenomenon. The ICO's revival as the IEO is interesting in that it is now functionally the same as the established IPO, with the main difference being that it exists on a different market. The function is broadly the same: a company submits a proposal to an exchange (stock or crypto), which then accepts or declines it based on its rules and discretion. Once an IEO/IPO is announced, participants on the exchange can then purchase tokens/shares directly from the exchange on the Initial Exchange/Public Offering date. [443]

With IEO's and the increasing institutionalization of exchanges, the crypto-economy has become an increasingly structured alternative to what we might call the established stock-market economy. A new company looking to raise funding from individuals can now consider the benefits and drawbacks of both systems; securities and tokens, and utilize both markets for the advantages they offer. The emergence of the IEO as a fundraising phenomenon, mirroring its mainstream counterpart, suggests that the blockchain economy is increasingly conforming to the image of its predecessor. While the 2017 ICO days may be reflected on as a time of irrationality, it was indicative of excitement regarding the opening of an entirely new market for increasingly legitimate ventures. As the crypto economy functions increasingly like the existing economy, one questions whether the two will naturally intertwine into one standard economy or if they will continue to exist as alternative economic plains. If they remain separate, in what ways can we expect them to interact?'

---

[443] Chavez-Dreyfuss, Gertrude. "Explainer: Initial exchange offerings flourish in crypto market." *Reuters*, 20 June 2019.

Challenging Authority

At the end of the day, tokenized money and securities are not quite so radical as they seem. This is because they do not change concepts of securities like stocks, bonds, or promissory notes. At their core, these are merely pieces of paper whose issuing entities promise that they represent something like equity, debt, voting rights, or gold in a vault. Blockchain tokens are merely a modern-day version of such signed notes, which were themselves improvements upon earlier systems which existed before printing, paper, or even writing. With digital tokens, whose control proves ownership, there is no need for a physical 'token' piece of paper. Long gone are the days when stock exchanges functioned as places where pieces of paper were bought and sold. Today, these papers (which are themselves mere abstractions of ownership) have been abstracted into computerized ledgers assigned to various market participants. These digitalized exchanges which control trading are themselves ruled by government regulations, at least in theory for the supposed benefit of society.

What is radical, is that cryptocurrencies and tokenized securities largely sidestep these institutions which have been built around the regulation of trading. They are a return to a financial wild west; a time before (and possibly after) strong central government and its ability to control, stabilize, and track economic activity. This emerging ability to *go wild west* as a company or investor is notable, because it pits budding entrepreneurs against the current economic-political model. This model depends on its ability to audit companies and individuals as well as regulate and track trading, to collect the taxes by which it functions. Blockchain facilitates the option of financial rebellion for some of society's most critical (in terms of potential tax revenue, innovation, and job creation) members.

If income, bank account balances, stock markets, equity holdings, and dividends can all exist outside of the regulated system, then they cannot be audited, seized, or effectively taxed. If this alternative system gets more user-friendly while it stands the test of time, more and more individuals, companies, and other actors can be expected to seek benefit from it. The greater the degree of this effect, the more it will impact governments' ability to collect taxes based on income and wealth. The severity of this disruption to civilization as we know it can range from inconsequential to extreme. As blockchain technology advances on all its fronts, the political and economic system which we cooked up in the previous millennium may well begin to approach its best-before date.

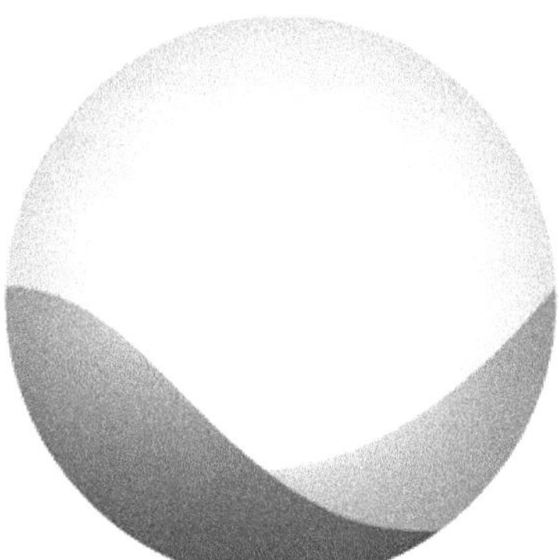

The Token Valley logo in green, blue, and silver.

1903 cartoon describing American industrialist Andrew Carnegie's philanthropy as a shower of gold.

CHAPTER 14

Cryptillionaire Values

There is a charitable side to the Bitcoin world that is quite the polar opposite of its popular image, which consists of rampant scams, dubious investment schemes, overnight millionaires, and excessive parties. As Bitcoin grew from a grass-roots movement based around the idea of giving power back to the people from what many saw as a corrupted system that manipulated the economy without regard for the masses, there was an undercurrent of compassion for those that were seen as having been victimized by that system.

Many early Bitcoiners were concerned with the negative depictions that Bitcoin was receiving in the media, particularly for its connections to drugs, extortion, and allegedly even terrorist activity. To counter these negative images, there were waves of community interest in bettering Bitcoin's public image by demonstrating its utility as a charitable tool. Despite some early Bitcoiners meeting a stereotype of arrogant computer geniuses who more desired to escape the masses rather than help them, there are others who gave their bitcoins away to what they saw as worthy causes. Indeed, many were involved for reasons far beyond mere monetary gain and saw themselves as trailblazers trying to transform the world for the better. Some entrepreneurs and investors entered the industry dreaming of riches, only to have their entire worldviews changed as they found their true calling was to bring positive change with their newfound influence and wealth.

Bitcoin 100

The first charitable Bitcoin venture was founded by Bruno Kučinskasin in November 2011 with the goal of spreading awareness about Bitcoin by donating 100 BTC to charities that agreed to add a Bitcoin donation address or button to their websites.

The idea came about after a failed campaign to get Wikipedia to accept bitcoins in their annual donation drive and a realization that there are hundreds of charities that may be willing to accept Bitcoin donations. The initial goal was to gather a public list of at least 100 (in practice, mostly pseudonymous) people who pledged at least one bitcoin to the collective, with charities then being told that 100 donors were ready to support the charity if they were willing to accept bitcoin. With well-respected charities beginning to accept BTC, it was hoped that Bitcoin would gain legitimacy. Roger Ver, who was among the first to pledge, promising 10 bitcoins per charity "*as long as Bitcoins are under $10 each*"[444], later became a sort of trustee entrusted with the Bitcoin 100 private keys as a safeguard

444 Ver, Roger. "Bitcoin 100: Developed Specifically for Non-Profits." Bitcoin Forum, 22 Nov. 2011.

should any accident befall Mr. Kučinskasin. The result was a resounding success:[445]

> *Since its inception, Bitcoin 100 endowed exactly 83 NPOs, most of which priorly were not familiar with Bitcoin specifically, let alone cryptocurrencies (or blockchain technologies) in general. Those 83 entities... received exactly 681.74286264 BTC valued near-$83K USD when endowed, with 49 of them still accepting bitcoin donations (some now accepting other cryptos) to this very day. The last charity endowed was Northern California DX Foundation over a year ago on July 22, 2015, which brings us to today where Bitcoin 100 still has 109.46781528 BTC in its coffer, the last anonymous [dust] donation of 0.00010168 BTC ($0.05 USD) contributed on January 12, 2016.*[446]
>
> - Bruno Kučinskas, 24 Oct. 2016.

In 2016 it was decided that the charity, which in true Bitcoin fashion had been never officially registered, had succeeded in its purpose and run its course, and that the leftover BTC should be distributed back to the original donors in accordance with their donations. This amounted to ~ 0.368 BTC per 1 BTC donated, which due to the significant BTC rise over four years amounted to a much larger dollar payout than had been originally donated. Perhaps in addition to its legacy as one of the first organizations to help popularize Bitcoin, it is notable for its structure as a *Bitcoin-like* entity that simply *was*, and successfully so, without subscribing to the existing ideas of what a charity should be and how it should be organized from a legal standpoint.

---

[445] Kučinskas, Bruno. "Bitcoin 100: Developed Specifically for Non-Profits." Bitcoin Forum, 22 Nov. 2011.
[446] Kučinskas, Bruno. "Bitcoin 100 Has Run its Course. This is the Rebate Thread." Bitcoin Forum, 24 Oct. 2016.

Sean's Outpost

One of the first successful Bitcoin charity projects was Satoshi Forest – a project of Sean's Outpost. Sean's Outpost, a homeless shelter in Pensacola, Florida, started accepting Bitcoin donations in March 2013 after its director Jason King posted on a Reddit:

> *When we break down cost, it runs about $1.25 to make a bagged lunch and get it delivered to a homeless person. 40 meals = $50. $50 is 1 BTC. Here is your chance to make a guaranteed, phenomenal return on your investment. Donating 1 bitcoin right now will put food in the tummies of 40 homeless people.*[447]
>
> -Jason King, 9 Sept. 2013.

This came at a time when Bitcoin was still effectively unknown to the media, and there was still little clarity amongst early enthusiasts whether Bitcoin was useful for anything in the real word. After seeing 10x monetary gains in the past 12 months from about $5 to $50, many Bitcoin investors were feeling generous, and grew excited by the prospect that feeding the homeless could essentially be a proof of concept for the burgeoning currency. With dozens of homeless people being fed and housed as a result of random people around the world running strange math equations on their computers, it would be difficult for anyone to claim that the Bitcoin experiment had borne no fruit.

With over $30,000 donated in three months, Satoshi's Forest, "*a homeless sanctuary, a place where the downtrodden can find respite from the 'crime' of simply being poor*", was established on a nine acre wooden lot located at 1999 Massachusetts Ave in Pensacola, Florida. The property was purchased for $89,000 with a

---

[447] Buterin, Vitalik. "Sean's Outpost Announces Satoshi Forest, Nine-Acre Sanctuary for The Homeless." *Bitcoin Magazine*, 9 Sept. 2013.

monthly mortgage payment of $600; the entirety of which the mortgage firm agreed to accept in BTC. On this property, King developed a project called Bithouses, which were essentially trailers that residents could live in and eventually take with them if they wanted to move out.

> *We envision Satoshi Forest morphing into an organic farm/makerspace with a Summer Camp feel. Apart from the obvious of growing food to further our operations, learning how to farm is an invaluable skill and one that is slowly being taken away by the corporate food monopolies. There's something damn near magical about showing someone how to plant and grow their own food. There's not much more pride to be had then eating food you grew. Construction/Makerspace is the same, it's showing someone that they have abilities to turn a stack of raw materials into something of value.*[448]
>
> -Jason King, 9 Sept. 2013.

Indeed, Satoshi Forest aligned perfectly with the values of the early Bitcoin community. This becomes even more apparent when we learn of the original motivation behind the concept and Mr. King's legal battle with the Pensacola Municipality. The city was aiming to institute ordinances which made it illegal to "camp" anywhere whether with a tent or even a simple blanket, or to use any public bathroom to wash, shave, or prepare food or drink. This was widely seen as an attempt to criminalize the very act of being homeless or poor, and Mr. King once confirmed that he had "*been told that if I bring someone freezing [while sleeping outside in the winter] a blanket, I will be aiding and abetting in a crime.*" As this would strike many people as wrong, it was the perfect injustice for the Bitcoin community to fight against.

[448] Buterin, Vitalik. "Sean's Outpost Announces Satoshi Forest, Nine-Acre Sanctuary for The Homeless." *Bitcoin Magazine*, 9 Sept. 2013.

The average Bitcoin user was at this time overwhelmingly libertarian and detested what they understood to be government overreach into people's freedom as well as a system that demanded people to fit into its established structures. Bitcoin itself did not fit into society's mold nor ask its permission, so it was a certain poetry that the shunned and misfit currency became a protector of the homeless. Around Thanksgiving, Bitcoin 100's Bruno Kučinskas drove all the way from Illinois to camp with Satoshi Forest's residents and cook turkeys for them in a pilgrim-themed event.[449] While this might seem nonsensical from a mere economic perspective of helping the homeless, it is important to remember that there was always a larger goal: the building of legitimacy, the gathering of positive publicity, and the spreading of Satoshi's message. This is clear evidence that Bitcoin and the tight-knit community around it circa 2013 was best classified as a movement, be it a religious, political or something else entirely.

Sean's Outpost also founded BITHOC, The Bitcoin Homeless Outreach Center, to expand its operations. Housing food pantries, donated clothing storage, and later a thrift shop built and staffed by paid homeless people, BITHOC became another beacon of positive light for the Bitcoin world. Mr. King remained active in the Bitcoin community, working on methods by which to publicly account for the charity's spending and even helping to develop a food-sharing app to combat the growing amount of food insecurity in the United States. With 733 BTC in donations from both individuals and companies in the first year, Sean's Outpost served 30,000 meals and distributed 1,000 blankets.

Some of these donations were however more notable than others. During filming of ESPN's *College GameDay* college football show

[449] Kučinskas, Bruno. "Pilgrim Kālua (theme): First Thanksgiving at Satoshi Forest." Bitcoin Forum, 9 Nov. 2013.

on November 30th, 2013, a student in a large crowd held up a large sign featuring a QR code and "HI MOM SEND [BTC]." The image was shared across the internet and within hours the student received over 100 transactions adding up to 23 BTC which were worth around $25,000 at the time. Days later, he sent 11.125 BTC of this to Sean's Outpost.[450]

Another curious donation came 2 months later on January 21st 2014, when a Reddit user named BitcoinDPRK sent 0.103 BTC to the charity from North Korea, in what was likely the first use of blockchain in the country, saying "*What better use case of bitcoin than to send money internationally from what is probably the most restrictive country in the world? And what better recipient of that money than /u/SeansOutpost? With bitcoin, borders mean nothing!*"[451] The Redditor explained that he was in the country to see basketball player Dennis Rodman play, and proved his location with a photo of a piece of paper with his username and date with the Pyongyang Schoolchildren's Palace in the background. Like some sort of missionary spreading the revelation of Satoshi, he told about giving paper wallets with small amounts of BTC to each of the local guides he encountered.[452] [453]

To raise more money for the growing charity, Jason King embarked on a 5,150 km Bitcoin Marathon from Miami to San Francisco, with wife and kids following behind in a branded motor home that

---

450 Bitcoinsignguy, Reddit.com user. "Here's the Famous ESPN Sign! I'm the Bitcoin Sign Guy. I Keep Losing My Throwaway Account Passwords. I'm Going to Be Interviewed Tomorrow by Someone Big. What Questions Would You Ask so I Can Be Ready? I'll Tweet the Interview Time/Place so You Can Tune in. Proof in URL." *Reddit r/Bitcoin*, 3 Dec. 2013.
451 Hong, Kaylene. "North Korea May Have Seen Its Very First Bitcoin Transaction This Month." *The Next Web*, 21 Jan. 2014.
452 BitcoinDPRK, Reddit.com user. "The First Bitcoin Transaction in North Korea." *Reddit r/Bitcoin*, 7 Jan. 2014.
453 Hong, Kaylene. "North Korea May Have Seen Its Very First Bitcoin Transaction This Month." *The Next Web*, 21 Jan. 2014.

was donated by a start-up and would go on to be used for meal deliveries.[454] Over nearly four months he averaged about 50 km per day and paid for most of his expenses using gift cards purchased with BTC. He stopped at Bitcoin meetups in various cities along the way and managed to raise 200 BTC, valued around $120,000 by the time he arrived in San Francisco on June 7th, 2014. Upon arrival, he was greeted by a crowd that included representatives of other Bitcoin charities including BitGive Foundation's Connie Gallippi; Bitcoin Not Bomb's Davi Barker; and Vitalik Buterin, who had written about Sean's Outpost in his *Bitcoin Magazine* nearly a year earlier. Among the more memorable running days was when he ran down a busy road in the middle of a swamp; a story he told WIRED: "*I was basically running through traffic above swamps and alligators. It was in the middle of nowhere, so I couldn't turn around and go back.*" To pass time, he listened to audiobooks by Neal Stephenson, a science fiction author who, according to King, predicted Bitcoin back in the 90's.[455]

North Korean Weed Adventures

Dennis Rodman himself went on to make crypto headlines three years later, when in June 2017 he headed back to North Korea while representing PotCoin, a "*community-based cryptocurrency for legalized marijuana*". Based in Canada, the currency was created to help give farmers and dispensaries in the legal marijuana industry access to banking, which is essentially inaccessible to US

[454] Wong, Joon Ian. "Sean's Outpost Founder Plans Ultra-Marathon to Raise 1,000 BTC." *CoinDesk*, 12 Jan. 2014.
[455] Hernandez, Danila. "The Man Who Ran Across America to Raise Bitcoins for the Homeless." *Wired*, 11 June 2014.

companies due to the full prohibition at the federal level.[456] To support the growing legal cannabis market, PotCoin developed a PotChain Block Explorer, a PotChain API, and PotWallet API. The plant is seemingly legal in North Korea, and a pound of "leaf tobacco" is reported to sell for $3 there.[457] Rodman is apparently a close friend and confidant of Supreme Leader Kim Jong Un, who happens to be a basketball fan. In addition to his close relationship with Kim, he was on the cast of Seasons 8 and 13 of Donald Trump's *Celebrity Apprentice* in 2009 and 2013, respectively. Donning a PotCoin shirt on the eve of his departure to the DPRK, Rodman appears in a hotel room video as a PotCoin team member sitting beside him declares that:

> *He is the only man to have a relationship and be friends with both [Kim Jong Un and Donald Trump], and he's going there tomorrow to try to bridge the gap and bring peace and dialogue between both nations, and PotCoin is the reason why we are going out there!*[458]
>
> - PotCoin spokesman, 13 June 2017

PotCoin sent Rodman on a second trip in December of the same year, this time on a multi-country "Peace Mission" in Asia. Before heading to North Korea, he met with locals and military personnel in the US Territory of Guam, which was suffering from decreased tourism due to North Korea's ongoing threats of a nuclear strike on the island's military base. Wearing a PotCoin shirt featuring a smiling and fur-coat wearing Rodman in between Kim Jong Un and Donald Trump, flanked by the flags of both nations and the word *UNITE* through the middle, he told media that:

---

[456] Cuthbertson, Anthony. "What Is Potcoin? Marijuana Cryptocurrency Flies Dennis Rodman To Trump-Kim Summit." *Independent*, 11 June 2018.

[457] Robinson, Melia. "North Korea Has Been Branded as a 'weed-smoker's Paradise' - but the Truth Is More Complicated." *Business Insider*, 6 Apr. 2017.

[458] PotCoin. "PotCoin Sends Dennis Rodman Back to North Korea." *PotCoin*, 13 June 2017.

> *I try and stay out of it. I try to just be his friend, and play sports, and that's my whole thing.... To me, he does not want to have war ... it may sound like that on the news, but I see that Donald Trump and him ... it's more like two big kids deciding who's the toughest.*
> *I don't know why he would, in my eyes, remotely even think about bombing anything in the world. I've never heard him say anything like that to my face, and we talk all the time.*[459]
>
> \- Dennis Rodman, 7 Dec. 2017.

A full year after starting with PotCoin, Rodman was in Singapore for the historic June 2018 meeting between the US and North Korean leaders, this time wearing a PotCoin t-shirt with the slogan *Peace Starts in Singapore* along with Trump's signature *Make America Great Again* red baseball hat.[460] It is unclear if Rodman met the two leaders together or what role, if any, he played in bringing them together. Though a spokesman for PotCoin told *The Washington Post* that "*We at PotCoin definitely believe that Dennis Rodman deserves the Nobel Peace Prize jointly with President Trump and the Marshal Kim Jong Un*", the US State Department clarified that "*we have no comment on Dennis Rodman's private travel. He's not a representative of the U.S. government.*"[461]

The summit itself made history, but what we may never know is whether PotCoin played a role as a global bringer of peace, merely used the situation as an elaborate marketing stunt, or something in between. In the month leading up to Rodman's first trip, PotCoin's market capitalization spiked from about $15 million to over $35 million before returning to previous levels, only to rocket from $26 million to $105 million in the week of Rodman's December peace

---

459 Tomas, Jojo Santo. "Rodman Visits Guam, Says North Korean Leader Doesn't Want War." *Pacific Daily News*, 7 Dec. 2017.
460 Deahl, Dani, and Shannon Liao. "Why Dennis Rodman Promoted Potcoin at a North Korea Summit." *The Verge*, 12 May 2018.
461 Hudson, John. "A Cryptocurrency for Marijuana Is Backing Dennis Rodman's Trip to Singapore." *The Washington Post*, 7 June 2018.

mission.[462] The media hype around his visit to the Singapore summit six months later produced only a modest peak of $23 million, followed by a steady decline to around $3 million by the end of the year.

The Pineapple Fund

One of the most impactful Bitcoin philanthropists is an anonymous person known only as Pine, who gave away over $55 million to 60 charities. On December 14th, 2017, he/she used Reddit to announce that he/she was giving away 5057 BTC, which represented the majority of his/her holdings.

> *I remember staring at bitcoin a few years ago. When bitcoin broke single digits for the first time, I thought that was a triumphant moment for bitcoin. I watched and admired the price jump to $15.. $20.. $30.. wow! Today, I see $17,539 per BTC. I still don't believe reality sometimes. Bitcoin has changed my life, and I have far more money than I can ever spend. My aims, goals, and motivations in life have nothing to do with having XX million or being the mega rich. So I'm doing something else: donating the majority of my bitcoins to charitable causes. I'm calling it The Pineapple Fund... Yes, donating ~$86 million worth of bitcoins to charities :)"*[463]
>
> \- Pine, 13 Dec. 2017.

We know little about Pine, other than he or she was a very early Bitcoin adopter who "*decided to mine/buy/trade some magical internet tokens*" when bitcoin's entire market cap was far below $55 million. At over 5,000 BTC, the fund was among the 250 largest bitcoin holdings in a single address at the time, and Pine realised

---

[462] Langone, Alix. "PotCoin Is Spiking After Dennis Rodman Promoted the Cryptocurrency in Singapore. Here's How Much Richer You'd Be If You Had Bought It Yesterday." *Money*, 12 June 2018.

[463] PineappleFund, Reddit.com user. "I'm donating 5057 BTC to charitable causes! Introducing the Pineapple Fund." *Reddit r/Bitcoin*, 13 Dec. 2017.

that "*the expectation shattering returns of bitcoin over many years has lead to an amount far more than I can spend.*" When asked where the name *Pineapple Fund* came from, Pine simply said that he/she really liked pineapples and that they "*cotain high levels of bromelain, which has been shown to be an effective anti-inflammatory, muscle relaxant, and digestive aid.*"[464] I suppose that is as good a reason as any.

Over 10,000 applications poured in over the next several months. Pine selected 60 of these to receive donations between $50,000 and $5,000,000 spanning medical research, education, poverty reduction, human rights, open-source software, environmental conservation, and psychedelic therapy. Altogether 5,104 BTC was sent to charities, amounting to $55,750,000 when calculated according to the times the donations were made. With each donation announcement, Pineapple Fund's website included links to the relevant bitcoin transactions to prove the donations. As per my analysis of these transactions, most charities quickly moved the bitcoins they received to exchanges. This suggests that the majority of them converted their BTC to fiat without much delay, which was beneficial considering the market value of Bitcoin dropped significantly in the following months.

The three largest donations of $5 million went to Give Directly, HOPE Open Medicine Foundation, and MAPS: Multidisciplinary Association for Psychedelic Research.

Give Directly - 5m

In addition to functioning as a more general charity supporting those in extreme poverty with cash, Give Directly is conducting a massive Universal Basic Income (UBI) trial in Kenya. The hope is

[464] pineapplefund.org (no longer available)

that it will lay the academic groundwork to institute Basic Income into the economic policies of countries around the world. According to the charity, the fullest form of Basic Income is unconditional and irrevocable, universal to all members of society, enough to cover all basic needs, and guaranteed for life. Though this could take various forms, the core idea is that society should guarantee a minimum standard of living for everyone. Give Directly counts Economists Milton Friedman and Friedrich Hayek as supporters of the idea on the basis that negative income tax could be used to both protect individual freedom and simplify the government welfare system. Dr. Martin Luther King Jr. has also supported the idea of a guaranteed income floor to replace "*indirect*" and "*piecemeal and pygmy*" anti-poverty policies.

The experiment that Give Directly is conducting is composed of 21,000 people in 190 villages receiving cash transfers for up to 12 years. The dataset consists of four groups of villages as follows:

- Long-term basic income: 40 villages with recipients receiving roughly $0.75 (nominal) per adult per day, delivered monthly for 12 years.
- Short-term basic income: 80 villages with recipients receiving the same monthly amount, but only for 2 years.
- Lump sum: 70 villages with recipients receiving the same amount (in net present value) as the short-term basic income group, but all up front as a lump sum.
- Control group: 100 villages not receiving cash transfers.

The goal of the research is to assess the impacts of the various forms of UBI regarding various metrics such as economic status (income, assets, standard of living), time use (work, education, leisure, community involvement), risk-taking (migrating, starting businesses), gender relations (especially female empowerment), and aspirations and outlook on life.

Basic Income is a divisive idea amongst Bitcoin enthusiasts, with both optimistic supporters and fervent opposers but not much in between. For those in support, I don't think this stems from Bitcoin per se but is, like the support of Bitcoin itself, caused in part by a belief in an approaching global crisis as technologies like Artificial Intelligence begin to increasingly supplant modern workers in practically all fields. Just as Bitcoin has removed international barriers when it comes to money transfers, the increasing efficiency by which people in poor and middle-income countries can attain and then transfer their skills & knowledge is resulting in the removal of the economic inefficiencies that currently allow for comparatively high standards of living in 1st world countries. I hold no doubt that these trends of techno-globalization will result in far-reaching instability, of which France's Yellow Vests Movement may well be among the first. If basic income were ever implemented, it may well go hand-in-hand with other radical economic models such as cryptocurrencies with unconventional coin-creation protocols.[465]

HOPE Open Medicine Foundation - 5m

OMF is focused on researching and improving the available care for ME/CFS (Myalgic Encephalomyelitis / Chronic Fatigue Syndrome), which usually goes undiagnosed and causes people to intermittently or constantly feel debilitating tiredness despite having enough sleep. This makes work, social activity, and even clear thinking exceedingly difficult. OMF communicated directly with patients in over 100 countries, and its researchers are searching for biomarkers which may be used to find an eventual cure. This matter does not appear to have a relation to the blockchain world; one might speculate that Pine suffered from such issues personally.[466]

---

[465] givedirectly.org
[466] omf.ngo

MAPS: Multidisciplinary Assc. for Psychedelic Research - 5m

MAPS' main work is to develop "*medical, legal, and cultural contexts for people to benefit from the careful uses of psychedelics and marijuana.*" Their most ground-breaking work is a $26 million Food and Drug Administration (FDA) trial to make MDMA an approved prescription medication for PTSD and emotional damage caused by things like sexual assault, war, and violent crime. One of the stated advantages is that unlike most drugs, which are needed for years, this treatment is reportedly needed only a few times. Other studies include pilot programs relating to the effects of LSD, Ibogaine, Ayahuasca, and Marijuana as psychiatric treatments for PTSD, palliative care, and drug addiction.[467]

When considering MAPS' subject matter, one is reminded again of Potcoin, Silk Road, and other industry anecdotes. There appears to be a certain correlation between cryptocurrency and drugs that goes deeper than the mere utility of using one to acquire another. Perhaps this is because both subjects – psychoactive drugs and cryptocurrencies, have a shared background of being underground and even subversive elements outside the approval of authorities. Just as official attitudes towards cryptocurrencies are changing as institutions begin to embrace the technology instead of fearing it, cultural and legal trends around the world are shifting towards the acceptance of both medical and recreational use of certain drugs. It makes sense to think that the type of person willing to question the status-quo and basic idea of money and trailblaze with cryptocurrency might well also support comparable developments in other areas.[468] It is also worth noting that the West Coast tech elite, who over-represent the blockchain world, are famously liberal with

---

[467] maps.org

[468] Griffith, Erin. "At This Crypto Event, the Attendees Really Were High." *Wired*, 6 Mar. 2018.

their attitudes toward drugs. One consultant from the region admitted that "*I don't know anyone under 35 in crypto that doesn't do drugs.*" The industry's fast-paced lifestyle combined with new money, youth, and an embrace of experimentation certainly support this co-occurrence.

Other Pineapple Charities

In addition to these major contributions, 57 other charities received disbursements ranging from $50,000 to $2,000,000. Researching the work of each of these charities has been a journey for me, and I am amazed by the breadth of their work. Especially inspiring to me is the futuristic nature of many of these projects as they anticipate needs too abstract and far in the future for profit-oriented businesses to tackle. I strongly encourage every reader to read more about the charities that interest them most and contribute, however little, to one of them in honor of the Pineapple Fund. They are part of the book because they are a window into the values and worldview of a very early Bitcoin investor, and seeing that the Bitcoin world rallied around Pine's efforts suggests that these values were not Pine's alone, but a collective expression of early Bitcoin spirit. It is likely that just like Pine, each reader will find some of the charities listed here utterly fascinating and worthy.

Watsi - 2m

Emphasizing advanced technology, people first, and radical transparency, Watsi is "*building technology to finance universal healthcare by crowdfunding surgeries and administering health insurance systems.*" Through its crowdfunding, patients in need around the world share their stories and receive funding for their surgeries. It has also developed Meso, a "*suite of mobile and web applications that manage enrollment, identification, claims submission, claims processing, and reporting*" for health insurance administration.[469]

The Water Project - 1m

This charity installs and monitors water pumps across sub-Saharan Africa. Monitoring over 1250 pumps with 225 added in 2018, it ensures their continued functionality to provide water security to over 400,000 people daily. According to the charity, $1,000,000 provides continuous water for nearly 30,000 people. All pump locations are tagged through Google Maps along with functionality stats.[470]

BitGive - 1m

Founded in 2013, BitGive was the first Bitcoin non-profit in the United States. They have collaborated with groups such as Save the Children and Medic Mobile to support projects from natural disaster relief in Nepal, Philippines, and Alabama, to building wells in Africa and homes in Brazil. BitGive has successfully "*built a positive philanthropic representative organization for the Bitcoin and Blockchain industry, bridging the gap between an innovative technology and its practical applications for nonprofits and humanitarian work.*" Indeed, it is clear from the charity's 5-year report that its early donors include many early blockchain companies and adopters.

BitGive has done more than just distribute aid. It's Bitcoin Charity 2.0 Initiative aims to bring the benefits of blockchain technology directly to charities around the world. It has developed *GiveTrack*,

[469] watsi.org
[470] thewaterproject.org

which is a donation platform through which non-profits can share their financials and project outcomes in real-time for maximum transparency and accountability.[471]

Electronic Frontier Foundation - 1m

The EFF has long been a favorite among the Bitcoin community and began accepting BTC in 2013. "*The Electronic Frontier Foundation is the leading nonprofit organization defending civil liberties in the digital world. Founded in 1990, EFF champions user privacy, free expression, and innovation through impact litigation, policy analysis, grassroots activism, and technology development. We work to ensure that rights and freedoms are enhanced and protected as our use of technology grows.*"[472]

OpenBSD - 50k

OpenBSD supports development and maintenance of free software based on the OpenBSD operating system. This security-focus is especially useful for developing IT security systems and has been in use since 1995.[473]

Sens Research Foundation - 2m

SEN's goal is to "*help build the industry that will cure the diseases of aging.*" The core belief is that the symptoms of aging caused by damage to the body's cells and tissues can be repaired through regenerative medicine. SENS stands for Strategies for Engineered Negligible Senescence, which "*refers essentially to a condition in which senescence (the progressive slide into sickness and frailty*

[471] bitgivefoundation.org
[472] eff.org
[473] openbsdfoundation.org

with age) is negligible - that is, so small as to not merit consideration." The goal is thus to give humans the same traits as lobsters and rockfish: that their bodies would simply not deteriorate with age.[474]

Charity: Water - 2m

All donations go directly to people brining clean water to those in need, with the location of each pump viewable through an interactive world map along with photos and detailed information. This charity has directly funded almost 30,000 water projects in 26 countries, giving clean water to 8,500,000 people.[475]

Mona - 1m

Mona funds grassroots educational initiatives around the world to educate children, with an emphasis on providing opportunities to women and girls. Since 1999, Mona has enrolled over 100,000 students and directly impacted over 250,000 people through provisions of tools, resources, and education materials.[476]

NEW STORY - 2m

NEW STORY is pioneering 3D printed homes; a ~700 square foot home can be constructed in less than 24h for a budget of around $4000. All money received goes "*directly to hiring locals, buying local materials, and building [homes]*" because the charity believes that that no human should have to live in survival mode without a roof over their head.[477]

---

474 sens.org
475 charitywater.org
476 monafoundation.org
477 newstorycharity.org

Internet Archive - 2m

This non-profit has an enormous mission: to provide "Universal Access to All Knowledge." They are building "*the digital library of the future - a place where anyone can go to learn and explore our shared human experience from books, web pages, audio, television and software. Forever.*" The current archive includes 330 billion web pages, 1.6 million TV news programs, 180,000 live concerts, 200,000 software programs, and over 20 million books.[478]

Pencils of Promise - 1.25m

Pencils for Promise is a literacy-focused organization that builds and supports schools in Ghana, Guatemala, and Laos. They use a data-driven method of tracking the reading fluency of their 98,000 students to measure positive impact across the 500 schools they have built.[479]

Green Steps - 100k

Green Steps has created an app to arrange community clean-up efforts as well as reward people, with up to $30 a month in gift cards, for picking up litter.[480]

PTSD - 50k

Professional Transformation Sports Development uses outdoor sports to help US veterans "*overcome personal struggles attained*

[478] archive.org
[479] pencilsofpromise.org
[480] greenstepschatt.com

through the military and break the habits that hold them back from successfully reintegrating back into civilian life."[481]

Quill - 1m

According to a 2011 study by the US Department of Education, 76% of eighth grade students are not proficient writers. Writing ability is critical for building critical thinking and producing new knowledge. By offering free online tools, Quill's goal is to help 30 million K-12 students in the US who struggle with writing to improve their skills.[482]

Possible - 1m

After the 2015 Nepal earthquake, Possible has developed an integrated electronic health record system to optimize care between the hospital and home, delivered through its 350 staff. They "*provide over 150,000 hospital visits and conduct over 8,000 surgical procedures annually.*"[483]

Hearts & Homes for Refugees - 100k

This grassroots humanitarian group that offers its "*talents, time, and expertise to identify and utilize resources that will offer hope and help to refugees, in keeping with the time-honored American practice of welcoming newcomers.*"[484]

[481] ptsdveteranathletes.com
[482] quill.org
[483] possiblehealth.org
[484] heartsandhomesforrefugees.com

The Focus Foundation - 1m

This foundation supports works to "*promote awareness, increase early detection, and to discover innovative treatments for recovery*" related to neurogenetic X & Y Chromosomal Variation Disorders which can cause learning disabilities like dyslexia and ADHD in untreated children.[485]

Erowid - 500k

Erowid works with medical, academic, and experiential experts to curate information relating to psychoactive substances because they "*believe that truth, accuracy, and integrity in publishing information about psychoactives will lead to healthier and more balanced choices, behaviors, and policies around all psychoactive medications, entheogens, herbs, and recreational drugs.*"[486]

OpenStreetMap - 250k

This project "*creates and distributes free geographic data for the world. We started it because most maps you think of as free actually have legal or technical restrictions on their use, holding back people from using them in creative, productive, or unexpected ways.*"[487]

Software Freedom Conservancy - 250k

"*Software Freedom Conservancy... helps promote, improve, develop, and defend Free, Libre, and Open Source Software (FLOSS) projects. Conservancy provides a non-profit home and infrastructure for FLOSS projects. This allows FLOSS developers*

485 thefocusfoundation.org
486 erowid.org
487 openstreetmap.org

to focus on what they do best – writing and improving FLOSS for the general public – while Conservancy takes care of the projects' needs that do not relate directly to software development and documentation."[488]

Neural Archives Foundation - 250k

This foundation stores brains in cryogenic tissue banking facilities, with the goal to "*preserve as much as possible the information content of the brain that includes identity and memory which is encoded by the vast interconnected network of cellular processes that comprise the human cerebral cortex.*" The technology to decode information in these frozen brains is currently being worked on, and NAF believes that eventually, "*whole brain simulations will... [allow] the information to be accessed. This will then become a slice of human history as seen through the eyes of an individual alive now.*" In addition to currency, NAF accepts donations of brains and other organs.[489]

Wings For Conservation - 250k

WfC operates in the Republic of Chad to protect elephants from poachers, by flying surveillance missions to monitor elephant herds and look for signs of poachers; the information is then relayed to local field rangers who follow up. It is worth mentioning this donation is enough to cover 2 year's budgets for 25 monthly flight hours.[490]

---

488 sfconservancy.org
489 neuralarchivesfoundation.org
490 wingsforconservation.org

Talk Life - 50k

Talk Life is a mobile app that creates a peer support group around each user.[491]

Reagent project - 100k

This project matches under-resourced researchers around the world with excess scientific equipment and goods sitting in US labs. They believe that science provides health, industry, and solutions to problems; however, modern science requires expensive equipment that is not always available. #givescience[492]

Wild Me - 250k

Wild Me has developed a system by which tourists' geotagged photos of animals are automatically sorted and analyzed with artificial intelligence. This is useful for wildlife researchers to gather and make sense of data much faster than otherwise possible.[493]

Empower Network - 100k

" *We provide confidential support for people facing tough, non-legal work situations. Anyone in the U.S. can immediately connect with a vetted and trained peer counselor via text or web chat.*"[494]

The Apache Software Foundation - 1m

The ASF supports nearly 8,000 people who "*collaborate to develop freely available enterprise-grade software, benefiting millions of users worldwide.*" This includes over 350 open-source projects relating to HTTP, data security, spam protection, search functions,

---

491 talklife.co
492 thereagentproject.org
493 wildme.org
494 empowerwork.org

and a myriad of other technologies upon which our digital world is built. Because of their importance, Apache believes they should be freely available.[495]

OpenMRS - 1m

OpenMRS is building an OPEN-source Medical Record System that can create and store complex personal medical records and be customized in creative ways, allowing for large-scale tracking of health trends across a population. The software is now in use across Africa, in various Asian countries, and the USA.[496]

Justice and Care - 1m

J&C has rescued 4,795 victims of human trafficking, and its work has led to over 1,000 prosecutions and 100+ convictions of modern-day slavers primarily relating to sweatshops, brothels, and domestic labor exploitation in India and Bangladesh. It offers a 3-year after-care program and has trained about 50,000 front-line professionals including police, judges, and community leaders to better understand issues of human trafficking.[497]

Enthea - 50k

"*Enthea is a research project assessing the hypothesis that the world would be better if more people had experiences with psychedelics... Our current view is that increasing access to high-quality psychedelic experiences is an impactful project.*"[498]

---

495 apache.org
496 openmrs.org
497 justiceandcare.org
498 enthea.net

The Organ Preservation Alliance - 2m

The OPA is working to advance and proliferate technology that will allow for organs and tissues to be preserved for extended lengths of time in between living hosts. While traditional organ transplants are a race against time in both waiting for a donor and then transferring the organ in mere hours, new technologies could allow for hearts, livers, and even brains to be stored for months or years. Among their subjects of study are animals with the ability to enter suspended animation.[499]

Wiki Edu - 500k

" *Wiki Education connects higher education to Wikipedia, ensuring that the world's most read source of information is more representative, accurate, and complete.*" They create educational partnerships with university faculties to expand Wikipedia's scope and teach faculty how to add their knowledge to the world's most popular reference work.[500]

The Indigo Project - 50k

The Indigo Project is a practice of over a dozen Sydney psychologists who run self improvement workshops and individual sessions. Their goal is to break the stigma behind mental health and approach it from a familial and loving perspective, as opposed to a doctor-patient model.[501]

---

499 organpreservationalliance.org
500 wikiedu.org
501 theindigoproject.com.au

Replate - 250k

40% of food produced in the US gets thrown away. "*Replate matches extra food with communities in need. Our platform enables charities and hungry individuals to recover food donations based on their needs and location.*" People and businesses with extra food use an app to summon food rescuers who drop the food off to families, communities, or non-profits in need.[502]

Methuselah Foundation - 1m

With the mission of "*Making 90 the new 50 by 2030*", the foundation seeks to accelerate breakthroughs in longevity by incubating relevant businesses, funding cutting-edge research, and support prizes such as the Methuselah Mouse Prize (M-Prize) for life-extension advancements.[503]

Experience Camps - 500k

"*Experience Camps are free one-week camps for boys and girls who have experienced the death of a parent, sibling, or primary caregiver. It's a place where kids can laugh, cry, play, create, remember the person who died, or forget the grief that weighs them down.*"[504]

Free Software Foundation - 1m

"*As our society grows more dependent on computers, the software we run is of critical importance to securing the future of a free society.*" FSF's mission is to promote the freedom of all computer

---

[502] replate.org
[503] mfoundation.org
[504] experience.camp

users and the rights of all software users. "Free software is about having control over the technology we use in our homes, schools and businesses, where computers work for our individual and communal benefit, not for proprietary software companies or governments who might seek to restrict and monitor us."[505]

ACLU (American Civil Liberties Union) - 2m

"*For almost 100 years, the ACLU has worked to defend and preserve the individual rights and liberties guaranteed by the Constitution and laws of the United States.*"[506]

Women Who Tech - 250k

WWT's mission is to "*bring together talented and renowned women breaking new ground in technology to transform the world and inspire change.*" They do this by breaking down barriers to funding, creating a network of start-ups founded by women, and highlighting the large exits that these businesses can have.[507]

Blueprint - 50k

"*Each year, teams of five [UC Berkeley] students work with non-profit organizations on projects to help them better serve their communities.*"[508]

Canine Therapy Corps - 250k

"*Since 1991, Canine Therapy Corps' volunteers and certified therapy dogs have been serving the Chicago metropolitan area, working*

505 fsf.org
506 aclu.org
507 womenwhotech.org
508 calblueprint.org

with health care, education, and social services professionals and helping people recover from physical and emotional trauma."[509]

Institute for Justice - 2m

"*The Institute for Justice is the National Law Firm for Liberty. IJ litigates to limit the size and scope of government power and to ensure that all Americans have the right to control their own destinies as free and responsible members of society.*" In addition, they support grassroots activism to train US citizens to be "*advocates for free speech, economic liberty, educational choice, property rights and liberty in their communities and beyond.*"[510]

Treesisters - 500k

Treesisters is planting over 200,000 trees per month in countries that are both in need of tree cover and lack opportunities for women. They hope that by planting trees they will "*empower women to step into their feminine nature-based leadership, in support of humanity's identity shift from a consumer species to a restorer species.*"[511]

Human-I-T - 250k

Human-I-T fixes and reuses old computers that would otherwise become e-waste. They distribute these refurbished computers to people in need and provide them with training. According to the charity, over 80 million Americans still lack a computer with internet access with cost being the primary issue.[512]

---

509 caninetherapycorps.org
510 ij.org
511 treesisters.org
512 human-i-t.org

The Adventure Project - 1m

This charity provides families with stoves, and helps women set up their own businesses making and distributing the stoves. According to the TAP, up to 3 billion people cook primarily using open flames, with the smoke causing many preventable cases of respiratory illness.[513]

SOA - 1m

The Sustainable Ocean Alliance supports over 1,000 ocean impact projects in the 80+ countries they operate in with the goal of preserving the ocean as much as possible from the negative effects of climate change. They run a leadership program that connects emerging leaders as well as a start-up incubator for businesses that offer promising solutions.[514]

Many Hopes - 250k

Many Hopes rescues, educates, and advocates for street children in Kenya. They create self-sustaining complexes to house them in a family-like setting and advocate for them in the country's courts. They have also built a school where both privileged and former street children study together.[515]

Lets Encrypt - 250k

Let's Encrypt is a free, automated, and open certificate authority (CA) that gives people "*the digital certificates they need in order to enable HTTPS (SSL/TLS) for websites, for free, in the most user-*

513 theadventureproject.org
514 soalliance.org
515 manyhopes.org

friendly way we can. We do this because we want to create a more secure and privacy-respecting Web."[516]

Snow Lovers - 50k

Snow Lovers works to encourage snow-related businesses and initiatives to track and reduce their carbon footprints. They focus on businesses like ski resorts and winter sporting brands, leveraging their love for snow into a desire to preserve it.[517]

SOGAL - 1m

SOGAL has created a mentorship community of diverse entrepreneurs and organizes high-impact events like conferences and start-up bootcamps for female founders. They also run SOGAL ventures, which is "*the world's first female-led millennial venture capital firm investing in diverse founding teams in both the U.S. and Asia.*"[518]

Tennessee River Gorge Trust - 250k

TRGT protects over 17,000 acres of land in the Tennessee River Gorge area and funds ongoing research about birds, water quality, climate change, and reptile populations. They also arrange various community engagement activities and upkeep walking trails.[519]

KDE - 200k

"*The KDE Community is a free software community dedicated to creating an open and user-friendly computing experience, offering*

---

516 letsencrypt.org
517 snowlovers.org
518 iamsogal.org
519 trgt.org

an advanced graphical desktop, a wide variety of applications for communication, work, education and entertainment and a platform to easily build new applications upon."[520]

<u>Nuzzles & Co - 1m</u>

" *We save the most vulnerable animals from our region's euthanasia shelters, giving them all the medical care, nourishment, training, socialization, TLC, and time they need till we find them forever families."*[521]

<u>New Incentives - 250k</u>

New Incentives provides Conditional Cash Transfers (CCTs), which are "*small sums of money that individuals in need can earn after meeting various education and health benchmarks such as school attendance or clinic visits.*" These are effective in ensuring babies are vaccinated against preventable diseases by making medical care a smart investment for their families.[522]

<u>#ME ACTION - 50k</u>

"*A global, grassroots network for people with Myalgic Encephalomyelitis and Chronic Fatigue Syndrome."*[523]

<u>Alter - 1m</u>

Alter seeks out the best entrepreneurs in developing markets such as Afghanistan, Cuba, Bangladesh, Haiti, and Myanmar and connects them with mentorship, financing, and other resources from Silicon Valley. This not only helps these entrepreneurs grow their

---

520 kde.org
521 nuzzlesandco.org
522 newincentives.org
523 meaction.net

businesses, but also to develop local economies by providing employment, infrastructure, and opportunity.[524]

Council for Spiritual Practices - 250k

The CSP is working to change the attitudes of the scientific, religious, and legal communities regarding the usage of entheogens; specifically psilocybin (magic mushrooms), because they believe that "*increasing the number of people who undergo mystical-type experiences under suitable conditions would tend to increase the amount of prosocial behavior in the world.*" Their work includes cutting edge research through Johns Hopkins University, and is a "*collaboration among spiritual guides, experts in the behavioral and biomedical sciences, and scholars of religion, dedicated to making direct experience of the sacred more available to more people.*"[525] Pine's choice to support the CSP and comparable initiatives suggests a fascinating fan-theory. Did Pine use bitcoins to purchase illegal substances on the dark web, only to experience some sort of mind-altered spiritual awakening that inspired him or her to give almost everything away for the benefit of all?

Conclusion

> *I kind of miss the old times when bitcoin was a small community, and you could count the number of 'altcoins' with one hand. Finding someone else who even knows about bitcoin was incredibly rare, and exchanges were semi-automated or running on PHP.*
> *Every development since then makes Bitcoin stronger and better at solving the problems of the existing financial and monetary system. It's created a new generation of crypto early adopters, cypherpunks or technologists using cryptography to*

[524] alter.global
[525] csp.org

> *change the world; and now having the power and responsibility of capital.*
>
> *5104 BTC was turned into $55 million for charities, from providing clean water, open mapping, to clinical trials of MDMA as treatment for PTSD.*
>
> *Thanks for following along with this experiment. I'm going to say goodbye now, but maybe there's room for dessert in a few years.*
>
> *If you're ever blessed with crypto fortune, consider supporting what you aspire our world to be. :)*
> *<3, Pine*[526]
>
> - Pine, 11 May 2018.

The world would be a better place with more people like Pine not only because of his/her generosity, but also their pragmatic and future-oriented approach to solve huge systematic problems despite being an individual. Pine's choices display brave and unconventional thinking, characteristics which likely drew Pine to Bitcoin in the first place. The people of Blockland are a most innovative, unconventional people and many of them have now attained significant wealth. Perhaps with time many more of them will see beyond the merits of merely possessing money and desire to put it to use, instituting the change they wish to see in the world. Influence, capital, connections, fame, and the attention of rulers are not merely advantageous possessions, but heavy responsibilities.

The head that wears the crown is a heavy one, and Pine decided that the greatest act would come from melting it down in order to sow seeds both literally and metaphorically for all of humanity to enjoy for generations to come.

That is true power, true wealth, and unshakeable legacy.

---

[526] Kelso, C. Edward. "Bitcoin's Anonymous $55 Million Pineapple Fund Gives Final Donation." *Bitcoin.com*, 11 May 2018.

All of us possess the power to mold the world according to our values. Do not squander it. Act!

The 1640 'A Satire of Tulip Mania' depicts speculators as monkeys in upper-class dress. One urinates on the previously valuable plants while others appear in debtor's court, and one is carried to the grave.

CHAPTER 15

Tulip Hangover

Bubbles

Late 2017 through early 2018 saw the peak of what will likely be remembered as the ICO Bubble. Part of this enthusiasm can be attributed to the fact that few ICO's so far had enough time to fail, and thus most news was positive. Bitcoin reached a high of up to $20,000 as the crypto market peaked at 830 billion dollars, of which Bitcoin represented 33%. Hoping to cash in on the riches of the internet during the DotCom bubble in the 1990's and early 2000's, new and existing businesses put *.com* behind their names.[527] In the *Coin Bubble*, these same types of companies created coins and tokens to access the legendary riches of the blockchain world. Though the DotCom Bubble is an obvious comparison, this was merely a fraction of its size. Another historical comparison for the ICO Bubble is that of the infamous Tulip Bubble, which rocked The Netherlands in the 1600's.

---

[527] Goodnight, G. Thomas, and Sandy Green. "Rhetoric, Risk, and Markets: The Dot-Com Bubble." *Quarterly Journal of Speech*, vol. 96, no. 2, 2010, pp. 115–140., doi:10.1080/00335631003796669.

Dutch Golden Age

The first IPO took place over 400 years ago in 1602, when the Dutch East India Company (VOC), the first multi-national company, offered shares to the public in order to raise 6.5 million Dutch guilders to expand its trade in spices, silk, tea, grain, rice, soybean, and sugarcane. This was a vast sum, considering a skilled craftsman would earn about 1 guilder per day (think something around one billion dollars for 6.5m guilders). The Amsterdam Stock Exchange was formed to facilitate the re-selling of these shares, thus becoming the first modern securities exchange which soon began trading both bonds and shares of other companies as well. Investors, in what was doubtlessly a questionable and novel system at the time, were handsomely rewarded for their part in ushering the world into a new economic age; VOC shares delivered an average annual dividend of 18% over the next 200 years![528]

These innovations in early 1600's Amsterdam quickly built on-top of each other to form the modern financial system with features including diversified investment funds and investment banking.[529] Only seven years after the establishment of the first stock exchange, the Bank of Amsterdam, the first central bank, was founded to support the network of international lending, trading, and investing.

[528] Stringham, Edward. "The Extralegal Development of Securities Trading in Seventeenth-Century Amsterdam." *The Quarterly Review of Economics and Finance*, vol. 43, no. 2, 2003, pp. 321–344., doi:10.1016/s1062-9769(02)00153-9.
[529] "Venture Shares of the Dutch East India Company." *The Origins of Value: The Financial Innovations That Created Modern Capital Markets*, by William N. Goetzmann and K. Geert. Rouwenhorst, Oxford Univ. Press, 2005, pp. 165–175.

Amsterdam became the economic center of the world.[530] This laid the foundation for 17th century development of modern investment speculation instruments. These includes *stock futures* (an agreement to buy or sell at a future date), *stock options* (the option to buy or sell for a specific price on a specific later date), *stock shorting* (anti-buying a stock; essentially borrowing a stock in order to sell it, with the intention of 'buying it back' for less when the price drops), and *debt-equity swaps* (a debt-holder cancels debt in exchange for shares).[531] This entirely new financial landscape created a wild-west environment ripe for market manipulation. It was in this time that *Confusion of Confusions* (1688), the first book on stock trading, was written by Amsterdam businessman Joseph de la Vega.[532] Indeed, there is nothing new under the sun.[533]

This century became known as the Dutch Golden Age and for good reason. The country achieved the world's highest per-capita income for a period of about 120 years.[534] The tiny nation was a world leader in not only trade and military power, but also art and science as well. This explosion of wealth and culture can, in my view, be attributed to a positive feedback loop stemming from the creation of an entirely new and more importantly, more functional

---

530 Daly, Jonathan W. *The Rise of Western Power a Comparative History of Western Civilization*, Bloomsbury, 2014, pp. 228–229.

531 Goetzmann, William N., and K. Geert. Rouwenhorst. *The Origins of Value: The Financial Innovations That Created Modern Capital Markets*. Oxford Univ. Press, 2005.

532 De la Vega, Josseph. "Confusion of Confusions [Hardback]." *Archive*, 1 Jan. 1970.

533 Petram, Lodewijk. *The World's First Stock Exchange: How the Amsterdam Market for Dutch East India Company Shares Became a Modern Securities Market, 1602-1700*. Columbia University Press, 2011.

534 French, Doug. "The Dutch Monetary Environment during Tulipmania." *The Quarterly Journal of Austrian Economics*, vol. 9, no. 1, 2006, p. 3., doi:10.1007/s12113-006-1000-6.

financial system, of course further compounded by convenient geography and a skilled workforce that valued education and thrift.

Tulip Mania

Tulip Mania is a most glaring example of Dutch new-money during the Golden Age and is considered the first speculative bubble. As tulips found their way to Europe from the Ottoman Empire, they became renowned for their unique shape and bright colors. They soon became coveted status symbols and were classified by color. A virus started spreading among some plants, splitting the color of individual petals into two. This resulted in spectacular, multi-colored petals with flame-like streaks which took 7-12 years to cultivate from "infected" bulbs.[535] The mania phase set in as French buyers became interested in the tulips, leading many to speculate that demand would soon outstrip supply due to increased demand across Europe.[536] As each tulip could only generate a limited number of new tulips over the decade-long growth cycle, supply was capped but future demand was potentially endless. Tulips were the country's 4th largest export in 1636,[537] and one apocryphal story from the time recounts a sailor who ate a tulip after mistaking it for an onion. The ship's merchant was horrified to find him "*eating a breakfast whose cost might have regaled a whole ship's crew for a twelvemonth.*"[538]

---

535 *Irrational Exuberance*, by Robert J. Shiller, Princeton University Press, 2005, p. 85.

536 Garber, Peter M. "Tulipmania." *Journal of Political Economy*, vol. 97, no. 3, 1989, p. 543., doi:10.1086/261615.

537 *The Embarrassment of Riches: An Interpretation of Dutch Culture in the Golden Age*, by Simon Schama, 1st ed., Vintage Books, a Division of Random House, Inc., 1997, pp. 350–366.

538 "The Tulipomania, Chapter 3." *Memoirs of Extraordinary Popular Delusions and the Madness of Crowds*, by Charles Mackay, 1856.

> *Many individuals grew suddenly rich. A golden bait hung temptingly out before the people, and, one after the other, they rushed to the tulip marts, like flies around a honey-pot. Every one imagined that the passion for tulips would last for ever, and that the wealthy from every part of the world would send to Holland, and pay whatever prices were asked for them. The riches of Europe would be concentrated on the shores of the Zuyder Zee, and poverty banished from the favoured clime of Holland. Nobles, citizens, farmers, mechanics, seamen, footmen, maidservants, even chimney sweeps and old clotheswomen, dabbed in tulips.*[539]
>
> - Charles Mackay, 1856.

Tulip trading was not an established practice and was therefore not practiced in "official" places like the exchange, but rather in bars and taverns where buyers would pay up to three guilders of "wine money" on top of any purchase.[540] At these organized trading events, some individual bulbs changed hands as many as ten times per day on paper.[541] Despite some bulbs going for well over 3,000 guilders (think $500,000; 10x a skilled craftsman's wage), many "investors" are said to have never seen an actual tulip.[542] These speculators were generally merchants or skilled craftsmen, not nobles.[543]

The mania phase lasted for four months, with prices crashing in February 1637, allegedly after news spread that no buyers had

539 "The Tulipomania, Chapter 3." *Memoirs of Extraordinary Popular Delusions and the Madness of Crowds*, by Charles Mackay, 1856.
540 *Tulipmania: Money, Honor, and Knowledge in the Dutch Golden Age*, by Anne Goldgar, Univ. of Chicago Press, 2008, p. 322.
541 Garber, Peter M. "Tulipmania." *Journal of Political Economy*, vol. 97, no. 3, 1989, p. 543., doi:10.1086/261615.
542 *The Embarrassment of Riches: An Interpretation of Dutch Culture in the Golden Age*, by Simon Schama, 1st ed., Vintage Books, a Division of Random House, Inc., 1997, pp. 350–366.
543 *Tulipmania: Money, Honor, and Knowledge in the Dutch Golden Age*, by Anne Goldgar, Univ. of Chicago Press, 2008, p. 141.

shown up to an auction in the city of Haarlem.[544] This lack of attendance was perhaps because the city was suffering from the bubonic plague at the time.[545]

Prices of the most expensive bulbs fell as much as 99%, leaving speculators with near-worthless contracts to buy tulips that were still years from flowering. Most losses were on paper, and people who thought they had made fortunes over the previous weeks soon learned that they had nothing.[546] According to some accounts, courts would not enforce the payments of tulip contracts because they considered them to consist of gambling debts instead of reflecting legitimate business transactions.[547]

The intermittent investor mania surrounding Bitcoin and cryptocurrencies has been long compared to the irrationality of the Tulip Bubble. As the price of Bitcoin approached $1,000 for the first time in November 2013, Nout Wellink, former president of the Dutch Central Bank, called Bitcoin "pure speculation" and "hype" during a lecture at the University of Amsterdam. "*Sooner or later the facade will fall... This is worse than the tulip mania... At least then you got a tulip [at the end], now you get nothing*" he told students.

Dr. Wellink was not entirely wrong; the early economics of Bitcoin, altcoins, and ICO's were virtually identical to that of tulip mania in several ways.

---

544 *Famous First Bubbles: The Fundamentals of Early Manias*, by Peter M. Garber, MIT Press, 2001, pp. 37–47.
545 Garber, Peter M. "Tulipmania." *Journal of Political Economy*, vol. 97, no. 3, 1989, p. 542., doi:10.1086/261615.
546 Garber, Peter M. "Tulipmania." *Journal of Political Economy*, vol. 97, no. 3, 1989, pp. 535–560., doi:10.1086/261615.
547 "The Tulipomania, Chapter 3." M*emoirs of Extraordinary Popular Delusions and the Madness of Crowds*, by Charles Mackay, 1856.

- Supply was limited, and the rate of creation of new [tulips] / [tokens] was predictable and slow
- Investors were mainly speculating on the idea that a much larger and more powerful contingent of buyers [European aristocracy] / [global institutions] would soon be desperate to enter the market at any price
- Buyers rarely took possession of the actual [tulips] / [tokens], instead letting them remain under the custodianship of a [grower] / [exchange], and often had no practical understanding of [horticulture] / [cryptography].
- Exchange did not happen in [the Amsterdam Stock Exchange] / [any "establishment" exchange anywhere], but in [bars and taverns] / [unregulated exchange sites run out of students' dorms or island tax havens]
- When disputes arose between buyers and sellers, the courts did not always recognize [tulips] / [tokens] to fall under their jurisdiction

The Dutch Golden Age presents us with two useful case studies in radical economic/financial innovations. The first is The Dutch East India Company which richly rewarded investors for 200 years and redefined business, finance, and economics to such an extent that it served as the basis for the development of institutions and systems that have lasted for centuries.[548] The second is the Tulip Bubble, which saw a value explosion in rare tulip bulbs which were ultimately nothing but multi-colored gimmicks for starry-eyed commoners to dabble in.

---

[548] Steensgaard, Niels. "The Dutch East India Company as an Institutional Innovation." *Dutch Capitalism and World Capitalism: Capitalisme Hollandais Et Capitalisme Mondial*, by Maurice Aymard, Cambridge U.P., 1982, pp. 235–257.

Bubble Flashbacks

It is mid-December in 2017 and after a month with clients in Canada. I'm off to China to visit miner-factories and meet Xavier, a recently introduced contact who wants to help Token Valley launch an ICO. Token Valley's co-founder met him at a crypto summit in Switzerland, and he has been eager to meet me. We hit it off over Peking Duck in Beijing, where we spend an evening sketching out the $10 million fundraiser on a hedge fund office's whiteboard. Xavier controls a Taiwan-based ICO investment platform, virtually guaranteeing millions in funding within the first days. In the following week, the whitepaper came together.

> *Abstract*
>
> *Token Valley is a blockchain education network promoting social interaction and knowledge sharing among the casual, academic, and professional blockchain communities. We combine educational resources, tools for investment analysis, and social networking into a hub allowing cryptocurrency users to share valuable ideas and insights with each other. Encouraging users to share their expertise requires a fair accounting system that provides incentives to users based on their contribution. To this end, Token Valley will integrate its own digital currency called the Token Valley Token (VAL). Users who contribute value to the platform will be rewarded in VAL based on our unique, Subjective Proof Of Stake (SPOS) consensus algorithm. A smart contract will then allow VAL holders to access a fund investing in the projects deemed worthy based on the data gathered and verified by members of the Token Valley community. The value of the Token Valley Token will be based on the growth of the funds invested and the ability of the platform to aid in investment decisions.*
>
> - Token Valley, Jan. 2018.

Our concept was the creation of an *open ICO hedge fund,* where literally anyone could come and work as an analyst and effectively get paid in shares of the fund's portfolio. The more valuable an analyst's contributions, the more interest they would gain in the fund. Everything was ready; millions in funding were a few clicks away. As an ICO about ICO's by a company advising ICO's, I believe Token Valley's experiences were archetypal for the wider ICO industry.

I stopped in Finland to celebrate the holidays with family. I then flew to Prague on January 2nd for a meeting regarding a mining operation and woke up the following day in Dubai, where I had eight hours to meet with a prospective ICO client before boarding for Hong Kong at 20:00. I managed barely an hour of rest at the Hong Kong hotel before I was off to meet Token Valley's new legal advisor, who mentioned over dinner that he was flying to Manila in a few hours and that I was welcome to come along and continue discussions there. Why not, I figured, and the next morning I was off to Manila. Though we were days away from launching the ICO, we were advised to hold off due to the lack of regulatory clarity with receiving money from global investors in the manner we intended. We were to reformat the ICO as an STO to designate the tokens as securities. This was expected to delay us by a few weeks but protect us from legal worries down the line.

After three days in Manila, I was off to Shenzhen to meet with the Chinese mining group looking for a place to put their machines. Days later it was time to head back to Dubai to sign papers with the client and meet Trevor[549], a potential business partner with whom I had connected on LinkedIn. Clients and coworkers began to know me as the high-flying hobo; I got most of my sleep in the sky on some weeks. Airplane cabins and hotel rooms blurred together into the same basic concept – a place to rest between meetings.

549 Name changed for purposes of this story

This lifestyle left little room for hobbies, but it did complement one: credit card churning. This involves a hacker-like online community who use spreadsheets to compare promotional credit card offers, and then constantly apply for new cards to collect their generous sign-up bonuses of airline or hotel points before closing the accounts within a year as to avoid the annual fees. This allowed me to fly around the world in Business class, enjoy lounges in every city, and stay in downtown hotels – all for free. Credit card companies make good money by taking advantage of people who go into debt, but they lose out to churners who turn their advantage-taking tricks against them. Not even the big banks can win every hand against every player.

With a few days to kill before needing to be in Dubai, I made a rest stop, a rare vacation if you will, in Nepal. Here, I found myself stepping off a specialized helicopter to eat breakfast at 5,000 meters (17,500 ft) above sea level at a Mt. Everest base camp, followed later that day by dinner at the sea-level foot of Dubai's Burj Khalifa. As this pinnacle-themed day fell on almost exactly the height of the market, it was the perfect embodiment of the speed, optimism, and euphoria then shared by nearly everyone in the industry. I was on top of the world.

In Dubai, a new opportunity arose. Token Valley lacked a userbase, and Trevor who operated the Telegram community for ICO investors lacked a platform; a merger was in the works. He had scheduled to meet his with his business partner in London later that week, so the natural solution was to scramble the rest of the Token Valley team from around the world to join Trevor for discussions at his London home on barely 2-day's notice. Two intense days were spent discussing the terms of the merger, after which a contract was written and signed in a make-shift ceremony involving applause, champagne, and cigars. The ICO market was booming and everyone was on their way to being rich. Trevor's family and friends came over, and though they varied by trade from landscapers and electricians to hotel staff, they had all invested heavily in ICO's on Trevor's advice. His brother had even become a crypto millionaire in the previous week.

The crash began on the night of our signing ceremony, and I woke up to having lost a quarter of my wealth overnight. I shrugged this off as normal, as it was for the crypto market. Trevor's brother soon lost 98% of his fortune as the chosen token failed in the court of market opinion. Perhaps expectedly, the merger was unsuccessful. With taking $1,000 1-year subscriptions from ICO newsletter readers during the run-up of the ICO boom, Trevor had failed to budget the money to cover the needed analysts over 12 months. As the market started falling and no new subscribers signed up, there was no money left to pay analysts. Trevor, who had quit his corporate job to pursue cryptocurrency, found both his finances, relationships, and marriage in severe distress as his wife equated his dabbling in cryptocurrency with gambling addiction.

Years later I heard that Trevor had left the industry, with his former business partner telling me that he now hated anything related to blockchain and once told him to "*never talk to [him] about crypto again!*" Such a reaction is typical for someone who has returned from Blockland empty handed; it becomes imperative for them to believe that it was a lie or mirage all along, for the idea that they squandered their opportunity is often a pill too bitter to swallow.

Cryptocurrency and Suicide

After a breathtaking high, an equal and opposite suffocating low cannot be unexpected. Though Trevor's case was not grave, these tumultuous times in Blockland led to numerous suicides by people lost fortunes and even their family's homes and savings. One of these was Trevor's business partner, who took his life after becoming involved in an ICO-type project only to see the loss of not only his own money, but that of his friends and family members who invested in the project based on his advice. As the bubble began to pop in early 2018, one crypto investor announced that they had sold their holdings and would not be buying back in until the suicide prevention hotline's phone number was the top post on the r/Bitcoin subreddit, as it had been at the desperate depths of previous crashes. A rather morbid market signal.

It is easy to understand how the cryptocurrency world could drive a young person over the edge after first giving them the certain means to earn even hundreds of millions of dollars, only to take it away at the blink of an eye. In December 2017 one anonymous mourner recalled his late brother, who in 2012 had up to 15,000 BTC and kept enthusiastically telling him and other relatives about how Bitcoin would revolutionize the financial world and make every investor a millionaire. Then in 2013, he lost his fortune after being hacked and panic-selling the rest.

> *As the price took off in late 2013-early 2014 you could tell he was distraught over it and became increasingly withdrawn from family and friends. Whenever I did manage to contact him he would sometimes end up ranting about how badly he had f--ked up and how he would never have a chance to be rich again. As the price climbed up to 10k over the past several months it became even more difficult to make contact with him, he just wouldn't reply to me or my parents calls and texts. A couple weeks ago my parents flew out to see my brother and found him dead by suicide with no note. He was 29 with 50 years of life ahead of him.*[550]
>
> \- Reddit user barking_bonerz, 5 Dec. 2017.

[550] barking_bonerz, Reddit.com user. "My Brother Killed Himself Because of BTC." *Reddit r/Bitcoin*, 5 Dec. 2017.

That same month a Vietnamese family died in an apparent double-murder-suicide, presumably after losing money borrowed from friends and relatives. It is understood that they invested this money in the mining service NiceHash, which was hacked days earlier, and the still running laptop with empty NiceHash accounts was found among the hung and poisoned bodies.[551] In January 2018, 23-year-old Bitcoin blogger and consultant Pavel Myakushin was robbed in his home of about $500,000, after posting images of himself posing with hundreds of thousands of dollars in cash. Myakushin then took his life because the money belonged to investors whom he was unable to pay back.[552] These examples are certainly not exhaustive, as there are numerous instances of traders[553] [554] [555] [556] [557], investors[558], and entrepreneurs[559] [560] taking their lives upon seeing their fortunes turn. This is a sobering reminder that while cryptocurrencies may exist in the ether and we may have ideological debates about the

551 Vanilla_Buddha, Reddit.com user. "Vietnamese Family Commits Suicide after Nicehash Lost Their Bitcoin Investment." *Reddit r/Bitcoin*, 15 Dec. 2017.

552 "Young Bitcoin Millionaire Dies in Suspected Suicide After Having Fortune Stolen." *NZ Herald*, 7 May 2018.

553 Delafont, Rick. "Indian Bitcoin Trader Commits Suicide Over Losses Trading Crypto for Local Officials." *NewsBTC*, 16 May 2019.

554 "Trader Threatens to Commit Suicide, as Millions Worth of Bitcoin Were Liquidated." *NewsBTC*, 30 Mar. 2018.

555 "Senior Cop Under Radar : Bitcoin Trader Commits Suicide." *Ahmedabad Mirror*, 20 May 2019.

556 Emem, Mark. "Chinese Bitcoin Trader Commits Suicide After Losing 2,000 BTC on 100x Leverage Bet." *CCN*, 12 June 2019.

557 Zafar, Shahzaib. "Bitcoin Volatility Resulted in BTC Trader Suicide." *Blockpublisher*, 23 May 2019.

558 Enomoto, Joshua. "Bitcoin Suicides: The Darker Side of Cryptocurrencies." *Crush The Street*, 8 Sept. 2018.

559 Radtke, Autumn. "Singapore Police Probe 'Unnatural' Death of American CEO of Bitcoin Trader." *South China Morning Post*, 6 Mar. 2014.

560 Grey, Micheal. "Bitcoin Firm CEO Found Dead after 'Suicide'." *New York* Post, 5 Mar. 2014.

"right" to tokens gained by hacking or market manipulation, this block-game is very much a serious matter.[561]

Being in Danger

While network security is of huge importance in Blockland, where hackers run wild, Pavel Myakushin's fate highlights another oft-overlooked matter of physical security for what can be termed *Crypto-Exposed People* or CEP's. The fact of the matter is that anyone who is known to have been materially involved in Bitcoin in 2017 or earlier can be reasonably assumed to control some amount of cryptocurrency. This amount of untraceable and immediately accessible money could range from thousands to millions of dollars. This presents the uncomfortable truth that while the average person would be generally uncomfortable carrying over $1,000, CEP's carry proverbial backpacks filled with gold bars whether they go out to the bar, for a late-night walk in the park, or check in to a hotel in a foreign country. When faced with a knife or gun, all but the most secure crypto holdings can be accessed and irretrievably surrendered in less than five minutes, provided a Wi-Fi connection is available. The sobering reality is that for as long as cryptocurrencies have value, being branded as a CEP is a permanent condition whether or not one actually has any cryptocurrency. Once a CEP, always a CEP.

CEP's are ideal targets for scamming, hacking, robbery, and extortion. While being a low level CEP, who is rumored among friends to have a few bitcoins, may not pose a major risk, a high-level CEP(++), who is well-known crypto trader, personality, or the Chief Technology Officer of an ICO-type project or exchange, could be interpreted as an overloaded walking piggy-bank waiting to be

---

[561] Premack , Rache. "South Korean Millennials Are Reeling from The Bitcoin Bust." *The Verge*, 3 Apr. 2018.

smashed for bits. An Ethereum investor, who was robbed of $1.8 million after having dinner with a business associate at New York's Time Square in December 2017, serves as a cautionary tale:

> *On leaving the restaurant, [the thief] Meza told his associate he had hired an Uber minivan to transport him home, and insisted he get in. Unfortunately, the "Uber" didn't get very far before a gunman popped up from the back seat and demanded the victim hand over his phone and apartment keys... the gunman also demanded the victim hand over a 24-word password to his Ledger Nano S– a device known as a hardware wallet that lets users store digital currency offline and safe from hackers (though not from kidnappers). The victim eventually escaped his ordeal by running into a deli, but not before Meza had used his keys to enter his apartment and steal the hardware wallet, using the password to transfer the Ethereum to his own account.*[562]
>
> -Jeff John Roberts, 1 Feb. 2018.

Comparable examples abound, including a Russian couple who were followed to their apartment while vacationing in Thailand, where they were left tied up after being forced to surrender their password to $100,000 worth of BTC.[563] Executives of crypto exchanges have been kidnapped for ransom from London[564] to Ukraine[565], and South Africa[566] has seen multiple kidnapping of children.

---

[562] Roberts, Jeff John. "Robbed for Bitcoin: How a Dumb Crypto Criminal Botched a Kidnapping." *Fortune*, 1 Feb. 2018.
[563] Popper, Nathaniel. "Bitcoin Thieves Threaten Real Violence for Virtual Currencies." *The New York Times*, 18 Feb. 2015.
[564] Murphy, Margi. "Bitcoin Exchange Chief Kidnapped as He Leaves Work." *The Telegraph*, 28 Nov. 2017.
[565] Polityuk, Paval. "Ukraine Kidnappers Free Bitcoin Analyst after $1 M Ransom Paid." *Reuters*, 30 Dec. 2017.
[566] Emem, Mark. "Kidnapped South African Tycoon Released for 50 Bitcoins Ransom." *CCN*, 18 Aug. 2018. Print.

Even in Singapore[567] and Canada[568], there has been a string of scams where callers claim to have kidnapped a partner or child and demand immediate payment of $10,000 in BTC for their safe release. The true scale of crime like these is likely much larger, as it is reasonable to presume that many victims do not come forward as to avoid attracting further attention towards their holdings, whether from the from the public or government.[569] [570]

While many are oblivious to their vulnerable position, other CEP's are all too aware. This was the case for Griff Green, who recounted the Ethereum DAO hacker-battle in which his White-Hat Robin Hood Group "stole" over $100 million of ETH. That night, Green placed a mattress by the front door of one of the groups members and slept with a baseball bat ready to bash anyone who might be coming for the precious private keys under the cover of night.

I myself fell victim to a digital attack when someone managed to access my Bitcointalk.org forum account, and view my recent messages requesting BTC payments for books to a specific Bitcoin address. Hours after I sent such messages, the hacker would send another message indicating that the original address had been incorrect and instead specifying an address they controlled, signing each message off with *Elias Ahonen.* Over the span of a few days, buyers sent the hacker several thousand dollars in BTC. One of these book-buyers became suspicious and included my editor in the discussion, with the hacker then convincing my editor that they were me. The hacker expertly deleted these sent and received messages,

---

567 "Singapore Police Warn of Kidnap Scams Targeting China Students." *Yahoo News Singapore*, 14 Sept. 2018.

568 "Fake Abduction, Bitcoin Ransom the Latest Scam in Metro Vancouver." *CTV News Vancouver*, 18 July 2018.

569 Deep, Jagdeep Singh. "Ransom Demand Made in Bitcoins, Six in Police Net." *Indian Express*, 1 Jul 2017.

570 Memoria, Francisco. "$3.5 Million: Turkish Kidnapping Gang Targeting Bitcoin Holders Busted." *CCN*, 17 Nov. 2017.

making the intrusion into my digital home invisible to me until I saw myself receive an email that disappeared before I had time to read it, indicating that I was not alone.

Phone hijacking, where *social hackers* convince phone companies to transfer them control of target's phone numbers, is another way in which cryptocurrency holders have been targeted. This method of hacking is highly effective, as phone confirmations often serve as security backups to access email, social media, or exchange accounts. As crypto users naturally have the most valuable online accounts, they are at increased risk for such attacks, prompting the New York Times to state that "*attackers appear to be focusing on anyone who talks on social media about owning virtual currencies or anyone who is known to invest in virtual currency companies, such as venture capitalists.*"[571] CEP risk confirmed.

Bitcoin has proved to be an excellent medium for criminals to demand payment. Perhaps the most notable of these was the WannaCry ransomware attack which spread to over 200,000 computers in May 2017, encrypting their files and demanding Bitcoin payments in order to release them.[572] In other cases, the data networks of municipalities and even hospitals have been hijacked and held for ransom.[573] In December 2018, businesses, schools, and government offices in Canada and the USA received emails threatening bomb attacks if they failed to make $20,000 ransom payments in BTC.[574]

---

[571] Popper, Nathaniel. "Identity Thieves Hijack Cellphone Accounts to Go After Virtual Currency." *The New York Times*, 21 Aug. 2017.
[572] Berr, Jonathan. "'WannaCry' Ransomware Attack Losses Could Reach $4 Billion." *CBS News*, 16 May 2017.
[573] Jr, Berkeley Lovelace, and Lizzy Gurdus. "Hospital CEO Forced to Pay Hackers in Bitcoin Now Teaches Others How to Prepare for the Worst." *CNBC*, 8 Apr. 2018.
[574] Hosenball, Mark. "Bitcoin Bomb Threats Sweep U.S., Canada, but Lack Credibility." *Reuters Canada*, 14 Dec. 2018.

Treasure in Landfills

As with tulip mania, paper fortunes were made and lost overnight. Just like the sailor who unknowingly ate a tulip that was worth a fortune, there is an abundance of stories involving the accidental loss of Bitcoin fortunes. Take that of James Howells, a ~24-year-old Welsh IT worker who mined 7,500 bitcoins in 2009 using his laptop. As mining difficulty increased and it became impractical to continue mining with his Dell laptop, he took his computer apart and sold its components on eBay. Though BTC had no recognized monetary value in 2009, he kept the hard drive containing his crypto fortune, believing that it might one day be worth something. It remained in a drawer for four years, when in 2013 he mistakenly threw it away after mixing it up with another empty hard drive in the same cupboard.

Speaking to the New York Post in 2018, he recalled the incident:

> *I looked up the price, did the calculation... and thought, 'Shit. [Those bitcoins are] worth around $2 [million] or $3 million.' A few months later it was worth $9.9 million. I was annoyed, pissed off, sick. I spoke to the people at the landfill and told them that I threw away a hard drive worth $10 million. They looked at me stupidly.*[575]
>
> -James Howells, 26 May 2018.

Howells has not given up hope and considers the bitcoins rightfully his, as if in a bank account to which he has forgotten the PIN code. He has offered the Newport City Council a 10% cut of the BTC if they allow the landfill to be excavated, a request that has so far been denied. "*The higher the value goes, the more chance I have to recover it, so it's just been a waiting game for the past few years ... waiting until the bitcoin price was high enough to make the drive a*

[575] Kaplan, Micheal. "I Accidentally Threw Away $60M Worth of Bitcoin." *New York Post*, 26 May 2018.

juicy enough treasure to hunt."[576] Ironically the cost of any future excavation increases every year, as new layers of trash are piled upon Howell's treasure.

A very similar story is that of Campbell Simpson, an Australian technology journalist who in 2010 bought 1,400 BTC for $25, only to intentionally throw his hard drive away while moving to a new house, thinking that there was nothing worth keeping on it. "*I'm generally pretty easygoing in life, I think, and I can laugh about it for like 95 per cent of the time, but also, man. Man. What if.*"[577] he lamented. A happier ending befell Kristoffer Koch, a Norwegian who paid the equivalent of $27 for 5,000 bitcoins in 2009 while writing his master's thesis on encryption. Koch forgot all about his purchase for years until he saw Bitcoin's rise mentioned in the media as it approached a value of $180 in October 2013. After some attempts trying to recall his password, he managed to access his wallet which was by then worth $886,000. He then promptly sold 1/5th of his newfound fortune to purchase an apartment in Oslo.[578 579]

Even companies have lost the private keys to huge amounts of BTC. Take the case of Bitomat, the third largest Bitcoin exchange in its time, which lost 17,000 BTC in July 2011. The exchange stored all its information, including private keys, using a virtual machine on a cloud server which eventually ran low on memory. When the administrator attempted to upgrade the server, it permanently deleted all stored information due to an apparently faulty

---

576 Molloy, Mark. "The Unlucky Man Who Accidentally Threw Away Bitcoin Worth $100 Million." *The Telegraph*, 3 Dec. 2017.
577 Molloy, Mark. "The Unlucky Man Who Accidentally Threw Away Bitcoin Worth $100 Million." *Daily Mail*, 3 Dec. 2017.
578 Lauritzen , Fredrik. "Kjøpte Leilighet for Internettpenger." *Okonomi*, 25 Oct. 2013.
579 Gibbs, Samuel. "Man Buys $27 of Bitcoin, Forgets About Them, Finds They're Now Worth $886k." *The Guardian*, 9 Dec. 2015

setting.[580] A similar fate fell upon Canadian exchange QuadrigaCX in January 2019, whose 30-year-old CEO Gerald Cotton had sole control of $145 million worth of cryptocurrency when he apparently died of illness while travelling in India.[581] As years go by and early Bitcoin adopters begin to die without arrangements for their heirs to access their crypto-assets, cases like this on the individual level may become commonplace.

There are thousands of stories of lost bitcoins; even I have an old hard drive containing 0.35 BTC to which I no longer remember the password. Another such man is Elon Musk, who was once given a quarter of a bitcoin but has no idea how to access it today.[582] All hope is not lost; American hypnotist Jason Miller asserts that for a base fee and 5% of recovered coins, he can use *hypnotic age regression* to help poor souls like Elon and I to access old photographic memories and thus remember long-forgotten passwords.[583] Another start-up called Wallet Recovery Services has reported a 30% success rate by using an algorithm to try out thousands of potential passwords based on wallet owner's vague recollections.[584] One bitcoin I will never recover is the 1 BTC physical Bitcoin which I carried in the pocket of my jacket for over a year, only to leave said jacket on a park bench in Toronto. So much for my "lucky coin".[585]

---

[580] Dotson, Kyt. "Third Largest Bitcoin Exchange Bitomat Lost Their Wallet, over 17,000 Bitcoins Missing." *Silicon Angle*, 1 Aug. 2011.

[581] Alexander, Doug. "Crypto CEO Dies Holding Only Passwords That Can Unlock Millions in Customer Coins." *Bloomberg*, 4 Feb. 2019. Print.

[582] Mayer, David. "Elon Musk Doesn't Know Where He Left His Bitcoin." *Fortune*, 28 Nov. 2017.

[583] Krause, Elliott. "A Fifth of All Bitcoin Is Missing. These Crypto Hunters Can Help." *Wall Street Journal*, 5 July 2018.

[584] Woo, Wilma. "Estimated 4 Million Bitcoin ISs Lost Forever By Users' Forgetfulness." *Bitcoinist*, 6 July 2018.

[585] It may well have become someone else's lucky coin, and if not, then it's every bitcoin-holder's lucky coin seeing as all BTC is now 1/21,000,000th scarcer, thanks to my misfortune.

John Ratcliff is recognized as a zombie researcher. A zombie Bitcoin researcher, that is. Ratcliff (who is a moderator of the popular r/Bitcoin discussion forum) classifies bitcoins as zombies if they "move" after 18 months of dormancy, specifically in 2013-2014 when he did his research. The theory behind his investigation is that it is very likely for anyone who acquired their bitcoins below $1 or even $10 to have at some point moved (sold, or moved into different wallets) at least a portion of their bitcoins as the price increased to $100 and $1000 in late 2013. This means that bitcoins in wallets that had been "motionless" for 18 months as of mid-2014 could be presumed *dead* (permanently lost). While some dead bitcoins did come back to life as zombies and continue to do so, it is ever-increasingly rare.[586] He found that as of June 18, 2014, 20% of mined coins (~2,580,000 BTC) had not moved in 18 months, with the same being true for ~4,386,000 BTC when calculated for 12 months.[587] Further analysis in 2017 by blockchain compliance company Chainalysis corroborates Ratcliff's research, estimating that between 2.78 and 3.87 million bitcoins (13.2%-18.4% of all bitcoins ever) are lost forever.[588] [589]

Conclusion

It has been said that the cream always rises to the top, but so do the bubbles and foam. This analogy could describe the entire blockchain industry, as its participants broadly consisted of various extremes rather than any kind of normal. While many insiders took the idealistic view that the entire industry itself was the concentrated

586 Ratcliff, John. "A History of Zombie Events." *LTB Network*, 1 Aug. 2014.
587 Ratcliff, John. "Rise of the Zombie Bitcoins." *LTB Network*, 22 June 2014.
588 Roberts, Jeff, and Nicolas Rapp. "Exclusive: Nearly 4 Million Bitcoins Lost Forever, New Study Says." *Fortune*, 25 Nov. 2017.
589 LI, Martin YK. "How Much Bitcoin Has Been 'Lost' Forever?" *Seeking Alpha*, 21 June 2017.

cream of economics and computer science, many outsiders dismissed it as nothing more than foam and bubbles that would soon dissipate into nothingness. Both views were incomplete as in truth the industry was made up of both cream and foam, but almost nothing of substance in between.

I am here reminded of a Dubai ICO which I advised, only to find out that another fellow "advisor" was a member of a European royal family which he represented in the Emirite by mingling with Middle Eastern royals. He would be an excellent advisor, I was told, because of his connections to both European "old money" and various royal families in the Arab world. The truth came to light as I conducted a due diligence investigation on the team members: the "royal house" my colleague claimed to belong to had been deposed 800 years ago! Our prince was a foamy phony.

This demonstrates the near-impossible challenge of separating the two extremes. Was it mostly foam and a tiny, chance amount of cream? Quite possibly. Did the foam ever doubt that it was cream? Barely.

The half-year period between 2017 and 2018 represented a historical technology bubble largely built upon ICO's, which were themselves often based on enthusiasm regarding exciting, though not-yet-profitable, or even viable, systems and technologies. Though it is true that the vast majority of ICO's failed outright, in the sense that their values dropped well below the ICO prices, it is incorrect to say as some do that "90% of ICO's were scams" because the majority were real, though often naïve, attempts of creating legitimate financial innovations. It is fair to describe this period as one where many felt that the old rules no longer applied and responded by throwing whatever they had at the proverbial wall to see if it would stick. Looking back, it was all mere experimentation, and surely something worthwhile would come of it.

The crypto-market's massive gains brought wealth to somewhat average people whose ideas of money were transformed in consequence. For the true believers who were not itching to convert their crypto assets into fiat, there developed a strange dichotomy between their crypto wealth and "real" money. This is well described by a person of average means barely flinching at an overnight paper loss of $10,000, only to be deeply bothered by a $100 parking ticket later that same day. If there was no immediate intent to sell out of crypto, its value became almost meaningless and disconnected from reality. One 23-year-old friend of mine recounted the day of his largest market gain near the height of the bubble – over $150,000, during which he stayed at a hostel while on a business trip in order to save the extra $30 per night which a private room would cost. The same people would paradoxically also display an opposite effect: "*what did it matter that I spent an extra $1,000 today? I either gained or lost 10 times that on crypto since I woke up!*" Perhaps much of the lavish ICO party-spending can be explained by this latter mechanism. In many ways, it didn't seem real.

This attainment and subsequent reduction or loss of significant wealth was difficult to handle for many, even resulting in tragedies. Some investors and companies found themselves unprepared for the realities of being associated with large amounts of untraceable money and fell victim to crimes ranging from hacking to murder. The markets became increasingly characterized by a rollercoaster, as personified by the *Bitcoin rollercoaster* meme, in which a Bitcoin is pictured in various positions of uphill, downhill, and horizontal depending on the relevant price movement. The experienced hodler is similarly represented by videos of people appearing bored on intense rollercoasters, implying that it is merely their unexciting daily go at an experience that would terrify the uninitiated. Stoicism can be understood as a collective ideal within Blockland and surviving the absolute terror of subsequent bubbles is seen as a sort of ongoing initiation into this new order. The more bubbles one has survived, the more battle stripes and thus the higher their status in the order of Blockland when the new order conquers the old.

Courtyard of the Exchange
in Amsterdam, 1653

CHAPTER 16

Traders' Games

Mt.Gox spawned an entire industry of exchanges dealing in cryptocurrency, crypto-assets, and blockchain tokens. They are based on the model of existing stock exchanges, which are themselves digitized versions of in-person markets where buyers worked to outbid each other while sellers offered lower prices to move their goods faster. The basic mechanism of a crypto exchange is to act as the marketplace which matches buyers and sellers who have already deposited their cryptocurrencies or national currencies within the exchange. Someone looking to sell cryptocurrencies like BTC, ETH, or DOGE could send them to any exchange in which they have an account before trading them into supported fiat currencies such as USD, EUR, RUB, GBP, or CNY. With the cryptocurrencies sold, the account holder could then have the exchange deposit the fiat currency in their bank account. The procedure to buy crypto with fiat was the opposite, with the buyer making a bank transfer of fiat to the exchange, where it could then be traded into crypto which could then be easily sent to the buyer's own crypto wallet. With each trade, exchanges would profit by taking fees ranging from ~0.25% to 5% or more.

After a successful ICO, a project could no longer be described as an 'ICO' but as a token. With each completed ICO at least one new token was launched, causing the number of cryptocurrencies to balloon to thousands in the space of a year. To have any legitimacy, a token had to trade on at least one reputable exchange. This was a golden opportunity for the exchanges, which could charge millions of dollars to list a token.[590] The news of a prestigious exchange accepting a token could of course be worth exponentially more as the market value could consequently increase by a hundred million dollars. Hundreds of exchanges were launched as thousands of token-projects vied to see their tokens trading on as many markets as possible.

This created a most unbridled market, where thousands of shady and unregulated tokens traded on hundreds of exchanges around the word. There were simply no rules and few exchanges required anything more than a username and password. The owners of many exchanges were anonymous, and the tokens were not always based in any particular country. Exchanges would fail in the way of Mt.Gox every month with trader's assets usually gone with the wind. For many, crypto trading began to look more like gambling than investing. As exchanges added new features, traders took on the ability of trading on margin with 2x, 3x, 10x, or even 50x leverage. This meant that someone with $20,000 could purchase up to $1,000,000 worth of cryptocurrency, profiting $1,000,000 if it doubled in value but losing everything if it fell by 2%.[591]

---

[590] Hussey, Matt. "Crypto Exchanges Charging Up To $3 Million To List Tokens." *Bitcoin.com*, 4 Apr. 2018.
[591] Bain, Benjamin. "Crypto Margin Trading Challenged by U.S. Derivatives Regulator." *Bloomberg*, 24 Mar. 2020.

As each exchange had separate order books, by which supply and demand determined prices on a second-to-second basis, there was often variance between exchanges. While these differences are usually insignificant, there have been instances where a given country's demand for cryptocurrency is so high that the popular exchanges operating there see prices much higher than the global average. On the flip side, exchanges suspected of being illiquid or suffering from slow deposits/withdrawals, such as Mt.Gox, have featured BTC at significant discounts.

Even minor differences in prices made it profitable for traders to employ 'arbitrage strategies', which involved the buying of cryptocurrencies on exchanges with low rates before selling them on ones with higher prices. This could take complex forms involving several different tokens. With time, trading bots were designed to automatically shift money between exchanges. This type of trading served a natural function to balance markets, as any 'market inefficiencies' could be immediately exploited and thus smoothed out.[592]

Bitcoin Dealers

This idea of arbitrage extended to the 'offline' sale of bitcoins. Sites such as localbitcoin.com allowed for anyone to make sell offers and buy requests, with sales taking the form of in-person meetings or buyers wiring money directly to the seller's bank account based on ratings of trustworthiness from previous clients. Even without the help of online platforms, this created a lucrative business for many who were well-connected within their local Bitcoin communities. In-person sales offered many advantages for which buyers were willing to pay high premiums above market prices such as speed, the lack of any paper trail, the option to use cash, and the ability to ask

[592] Blenkinsop, Connor. "Arbitrage Trading in Crypto, Explained." *CoinTelegraph*, 10 Sept. 2019.

the seller for advice. Methods like these were among the first ways in which one could buy BTC before automated exchanges were available and reliable. Bitcoin sellers of this type have at times faced prison due to the unregulated nature of their activities.[593]

Bitcoin ATM's (also known as BTM's) represent a branch of these offline sales and were at times set up by the same people who were already active as local bitcoin dealers, with the first of these being installed in Vancouver, Canada, in July 2013.[594] Anyone could walk up to an ATM and deposit money, receiving a slip of paper with a QR code and private key by which to access the bitcoins that had just been purchased. Some ATM's even allow users to send BTC directly to the ATM and receive cash without the collection of any personal information. While the ATM's offer the convenience of not having to wait for exchange account creation or bank transfers, they do charge a corresponding premium usually by quoting rates significantly above or below the market prices according to whether BTC is being bought or sold. While crypto ATM's have proven profitable to many of their operators, some have expressed caution towards investing in larger networks of them because large banks could add 'crypto ATM' function to their existing machines almost instantaneously.

OTC Markets

Over The Counter (OTC) deals were another interesting avenue of trading that developed. In cryptocurrency, the term refers to the off-exchange trading of (mostly) BTC and cash. These primarily refer to very large-volume orders which would influence exchange

---

593 Liao, Shannon. "Bitcoin dealer gets two-year prison sentence for unlicensed cryptocurrency exchange." *The Verge*, 9 Apr. 2019.
594 Sanghani, Radhika. "World's First Bitcoin ATM to Launch This Week." *The Telegraph*, 28 Oct. 2013.

prices in an undesirable way.[595] Other reasons to avoid exchanges include desires for greater privacy, wanting to avoid *exchange risk* – referring to the possibility of exchanges shutting down unexpectedly, and sometimes the possibility of avoiding KYC (Know Your Customer) requirements demanding that the other party to the transaction is known. The typical OTC participants are large institutions like investment funds, banks, crypto exchanges, large-scale miners, ultra-high net worth individuals, very early Bitcoin investors, and governments. The US Marshal's series of Bitcoin auctions in the wake of the Silk Road seizures among others is an example of OTC dealing, though they are almost never public like the auctions were.

Large OTC transactions almost never happen at the market price of BTC. This is because trading that amount of BTC on the open market would have a significant effect on the market price. Instead, a market average is determined at a specific hour such as 12:00 GMT and a discount or premium of 0.5%-15% or more is added or subtracted. This is a huge range, and it depends on market conditions and the specific factors surrounding the transaction.

Suppose that some institution holding 200,000 BTC foresaw an imminent 30% crash in the markets. Simply moving such amounts onto exchanges would likely set off all kinds of alarm bells leading to immediate market reactions, much less if the 200k BTC were actually liquidated out in the open. In this case it could be a godsend if the sellers were able to find a buyer willing to purchase the entire lot at 10% below market value and pay directly by bank transfer, even if they are losing 20,000 BTC on paper. The reverse can take place when the market is in the middle of a bull-run or about to start one. As bank transfers to exchanges can take multiple days

595 Bradley, Elijah. "Crypto OTC Trading, Explained." *CoinTelegraph*, 6 June 2019.

and BTC has been known to see double-digit gains for days on end, it can be reasonable for an entity wanting to get in on the action immediately to offer 15% above market price to immediately purchase 10,000 BTC. There are also the peculiar cases where someone with duffel bags of large-denomination notes wants to get rid of them as fast as possible and is willing to take even half their value in untraceable and easily transportable Bitcoin.

This is where the James Bond-esque OTC Bitcoin Broker comes in. The qualification for such mysterious work is not only knowing the right people, but for the right people to know that you know the right people. It further requires the street-smarts to avoid getting killed, caught up in some sort of dictator-financing scandal, and knowing when to stop dealing with a timewaster. It is as lucrative as anyone might imagine; 0.5%-4% of the entire lot's value is the standard fee, usually split between two to four brokers in a daisy-chain of who-knows-who and escrow lawyers. As with many jobs in the crypto-economy, getting out of bed is optional.

Historical Heists

In addition to coders, traders, and brokers ranging from small-town to intercontinental, good old-fashioned thieves are not to be forgotten from the assemblage of characters in the crypto-trading landscape. Despite lacking weapons, dynamite, or facemasks, these keyboard-based safe-crackers have pulled off some of history's greatest heists without ever stepping foot in a bank nor taking anything that a normal bank would consider real money.[596] [597] [598]

Perhaps the greatest heist ever occurred when hackers exploited a bug to make fraudulent withdrawals from Mt.Gox's *hot wallets* (wallets that are used for everyday transactions and thus more at risk) over a period of several years to steal a total of 650,000 BTC.[599] This gradual debasement of the exchange's holdings is understood as the primary reason for its collapse, leading to 127,000 creditors suing the company in bankruptcy. Eventually, Gox's victims got back everything they lost in dollar terms after the value of the BTC remaining with Mt.Gox's trustees grew exponentially. It's worth noting that when Mt.Gox was still operating, it was often blamed for various drops in the BTC market prices, and traders soon began to refer to such drops as being *goxxed.* Gox's bankruptcy was the ultimate goxxing, though when the company's trustees sold portions of the remaining bitcoins and thus allegedly triggered further market tremors, traders joked about being goxxed again by Mt.Gox's ghost.[600] [601] [602] Alexander Vinnik was arrested by US authorities in Greece in July 2017 for allegedly laundering four billion dollars of

---

[596] Helms, Kevin. "Biggest Heists in Bitcoin History and How They Were Pulled Off." *Bitcoin.com*, 1 June 2019.
[597] dree12, Bitcointalk.org user. "List of Major Bitcoin Heists, Thefts, Hacks, Scams, and Losses [Old]." *Bitcoin Forum,* 26 May 2012.
[598] Comben, Christina. "Top 5 Biggest Crypto Exchange Heists in History." *Bitcoinist*, 9 May 2019.
[599] Gox, Mt. Hack Flasback: "The Mt.Gox Hack – The Most Iconic Exchange Hack." *Ledger*, 18 Feb. 2019.
[600] Comben, Christina. "Mt. Gox Hodling Funds Worth Over Half A Billion Dollars." *Bitcoinist*, 21 Mar. 2019.
[601] Baydakova, Anna. "$2 Billion Lost in Mt.Gox Bitcoin Hack Can Be Recovered, Lawyer Claims." *CoinDesk*, 12 Sept. 2019.
[602] Norry, Andrew. "The History of the Mt Gox Hack: Bitcoin's Biggest Heist." *Blockonomi*, 31 Mar. 2020.

stolen Mt.Gox bitcoins on the Russian-based BTC-e site he operated, which was ironically Mt.Gox's largest competitor.[603 604] As with Silk Road, BTC-e's website was subsequently seized by authorities.[605]

Another form of heist common in Blockland is known as an *exit scam*, where the thieves are the owners of the exchange itself. This is especially easy in the case of exchanges and other cryptocurrency services whose owners are anonymous. A perfect example of this took place on Sheep Market, a drugstore on the dark web. After years of operation, both buyers and sellers had the sheep-like trust to store $6 million of BTC within the platform. One day, the site simply went offline as its alleged Czech owners made off with all the money.[606] It was the perfect crime, as the victims were not exactly incentivized to report their losses to authorities.

A legendary exploit took place in 2016 on Bitfinex, from which hackers made off with 120,000 BTC. Bitfinex issued *BFX Tokens* representing debt to affected users and finished buying them back (repaying the debt) ten months later.[607] Similar hacks took place on exchanges such as Coincheck, which lost 500 million NEM worth over $530 million in 2018, and BitGrail, which saw the loss of 17 million Nano Tokens worth $170 million that same year. In 2019, the largest exchange, Binance, lost 2% of its holdings[608], leading

---

603 Khatri, Yogita. "Alleged BTC-e Operator Alexander Vinnik Seeks Extradition to Russia." *CoinDesk*, 21 Mar. 2019.
604 Baydokova, Anna. Mt Gox Trustee Asked DOJ to Share Info on Jailed BTC-e Owner Alexander Vinnik. *CoinDesk*, 1 Oct. 2019.
605 Khatri, Yogita. "Crypto Exchange WEX Linked to Iranian Ransomware Operators, Says PwC." *CoinDesk*, 5 Mar. 2019.
606 Greenberg, Andy. "Silk Road Competitor Shuts Down and Another Plans to Go Offline After Claimed $6 Million Theft." *Forbes*, 1 Dec. 2013.
607 Bitfinex Team. "Announcements & 100% Redemption of Outstanding BFX Tokens." *Bitfinex*, 3 Apr. 2017.
608 Lam, Eric. "Hackers Steal $40 Million Worth of Bitcoin from Binance Exchange." *Bloomberg*, 8 May 2019.

CEO Changpeng Zhao to assure everyone that Binance would be covering all losses and that "*all funds are safu*", meme-fying the word *safe* in the style of *hodl.*

Despite the regularity of hacks, many crypto owners store most or even all their holdings directly on the balance sheets of exchanges, citing the ease of accessing and trading their tokens. This is frowned upon by many industry veterans and ideologues, who posit that one does not actually own any cryptocurrency to which they do not actually control the private keys. This *not your keys, not your coins* mantra has however fallen on deaf ears partly because of exchanges offering incentives, such as the opportunity to lend held funds to the exchange or to other traders at attractive interest rates.

To keep exchanges accountable, influential Bitcoin personality Trace Meyer promoted the inaugural *Proof of Keys* event for January 3, 2019; the 10th anniversary of the Genesis Block.[609] On this day, everyone was encouraged to move their cryptocurrencies out of exchanges and into their own wallets, if even for an hour. By doing so, each owner of cryptocurrency could prove to themselves that they do indeed own what they think they do. Traditional banks practice fractional reserve banking, which means that they lend out much more money than they receive. If even a quarter of a bank's client base were to suddenly withdraw their entire accounts, there would simply not be enough money and the bank would collapse. The dominant rhetoric around blockchain currency generally views this system as a scam, variously blaming it as a cause inflation (which it views as bad), recessions, and financial instability.

Depositing cryptocurrency into the custody of a third party exchange is thus somewhat antithetical to the early vision of Bitcoin,

[609] Comben, Christina. "Trace Mayer Gives 60-day Reminder of Proof of Keys 2020." *Coin Rivet*, 5 Nov. 2019.

though this ideological issue is minor as long as the exchanges function more as safety deposit boxes for the safe-keeping of private keys rather than as traditional banks that could hold more bitcoins on their balance sheets than they actually control. A situation of fractional reserves can even be created unintentionally, for example, when an exchange becomes a victim of theft or simply loses access to a portion of their private keys. Proof of Keys is thus essentially a bank-run meant to remind the "banks" that the cryptocurrency they hold belongs entirely to the clients and that it is unacceptable for them to carry more cryptocurrency liabilities than they can cover with their holdings. There can never be more than 21 million bitcoins.

Trading Culture

Insider trading and market manipulation, at all levels, was so heavily integrated as part of the game that the mere suggestion that it could be illegal, improper, or *against the rules* was simply quaint to all but the most naïve traders. Indeed, the formalized concept of an *insider* or *insider information* as understood in traditional markets was essentially foreign. It was an ultra-competitive dog-eat-dog world without rules or boundaries where everyone was out for themselves.

Boiler-room *pump groups* flourished. Such a group would consist of a hidden individual or group which would acquire a large amount of a specific low-volume token over a few days before announcing it to a wider group. The price would immediately begin rising, at which point a third group (usually the public) would be informed of the ongoing pump. These masses of people would then begin buying, creating high liquidity, thus allowing the pump's instigator(s) to sell their accumulated coins to them at 30%, 50%, 100%, or 500% profit. Once most insiders had sold at a profit, the price would usually crash quickly leaving the most recent buyers with losses. The surest losers were those who did not understand the game, and simply bought tokens that had begun a meteoric rise, thinking that the spike was the beginning of some long-term upward trend.

These pump groups came in various structures, but the result was usually the same. McAfee's weekly pumps were a particularly unique version, as they allowed anyone with enough money to buy into a forgotten token and pay McAfee to promote it. Some groups charged thousands of dollars per week to subscribers wanting to receive pump-announcements – even 15 minutes before publication, while others allowed *whales* with 50 or 100 BTC to join a higher echelon of the pump group's hierarchy. Pumping was by no means secret; most traders knew what was going on and were simply hoping that they could get off the gravy-train before it fell off the eventual cliff. It was a game. A 2018 study by the Social Science Research Network found 4,818 such pump-and-dump groups operating primarily on Telegram and Discord chat apps.[610]

Trading bots that could automatically trade cryptocurrencies based on pre-programmed formulae became popular not only among coders, but somewhat normal traders who could effectively purchase access to such pre-programmed bots with monthly subscriptions. The most famous among these was the Willy Bot, whose trading activity on Mt.Gox has been suggested as a major contributor or even cause of Bitcoin's first rise to $1,000.[611]

---

[610] Li, Tao, et al. "Cryptocurrency Pump-and-Dump Schemes." *SSRN Electronic Journal*, 2018, doi:10.2139/ssrn.3267041.
[611] Buntinx, JP. "What Is the Willy Bitcoin Trading Bot?" *The Merkle*, 23 Apr. 2017.

Terms, metrics, and methods used by traditional market analysts have found their way into the crypto markets, often applied in unorthodox ways. While online discussion regarding the movement of individual stocks is nothing new, I would suggest that the scale at which social media responds to and influences traders is unprecedented. This can perhaps be demonstrated by imagining how hundreds of amateur traders spend hours each day in public chatrooms discussing esoteric market analysis charts, with these discussions ranging from 5-minute movements to eccentric 50-year projections. Chat channels with hundreds of participants are dedicated to each of dozens of cryptocurrencies, and participants share screenshots of charts, memes, and banter about how various exchanges are about to go bankrupt and how the next hour of market activity will determine whether they the commenter will buy an island or move into a local homeless shelter next week. This surely does not describe your average commodities trader sitting in an institutional cubicle nor even a self-directed tech investor focused on FAANG (Facebook Amazon Apple Netflix Google) companies; this is clearly crypto territory.

One of the arenas in which these pumps played out were the infamous *trollboxes* on exchanges such as BTC-e and Poloniex. These were ever-present public chat boxes where traders could chat with and broadcast messages to all other traders using the exchange. I interestingly recall this exact type of behavioral mechanism taking place years before cryptocurrency on online multiplayer games such RuneScape, where players would form “merchant guilds”, purchase large amounts of a specific in-game item, and repeatedly announce the ongoing pump within the game’s open chatrooms.

Crypto Game: Origins

I suggest that the concept of digital scarcity, upon which cryptocurrencies are based, has its roots in Massively Multiplayer Online Role-Playing Games (MMORPG's) like WoW, RuneScape, and Second Life. These games featured in-game money and allowed players to freely trade items and "gold" between each other. Naturally, some players managed to acquire large amounts of in-game wealth through various means including simply gathering items to sell, running in-game businesses of various kinds, battling other players, or speculating on various items and even manipulating in-game markets. This elite 0.1% of gamers however found it challenging to preserve their wealth due to continuous inflation within the game. This was partly because the game kept "printing" gold which was needed for game play. With the value of gold decreasing and more items being created by the players and generated within the game, the only way to preserve wealth was by purchasing *rare items* which could no longer be created within the game. These items were deflationary in nature as the amount of them in circulation would only decrease as players lost them, forgot their passwords, were banned for rule-breaking, or simply stopped playing. Despite the dwindling supply, the number of gamers would generally increase; causing the rare items to grow only more legendary and sought-after.[612]

Within the RuneScape world, some of the rarest items are "Christmas crackers" and "party hats". The former were strewn across the map during Christmas holidays in 2001, to be picked up and 'pulled' (and thereby consumed/destroyed) by players. They were utterly worthless at the time but as the holiday ended and players

---

[612] Bilir, Tanla E. "Real Economics in Virtual Worlds: A Massively Multiplayer Online Game Case Study: Runescape." *SSRN Electronic Journal*, 2009, doi:10.2139/ssrn.1655084.

consumed most of the crackers, some players realized that they were suddenly rare. During the next year's holiday, the crackers did not re-appear. Adding to this element is that only a tiny portion of 2010's players were online in 2001. Despite their value, they are utterly useless in the game and cannot even be used to 'show off' by being wielded or worn. The other famously rare item, the Party Hat, could have been nominally purchased for one 'goldpiece' but sells today for billions of gold.[613] Both rare items can be purchased directly from other players for thousands of real-world dollars. With both these items, the similarity to sub-$1 bitcoins is undeniable. Maybe the people who happened to spend much of their time in this type of environment were better equipped to understand the concepts behind Bitcoin before older generations could wrap their heads around it.

When we broadly outline the average cryptocurrency user in the 2010's, we roughly arrive at a 20-35-year-old tech-savvy male who is connected to online culture. Not surprisingly, this is also the demographic which spent a good portion of its middle, high school, and college years playing video games, including the above-mentioned and other similar multi-player role-playing games. As such, I wonder to what extent the crypto-economy and especially crypto-trading culture is directly derived from online multiplayer games, where anonymous players created complex communities within a free-form libertarian environment that tacitly tolerated "scamming" by way of wit. I certainly gained my first leadership experiences through running "companies" and managing alliances of hundreds of players within such games. In this sense, I suggest that certain levels of the cryptocurrency phenomenon can be understood as a sort of blurring between fantasy and reality, where the ethics, mores, and culture from the gaming days is supplanted into the real-

---

[613] rouse, Medium.com user. "Bomb Token, Runescape Partyhats and Rubber Turkeys — A Game of Scarcity & Desire." *Medium*, 15 July 2019.

world crypto-game economy. Indeed, the Bitcointalk.org forum itself had the same structure as most online-gaming forums of the time, and "Bitcoin players" used aliases and screen-names just like gamers.

Mt.Gox's origin as an exchange for digital trading cards speaks to this on many levels. In addition to online games, trading card games such as Magic: The Gathering, Pokémon, Digimon, and Yu-Gi-Oh played formative roles in the childhood, teenage, and later experiences of much of the same demographic. In many schoolyards, these various games formed a sort of ongoing meta-game, which was not only just about winning individual battles but also of acquiring the right cards in the right games. Desirable cards could be gotten not only from the store, but by trading, playing for keeps, and even stealing from schoolmates. Among the relevant demographic, these various card games variously formed the basis of in-school economies from first grade onwards. Unlike games like basketball or checkers, success in these games lay not only in gaming ability but also in the ability to set oneself up to win with the right cards and by getting the opponent to agree to desirable rules. Having a powerful card-deck meant status, and cards could well be traded for desirables like candy or money. It might be interesting to investigate to what extent these long-standing schoolyard meta-games primed youngsters to embrace online free-form multi-player games.

Perhaps these early experiences with trading cards contributed to a trend in which "games" are becoming "real life", and virtual reality is becoming so intertwined with physical reality as for the two to be indistinguishable. Just consider the multi-million-dollar cash prizes regularly won by top players in various gaming leagues or the phenomenon of players in countries experiencing hyper-inflation, earning enough dollars to feed their families by producing in-game items for other player's convenience.[614] For an extreme example, there is even an online community called RiftintotheMind centered around the taking of dissociatives while wearing immersive Oculus Rift virtual reality goggles, apparently leading "players" to temporarily forget that any external reality exists outside the game at all.[615]

Trader's styles of communication are highly comparable to the way both online gamers and gamblers interact and discuss both micro and macro matters relating to the game. This type of ongoing interaction relating to the game's "real world" happenings — forms a sort of culture and identity around the game complete with inside jokes, memes, and humor. The stock market itself could be described as a massive multiplayer online game, and we can perhaps predict how it too will evolve as the crypto reality that *memes move millennial markets* spreads to traditional finance. It appears that Teslas's CEO Elon Musk who is known to engage via memes on Twitter and has jokingly embraced a role as a fictitous CEO of Dogecoin is an early example of this.

On that note, what even *is* traditional finance? Can such a thing exist, considering that our current fiat-based monetary system has existed for only 50 years and Bitcoin a significant fraction of that? Can we even think of economic systems as long-lasting institutions that can withstand generations of change, when each generation is bound to see it in a different light? There is also the argument that blockchain-based digital scarcity is in practice *more traditional* than anything we have today, taking us back to the time when currency represented some limited, tangible thing.

---

[614] Dubrowski, Doug, et al. "Playing for Their Lives: How a 2001 Video Game Is Feeding Venezuela." *National Interest*, 26 Mar. 2019.
[615] Neal, Meghan. "Real Drugs, Virtual Reality: Meet the Psychonauts Tripping in the Rift." *Vice*, 23 Nov. 2015.

This intrusion of video games into the "legitimate world" is a similar phenomenon to what the "ICO Game" and "crypto game" have exhibited, with both revolving around the Blockland game's primary in-game currencies. I think that this in part explains a sort of general confusion or blurriness among the people of Blockland regarding their place in society. Are they really in some far-off new world of gaming, experiments, and fantasy where the old world's rules simply no longer apply, or do they remain (a troublemaking) part of the established system while redefining or even transcending it? This can perhaps be supported by the observation that the crypto-game has two different ways to measure one's score that are not really tied to one another: some players measure their performance in terms of fiat money like dollars, wheras others disregard "traditional" monetary value and aim instead to increase their bitcoin-score regardless of its day-to-day dollar value. Of course, others choose to measure their portfolios in ETH or by some other digital yardstick.

When puppies play-fight, they are not engaging in some sort of scheduled puppy-activity that is set aside upon graduation to dogdom. They are testing limits, learning their strengths, and sizing up their competitors; the methods they learn may well be different than those of their parents, particularly if the environment they grow up in is somehow different. These skills and techniques learned in play become the bark and bite of the adult dog; its means to defend territory and fight for mates. In this sense, the very concept of a *game* may be a misnomer; perhaps all these games and play-money are as real-life as it gets: Just look at Dogecoin.

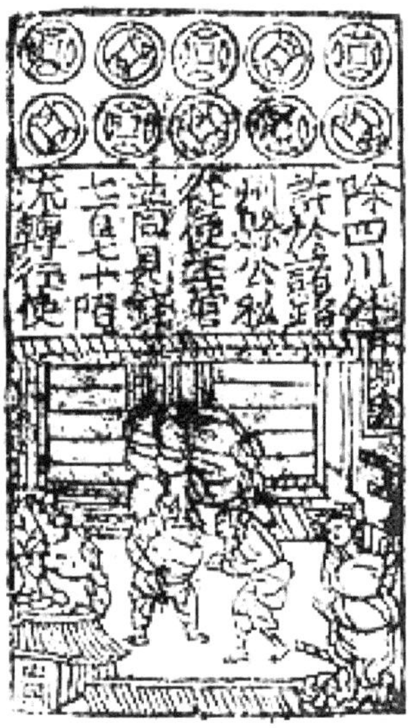

Earliest banknote, known as "Jiaozi" from 10th century Song Dynasty China. They were receipts for copper coins, and the central government soon realized the economic advantages of printing money and thus became the only entity allowed to issue such certificates.

CHAPTER 17

Crypto Evolution

It's the year 2000 and 7-year old Sam is obsessed with Trading Card Monsters. He spends his allowance on trading cards and his art classes on designing new Monsters with various abilities and backstories. At recess he battles his friends and as new episodes air each Wednesday at 5pm, he is glued to the television as if his life depends on it. Every night he dreams of life as a Monster Master, travelling the world searching for new Monsters and training them. After he tells his teacher that he will become a Monster Trainer, a parent-teacher meeting is called. Sam seems not to understand that Monsters are not real and that he cannot train Monsters in real life; he needs to come back into the real world. Eventually, Sam comes to his senses and understands what he needs to do. This happens in 2025, when he drops out of his PhD in Software Engineering, bids his parents goodbye, and embarks to travel the world in search of rare Monsters – on a mission to become the very best Monster Trainer and Tame'em All.

This is possible because Monsters are now real. The company that developed Monster Cards has now put them on the blockchain, allowing them to be interacted with through a smartphone one keeps in their pocket. Each phone is a Monster Receiver and different Monsters live in different places throughout the world. Sam has now camped in the rainforests of Borneo, hiked the Great Wall of China, and for a brief stint lived with Bushmen in Botswana, while lugging around a solar-powered setup with 10 smartphones and several sets of virtual reality goggles.

The various Monsters are geo-tagged to different locations, with the rarest being in places where few people ever go. Indeed, the algorithm is designed in such a way that the Monsters with you gain experience faster if you take them to harsh climates, and the further from civilization a Monster is found, the higher their stats. Whenever one of his phones vibrates, he puts on a set of virtual reality goggles and battles the Monster nearby, hopefully capturing it. Sam is now a bona fide Monster Trainer who sells his Monsters on the decentralized Monster Market to cover his expenses. He is on his way to becoming The Most Best; he has even competed in tournaments held in soccer stadiums with thousands of spectators in attendance. After just a few years of adventuring, his Monster collection is worth over a million dollars.

This story is fictional and hypothetical, but its substance is not far from reality. Decentralized Applications or dApps for short are the next-generation evolved form of what we know as Apps. Instead of a back-end based on C++ running on a corporate server, a decentralized application runs on a distributed peer-to-peer network (blockchain) according to smart contracts. In a sense, this makes them "real" entities instead of just mere projections displayed by a controlling company back-end. Though most dApps are created by companies, their influence over them is very limited by design. In the case of the Monster dApp, Monster Corp has no control over who owns which Monster, how they evolve and gain stats, or whether they can be sold or for how much. Just like a company manufacturing gardening tools or physical trading cards has no control over how they will be used or who will use them, Monster Corp. has long ago lost control of its monsters.

Crypto Gambling

It is said that gambling, gaming, and pornography are the first three industries to adopt new internet technologies. The first two of these have taken the dApp world by storm, with gambling leading the way. Some of the first gambling dApps were manual proofs of concept, operating on Bitcoin without any real smart contracts. They were run by dark-web entrepreneurs, who invited anyone to send them a bitcoin with the promise of returning it with a specified multiple depending on the numbers appearing in the transaction's public hash-code.

Suppose for example that the last number of a transaction hash code had an equal chance of landing between 0 and 9; the lottery might promise to pay back 1.9 BTC for an odd-numbered result while paying nothing for an even number. This would amount to a transparent house edge of 5%. Another example might be one which pays a 9x multiple, leaving a house edge of 10%. While no one could force these "lottery entrepreneurs" to pay out for winners, it was in their self interest to do so as a failure to pay a successful "roll" would be clearly visible on the blockchain and thus destroy the lottery's reputation. Beginning in 2012 with the likes of Eric Voorhees' SatoshiDice, which had its "IPO" on MPEx, these primitive operations made way for automated "dice games" with specific addresses for various odds from 1.1x to 999x or more. These addresses would hold large BTC balances and have a backend automation feature to send certain multiples of BTC back based on certain hash codes. At times, they faced criticism for spamming the blockchain by producing huge amounts of transactions. Despite automation, gaming was not instant as Bitcoin transactions took time.

A more fast-paced type of dice game emerged, which functioned more like an exchange. A user would create an account and deposit BTC, after which they could "roll the dice" as many times as desired. Players could set their odds at will, betting as little as 1 Satoshi per roll for payouts as high as 99,999x provided a static 1%, 0.5%, or even 0.1% house edge (depending on the casino) was accounted for. Some such casinos allowed players/users to invest in their bankrolls by providing liquidity, with such investments paying daily dividends based on the casino's performance in what can be understood as a proto-yield farming. These investments were however not foolproof, as demonstrated by a legendary "whale" gambler called Nakowa who once withdrew 11,000 BTC after a weekend of gambling success in 2013.[616] Like the trollboxes of exchanges, these games had a social element that allowed players to chat about while playing and watching other's rolls. Despite their transparent nature, these games still generally depended on their owners to not *exit scam* by shutting the website down and keeping everyone's BTC. Not all these casinos were honest, as the internal back-end mechanisms were difficult for outsiders to audit.

Along came the decentralized casinos. They operated primarily on blockchains such as ETH, EOS, and TRON, whose fast transaction speeds and smart contract capabilities made it possible to create decentralized casino-games that required little to no trust in the game's developers or operators. No longer would payouts be manual or automated by the operator's back end, but they would be

[616] O'Neill, Patrick Howell. "The Biggest Bitcoin Win in Gambling History." Daily Dot, 2 Mar. 2020.

executed according a pre-programmed auditable smart contract in the way of a Rube Goldberg gambling machine. Often, these casinos would make use of a *native token* which would function as a casino chip, and secondarily as a way for anyone to invest in the casino's success. While theoretically not casinos, some crypto exchanges, such as Binance, have opted for a similar structure where *branded tokens*, such as Binance Coin, can be used to pay discounted trading fees and held in certain quantities to access special privileges.

Non-Fungible Tokens

Bitcoin, Ethereum, and other cryptocurrencies are based on the concept of fungibility; it means that each Bitcoin or Ethereum token are equal to all others in the same way that every US Dollar is equal in value to all other US dollars. *Non-Fungible Tokens* or NFT's are different in that they cannot easily be exchanged for a direct equivalent. While shares in a company are fungible, an asset like a house is non-fungible. Similarly, an individual US dollar bill expertly folded into a complex paper airplane by a famous artist or featuring a one-of-a-kind printing error would be non-fungible.

CryptoKitties was the first NFT game, unveiled in October 2017 at an Ethereum hackathon in Waterloo. It featured Ethereum-based non-fungible tokens taking the form of unique virtual cats. Players could collect cats and mate them, randomly passing on the parent-cat's "DNA" to the next generation of offspring. These *cattributes* included things like fur color and the shapes of facial features, making each cat unique. As each cat was an Ethereum token, they were entirely controlled by their owners in the same way as any other cryptocurrency. The difference was that each token represented an entirely unique cat or digital good. As certain cat-features came to be sought after, external marketplaces for NFT tokens such as

RareBits and OpenSea were quickly launched. The first CryptoKitty named *Genesis* sold for 246.9255 ETH ($117,712) in December 2017[617], and CryptoKitties soon had so many users that its transaction volume was crowding out the Ethereum blockchain's capacity as miners had failed to prepare for the increased usage.[618] A few months later, the game's developer Dapper Labs raised $12 million in venture funding.[619] While many in the industry mocked the concept of useless internet cats, others began to take NFT's seriously.

After the successful proof of concept, more dApp games making use of NFT's emerged. Many of these took the form of card games such as Steem Monsters and Gods Unchained, giving a modern twist to the baseball, hockey, and various battle-monster cards of old. These cards were made up of limited editions and instead of being merely controlled within a game platform, they were legitimately owned by the players. Digital card decks could be purchased from the game creators, and they could then be battled with for rank and bonuses, held as investments in the game's growth, or traded for other cards within the game's internal marketplace or on external third-party markets. Players with especially rare and powerful cards could even rent them to other players, with self-enforcing smart contracts ensuring that payment was made and that the cards were returned on time. Even if the game designers went bankrupt and shut down their websites, players would continue to own the cards and could build any type of game infrastructure in which to play with them. Leagues and tournaments with real prizes could

---

[617] Tepper, Fitz. "People Have Spent Over 1M Buying Virtual Cats on the Ethereum Blockchain." *Tech Crunch*, 4 Dec. 2017.
[618] Kharif, Olga. "CryptoKitties Mania Overwhelms Ethereum Network's Processing." *Bloomberg*, 4 Dec. 2017.
[619] "CryptoKitties Receives $12M in Funding." *Dapper Labs*, 20 Mar. 2018.

still be organized. The game creators can act only as mere custodians, able to be overthrown at any time by a *player's fork* (people's revolution).

Decentralized Finance

Consider this realisitc example: by depositing $1,000 of hard-earned money to a bank, Joe might earn $2 (0.20%) of interest per year, well below the 2% inflation rate which at the same time reduces the account's buying power by $20. At the same time however, with $1,000 in new holdings the bank can now lend $5,000 to Lisa at an interest rate of 5% to earn $250 on the back of Joe. Indeed, the inflation that eats away Joe's meagre interest is arguably caused by this very process of new money creation (inflating the money supply). Is it a surprise if Joe feels cheated, and begins to question who the system is really created for? This explains why many cryptocurrency proponents want to upend the financial system, and provides an apt description of the economic views of the Austrian school of economics which continues to oppose the monetary policies developed in response to the Great Depression. From the micro perspective of the individual, banks are here imagined as exploitative in that they pay small interest while charging more for loans, wheras from the macro perspective of societal structure, their practice of fractional-reseve banking is imagined as somehow fundamentally corrupt.

Bitcoin may theoretically fulfill the requirements of an absolute unit of value for the digital age, but it does not quite offer a solution to the "problem" of banks, which are centralized financial institutions. Enter Decentralized Finance, DeFi for short.

As an experimental form of finance, DeFi does away with intermediaries like banks and exchanges, allowing individuals users to lend to and borrow from each other through DeFi dApps (most of which operate on Ethereum as of writing). This effectively cuts intermediaries out of the equation, to the point that CEO's of some of the largest exchanges including Binance and OKEx have acknowlaged that they must innovate in DeFi as their exchanges will likely become obsolete. The implication is that Decentralized Exchanges (DEX's) will come to dominate much of the cryptocurrency trading sphere. The Difference between a Dex and a centralized exchange is significant: a centralized exchange operates much like a bank, in that a user deposits their funds into it and must trust that the exchange will keep them safe. The centralized exchange could be hacked by an employee, and they could potentially choose to freeze a specific user's account for some reason, or the entire exchange could be frozen by an act of government, such as what happened when Silk Road was seized and shut down. A Decentralized Exchange offers no such options, as they are in effect pre-programmed machines that now exist outside the control of any individual.[620]

Since Decentralized Finance operates on Decentralized Applications and Smart Contracts which all run on blockchains, these various DeFi systems can effectively be stacked on top of an connected to one another as if they were "financial legos", an expression which Ethereum proponents have used to explain their future vision for the blockchain.

Launched in 2015, MakerDAO, which allows users to profit by helping to stabilize the USD-peg of the DAI stablecoin, is credited as the first DeFi platform.[621] The DeFi industry reached the 1-billion-dollar mark in early 2020, passing 10 billion later in the year.

---

[620] Keoun, Bradley, et al. "First Mover: Binance's CZ Doesn't Even Dispute That DeFi Might Be Inevitable." CoinDesk, *CoinDesk*, 18 Sept. 2020, www.coindesk.com/first-mover-binance-defi-inevitable-federal-reserve.
[621] Kharif, Olga. "Why 'DeFi' Utopia Would Be Finance Without Financiers: QuickTake." *Bloomberg*. 26 Aug. 2020.

As with any substantial cryptocurrency project, an internet culture has formed around the DeFi phenomenon where the lending of money into various liquidity pools or even to individuals has come to be known as *yield farming*, the most committed farmers of which may change the subject of their lending on a daily basis in order to chase the highest interest rates available. This yield farming phenomenon is comparable to mining, only that it uses a different methaphor and that the computing power of mining is replaced with financial liquidity. Unsurprisingly, a new crop of variously complex "DeFi tokens" such as SNX, YFI, and AAVE have popped up in Blockland, as well as tokens like DeFi Pulse Index (DPI) which act as index funds made up of the former. These can be expected to propel the next age of this ever-developing story, perhaps mirroring the ICO craze.

The New Ownership

As fungible cryptographic tokens are redefining the concept of money and value in the Information Age, Non-Fungible Tokens are redefining the very concept of an "item" to better fit the digital reality in which we increasingly exist. Owned property now no longer needs to be physical, nor do they need to be confined to some specific platform. They can be immaterial yet tradable, unregulated yet finite in number. These digital goods can even be owned by practically living, breathing, Decentralized Autonomous Organizations (DAO's, also known as Decentralized Autonomous Corporations or DAC's) whose shares are owned by yet other autonomous digital organizations which have no worldly rulers.

An NFT can represent anything, such as a ticket to a specific seat at an event, a coupon for half-priced pizza, a playing card to a decentralized game, or a piece of digital art. NFT's make it possible for anyone to create limited or one-of-a-kind pieces of digital art which cannot be replicated any more than the Mona Lisa can be duplicated using a camera. An artist can, for example, create a digital image which is represented by a unique digital token. Whoever controls the token then owns that piece of art and can then sell it to a third party by listing it for sale on an NFT art marketplace such as SuperRare.io. Just like with physical art whose pictures spread around the internet, anyone can view the art but only one entity may own it. As in the analog world, the art's value can be expected to increase according to the artist's reputation. In the blockchain world this can benefit the artist very directly; the art can for example be programmed in such a way that the artist (or their estate) receives a 5% royalty every single time that the work is re-sold.

There is of course nothing to stop the tokenization of physical art or any other thing, such as a house or car. Imagine for example the $155 million *Le Rêve* (*The Dream*) by the surrealist painter Pablo Picasso, which is owned by an individual. This enterprising art owner might do quite well to tokenize the piece by dividing its ownership into a billion tokens and selling them for 25 cents each. Now instead of being owned by a single person, millions of people could effectively buy stock in their favorite painting, likely increasing its value far beyond that which a single individual would be willing to pay. A Decentralized Autonomous Organization could be created to manage the painting's physical form, with "shareholders" voting on things like restoration efforts and insurances, while individuals and museums could bid to rent the physical version of the painting. It is even feasible that the money earned by renting and licensing the work could allow *The Dream DAO* to initiate share buybacks, until the painting owns itself outright and goes on to purchase other paintings by Picasso or his rival Matisse. Perhaps artificial intelligence can be added to the mix one day. Surreal. Picasso would be proud.

This fact of un-incorporated enterprises that can function within the global marketplace without any human director is a pandoras box when it comes to things like law and business ethics. When a DAO does something, who is legally and morally responsible for negative consequences? In a normal company that is incorporated within a jurisdiction, there are plenty of potential people formally associated with the corporation who the courts can go after from employees to CEO's and theoretically even shareholders. With DAO's, there is little possibility for such jurisdiction because unlike corporations that are attached to an established societal framework and are ultimately human organizations, DAO's are in effect alien associations with no human element and thus leaves uninvolved humans with very few tools by which to police their actions. How the world deal with this coming invasion of alien entities? Nobody knows.[622]

The idea that real goods like houses and land could be tokenized in the same way as *The Dream* inspires one to consider a limitless number of radical applications and their effects on the world. Indeed, these applications of tokenization can be ones that were previously unimaginable from an investment perspective. Consider that a professional of some type could tokenize blocks of their time, selling them to the highest bidder either to raise money for a house deposit or to finance their education. An investor could pre-purchase 1,000 units of a promising 1st year law student's work-hour tokens. The investor could then redeem them over the years whenever in need of legal services, barter them for the services of other professionals like plumbers or veterinarians, and eventually sell

[622] Kypriotaki, Kalliopi, et al. "From Bitcoin to Decentralized Autonomous Corporations - Extending the Application Scope of Decentralized Peer-to-Peer Networks and Blockchains." *Proceedings of the 17th International Conference on Enterprise Information Systems*, 2015, doi:10.5220/0005378402840290.

them for a huge return after 10 years of holding due to the lawyer now being a highly respected specialist in a niche field. As the law students would issue the tokens themselves, they would be in full control of their terms with the ability to create pre-programmed rules such as maximum redemptions per month, buy-back options, or an annual *evaporation rate* of 3%. The questions arising regarding ethics and legal aspects are innumerable.

Despite this unfathomable opportunity, anyone looking at these digital capabilities as solutions only for the physical world suffers from a certain myopia. It is in the virtual world that tokens of all types operate naturally, for there they are not abstractions but the very makeup of reality. With virtual reality, seemingly physical items can exist in cyberspace in the form of "wearable" clothing, paintings, special items, or virtual land. A fascinating example of this is Decentraland, which is built on Ethereum and consists of a virtual reality universe whose first "world" is the 9 square kilometer *Genesis City*, where *Mana* is used to purchase 10m x 10m parcels of land upon which owners can build anything they want. Anyone can design and sell items which can be used within Decentraland or taken out and utilized elsewhere. The project is rather comparable to the concept in Steven Spielberg's *Ready Player One*, in which people live their lives in a virtual reality game. For the budding generation born in the 21st century, to whom virtual reality goods and digital currencies have "always" existed, these concepts are not any more alien than television was for the boomers. The eternal flames of crypto-land belong to the crypto natives; those before them are mere torchbearers.

It seems clear that there is indeed more to blockchain than just mere digital gold. The smart contract's inventor, Nick Szabo, seemed to predict this. When paired with the blockchain technology inherent in Bitcoin, smart contracts could be used to create digital scarcity beyond that of fungible gold. Cryptographically based items, such as artworks, could have value due to the actual human effort involved in their creation allowing for an alternative proof-of-work to machine-mining. Now both precious metals and collectibles have counterparts which can be integrated with the virtual world of the Internet Age.

> *Precious metals and collectibles have an unforgeable scarcity due to the costliness of their creation. This once provided money the value of which was largely independent of any trusted third party.*[623]
>
> - Nick Szabo, 29 Dec 2015.

Surprisingly enough, the first NFT's were unknowingly created by Mike Caldwell in 2011 when he sealed digital bitcoins into physical brass, silver, and gold coins. These coins, despite having the same amounts of fungible BTC, became non-fungible due to their varying physical condition and provenance. This non-fungibility made the coins collectible and much more valuable than the actual BTC inside. You may recall my earlier mention of the *Autographs Edition* of my encyclopedia of these coins, which featured dozens of signatures by the earliest manufacturers of these proto-NFT's. Each of these books were also assigned an empty Bitcoin address with the private key sealed under a security sticker, making them the first non-coin NFT and meta-NFT, before the idea of an NFT even existed. Admittedly, I was merely playing around without any intention of doing anything revolutionary.

Magna Carta Novum Libertatum

As we ponder upon the idea of decentralized games whose game-pieces are owned by the players and whose game-designers are mere custodians rather than rulers, one might wonder if something

[623] Szabo, Nick. "Bit Gold." *Satoshi Nakamoto Institute*, 29 Dec. 2005.

significant is in the works. Consider the western system of democracy, the modern version of which was underpinned by the 1215 Magna Carta Libertatum, which was a charter of rights for the barons who complained of arbitrary imprisonment, lack of justice, and unreasonable taxes under King John of England. By signing the charter, King John effectively gave up his right of absolute rule. Until this point, the landowning barons had no more real rights than their peasants. Now consider what life was like in those times: before the charter for the barons, and still after it for the peasants and other classes. They had rights to neither a fair trial nor even life, with the barons existing at the pleasure of the king and the peasants living on the baron's lands without any rights despite generations of feudal service.

In these dawning days of the information age that the early 21st century represents, we live in a structurally comparable time. Consider a multiplayer game played by millions, played for eight hours per day, for 20 years from the age of 15 to 35 by someone physically disabled in such a way that he cannot leave his remote home to go to school, work, or social events. It is quite conceivable that for this person, the game in question contains the majority of his entire meaningful life experiences, social connections, self-image, and societal role. Perhaps he is even able to support himself by creating instructional videos and blogging about the game. For him, existence within the game is the very definition of real life.

Is it not on some level disturbing that after all this time, this player's account can be permanently banned based on unintentionally breaking a minor rule, voicing a negative opinion about some aspect of the game, or even commenting on an unrelated political event in a way that is counter to the game operator's interest? With a moderator's single cold click, the items, close friends, achievements, in-game money, and livelihood collected over a lifetime are gone forever. To his in-game friends, he is gone without a trace:

dead. Though he could begin again with a new account, it would be more akin to reincarnation than redemption. This is digital execution.

While many might write off the example of the obsessive gamer, consider instead your email, social media, instant messaging, and online payment accounts. We depend on these services to keep record of our personal and professional lives. This is especially true for those who make their money online, working for years to grow their social media followers and depending on payment services to receive money from their various subscribers and clients. Despite years and even decades of relying on these specific platforms, to which there may be no immediately obvious or reasonable alternatives, users can be "terminated" for any reason and have no rights to access the data they have gathered within these services. This means that everyone who makes use of the conveniences of the modern day is effectively walking on eggshells, existing (in their entire digital personas and real-world extensions) at the pleasure of their corporate rulers who owe them nothing and consider them a mere resource. This state sounds rather like that of a medieval peasant who must live without encoded rights, under the absolute rule of a potential tyrant, if they wish to exist within society instead of living a feral life in a nearby wilderness.

Decentralized applications certainly appear to provide a more client-rights oriented approach, with users remaining in active control of their data and interactions. This brings us to the big question: could tokens and smart contracts provide us a new basis of rights and freedoms in the Information age, possibly coming together to enforce a new kind of Magna Carta, underpinning an equitable and mutually respectful relation between the users and creators of technology?

As virtual word goods produce physical-world money, we witness fantasy become reality. Simultaneously, certain established realities are becoming fantasy as the virtual begins to compete with the physical for the title of accepted base reality. Surely, perceptions and experiences are realities regardless of in which realm, whether physical or virtual, they occur. Perhaps Decentralized Applications will eventually play a key to role in bridging the gap regarding rights and the general experience of existence between the physical and the virtual while Decentalized Finance connects people directly without need for centralized banks and Decentralized Autonomous Organizations revolutionize the way we conceptualize companies/organizations and the basis of their ownership/control.

A 13th-century Belgian manuscript illustrating a debate between a Jew and a Christian.

CHAPTER 18

Debates in Blockchain

We know that the blockchain world is a big tent in that its participants come from all walks of life. It is practically impossible for this diverse group to agree on anything, starting from the basic question of what token should rightfully be called *Bitcoin*, and what, if any, meaning blockchain has value beyond this ill-defined *Bitcoin chain*. Perhaps the only thing they can agree on is that blockchain technology, *however they may understand it in their minds*, is so revolutionary and powerful that it will radically change society.

Beyond this most basic yet powerful conviction of blockchain's revolutionary power, there is no shortage to the different ways that the blockchain concept is conceived. As is common with religious or political alignment, viewpoints and "blockchain identities" tend to be set in stone according to a person's interests and worldview. There is certainly a tendency for people to imagine blockchain as exactly what best suits and to disregard evidence and viewpoints that run contrary.

Bitcoin Maximalism vs. Multicoinism

The first alt-coins were commonly understood as experiments to help Bitcoin grow, but soon various people started taking them too seriously to the traditionalists' liking. This is perhaps the earliest major division of the blockchain community and while it has roots from 2015, it was solidified by the aftermath of the 2017 Ethereum fork. This split focused on the question of whether Bitcoin and Blockchain were one single concept or whether non-Bitcoin blockchains could be legitimate. While many Maximalists take an uncompromising view regarding all blockchains, others only take the Maximalist stance regarding *currency* blockchains while remaining open-minded towards other use-cases. As for this debate, the market will decide.

Immutability vs. Consensus

This is the classic conflict between Ethereum and Ethereum Classic. Immutability commands that code is sovereign and unchangeable, even when the creators of the currency, and most stakeholders, agree that what the code "allowed" was an unintentional bug and against the will and interests of the users and owners. If we think of code as law, then the support for immutability can be described as a type of legalism. This refers to unforgiving and unquestionable adherence to the code as it is written. For a proponent of blockchain immutability, there is no valid concept of a *spirit of the law,* unless of course its spirit is to do nothing but to robotically follow the letter of the law. In contrast, community consensus is driven by the wishes of stakeholders; it is open to amendment towards the collectively desired spirit of the law, if and when the consensus decides that the *letter of the law* is opposed to more important principles.

Blockchains indisputably operate primarily on the immutability principle, and it is widely recognized that casual alterations would cause chaos. The main point of controversy is whether such alterations can ever be made for any reason, regardless if 99.99% of stakeholders agree. It boils down to the idea of whether a blockchain is a mere human construct akin to our institutions or whether it should be placed above us as if it were a type of law of physics, mathematical principle, or divine revelation.

The beauty of blockchain currencies is that there ultimately need be no debate as users will vote with their feet and use the version they feel is best suited for them. This means that while someone may indeed be "right" by the code, they may end up alone with worthless tokens when everyone else decides otherwise and simply begins to use a new version of the currency. No matter what one believes about s*trength in numbers*, the human factor can perhaps never be discounted because the value of any blockchain is ultimately derived from the consensus of others.

Private Blockchains vs. Public Ledgers

Decentralization is not a universally recognized good. Further, the world is made up of systems built upon systems, built upon even more systems. Just how many of these systems can be decentralized, and would that be desirable to anyone, much less an entire population? Decentralization is a concept close to the heart of many in the industry, but it does not often go beyond an ideal. It is most valued by more idealistically driven individuals at the grassroots level; and decentralized start-ups and projects are primarily born of them. Larger corporations that adopt "blockchain" for whatever purpose generally do little more than pay lip service to decentralization, while keeping their blockchain solutions primarily closed, in-house, or otherwise in their control. Governments exploring blockchain solutions generally place little to no value on decentralization.

Many argue that decentralization is a definitional aspect of any blockchain and that nothing less than the anonymously created and leaderless Bitcoin can truly be called decentralized. The idea of decentralization can be interpreted in many ways: From being open access to anyone, to merely some basic form of decentralization within the confines of an otherwise closed organization. The concepts of *ethernet* and *internet* come to mind, with many interpreting *blockchain* as a new type of *net*, but without a designation of, nor understanding of the difference between internal/closed and external/open versions of this new *net*. These *ethernet blockchains* are often called *private blockchains*, whereas *internet blockchains* take form as a *public ledger*. As these concepts are new and foreign to most and ultimately still evolving, there is not yet a consensus understanding of nor differentiating between the two. What we do know is that even after 30 years, ethernet networks still exist despite the proliferation of internet. In this same vein, we are likely to see blockchains ranging from centralized to decentralized for the foreseeable future. It is difficult to argue that either type is inherently illegitimate; they both (along with hybrid systems) serve various functions that can be entirely valid and worthwhile to the entities making use of them.

Environmental Costs of Blockchain

In 2019, it was reported that Bitcoin mining consumed 64 TWh of electricity, more than Switzerland.[624] This naturally put many environmentalists up in arms, labeling Bitcoin a vile, planet destroying experiment in make-believe money. True enough, the reality of Bitcoin mining consists of an arms race towards ever-increasing amounts of computing power. While this is an arguably needless waste, there are not exactly many alternatives save for some sort of untenable cease fire in competition. These concerns have also been voiced from within the crypto-sphere, with early proponents of Litecoin touting its relative energy efficiency. Some newer blockchain platforms, like EOS, have done away with the proof of work concept of mining entirely, partly to avoid the environmental costs associated with ever-competitive mining.

The argument can be made that while mining, as with flying between endless blockchain conferences, certainly contributes to pollution and waste, the promise of blockchain is so large that it is worthwhile. Consider the non-controversial, yet comparably massive amounts of power consumed by normal internet and banking servers. Naturally if one does not believe in or is explicitly anti-blockchain in the way of a Nocoiner, then any amount of power consumption is too much. For those who believe that mining-based blockchains will somehow elevate humanity to a new level, there is likely no maximum limit. Perhaps there is a balance somewhere.

---

[624] Vincent, James. "Bitcoin Consumes More Energy than Switzerland, According to New Estimate." *The Verge*, 4 July 2019.

Goal of Fiat Profits vs. BTC Gains

> *What are you trying to tell me, that I can trade my bitcoins for millions someday?*
>
> *No Neo, I'm trying to tell you that when you're ready... you won't have to.*

This is the *lifer divide* in Blockland. Some people moved to Blockland hoping to find fortunes which they can eventually bring back home and convert to the local currency. Others believe that not only is it possible to stay in Blockland forever, but that Blockland will become so powerful as to conquer (even enslave) *everyone's* homeland. The idea is that Bitcoin, a mix of coins, or perhaps even some new cryptocurrency will become so powerful as to become the new lynchpin of the global economy. A practical example of this is the idea that Bitcoin will eventually come to rival or even replace gold. When estimating the future price of Bitcoin, those who are most optimistic and start suggesting values approaching 8-figures will typically acknowledge that at such a point, measuring in dollars would become meaningless as government issued money could no longer exist in its present form or valuation. Others will naturally consider thinking like this to be overly theoretical or even a bizarre post-apocalyptic fantasy. These *temporary residents* are in Blockland for the "gains", seeking a 5x, 10x, or even 100x return on their investments and ventures before intending to "exit".

Banking the Unbanked vs. Leaving the World Behind

Banking the unbanked is one of the rallying cries of Bitcoin, and blockchain in general. 1.7 billion of the world's poor lack bank accounts, and this is often seen as a barrier that is perpetuating their poverty.[625] Bitcoin democratizes finance and, in theory, allows anyone to save and transact more efficiently. This is understood to be a universal good, ideally helping hundreds of millions of people rise out of poverty by giving them a sound and stable means of "banking." This would be an example of a *technological leap*, where less-developed regions jump right to the newest technology without incremental improvements. An example of this is the direct adoption of cell phones and mobile internet in developing regions that never implemented landlines.

But perhaps the reason that the *unbanked* are poor is not because they are unable to easily store, save, and transact money, but because they lack access to debt? If Bitcoin is *digital gold*, how much will it really help those who are economically most disadvantaged? For such a population, the conventional wisdom would be not to save the meagre amounts they can scrounge together, but to invest in education, infrastructure, and local businesses. Outside of theoretically investing meager amounts in cryptocurrency for 100x returns (which, for a low-tech and low-information group of people to do successfully and "early enough" is entirely unrealistic), there are not many direct ways that any blockchain alone can be expected to lift millions out of poverty.

"*Gold is the money of kings, silver is the money of gentlemen, barter is the money of peasants - but debt is the money of slaves*"[626] is a good summary of many Bitcoiner's financial worldview. The idea

---

625 "The Global Findex Database." *The World Bank*, 2017.

626 Franz, Norm. *Money & Wealth in the New Millennium: A Prophetic Guide to the New World Economic Order*. WhiteStone Press, 2001.

that debt is universally bad and that "hard money" like gold or Bitcoin is anchored in the idea of scarcity; that there is only so much wealth in the world and people must thus protect their wealth to avoid losing their share. This comes with the uncomfortable implication that to benefit from these hard money principles, one must already have access to some type of wealth which to "solidify."

Perhaps the opposite end of this spectrum is equally valid. In Silicon Valley, it is often said that "s*oftware will eat the world.*"[627] As a result, the software-barons have become the richest men in the world with almost unspeakable global political power, even beyond the realm of governments. What if Bitcoin not only eats gold/money/derivatives markets by way of hyperbitcoinization, but also blockchain consumes everything in its wake from businesses to institutions and, like the internet, our society as we know it? Such a zero-sum game would suggest the formation of a new generation of super-rich unlike anything seen before. Consider the greatest wealth transfers of recent history: railroads, the industrial revolution, gold rushes, the oil boom, computer hardware, and more recently, software. Each of these have formed a wealthy, even global elite with large amounts of concentrated power and wealth. While this is not an inherently bad thing, it is the natural flipside of the *banking the unbanked* ideal of Blockchain's effect on the world.

How the world should deal with, or perhaps more accurately how this new class of billionaires might deal with the world, is an important question. If we continue to think of Bitcoin as gold and consider gold the money of kings, then large *hodlers* will quite simply become modern kings. Though past wealth transfer events have largely remained "under control" of governments by virtue of the wealth being created by physical goods in certain geographical

[627] Andreessen, Marc. "Why Software Is Eating the World." *The Wall Street Journal*, 20 Aug. 2011.

locations and in a certain national currency, this time is different. We can already see how the western political establishment has effectively lost its grip on software and data giants which operate global tax-avoidance systems and transact with all manner of governments. These titans have given us a taste of what happens when governments lose their effective control to even observe the means of production.

Unlike with resources, railroads, or computer hardware, identifying the means of production is difficult when it comes to software. A few employees and contractors around the world program something, it comes to be used by a billion people, and businesses, organizations, and political parties in a hundred countries pay for ad space by dealing with a number of regional marketing departments that are all incorporated in different countries. Whose laws apply, where should taxes be paid, and what country is responsible? No one really knows and that is despite established corporate structures with teams of lawyers and accountants, counting things like Dollars, Yen, and Euros. While the means of production might be an elusive concept in the software era, at least there is some type of discernible product being sold – adspace (user attention) and user data.

One of the major movements of the last century, Communism, called for the collectivization of these means of production to prevent the exploitation of workers (who both produce and purchase the goods). To allow for peace, modern society has effectively struck various rough truces between the bourgeoisie and the proletariat, with both contributing to taxes which are then used for the collective good. What happens to this order when companies become international and without tax liabilities, but workers remain tied to a specific country's system? If the wealth propping up the blockchain neo-bourgeoisie is not the direct result of any visible means of production nor any product that has been sold, can the modern ideal of the hardworking entrepreneur be used to believably justify their wealth in the eyes of the poor and middle-class?

In the blockchain era, even the remaining appearances of societal organization and control break down. In the case of Bitcoin, the creator is anonymous, no one is in charge, and there is no product being sold. Mining activity could be thought to have a physical location, but operations can be moved around the world on a week's notice or decentralized amongst hundreds of international servers. Further, no one can know how much BTC someone has, nor can it be forcefully seized or invalidated. What's more, BTC does not have to be sold for traditional currencies; it is wealth in its own right as it can be increasingly converted directly into goods and other assets around the world, without national currencies playing even an intermediary role. If national governments are already at a loss of how to reign in formally structured foreign companies selling the data of their citizens while showing them ads without paying taxes, then how can they dream of reigning in the coming clown-troupe of potentially anonymous global-citizen blockchain billionaires? Can the social contract that underpins western civilization remain valid?

A clown-troupe of billionaires? Indeed. The thing to understand is that these people who bought large amounts of bitcoin in the early years and intend to hold them into perpetuity, are not *normal* people. I would argue that they are more ideologues, technologists, and futurists than entrepreneurs, businesspeople, or investors. Their common thread is a belief that they could work together to reform the entire global monetary system, even if it meant contributing to the downfall of the existing one. Should they achieve a place as the next Gates', Brin's, Page's, Jobs', Bezos', and Zuckerberg's of the world, then they will do so not by individually building or creating anything per se, but by merely jumping on the ideological bandwagon of a very specific financial revolution early enough. They are an unconventional bunch and will absolutely work to bend the world towards their will. When we consider who may be lifted from poverty through blockchain or who might use it as a ladder to ascend to the highest echelons of power, we must also consider who will be left behind.

Perhaps this question can most succinctly be described as that of *Bitcoin Gentrification.* While many idealized Blockland as a sort of *Sean's Outpost* for the tired, poor, tempest-tossed huddled masses of the world, the once-free *Bithouses* are now million-dollar mansions that only relatively wealthy and risk-tolerant investors can benefit from. Blockland has become a place of privilege with little room for have-nots, and one is left to wonder if cryptocurrency is more a vehicle of individualist domination rather than collectivist liberation. Put bluntly, is *the revolution* merely a convenient façade for a private conquest?

Cash vs. Gold?

Related to the idea of banking the unbanked is the question of what role Bitcoin could theoretically play in a future global economy. This debate has been the core of the bitter block-size civil war. The question is whether Bitcoin should firstly be an efficient *cash* system that anyone can use for casual purchases such as cups of coffee, or if it is better placed as a type of money-of-kings *base asset* that does not prioritize speed, agility, or low usage costs. The analogy to gold is again appropriate, considering that gold trading is done with 400-ounce bricks that often remain in the same vault after changing owners. While common people may own gold, they do not shave off little slivers of their bullion to purchase food or clothing – cash and electronic methods are much more practical. If Bitcoin were optimized to function with such efficiency, it is argued that its blockchain could become overloaded and see its security compromised, whereas a focus away from the purely *common cash* system can be accused of straying from Satoshi's vision.

It is foreseeable that Bitcoin could one day fulfill both gold and cash functions without compromise, but it is not immediately practical. One option is for a *layered* system where separate cryptocurrencies, whether different versions/forks of Bitcoin or otherwise, are used for different purposes while being exchanged seamlessly. Until there can be one coin to rule them all, this controversy will likely continue.

Money, Security, Property, or Commodity?

Since the beginning it has been unclear what financial product cryptocurrencies and other crypto-assets most resembled. Though there have been many attempts to pigeonhole Bitcoin under a specific term, it seems that the most appropriate action is to consider tokens to constitute a new category altogether. Securities are issued by companies, which many cryptocurrencies like Bitcoin are not but many company-issued tokens are. Bitcoin certainly resembles a commodity like gold in many respects and often functions as money as well. Someone can certainly solely control and thus own a blockchain token, supporting the idea that tokens are property. There does not seem to be an imminent consensus on terminology – digital gold, digital cash, crypto assets, blockchain commodities, security tokens, and an endless list of terms appear to be equally valid descriptors.

Individualism vs. Collectivism

Bitcoin, like gold, can be understood as a currency based around individualism. The amount is finite, scarce, and must be protected even at great cost. Possession is law when it comes to Bitcoin, and the amount of BTC one controls cannot readily be proven by others. Fiat currencies, especially those held in bank accounts, are not this far right on the individual-collective spectrum. This is because governments can regularly inspect bank accounts and income reports, primarily to determine taxation. The utility of this system is not only to allow individuals to hold wealth, but to ensure that transactions in an economy are taxed for the (collectively decided) collective benefit. Looking back again at the Ethereum fork, we can see that the collective turned out more powerful than the individualist "attacker." Despite the common focus on individualism, there are powerful collectivist sentiments in the blockchain community. While *blockchain anarchism* or *crypto patriotism* may be on its way to becoming a relatively significant movement, neither *blockchain socialism* nor *crypto communism* have yet emerged though they very well may. If used for collectivist or redistributive ends, a specially programmed cryptocurrency could be quite the experiment, though going directly against the most basic ideals that spawned the technology. Good or bad, innovation nor experimentation are unlikely to stop.

Transparent Anonymity

Many people falsely assume that Bitcoin and most other digital currencies are anonymous. The contrary is true: all transactions are recorded forever and publicly. While it is true that there are no names per se involved in most transactions making the system pseudonymous (instead of anonymous), it is not unreasonable to assume that a large number of transactions can now and in the future be traced back to individuals. This is because exchanges and the sellers of physical goods often require personal information. What this means is that if Joe has 0.563 BTC in a wallet and sends portions of it to 10 different businesses over a few years, any one who knows that *Transaction X* was sent by Joe will be able to see the nine other transactions Joe made from that wallet (address / account). If one of those receiving accounts were then identified as having been used to receive money for illegal goods or services, Joe could find himself in trouble even 10 years down the line. Imagine a cash-based economy where the serial numbers of each bill ever transacted, whether legally or illegally, had to be publicly recorded at each point of exchange!

Bitcoin Mixers are one service which has been created to launder bitcoins in such a way that their origins are obfuscated, often used to hide illegal purchases, or avoid taxes. These methods are analogous to shuffling sums of money between several personal accounts and corporations in various tax havens around the world. While this would indeed make it difficult for others to track one's cryptocurrency, algorithms will most certainly be developed to identify certain patterns and make reasonable assertions as to which Bitcoin addresses are connected to the same owners. *Privacy blockchains* are another weapon in the arsenal of anonymity, including tokens such as Monero and BitcoinDark. These are obfuscated public ledgers, which allow anyone to transact but no observer can easily determine the source, destination, or amount of coins being sent. For this, Monero has earned a long-standing position as a widely respected and used cryptocurrency, even among many who otherwise tend toward Bitcoin maximalism.

Philosophically, both support for total anonymity and radical transparency can be found within the crypto sphere. My good friend Gary Lachance is a rare example of the latter variety – a decentralization activist who believes he might just have an answer to the modern question of privacy. He has published a manifesto titled *Privacy is the Enemy: A Grand Decentralization Theory*, where he reasons that "*privacy is dead and total surveillance is inevitable.*" The only way to combat mass-surveillance is to turn the other cheek and build our own surveillance society first. His thesis is that true freedom will be attained when all information is liberated, and Gary believes that this could be attained by building a consent-based *Open Society*, where everything is based on reputation. At the base level of his vision, people would voluntarily carry around a *black box* while in public, recording and publicly archiving all interactions. AI could then parse the videos through facial recognition, building an open database on practically everyone. This would disincentivize not only things like assault or theft, but even rudeness. With the recent proliferation of DeepFake videos, which make it nearly impossible to determine the validity of video, Lachance admits that this may no longer be workable.

Lachance envisions further steps of this Open Society, which include publicly-recording dash-cams in vehicles, mounted cameras in public streets and facilities, and camera-drones to monitor entire cities' traffic patterns and identify things like poachers or illegal fishers over wide stretches on wilderness or ocean. All this would culminate in an *Open Profile* on every person, which publicly presents "personal" records of *everything* from employment, education, and legal to medical and financial. Now friends, family, prospective employers, business partners, or love interests could come to know *everything* about you, along with any personal commentary or notes you have added to explain things like past criminal history or commendable achievements. While this may seem an insane proposition, it is based on the notion that all these records already exist anyway but collected against our consent by companies that will inevitably experience data leaks. These records are effectively used against us by marketers or background-researchers without our consent, or ability to comment or clarify. The secondary notion is that if all data was made public, we would see how flawed everyone is and lose our collective need to present a perfect image. This is pre-emptive transparency; truth will set us free.

What this manifesto presents is essentially a proposal to place our *existence* on *a blockchain of verified, transparent & indelible truth.* It goes on to assert that this type of system would radically change society into a place that effectively disempowers greed, sociopathy, monopolies, and the lust for power while allowing for all kinds of new collectives and civil discourses to develop. Privacy may be a desirable ideal for Lachance, but we are losing it anyway so society may as well embrace transparency instead. As one might guess, Lachance identifies as a decentralist.

The opposite and more common position held by blockchain enthusiasts is that of the privacy activist. The basic belief here is that privacy is a sacred right that must be protected. This idea is traced to early American thinking, by which authorities were not legally allowed to search residences or open letters without special warrants. Such constitutional laws have not been officially repealed, so there is a logic in asserting that similar protections should prevent random searches of electronic devices, communications, or financial records. Though Bitcoin's early applications involved the anonymous purchase of drugs, subsequent police action has shown that these transactions have not been nearly as anonymous as many assumed. In 2019, there was even a ring of hundreds of child abusers who were arrested around the world after having their Bitcoin transactions uncovered by a multinational investigation.[628] It is interesting to note that in the 90's and early 00's, every child knew that they must never reveal their real identity online; however, this changed

[628] "Dark Web Child Abuse: Hundreds Arrested Across 38 Countries." *BBC*, 16 Oct. 2019.

with social media, and anonymous use of computers is getting increasingly difficult, rare, and for many, suspicious.

National Economy vs. The Crypto Economy

The crypto economy refers to the (often cryptographically hidden) economy between actors in the blockchain industry. This economy often operates with cryptocurrency that rarely or never gets exchanged for fiat. This economy is global; as participants hail from around the world, nations and borders are considered irrelevant in the same way as in an online multiplayer game. The players in this economy consist of developers, marketers, designers, writers, and others.

A classic 2017-18 ICO is a perfect example of this economy at work. The first investor's BTC would be used to pay for sponsored articles & ads on blockchain-focused websites, booths & sponsorships at blockchain conferences, and various website designers and blockchain developers. While some of these recipients would exchange for fiat, many would hold all or most of their earnings and potentially invest them in other cryptocurrencies. With time, it has become increasingly practical to use Bitcoin and other major cryptocurrencies to buy almost anything.

The global crypto economy can be compared to the more local-regional concept of informal economy, as neither economies' activity is tracked by government. Much of *crypto labor* could as such be classified as grey market labor that goes unreported. Many of the crypto economy's participants would consider that there is no moral basis for taxation if everything is done in cryptocurrency, just like one would not imagine being taxed for finding a rare item in a video game that could theoretically be sold for money. While one might accept taxation if such in-game items were actually sold for money, it would appear absurd to tax items if they were only used or traded within their relevant games. Based on this thinking and the US tax concept of *like-kind* exchange, many have avoided ever converting their cryptocurrencies into fiat. Some have experimented with the alternative of trading them between other tokens or even stablecoins pegged to fiat, albeit with mixed results. Notably, no legal concept of insider trading exists in this economy because none of its markets are regulated.

Many governments from the local to national have expressed excitement at the economic benefits of attracting and encouraging blockchain business, which appears somewhat in contrast with the idea of a sovereign crypto economy. In the US, lawmakers have spoken about the high level of innovation in blockchain and how it would be important to attract such businesses to the country. Island nations such as Malta, Cyprus, Puerto Rico, and several of the smaller Caribbean islands have positioned themselves to attract blockchain companies with favorable legislation, including open-minded tax policies. A large piece of the thinking here is that by attracting such businesses, the localities will benefit from the mere presence of entrepreneurs spending money both for local hiring, services, and living expenses.

At conferences and summits around the world, local government representatives have sat on panels with business leaders to discuss blockchain's many benefits to the local economies, be it from the mining industry, local exchange start-ups, or from established companies hiring blockchain talent. An example of this is *Crypto Valley* in Switzerland's Zug, a fintech counterpart to California's Silicon Valley. Since 2016, Zug has attracted dozens of blockchain start-ups and numerous events which have identified it as an excellent location at both the geographical center and financial hub of Europe.

Global Perspectives

Having visited no less than 30 cities in 15 countries on blockchain business, I have come to see certain differences regarding the perceptions of Bitcoin, blockchain, and cryptocurrency. These patterns have repeated themselves and have been reaffirmed by many others. The variances are subtle and evolving which means that this analysis is merely a subjective snapshot in time.

North America

If we think of America as a culture of settlers that gained its independence through rebellion and created a government *by the people for the people* based around protecting each citizen's rights, it is easy to see how it would make fertile ground for Bitcoin to take root. With its established tech and finance sector, individualist and entrepreneurial culture, and cowboy/pioneer roots, North America has taken a role as the cradle of blockchain. Here lies most of Bitcoin's ideological roots, which consist of ideals including immutability, privacy, and individual sovereignty and autonomy. These ideals closely resemble the classical American understanding of negative liberty, which is the *freedom from* outside interference. This is related to anti-government, anti-fiat, and anti-taxation sentiments which in themselves are pillars of anarcho-capitalist and libertarian thought which is relatively popular and accepted there. Even the negative feelings towards inflation, the basic ascribed "evil" of fiat money, can be explained by this ideal of negative liberty by which the de-valuing of one's hard-earned money by an institution like a central bank is taken illegitimate infringement and personal attack. North America can thus be considered the ideological homeland of both Bitcoin Maximalists and Decentralites, both of which can be said to be driven by ideology. Both groups are largely organized at the grassroots level in various locales.

Though Canada does not share America's history of revolution, the same themes are largely present in crypto circles and we can therefore place both in the same boad category. Indeed, differences are more pronounced when comparing East and West as opposed to North and South.

I have made the interesting observation that American Bitcoiners are highly likely to be in support of 2nd amendment gun rights, including both automatic weapons and concealed carry without a license. The logic is rather straightforward; if you are to *be your own bank* without a need to rely on governments or corporations to safeguard your money, then you should naturally *be your own defense* without the need to rely on a police force to protect the *Swiss bank account in your pocket.* One should not need permission to protect one's assets, and the freedom-branded company Guns N' Bitcoin, whose tagline reads "*Thrive and survive the cyberpunk dystopia*"[629], demonstrates this cultural sentiment which overlaps somewhat with the doomsday prepper and goldbug subcultures. Notably with the advent of 3D printing, guns today are theoretically decentralized just like Bitcoin: it is possible for anyone to produce an effective semi-automatic weapon with only $100 worth of legally available parts and $300 worth of tools.[630] While many would consider this fact horrific, a large portion of blockchain ideologicals would see this democratization of weapon-access a natural, if not wonderful, development.

This trend of vocal support of gun rights is pronounced with those who focus on Bitcoin and less apparent with Multi-coiners and the like. The focus on *constitutional right* is a direct reference to immutability, which is a relevant and understood concept in American culture owing to the common idea that the nation's constitution is

---

[629] gunsnbitcoin.com

[630] Stella, Rick. "This 3D-Printed Gun is Semiautomatic, Untraceable, and Totally Legal." *Digital Trends*, 3 Feb. 2016.

set in stone and unchangeable whereas such rhetoric is less common and less passionate elsewhere. There is also the common idea that rights flow from the immutable written constitution and not from the group's current consensus of what is right. It is for this reason that if someone tried to change this written constitution to remove gun rights entirely, it is likely that a civil war would break out as many gun owners would reject such a constitutional fork.

Europe

When we look at the European blockchain ecosystem, we can see that it largely mirrors the North American ecosystem but without the same level of ideological conviction. Both Maximalism and Decentralism are largely absent from the common rhetoric, and the anarchistic fight-the-man zombie-survival instincts of North Americans are, while conceptually present, more akin to distant and abstract constructs rather than an intense, emotional, and immediate raison d'être. Blockchain is widely seen as an exciting technology by entrepreneurs, corporations, and governments, but Bitcoin itself is less prominent than in North America as a point of primary focus and discussion. There are certainly cultural differences at play; consider for example that while Switzerland is famous for its financial secrecy, in Scandinavia everyone's tax returns are publicly available. As one can see, the values of financial sovereignty and privacy are not universal. Whereas Americans may talk about Blockchain *replacing* or *bringing down* government or "the system", be it political or financial, Europeans are more likely to discuss how governments and corporations might be able to implement blockchain for efficiency and the public good. There is decidedly less discussion about a theoretical coming collapse that saturates American precious metal circles, and while such discussions in America tend to be action-oriented regarding individual survival in an unstable situation, Europeans are more likely to approach the subject from a theoretical direction with an eye on preventing instability. Certainly, very few Europeans are actively waiting for or excited by the idea of societal collapse.

Asia

In Asia, the viewpoint of blockchain as a political tool, mechanism, or actor is largely absent. Blockchain is almost invariably understood as a technology rather than a philosophy, and its highly ideological origins and continuing philosophical and political debates are effectively lost in translation to most participants in the Asian blockchain industry. Even those who understand Bitcoin's origin are likely to consider the cypherpunk ethos a mere foreign footnote. As such the Asian industry does not have substantial openly expressed anti-fiat and anti-government sentiments which are popular in North America and a minority viewpoint in Europe. The Asian blockchain sphere consists almost entirely of previously qualified technologists and business professionals, who have transitioned towards the industry due to the opportunities it has presented. Unlike in North America and Europe, there is no established grass roots blockchain community, making gatherings effectively industry socials or professional events more comparable to a meeting of accountants than misfit financial revolutionaries.

Unlike on the western continents where crypto-buyers tend to *buy in* on a deep emotional level and believe in the projects and cryptocurrencies they invest in, Asian crypto-buyers display a more open (or more honest) gambler mindset, and are, in my experience, less emotionally attached to given projects and the *big ideas* attached to them. This is almost certainly because these various tokens and companies are viewed mainly as a volatile and exciting market where the western philosophical, political, and social experiences and narratives are effectively absent.

The major Asian markets of course have somewhat different industry landscapes. In Japan for example, the industry's primary focus appears to be around the idea of cryptocurrencies and tokens presenting a new financial asset class to compliment the established system. This can be contrasted with South Korea, where there is a greater focus on the technology's use as a tool for fundraising such as in the case of ICO's, ITO's, and IEO's. China's industry landscape differs in that it largely rejects theoretical applications, even in the financial space. The Chinese approach focuses on immediately practical applications and development is swift.

Summary

To summarize the global approaches to blockchain, my general findings are that North American attitudes include more philosophical flair when contrasted to the primarily practical approach in Asia. North Americans entrenched in the industry tend to consider blockchain as entirely revolutionary, destined to replace massive industries and dethrone institutions. Asian participants tend to take a more cautious approach in considering it a primarily technological revolution (as opposed to an economic or ideological one), allowing for existing systems to be improved and made more efficient.

Considering this, I would propose the rough Global Blockchain Ideological-Practical Continuum. It runs from West to East, with the West Coast cities of San Francisco, Los Angeles, and Vancouver representing the pinnacle of blockchain idealism. Here lives many of the ideologues, futurists, and technologists who played an early and pivotal role in Bitcoin. As we head east to New York, Washington, and Toronto, we find that the focus becomes more corporate with the influence of Wall Street and government centers. Ethereum, which began in Toronto and took influence from the west coast, can appropriately be positioned right of Bitcoin on this spectrum as a mid-point between these *ideological* and *institutional* coasts.

The climate in Europe is comparable to America's east coast, and as we continue to Dubai in the Middle East the focus on technology and futurism is clearly surpassed by a business orientation. East Asian cities such as Singapore and Hong Kong lie on the right side of this spectrum, and the purest focus on capitalist practicality is found on the continent's easternmost edges in Beijing, Shanghai, Tokyo, and Seoul. South America, Africa, and Australia/Oceania are comparatively minor players in the global blockchain industry, so their positioning is more difficult to define at this stage. Of course, all perspectives exist everywhere to some degree, but there seems to be a clearly perceptible difference in attitude as we move along this axis.

1889 depiction of Cicero accusing Catiline of leading a plot to overthrow the Roman Senate.

CHAPTER 19

The World Weighs In

The only thing that's even kept Bitcoin alive this long is its novelty. Either it will remain a novelty forever or it will transition from novelty status to dead faster than you can blink.

- Dec. 2011, **$0.23** per BTC

Like the gold standard, a successful bitcoin would send our economy back into the dark ages. ... Even if it became popular, governments would squash it because of #1 and because they like being in power.... With bitcoin, a single failure of the cryptosystem could result in an utter collapse of the entire financial network.

- May 2011, **$3.12** per BTC

[Bitcoin will fail as a currency] because, by design, there will never be more than 21 million Bitcoins in existence. And thanks to hoarding and attrition, we can be sure that it will eventually serve as nothing more than as a collector's item... I would like to call upon the Bitcoin community to stop referring to it as a digital currency. This is misleading and harmful.

- June 2011, **$19.73** per BTC

So read the first three of hundreds of *Bitcoin Obituaries* collected by *99bitcoins.com.* Since 2011, these death notices have been published with increasing frequency, with 127 predictions of Bitcoin's imminent demise in 2017 alone. Though the first such obituaries were written by niche bloggers, mainstream media eventually took notice of Bitcoin and began to weigh in. These writings give us a clear idea how Bitcoin and later cryptocurrencies were perceived by governments, businesses, the media, and average people throughout the first decade of blockchain. Despite this, at least as of writing, Bitcoin is not dead.

A saying often misattributed to Gandhi reads that every movement goes through four phases: "*first they ignore you, then they laugh at you, then they fight you, and then you win.*" Gandhi was a lawyer who developed a philosophy of non-violent, passive resistance against apparent unjust rule called Satyagraha, which is Sanskrit for *holding firmly onto truth* or *truth force.* Satyagraha became central to the Indian Independence Movement and the famous saying has been interpreted as a summation of Gandhi's philosophy. The implication is that by the time *they* understand a movement well enough to consider it worthy of attack, it is too late to snuff it out. By openly oppressing the movement, it only becomes more resilient while making *them* appear increasingly illegitimate and resulting in the movement's triumph. With Bitcoin considered by many as a revolutionary movement, this Gandhian concept has continuously surfaced as a rallying cry asserting that *enemies* will eventually be conquered or made obsolete by blockchain's superior *truth force.*

Though *they* is commonly understood to stand for an oppressive financial order, it can be used to refer to any "haters" who have inevitably brushed off or laughed at the early Bitcoiner, in the way of a caricatural high school bully mocking the apparently wimpy and nerdy loser. Here, the ideal of the triumph of blockchain in supplanting the financial system can be read as a technologist's fantasy of an ultimate revenge of the nerds. It may very well be that *they* live mainly in the head of the blockchainer with a persecution complex – *they* are everywhere yet nowhere, everyone, yet nobody in particular. It is difficult to point out any specific government or institution that is continuously and unconditionally "oppressing" Bitcoin, much less blockchain.

In addition to public perception as reflected in pop culture and the media, government's perceptions of and reactions to cryptocurrency and blockchain are fascinating to study. Though blockchain got its start through Bitcoin, which was derived from a largely unapologetic anti-government movement, there is plenty for governments of all stripes to love in the capabilities offered by all manner of blockchains. The same goes both for central and retail banks. With time, the public statements issued by government and banking elites has slowly shifted from dismissal, first to apprehension and then towards cautious acceptance and even optimism.[631]

Among the first prominent people to take a stand in the Bitcoin world were Tyler and Cameron Winklevoss – famous after their successful *The Social Network* lawsuit against Facebook's Mark Zuckerberg. In April 2013, the pair announced that they had purchased $11 million worth of BTC.[632]

[631] Brito, Jerry. "Online Cash Bitcoin Could Challenge Governments, Banks." *TIME*, 16 Apr. 2011.
[632] Strydom, Martin. "Winklevoss Twins Plan $20m Bitcoin Float." *The Telegraph*, 2 July 2013.

> *A lot of people laughed at Tyler and Cameron Winklevoss when they announced in April that they had acquired $11 million worth of bitcoins. The announcement came on April 11, the day after the virtual currency hit a record high of $266 and then plummeted to $120. Over the next few days, it would fall as low as $50, cutting the value of the brothers' bitcoin stake in half.*[633]
>
> -Timothy B. Lee, 9 Nov. 2013.

Despite the dire news, the brothers reportedly used the opportunity to only buy more.

> *People say it's a Ponzi scheme, it's a bubble," said Cameron Winklevoss. "People really don't want to take it seriously. At some point that narrative will shift to 'virtual currencies are here to stay.' We're in the early days."*[634]
>
> - Nathaniel Popper, 11 Apr. 2013.

Statements from Superpowers

In the earliest of days when there was no word regarding Bitcoin's legal status, many worried that it might be seen in a sinister light and presumed entirely criminal. As my friend Daniel Mross filmed *The Rise and Rise of Bitcoin,* the first documentary exploring the subject, it was important for him that viewers would see him spending family time with his wife and young children in his stately, idyllically American home– complete with a flagpole and well maintained lawn. He was a normal family man and computer professional, not some terrorist financier nor underworld drug kingpin. The documentary featured interviews with eminent men like Roger Ver and Charlie Shrem, the latter whose arrest for laundering millions of

---

633 Lee, Timothy B. "The $11 Million in Bitcoins the Winklevoss Brothers Bought Is Now Worth $32 Million." *The Washington Post*, 9 Nov. 2013.
634 Popper, Nathaniel, And Peter Lattman. "Never Mind Facebook; Winklevoss Twins Rule in Digital Money." *The New York Times – DealBook,* 11 Apr. 2013.

dollars in Silk Road drug money made headlines days before the documentary's preview. Mross was horrified, as it appeared that Bitcoin's chance at legitimacy was crumbling like a house of cards.

These fears were well founded; already in July 2013, Thailand had effectively banned Bitcoin in an apparent ruling which made it "*illegal to buy and sell bitcoins, buy or sell any goods or services in exchange for bitcoins, send any bitcoins to anyone outside of Thailand, or receive bitcoins from anyone outside the country*", after a Bitcoin company made an informational presentation to Thai banking authorities.[635]

In an October 2013 meeting, "*The president* [Barack Obama]*, whose most important job is surely to protect the integrity of the monetary system, smugly asked* [Google's CEO Eric] *Schmidt if Bitcoin, one of many growing challenges to currency hegemony, was anything he had to worry about.*"[636] Schmidt himself had recently learned of the currency from conversations with Wikileaks' Ecuadorian-embassy-dwelling founder Julian Assange.

The first US congressional hearing on the future of Bitcoin took place on November 18th 2013, eight weeks after Ross Ulbricht's high profile Silk Road arrest. This hearing began with government and law enforcement officials airing concerns regarding activity like money laundering, drug dealing, and child exploitation and summarizing their successes in apprehending criminals using Bitcoin.

> *After the officials gave their opening statements, [chairing Senator] Carper's first question drew a parallel to the Internet. He pointed out that in the early days of the Internet revolution, many people raised concerns about illicit use of Internet technologies. Yet in the long run, he argued, the Internet has had a*

---

635 Trotman, Andrew. "Bitcoins Banned in Thailand." *The Telegraph*, 29 July 2013.

636 Wolff, Michael. ""How CEOs Are Clueless about Technology." *USA today*, 27 Oct. 2013.

> *hugely beneficial effect on peoples lives, making possible previously unimagined services like Facebook and YouTube. Carper wanted to know if the witnesses saw Bitcoin in the same light.*[637]
>
> -Timothy B. Lee, 18 Nov. 2013.

This marked the hearing's turn to a more positive light, with the government representatives generally agreeing with the Bitcoin industry leaders on the technology's obvious utility, its inherent legitimacy, and the importance of innovation. Despite stated concerns, the Senate's overall message "*stressed that Bitcoin has important legitimate uses and that regulators need to be careful not to stifle innovation in virtual currencies. And they seemed to believe that the situation was under control, and none asked for new regulatory powers to crack down on illicit uses of the currency.*"[638] This news was the first affirmation of Bitcoin's legality and set the stage for the price to double from $500 to pass the $1,000 milestone just 10 days later, on November 28th.

The next volley came one week later on December 5th, when China's central bank issued a statement banning banks under its jurisdiction from dealing with Bitcoin, mirroring concerns brought up by US lawmakers including unpredictable volatility and association with both money laundering and illicit markets. The bank declared that "*Judged by its nature, Bitcoin is one particular kind of a virtual product. It does not have the legal status of a currency, and it cannot and moreover should not be allowed to circulate in the market as a currency.*"[639]

---

[637] Lee, Timothy B. "This Senate Hearing is a Bitcoin Lovefest." *The Washington Post*, 18 Nov. 2013.
[638] Wille, Rob. "Bitcoin Crosses $700 As Senate Hearing Wraps." *Business Insider*, 19 Nov. 2013.
[639] "China Bans Banks from Bitcoin Transactions." *Financial Times*, 5 Dec. 2013.

Despite clarifications that individuals were free to purchase bitcoins at their own risk, the statement was widely misconstrued as an outright *China Bitcoin ban* and sent markets immediately tumbling from ~$1,200 to a low of $450 on December 18th, lower than before the US Senate hearing only a month before.[640] [641]

Blockchain Arms Race

With the existentially uncertain days of 2013 behind, practically all governments began to investigate the Bitcoin, and later, cryptocurrency phenomenon. The global interest in and recognition of blockchain technology kicked into high gear in 2017, when it was becoming clear that blockchain was no passing fad. Governments around the world began to consider blockchain not only as a potential source of wealth, but as a structural component of voting systems, identity verification, land registration, and more. With time, this developed into a sort of collective acknowledgment that blockchain technology itself was an entirely legitimate, powerful, and useful innovation beyond just the currency application. With this realization, a sort of blockchain arms race has begun to develop between major powers seeking to control the blockchain space as much as possible, while small nations and even cities have worked to create an edge by differentiating themselves as "*blockchain / Bitcoin / ICO / crypto friendly*."[642] [643] Among the first big players to

---

[640] Rizzo, Pete. "BTC Price Declines Following False Report of Bitcoin Ban in China." *CoinDesk*, 21 Mar. 2014.
[641] Hill, Kashimir. Bitcoin in China: "The Fall-out From Chinese Government Banning Real World Use." *Forbes*, 6 Dec. 2013.
[642] Milano, Annaliese. "Bermuda Drafting ICO-Friendly Legislation to Draw Crypto Businesses." *CoinDesk*, 20 Mar. 2018.
[643] Tassev, Lubomir. "Malta Sees No Issue with Unlicensed Crypto Firms, Valletta Mansion on Sale for Crypto." *Bitcoin.com* 11. Sept. 2018.

make a move was Russia, with President Vladimir Putin notably meeting with Vitalik Buterin in June 2017.[644] [645]

> Putin was attracted to Ethereum as a *"potential tool to help Russia diversify its economy beyond oil and gas."* After meeting Ethereum founder Vitalik Buterin, Putin said that *"the digital economy isn't a separate industry, it's essentially the foundation for creating brand new business models,"* - critical after Russia's recession. Vlad Martynov, adviser for nonprofit organization The Ethereum Foundation, compared blockchain to the internet. ... *"Blockchain may have the same effect on businesses that the emergence on the internet once had - it would change business models and eliminate intermediaries such as escrow agents and clerks. If Russia implements it first, it will gain similar advantages to those the Western countries did at the start of the internet age"* ... Putin's endorsement of Ethereum means that *"blockchain is no longer a bogeyman. It is more important for the attitude of the judiciary, which interprets and applies the law of Russia, than industrial applications. It will also drive the development of the government cryptography standard by security services, enabling future government use."*[646]
>
> \- Madhvi Mavadiya, 29 Aug. 2017.

This was put more bluntly by FSB (Russian Security Services– the successor of the KGB) agent Grigory Marshalko who, while leading the Russian delegation at an International Standards Organization meeting later in 2017, said "*Look, the internet belongs to the Americans – but blockchain will belong to us*"[647], after being questioned why Russian intelligence was getting involved with setting global standards for the industry. This was also echoed by Russian fintech executive Alexander Dunaev, who told a *Forbes* reporter that:

644 Anslow, Louis. "Vitalik Buterin: Putin's Useful Genius." *Medium*, 16 July 2018.
645 Higgins, Stan. "Vladimir Putin Mandates New Rules for Cryptocurrencies and ICOs." *CoinDesk*, 24 Oct. 2017.
646 Mavadiya, Madhvi. "Putin And Ethereum: A Match Made in Fintech." *Forbes*, 29 Aug. 2017.
647 Popper, Nathaniel. "Blockchain Will Be Theirs, Russian Spy Boasted at Conference." The New York Times, 29 Apr. 2018.

> *The last time the world saw such an unprecedented change was in the second half of the 20th century with the adoption of personal computers - which Russia missed due to geopolitical isolation. There is a lot of will to avoid this pitfall in the future.*[648]
> - Alexander Dunaev, 29 Aug. 2017.

Russia is not the only one to jostle for dominance in the blockchain industry. The Chinese government has also taken notice of the ways it can benefit from the technology. Despite many westerners in the industry having a certain apprehension towards China regarding its negative comments regarding currencies like Bitcoin and bans on ICO's[649], the government has invested heavily in blockchain development by way of numerous 9-figure government grants. President Xi Jinping made clear the Communist Party of China's desire to *seize the opportunity* presented by blockchain in a substantial 2019 speech as reported by Xinhua News:[650 651]

> *[Xi Jinping] emphasized that... we must take blockchain as an important breakthrough... the application of blockchain technology has extended to digital finance, Internet of Things, intelligent manufacturing, supply chain management, digital asset trading and other fields. At present, major countries in the world are accelerating the development of blockchain technology. China has a good foundation in the field of blockchain. It is necessary to accelerate the development of blockchain technology and industrial innovation, and actively promote the development of blockchain and economic and social integration.*
>
> *Xi Jinping stressed that it is necessary to... strive to let China take the leading position in the emerging field of blockchain... It is necessary to build a blockchain ecosystem, accelerate the*

---

648 Mavadiya, Madhvi. "Putin And Ethereum: A Match Made in Fintech." *Forbes*, 29 Aug. 2017.

649 Leng, Sidney. ?Why Has China Declared War on Bitcoin and Digital Currencies?" *South China Morning Post*, 16 Sept. 2017.

650 Foxley, William. "President Xi Says China Should 'Seize Opportunity' to Adopt Blockchain." *CoinDesk*, 25 Oct. 2019.

651 Li, Jane. "China's Leader, a Fan of Centralized Power, Is Suddenly the Darling of the Crypto Community." *Quartz*, 28 Oct. 2019.

deep integration of blockchain and cutting-edge technologies like artificial intelligence, big data, and Internet of Things, and promote integrated innovation and integration applications.

Xi Jinping pointed out that it is necessary to seize the opportunity of blockchain technology ... and play the role of blockchain in promoting data sharing, optimizing business processes, reducing operating costs, improving synergy efficiency, and building a credible system. It is necessary to promote a deep integration of the blockchain and the real economy. It is necessary to use blockchain... for creating a convenient, efficient, fair, competitive, stable and transparent business environment... [and to support] *economic development.*

It is necessary to... actively promote the application of blockchain technology in the fields of education, employment, poverty alleviation, health, anti-counterfeiting, food safety, public welfare, social assistance, etc. ... It is necessary to promote... blockchain and the construction of new smart cities, explore the promotion and application in the fields of information infrastructure, smart transportation, energy and power, and improve the level of intelligence and precision of urban management. It is necessary to use blockchain technology to promote greater inter-connectivity between cities in terms of information, capital, talents, and credit information. . . It is necessary to explore the use of the blockchain data-sharing model ... for government data across departments and regions... to deliver a better government service experience to the people.

Xi Jinping emphasized that it is necessary to strengthen the... regulation of blockchain technology, and actively explore development laws. It is necessary to explore the establishment of a safety guarantee... and guide [developers and operators] *to... implement safety features. It is necessary to implement the rule of law network into the management of blockchain and promote the safe and orderly development of blockchain.*[652]

[652] Chun, Chen. "During the 18th Collective Study of the Politburo, Xi Jinping Emphasized on Using Blockchain as an Important Breakthrough in Independent Innovation of Core Technology to Accelerate the Development of Blockchain Technology and Industrial Innovation." *Xinhuanet*, 25 Oct. 2019.

- President Xi Jinping, 25 Oct. 2019.

Contrasted with its rivals Russia and China, The United States federal government has not taken clear actions to promote blockchain innovation or implementation, whether related to Bitcoin specifically or its non-currency forms. Comments made by President Barack Obama regarding FBI-accessible back-doors in Apple devices has been seen as relevant to cryptocurrency:

> *And the question we now have to ask is if, technologically, it is possible to make an impenetrable device or system, where the encryption is so strong that there's no key; there's no door, at all. Then, how do we apprehend the child pornographer, how do we solve or disrupt a terrorist plot, what mechanisms do we have available to even do simple things like tax enforcement? Because if in fact you can't crack that at all; government can't get in, then everyone's walking around with a swiss bank account in their pocket. So there needs to be some concession to be able to get into that information somehow.*[653]
>
> - President Barack Obama, 5 Apr. 2016.

President Donald Trump has also commented on the matter via Twitter, showing clear disdain for Bitcoin and other cryptocurrencies without making mention of blockchain as a technology. He made the shockingly bold prediction that the US dollar was not merely the most dominant currency at the time, but that it would *always* remain so. One might, however, question why an American President would feel a need to make such an overconfident statement at all. Trump's official rejection of Bitcoin and other anonymous and uncontrollable currencies is actually in line with Russian and Chinese views, with the difference being his lack of comment

[653] Ryan Conley, Youtube.com user. "Obama admits Bitcoin is a 'Swiss offshore account in your pocket' - BitClub Network Ethereum." *YouTube*, 5 Apr. 2016.

on *non-currency blockchains* which Xi and Putin have acknowledged positively.[654] Despite relative silence at the federal level, some state-level governments have taken bolder steps to welcome the cryptocurrency age.[655 656]

> *[Tweet #1:] I am not a fan of Bitcoin and other Cryptocurrencies, which are not money, and whose value is highly volatile and based on thin air. Unregulated Crypto Assets can facilitate unlawful behavior, including drug trade and other illegal activity*
>
> *[Tweet #2:] Similarly, Facebook Libra's "virtual currency" will have little standing or dependability. If Facebook and other companies want to become a bank, they must seek a new Banking Charter and become subject to all Banking Regulations, just like other Banks, both National*
>
> *[Tweet #3:] and International. We have only one real currency in the USA, and it is stronger than ever, both dependable and reliable. It is by far the most dominant currency anywhere in the World, and it will always stay that way. It is called the United States Dollar!*[657]
>
> - President Donald Trump, 12 July 2019.

While it is easy to understand why major governments may not like the idea of everyone having a Swiss bank account in their pocket, this official rejection has only encouraged the more anti-government portions of the blockchain movement who reject the idea of government blockchains. Under the cypherpunk blockchain ideology, blockchain should not be like a program controlled by an authority, but like a law of nature by which all would function: no Pharaoh can command the sun to set an hour earlier or later. To

---

654 Partz, Helen. "Russian President Putin Orders Government to Adopt Crypto Regulation by July 2019." *CoinTelegraph*, 27 Feb. 2019.
655 Suberg, William. "US: New Hampshire Bill Aims to Legalize Bitcoin for State Payments in 2020." *CoinTelegraph*, 24 Jan. 2019.
656 Kuhn, Daineal. "US State of Nevada Passes Flurry of Blockchain Bills." CoinDesk, 14 June 2019.
657 Trump, Donald J. *Twitter.com account @realdonaldtrump*, 12 July 2019.

them, official apprehension is a sign of weakness and fear regarding something that cannot be controlled, making "*a Swiss bank account in every pocket!*" a sort of anarcho-capitalist rallying cry. Swiss pockets cannot be picked.[658]

Perhaps the most unified global position of cryptocurrency and blockchain was reached at the June 2019 G20 Summit in Osaka, where representatives of the world's most powerful economies agreed on a common declaration concerning the phenomenon:

> *Technological innovations can deliver significant benefits to the financial system and the broader economy. While crypto-assets do not pose a threat to global financial stability at this point, we are closely monitoring developments and remain vigilant to existing and emerging risks. ... We reaffirm our commitment to applying... anti-money laundering [regulations] and countering the financing of terrorism.*[659 660]
>
> - G20 Leaders, 29 June 2019.

Redefining Currency

Considering the reactions of some of the most powerful people in the world, it now seems safe to say that blockchain, be it in whatever form, has opened pandora's box and is here to stay.

The public perception of cryptocurrency has increasingly divided *Bitcoin*, *cryptocurrency/crypto assets*, and (other) *blockchain technology* into different and only tangentially related concepts; a fact attested to by the very title of this book. While this state of things will frustrate some, I suggest that it is by now a lost cause, and even bordering on foolishness, to assert that any of them are illegitimate,

---

[658] Torpey, Kyle. "U.S. Lawmakers Are Realizing They Can't Ban Bitcoin." *Forbes*, 30 July 2019.
[659] "G20 Osaka Leaders' Declaration." *G20.org*, 29 June 2019.
[660] Helms, Kevin. "Modi Discussed Crypto Standards at G20 Summit – How They Apply to India." *Bitcoin.com*, 3 July 2019.

ill-conceived, or that they are intrinsically one and the same. *Blockchain* has become an accepted, mysterious new method of doing things to such an extent that it has become a corporate buzzword. The idea of *crypto-assets* controlled by companies or governments have followed this trend, becoming acceptable-in-theory to large portions of the public, while *Bitcoin* has not yet been able to shed its simultaneously awkward and bad-boy persona.

With increasing global openness to blockchain solutions, many governments have begun to flirt with the possibility of issuing digital versions of their national currencies. These would in most cases be centralized, with the currency-issuer "printing" digital currency and then sending it to bank-controlled addresses, this being an alternative to printing physical bills to sit in vaults. This would eliminate the cost of printing, storing, counting, protecting, validating, and investigating fraud of government-issued paper money. In late 2018, the International Monetary Fund's Managing Director, Christine Lagarde, published a blog post titled *Winds of Change: The Case for New Digital Currency* in which she confirmed that "*I believe we should consider the possibility to issue digital currency. There may be a role for the state to supply money to the digital economy.*"[661] The following year, she took up a post as the President of the European Central Bank. Venezuela's President Nicholas Maduro was among the first to announce plans for a national cryptocurrency in February 2018, with the Petro being reportedly backed by the country's natural resources.[662] [663] [664]

---

[661] Lagarde, Christine. "Winds of Change: The Case for New Digital Currency." *International Monetary Fund*, 14 Nov. 2018.
[662] Popper, Nathaniel, and Ana Vanessa Herrero. "The Coder and the Dictator." *The New York Times*, 20 Mar. 2020.
[663] Markovitz, Leon. "Venezuela's Petro Cryptocurrency Is a Gift to Future Generations." *CoinDesk*, 2 Sept. 2018.
[664] Sharma, Rakesh. "Why Venezuela's Cryptocurrency, Petro, Is A Failure." *Investopedia*, 7 Sept. 2018.

While not a country, Facebook has also joined the currency-issuing fray by announcing plans for the Libra, a currency backed by the social media giant instead of by any government.[665] [666] Not everyone has been receptive towards the idea that multi-national companies could start "playing government" and issuing their own money, with Germany's Minister of Finacne offering a particularly transparent condemnation:

> *A wolf in sheep's clothing is still a wolf... We must do everything possible to make sure the currency monopoly remains in the hands of states.*[667]
>
> - German Finance Minister Olaf Scholz, 7 Dec. 2020.

Blockland is hereby revealed as a borderless battleground for not only ideologies, but for the very concepts underpinning governments and croporations as they fight to defend and expand their legitimacy and domain.

---

665 Chohan, Usman W. "Social Media Monopolies and Cryptocurrencies: Facebook's Proposed Coin." *SSRN Electronic Journal*, 12 Mar. 2019, doi:10.2139/ssrn.3351630.

666 Popper, Nathaniel, and Mike Isaac. "Facebook and Telegram Are Hoping to Succeed Where Bitcoin Failed." *The New York Times*, 28 Feb. 2019.

667 Shalal, Andrea, et al. "G7 finance officials back need to regulate digital currencies: Treasury." *Reuters – Future of Money*, 7 Dec. 2020.

Society and government imagined as a sovereign made up of its subjects, as depicted in Thomas Hobbes' 'Leviathan' in 1651.

EPILOGUE

The Future of Blockland

The Schism

Getting to the heart of the conflicts between the various tribes of Blockland, it appears there is a certain ideological question regarding the future and ultimate legacy of blockchain technology. What will we make of blockchain or perhaps more accurately, what will blockchain make of us?

The anarchistic cypherpunks had a very clear vision: blockchain would liberate humanity from control from governments and other societal institutions which they see as coercive, illegitimate, and even evil entities whose rule citizens are forced into by way of birth. Their idea is that blockchain serves as a fundamental antithesis of the surveillance and control that such institutions require to operate. Like the 2nd Amendment which gives Americans the right to bear arms and thus overthrow their government, blockchain is imagined as functioning like a wrench that, when thrown into the internal machinery of the Leviathan, will send it crashing down and decentralize and distribute its power. Out of one, many.

The establishment or international community as we might call it has a different vision. For governments and corporations of all stripes, blockchain presents a clear opportunity to solidify, harden, and improve existing systems in ways that tend to boil down to easier surveillance and control on all levels. Certainly, blockchain can be used within these existing frameworks to benefit normal people. For these mammoth organizations, blockchain can represent a sort of lubricant which will make their gears run even more smoothly and reliably. As the inherent inefficiencies related to multiple layers of governance or management are reduced, it becomes easier to centralize and consolidate power. Out of many, one.

While blockchain-run utopias can be imagined under both extreme decentralization and centralization, jungle-style anarchy and oppressive dictatorship reveal extremist dystopias on both sides of the coin. In 2013, Mastercoin's founder and ICO inventor J.R. Willett was among the first to air worries of competing dystopian futures powered by blockchain. In his vision, Bitcoin or its descendants replace government issued currencies causing their values to crash while making tax collection impossible. Governments and all they do will be thrown into chaos and even fail. Retirement savings will vanish and normal people, who will see a small elite having usurped all their wealth, may well round up and execute every blockchain investor. At the same time, money laundering, insider trading, and black markets will flourish without end. Kidnappers could even publicly auction off children for untraceable money, giving the highest bidder the coordinates from which to find their restrained "purchase". Others have also imagined a future *execution marketplace,* in which anyone could freely and anonymously bet a large sum of money that a specific person will NOT DIE in a specific year, indirectly giving freelancing assassins an incentive to bet against them and go on to influence the outcome directly by way of a bullet.

Does anyone really expect the government to sit back quietly and watch while their currency is debased, terrorism is funded, and children are kidnapped? The only question is when and how they will strike back against these forces. While the government does have a lot of options, ultimately those options only slow things down. At some point, we collectively with our governments face a difficult choice between trying to survive this deadly storm or attempting to destroy all decentralized computer networks (including the internet). The former seems unthinkable, the latter, impossible.

I wouldn't be surprised if this chaos gives rise to a strong, centralized, [blockchain powered] one-world government which gets its revenues by tightly reigning in freedom of commerce in order to collect taxes. For instance, I will not be surprised to see a requirement someday that every person buying or selling have an implant which tightly binds their identity to the sale. Perhaps the implant will even be located on the back of the right hand or the forehead! This may seem repugnant to you now, but wait until you have lived in the storm for a while before you call it impossible. The natural reaction to the deadly chaos of decentralized currency is for the populace to embrace increasingly centralized controls on commerce. The battle lines are only just starting to be drawn, and your guess is as good as mine for how it will play out.[668]

- JR Willett, 19 Apr. 2013.

Blockland United

Blockchain in and of itself is nothing but a technology or method and can hold no inherent political agenda anymore than other wide concepts like math, logic, computing, or accounting. The basic function of a blockchain might even be demonstrable in nature.

---

668 Willett, JR. "Bitcoin's Dystopian Future." *Bitcoin Forum*, 19 Apr. 2013.

To understand the idea of a naturally occurring blockchain and chain-splitting fork, imagine a tribal tradition where an ancient creation story is always passed down orally on the summer equinox. As most of the attendees have heard the story perhaps a dozen times before, they rely not on the memory of the individual storyteller but on their entire collective recollection. If the storyteller forgets or changes an aspect from the previous year, someone might interrupt to say "*Story Teller, I don't think the fairies were green as you say; I remember when my late grandmother told it years ago and she said that they were blue!*" the tribe might then vote upon their recollection. If 45 of the 50 spectators around the fire are confident that previous recitations featured blue fairies, then it will collectively be confirmed that the correct version of the story is one with blue fairies while the green-fairy version is ignored and forgotten.

However, if the split was 20 for blue and 30 for green, the story might become uncertain. One might contemplate a situation where this difference in fairy color is so important that the tribe splits in two, leaving the stories to continue developing on their own for generations without ever again being reconciled. One might even make the adventurous claim that the historical splitting up of languages, religions, and even the conflicts between political parties can be explained as natural consensus-of-reality blockchains operating on the 'human system', where each individual is a node of sorts. Perhaps blockchains have always been with us, and its institution onto the digital plane was simply the recognition and modernization of something ancient. In a sense, the basic function of DNA replication is a blockchain; an automatic copying and confirmation with occasional forks (mutations). It's blockchains all the way down.

Reflect again on the Mythology of Blockland, as presented early in the book.

Read together, the stories of Blockland convey an epic, true legend that recounts the formation of the modern phenomenon of blockchain. As with the early mythologies that were originally passed down orally, archetypes which represent basic symbols, characters, and ideas are of prime importance in communicating ideas through vast stretches of time, culture, location, and language. This new saga of Blockland has no shortage of such archetypal characters. These include The Creator, as symbolized by Satoshi, as well as the creators of various other cryptocurrencies and tokens. Another is The Outlaw, who seeks to overthrow existing power structures and is well represented by the Cypherpunks in general, and in particular by Assange and Ulbricht, whose efforts indirectly contributed to the legitimization of blockchain in the real world. You may recall the powerful phoenixes mentioned in the Mythology of Blockland: their names were simply ananyms derived from Assange and Ulbricht.

The Magician who stretches reality to create win-win solutions may be reflected in JR Willett's early ideas to improve upon Bitcoin or Vitalik Buterin's creation of a very different system altogether. Likewise, The Innocent or Utopian who wishes to *do the right thing* is apparent in the early Ethereum community, which rejected the powerful hacker's "rightful" claim to its wealth. Though there are plenty of The Ruler or King characters who seek power and control such as the Ethereum hacker and MPEx entrepreneur – Mircea Popescu, there is also The Caregiver or Saint who sacrifices themselves for others in the way of the Pineapple Fund and Shaun's Outpost. While The Sages of Blockland spend their time prophesying about how blockchain will radically transform the economy, society, and governments, The Everyman can be seen working at the grassroots to increase actual adoption and every day use of cryptocurrency among others like him, despite often falling victim to various scams and frauds.

The Hero, who attempts to attain mastery and is always seeking a new battle, can be found in recurring characters such Jed McCaleb, Dan Larimer, Roger Ver, and Andreas Antonopoulos, while The Jester, who lives for today can be speeding away in a Lamborghini bought with the gains of trading success. The ambitious and autonomous Explorer is apparent in the many entrepreneurs who have created all manner of companies and services around blockchain. Finally, The Lover is found in fervid artists who seek to glorify blockchain as the subject of their fiery passions. Each of these basic characters are pure; they stand on their own, as legitimate as any. Though each character tends to see the world from their limited perspective and consider their contemporaries as mere others, they are all important and together form a cohesive and complete whole that is greater than the sum of its parts.

Though the first decade of this prima nullius was a magical age of wonder, the legend of Blockland continues today. The men and women who were called to Blockland in its early years were not quite average people; they possessed a certain curiosity, freedom, and fearlessness which makes them somewhat extraordinary when compared to their neighbors. There is a special magnetism to this mysterious land which has attracted to it the most interesting of people from across the spectrum of wealth, ideology, and profession. These early settlers largely exhibit free, unconstrained minds divorced from mundane day-to-day reality and, due to their early investments, possess the financial resources to spend their days playing in this grand adult sandbox, in which they believe the designs for a new basis for civilization are being laid.

As Shakespeare once declared that "*all the world's a stage and all the men and women merely players*", so are the many characters of Blockland unknowing actors in a global drama. These actors appear, exit, and reappear – playing many different characters and roles across their many ages. As in any good play, these actors deal with deep conflicts and philosophical rifts that naturally arise between them. Such differences in values and culture are only natural, as Blockland is a multicultural immigrant nation to which settlers have arrived on proverbial boats from all the most distant shores of humanity. Though the earliest of settlers were loosely united under a common flag, the Blockland of today is a fractured and unstable place with few clearly defined borders and little sense of common history, belonging, or destiny. In this sense, it has come to represent a sort of cross-section or reflection of the world at large.

You might wonder what this *Blockland* really is. Is it a metaphor? Perhaps. The concept we understand as a *land* or *nation* is being quickly evaporated by globalization. Many people identify with our extended families, hometowns, cities, countries, and even continents and ethnicities less and less. However just as energy never dies, neither have nations; they are simply beginning to take different forms. One can consider nations as living, breathing entities that are ever-changing, reproducing, and dying.

At its core, a nation is a naturally forming entity that unites a population based on commonalities such as language, history, territory, ethnicity, and culture. The true requirement for the creation of a nation is for its members to become conscious of their collective autonomy, unity, and interests. When individuals and tribes unite in the creation of a nation, their collective power and influence grows exponentially. As per *The Ethnic Origins of Nations*, this is generally achieved through collective "*myths, memories, values and the symbols*".[669]

Let us continue to imagine Blockland as the entire crypto-sphere; a large group of crypto-nations inhabiting a common conceptual territory. Bitcoin is the oldest and most culturally, financially, and politically influential, while the powerful nations of Litecoin,

---

[669] Smith, Anthony D. *The Ethnic Origins of Nations*. B. Blackwell, 1988.

Ethereum, Monero, and Ripple were also established in the ancient pioneering times. Each of these crypto-nations has a different history and culture, and thus different founding principles and values which are in a constant state of political flux. Some citizens are loyal only to their own crypto-nation and even believe all others to be illegitimate, while others may hold multiple citizenships and accept the differences between all or most nations as minor.

Though the nation of Blockland is multi-ethnic and multi-lingual, its members share common memories of the historic and even mythical rise of cryptocurrency. They largely share common dreams for a bright blockchain future and have together endured the despair of both long crypto-winters and public ridicule. They recall the day *it clicked* and blockchain graduated from a mere point of curiosity into a passion. This Crypto Nation is an enigma; it has no accepted leader nor registered population. Its government is composed of unofficial self-forming political parties, which each espouse competing and evolving variations of crypto-values.

Blockland has the capacity to once again unite under a single banner. This nation is collectively composed of great wealth and great minds as well as a nimble and inventive populace that is incredibly well-adapted to the digital realm that increasingly dominates and defines our age. Together the people of Blockland form a loosely defined international class that at times supersedes national identity. Together, we can move mountains!

Let us acknowledge our differences as diverse perspectives, which allow this international blockchain movement to sparkle like a globally recognized multi-faceted diamond. Allow us to find common ground in our collective history. Let us put behind overly ideological squabbles so that we may face the world not as fractured techno-tribes but as a mighty force which must be reckoned with. Not so that we may benefit from the world, but so that the we may enrich the world as brave digital adventurers returning with the good fruits of Blockland.

Join the forefront of a technological revolution, there is room for all. Blockchain holds keys to the future and though we do not know where it will lead us, it is ours to discover!

People of Blockland, unite! May your only chains be the ones you own!

The Essence of Blockchain

What do ideas like *decentralized money* really mean, then? Perhaps we can boil down this idea of money to a simpler concept; energy, which equally describes power, force, influence, and strength. Energy, like money, cannot be meaningfully measured in the absolute, but only according to its equivalence to another, somehow opposite energy.

Many true believers will read the story of Blockland as one of a chosen people's glorious revolution against and liberation from a given oppressor be it individual, secret society, government, belief system, economic model, or political order. They believe that the structural ills of the Current Era can be forever fixed by giving rise to a universal one-world currency that is a supreme entity to itself, untethered from the direct influence of any worldly human organization. A new cryptographic Leviathan of sorts to replace the power of mortal kings and human organizations. They imagine that the blockchain will bring calamity after calamity to these oppressors until these Satoshists or Decentralites are able to go freely to their land of milk and honey. In this coming turning point, they imagine, those who willingly adopted this new value will ascend to the place of the victors from where they will rule the world as the blockchain, which is on their side, protects them and guides the wealth and influence of the world to them. They may even fantasize of the ability to cast away their former rulers and storm their palaces. This is exactly what took place during the 1917 February Revolution in St. Petersburg, after which Johan Fredrik Ylkänen, my maternal great-grandfather, volunteered to drive the train carrying the deposed Romanov family to exile in Siberia where they were soon executed.

The Greek Titan Prometheus is said to have stolen fire from the gods of Mount Olympus and gift it to humanity so that they could use it to build civilization with all that it entails, making men akin to gods. As we have seen in the many dramas of Blockland, blockchain has at times given individuals the power to behave as if they were above-human, at least from the perspective of governments that have tried to rein in that which may be fundamentally unreinable.

For millennia, it is these civilizations and societies that have regulated human life by way of the courts, social contracts, and enforced morality. They have brought peace and technology, but also wrought war and destruction. One might think of blockchain with all the possibilities it brings as a new sort of fire brought down by a contemporary Prometheus. Once had, it cannot be taken away, and gives its wielders a sort of godlike power to supersede limitations in the systems they inhabit. This means they have gained the ability to act on a level that is in certain ways outside of the reach of their governments and thus outside of organized society. This technology by which one can hold and trade unseizable and un-accountable property, communicate without detection, and by which companies can operate without human agents, is alien to and potentially at odds with societal dynamics that have been established since the dawn of time. The ideal image of civilization and society is that of a peace-promoting platform of mutual collaboration that breeds order and advancement while banishing war, brutishness, disorder, and chaos to forsaken lands beyond its mighty walls. Thus, civilization necessarily limits its members in some manner, often regulating their lives, property, and work.

If we imagine blockchains as chains by which anyone can climb undetected and repeatedly over the walls that separate civilization and the jungle, then the fortifications of the established order have been corrupted and its days are numbered. Some new balance must replace it.

This leads to a most fundamental question: the nature of humanity. If given the metaphorical fire of the gods, will we tear apart the artificial society that binds us and return to our natural-state lives that are in the words of Thomas Hobbes "*solitary, poor, nasty, brutish, and short*" or, will we supersede the fetters of society and arrive to an eternity of blissfully holding hands while singing Kumbaya?

Just as the communist revolution failed to bring about world peace and prosperity as promised, the true story of Blockland may not be an overarching and eternal fairy-tale of the light defeating the dark. This may be for no other reason than that lightness and darkness, and oppression and freedom, can be matters of perspective. The awaited savior to one can be a feared enslaver to another. Like physics and math, blockchain is beyond good and evil and can be equally useful for all ends and by all players. Simply put, it is a new factor of the eternal playing field.

What has been created is a renewed, firm platform on which and even a material of which a new type of digital era can unfold.

The undetermined future of centralization versus decentralization reminds one of the ancient Chinese concept of *Yin and Yang* (literally *dark-bright* or *negative-positive, but also understood as feminine-masculine*), which describes an unending universal dualism in which seemingly opposite forces or concepts are intertwined, forever giving rise to each other and ultimately being equal or the same. In this cosmological worldview, the *material energy* or *reality* that makes up this world is called qi.

This foundation stone, that is now in place, regardless of the intentions of its erectors, is impersonal and without bias or capacity for corruption. It is a digital constant that does not bend or regulate reality in favor of any side nor distinguish between right or wrong; it simply is, regardless of our ideas or preferences.

Thus, is its essence; it is what it is.

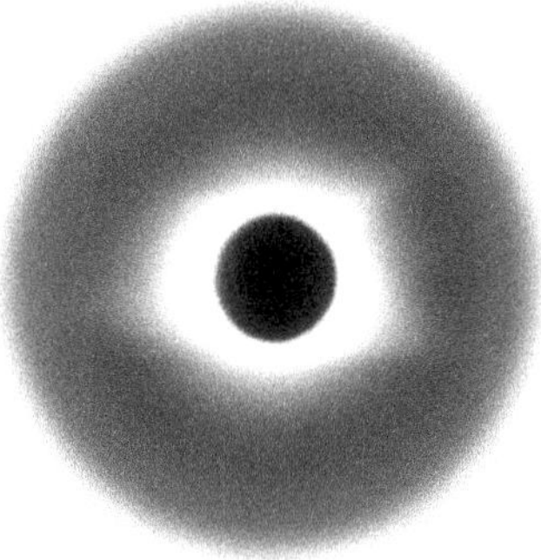

An eclipse; associated historically with a time of rapid change and exponential growth.

AFTERWORD

Among my earliest childhood memories is a briefcase filled with treasured bottlecaps, which I apparently had a habit of spreading on the floor. This curiosity was among the first of a string of all-consuming obsessions, be the target dinosaurs, knights, bugs, or Pokémon. As I gathered specimens related to my interests, my early identity became that of *the collector* and *the scientist* who presented collections of coins, stamps, rocks, shells, and cards to every visitor from electrician to grandparent. LEGO later dominated my formative years as I would spend weeks on end silently adding to and interacting with an expansive imaginary world in which each building, vehicle and mini-figure had a history spanning several years. Scouting with the 1st Elmira Scout Troop came to fulfill my passions in the early teens as I earned almost every badge including the *Chief Scout* and *Queen's Venturer Awards*, the latter technically bestowed by Elizabeth II herself. Later areas of interest included online gaming, in which I once led a 400-member clan, and photography, around which I built a summer business through a government grant program called *Ontario Summer Company* which aimed to mentor young people in entrepreneurship. Next came a short-lived business selling drop-shipped knives from China to buyers around the world with eBay, soon thwarted by issues with online payments. From there followed an immersion into the stock market

Looking back, it was my obsessive collecting of coins and deep-dive personality that paved the way for my early immersion into the Bitcoin world. While my thirst for adventure can only be blamed on being a boyscout, it was the volunteer mentors of the *Summer Company* program that introduced me to the world of business. My troubles with PayPal surely helped grasp the concept of a global permissionless payment system.

Eight years after my photography days, I found myself as a 24-year-old blockchain consultant in Calgary, a city where I had spent nine months and whose oil-based economy was in severe decline. Everyone wanted *a blockchain* as the back-end of their new business, as the way to fund their business, or as a buzz-word to raise millions of dollars; however, few who hired me truly knew what they wanted or what I could do for them. It was apparent that blockchain was a realm of magic and I was as a mysterious priest of this ethereal altar of plenty. Everyone from large oil companies to budding entrepreneur figured they could consult the local crypto-wizard who might write out some magic spell, perhaps "*Crypto-ICO-Blockchain-Bitcoin-Alakhazam!"* to churn millions in investment and government grants from thin air. This priest however lacked faith – blockchain was not magic, and if it was, no one had yet agreed on what it did, who should wield it, how it worked, or whether it was in any way reliable or a one-trick-hat-rabbit. That did not seem to matter – one needed only faith in blockchain, reminding me of the Finnish bible college where I spent a semester after high school.

As I got an urgent call for assistance from a client in Vancouver, I took the excuse to pack my bags and seek greener pastures in a move comparable to the time I dropped out of said insular bible college to attend a "real" university where I could think freely and honestly. With a few days to spare and accompanied by two executives from Calgary crypto exchange NDAX, I took the long way through Los Angeles where the *Crypto Invest Summit* was taking place.

There I met Steve Wand, a neighbor from my time in Waterloo, who introduced me to Daniel Mross at a bar to which I had lugged my large suitcase as I was on my way to the airport for my move to Vancouver. Daniel had produced the first Netflix documentary about Bitcoin and was a fan of physical Bitcoins. We hit it off as we reminisced about the early wild-west days, and I gifted him a book. After perhaps 15 minutes of discussion, I had a thought. Someone should write a book that presents all the different facets and perspectives involved in this insane, confusing industry so that others can understand how it became what it is today. The problem was that everyone from miners and traders to large businesses and governments had entirely different interests and ideas about what blockchain was, only looking at it from their limited, myopic perspectives without understanding the larger picture. Minutes later I realized the responsibility had fallen on me; *be the change you wish to see*, I thought. I had been handed a new life quest. SELECT: [ACCEPT].

Days after I arrived in Vancouver, the company I was there to advise was already collapsing, as was typical in the industry. I saw an email from Daniel; he had an extra VIP ticket to the *World Crypto Con* in Las Vegas which was two days away. I took off for Vegas without a care in the world. I had packed everything I needed for a year and my destination did not matter. All I knew was that I would spend some time discussing the book, and then find some convenient country to write from.

As I arrived on the conference floor, I was surprised to see a booth selling my books. I realized I had what amounted to a small fanclub of physical Bitcoin collectors who I had never met, despite working with for years. As the last night of the event rolled around, I found myself in a VIP booth at a Steve Aoki concert with a company that was celebrating a $30 million investment in the previous week, all while throwing actual money around the dance floor. That is when I saw Christy, whom I recalled meeting a few months earlier on a boozy pirate schooner in Toronto. This pirate ship was a party boat run by another ICO, onto which my business partner Dave and I had snuck uninvited at the Toronto *Blockchain Futurist* conference. Christy then introduced me to her friend Kieran and invited me to join them on a road trip to a blockchain event in Los Angeles the next day. After that we planned to fly to Puerto Rico for another conference, and I figured could write from there for a few months while learning Spanish. Carpe Diem.

We checked in to an LA Airbnb, only to have it burglarized while we went out for dinner (almost certainly by the owner, and almost surely because we were dumb enough to tell him we had arrived from a crypto conference). I lost my passports, the others their laptops and even some private keys. We drove to another blockchain conference in San Francisco, but as I could not fly home to Canada without a passport, I flew to Buffalo and walked over Niagara Falls, arriving at the border with only my learner's driving license. I felt like a child knocking on the door at 3am after sneaking out and losing the key.

I considered staying for an MBA degree, but lost enthusiasm for what seemed like an overly beurocratic and "inside the box" structure. I realized it had been years since I had even interacted with any agent of normality, that is, the analog society that the insular globe-spanning crypto-bubble which I had entrenched myself into collectively seeked to escape from. Being untethered to any place and without any role in society, I felt that my future, while surely bright and exciting, was especially difficult to grasp or conceptualize. The crypto markets were crashing to all-time lows. A two-week-old book idea was the only prompt for me to follow into the unknown, and I felt deeply that I would not arrive to my destiny until my quest was complete. It was a distant dragon, egging me on to come and slay it.

After a short interlude of waiting for new travel documents and exploring the recesses of my mind for inspiration, I was ready to again take on the world on my own terms. Sopping to visit Daniel in Pittsburgh to go over my writing plans, I took off for the warmer climes of Thailand where I met with a friend from Calgary. We were however in rather different states of being; he had just landed to a sunny vacation destination, whereas I had just arrived home, where I expected to get busy writing. I was now a digital nomad – everywhere was my home, and I was free to roam the world as I worked on my 22-inch external monitor which I carried in my single medium-sized backpack. There was no shortage of adventure, not the least of which was sitting in the passenger seat of J's legendary Bitcoin Lamborghini as it tripled the highway's speed limit in the wee hours of the morning. As I wrote, the scope of the book evolved from a mere 21 perspectives on the industry into an attempt to write the collective history of a historical movement.

While staying on a neverland-esque jungle island where several lost-boy blockchain entrepreneurs had set up a sort of crypto commune where they could work and adventure with like-minded people (that's a story for a different book), I invited Kieran to visit. He unfortunately suffered a tragic motorbike accident which left him permanently paralyzed from the waist down, and in a Thai hospital without travel insurance. To get him back home to Canada, his friends in the industry created a fundraising campaign which raised ~$70,000. He has hung on to his blockchain start-up despite his monumental struggles, even travelling to conferences around the world in hopes of raising money both for his company and treatments. He has been a great inspiration to me.

Behind on my writing, suffering the noxious air of Thailand's annual field-burning season, and rather shaken by my friend's accident, I changed my surroundings to ones of tranquility. I moved myself into a lakeside forest shack on my indigenous lands in Eastern Finland, within the township that my ancestors have lived in since before the time of Vikings. Each weekend I would spend time on the homestead, which had been passed down for perhaps 300 years, soon to the lakeside to immerse myself in writing and its related contemplation. I even cleaned an old barn that my great-great-step-grandfather had left messy, generations ago.

Time did not exist here, with the summer sun staying up for an entire month to create glorious 16-hour sunsets that were never punctuated with darkness. Fishing with self-made traps and heating up the wood-burning sauna to prepare my meals, I felt truly human – a sublime and timeless feeling which I worry that all too few humans know. Except for my ongoing writing about the most abstract of virtual futurisms, my life in a small log-built monkey-box in the forest was not materially unlike that of the people thousands of years before me in those same woods. I had no master nor timekeeper; I simply was. An anonymous sovereign.

Some things can only be seen by an outside observer. Having effectively abandoned society to live as a hermit in a self-sufficient balance with my immediate nature, I gained a unique perspective on not only the blockchain industry but also on human society and its social, political, and economic peculiarities. I took a break from forest-life in July by flying to Berlin for *Blockchain Week* – and saw my worlds collide. As I again donned a tailored suit and rubbed shoulders with the global crypto-elite in high flying clubs and exclusive party-boats, I reflected on the fact that I had just used a real toilet for the first time in over a month. Everyone around me was striving for something, trying to convince people that if they would give their time or money for whatever project, they would reap more money, by which they could buy things and other people's time. I was selling nothing, and it seemed to confuse and even bother people who kept asking "*but really, what are you looking for here*" at a networking event with penthouse views of the city. I did not know what to say – seeing the industry's development made me proud of its progress, like an uncle watching his nephew play sports, but that sounded like an invalid reason to be where I was. A year later, perhaps half the people I met there had made millions due to the Decentralized Finance boom.

Many seek a concept called *F-U money*, an amount that allows them to (metaphorically) shout, "*f--k you!*" without negative consequences to anyone and anything that wants something from them. With F-U money, a person is free and sovereign, thus able to retire from the oppression of work. This does not necessarily mean the end of work, but the end of, as Nietczhe described, an external "*Thou Shalt*" being replaced by an internal "*I will*" as work becomes entirely optional. Cities are full of people who sit at dull desks for 40-60 hour work weeks punctuated by hour-long traffic jams, with barely time to enjoy their income whilst dreaming of reaching F-U sovereignty by the time they turn 65 or perhaps 55, if they are lucky. The blockchain space and many other daring industries are full of hungry, even bloodthirsty entrepreneurs working 80-100 hour work weeks. They sacrifice sleep for dreams of ultimate F-U fortunes. At the end of the day, this money that they seek is merely a vehicle by which they hope to attain the freedom to live life on their own terms. Paradoxically, they sacrifice their very lives for it as sheep-like wage slaves or sheep-dog executives who are actually mere servants to their own fears.

I realized that I didn't want material things, nor did I really *need* to chase expanding eight-figure fortunes as such things were not worth my time, nor were they necessary for happiness or internal balance. I had transcended the F-U barrier; I owed the world nothing, and I had the land and space where I could live off the land to the end of my days with barely any interaction with the rest of society, if and when I so desired. Indeed, some of my relatives living nearby seemd to be doing just that in a place not dissimilar to The Shire as imagined by Tolkien, a place which felt to me like a generations-ago forgotten haven to which I had somehow washed up after a life of adventure. Here I had all I needed at my fingertips: land with home-grown fruits and vegetables– bursting with wild berries and mushrooms for eating, lakes full of fish and crustaceans, forests with wood for heating and building, and wild game for hunting.

From 25 till my old age, I was free from nearly all obligations, and could enjoy unspoilt nature, clean air, nine hours of sleep, no alarm clocks or schedules, and the company of good friends and family. These things are priceless and timeless, paradise and true freedom. I had returned to my forgotten citadel, a place of maximum stability and soundness whose intrinsic value could not be inflated away. How great it would be if everyone could join me in this freedom!

Instead of pursuing new material fortunes like my crypto-compatriots, I applied to grad school for Philosophy & Economics in Germany. With classes cancelled due to covid-19 I soon retreated to the cabin where I had the pleasure of listening to the ice melt in a continuous months-long banging roar which sounds like airplanes landing above at all hours. In view of practicality, I transferred to law school in Finland where I could specialize in this emerging technology. My return to academia was a result of a realization that I was effectively existing outside of society – having left its pull upon reaching escape velocity. Looking down however, I saw that this demanding gravity of civilization was not something that needed to be escaped by way of F-U booster rockets with which to leave earthly problems behind, but a work-in-progress that can be improved. I did not wish to retire on the moon, not yet at least, but, on my own terms, to offer my service and participation to a greater whole.

What is quite fascinating is that when one leaves the safe confines of society to fulfill some personal quest and returns upon its completion, they arrive back not as serious dragon slayers but as experienced yet playful children without worry or uncertainty and with nothing to prove. In my case this Jungian experience was not merely in my head. As I arrived for my first day at the law faculty of the University of Turku on what happened to be the day after receiving the first test-print of *Blockland*, I was struck by the peculiar feeling of being in a new place that was somehow familiar but long-forgotten. After a google image search, I understood – judging by the grounds, architecture, materials, furniture, and colors, my law school was virtually identical to a certain day-care center a short drive away, the destination of my first adventure as a newly independent 3-year-old exactly 23 years earlier. I had come a full circle.

I have here and in the Foreword described parts of my life's journey so far. Why? Perhaps only because this is the Afterword, and the only reason anyone reads an Afterword is to get into the author's head. Welcome, make yourself at home and enjoy your stay. The journey is lifted from a meticiulous and peculiar spreadsheet, in which I record and quantify the details and interpretations of my life and its phases. Doing this helps me give context to existance by finding various patterns and storylines within it, all in different stages of completion, and many abandoned partway through. Here, a certain snapshot escaped Excel and resettled in Word. There is however a deeper reason for sharing my recollection: I believe it contains pieces of universal truth that apply to not just individuals but to the lifecycles of greater socio-cultural movements including Bitcoin, Blockchain, and Cryptocurrency.

The Bitcoin movement can be understood as having a strong countercultural element comparable to things like punk rock, skateboarding, hippies, small-scale organic farmers, and many others in their time. These movements are similar in that they reject blind obedience to mainstream culture, while encouraging members to *do their own thing*. These countercultures represent a rebellion toward a mainstream culture with which participants have become disillusioned, most probably for good reason. It is from here that these movements embark on a journey in search of sovereignty.

Whether through the creation of music scenes to generate income, collectives to reduce living costs, or farms to generate food, these movements have often created the means for dedicated members to effectively exit the mainstream and take residence in the movement's micro-societies on a fully dedicated basis. Worth remembering however is the common pitfall of such movements, where this obedience to the mainstream is simply replaced with blind obedience to itself as in a cult. As they mature, successful movements redefine the world around them and allows even the mainstream to see itself from a different perspective, resulting in significant cultural shifts. For this reason, I am excited to see what change the blockchain revolution will bring. I hope it is a net-positive, whatever that means.

These brave counterculturalists are bound to see themselves as revolutionary heroes defeating an old, ancient oppressor and fulfilling some sacred quest. For many in the crypto-culture, this quest is a re-invention of money and value. Indeed, with the transfer of hundreds of billions of dollars to the early believers of cryptocurrency, blockchain represents perhaps the most lucrative or well-financed of these countercultural movements. As a result of these radical and anti-establishment investments, thousands upon thousands of people have gained the financial means by which to break norms and traditions, follow their dreams, and simply be themselves without conerns of serious societal disapproval. It is however important to remember that no solution is permanent; new will eventually conquer the old, and it is in everyone's interest for the old to recognize its time to yield. This goes doubly for innovation within the blockchain sphere itself!

With this newfound freedom to build their own realities in whatever way they desire, they can live their very best lives and create their very best work to share with the community and world. It is when people are liberated to be their true selves without need to justify themselves to anyone, that they can truly shine like diamonds and rock the world. From a lifecycle perspective this can be understood as old age; a point at which one can pursue limitless creativity without expectations or concerns. Like punk rock in its time, blockchain has given many the opportunity to break the chains which bind them and self-actualize. It is my greatest wish that this collective experience will be a great boon to not only individuals, but also to all of humanity in everything that will sprout from it.

If Blockland's people are self reliant and secure, they form a sort of sovereign nation. All this was not quite about money after all, but of a quest to coming at peace with oneself and free to live one's life on chosen terms. This life which people waste away is all too fragile and temporary to focus on anything less. We must discover and define it ourselves. Perhaps we will play a notable role in reshaping society in the 21st century. What changes are the people of Blockland likely to bring? Will we usher in a new era where civilizational wealth cannot be counted in dollars but in the number of people who have reached some level of self actualization, or will the economy return to a top-down model of the middle-ages? One thing I am certain of is that Blockland will be leaving quite a mark on history. What kind? Time will tell.

I am lucky to count myself among these who have escaped the pressures of the default life, where one must attempt to fit themselves into the boxes defined by others. The alternative world of Crypto has opened to me a world of privilege, giving me the platform by which to make deep lifelong friendships, find reliable colleagues, and create a unique network to which doors have opened in part due to *crypto cred.* It has been for me the most exciting of classrooms, teaching lessons in life, leadership, business, and psychology. The concept of limited, deflationary money has radically changed the way I see not only monetary value, but time, wealth, relationships, and nature. These are all finite and we must conserve, care for, and enrich them, as infinite exponential growth cannot go on forever. Unlike my peers, I have had the privilege of spending an entire year in leisurely writing and enjoyment. I have been allowed to experience life free as a bird, flying freely while moving south towards a roughly defined destination to which there is no deadline. How could I think to go back?

To be a global citizen who moves between cultures comes at the cost of never being fully integrated or in-step with the masses of any one place. This is because culture comes from shared experi-ences, and no cultural straddler nor peretual traveller can ever keep up. Perhaps that was part of the draw of Blockland on my part: a desire to cement a record of the ethereal crypto-world which shaped me into who I am. To create an account of the already-ancient place from which I am partly derived, comparable to the way my eponym once did of the mythic world of ancient Finland. In this sense, *Blockland* is a work of quite literal self-actualization, written from a sense of calling and even destiny. Few people can imagine doing work on this premise today, and that is too bad. Work of passion may just be the only type of work worth doing.

Having finished writing for now, it again comes time to start something new. This includes many things, such as the reinvention of Token Valley into an investment fund where the lessons learned, friends made, and visions had on this grand trek can again be leveraged into something greater.

As this adventure ends, new ones await. Blockland continues to evolve. This book is already mere history, an explanation of the early days that brought us to the present, which at the time of writing, was the future. Time rhymes around in waves. What comes next will reflect the past, which has always been driven by little more than an image of the future. Thus, by drawing from our roots we can bring our branches to bloom.

Perhaps you will join me on new adventures. Keep in touch, this is only the beginning.

May we meet again,

November 2019
Bayreuth, Germany

(Revised September 2020 – Turku, Finland)

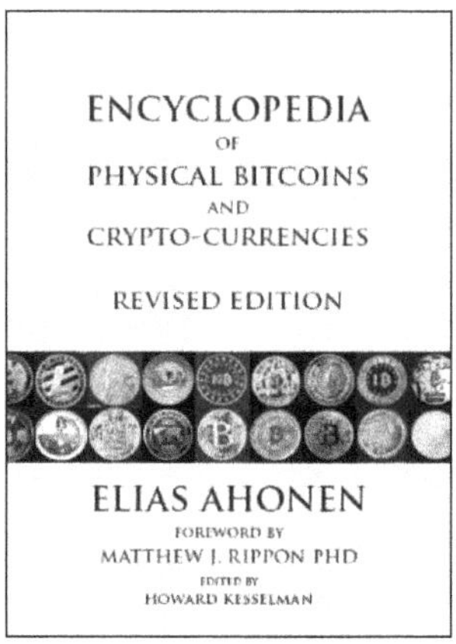
ENCYCLOPEDIA
OF
PHYSICAL BITCOINS
AND
CRYPTO-CURRENCIES
REVISED EDITION
ELIAS AHONEN
FOREWORD BY
MATTHEW J. RIPPON PHD
EDITED BY
HOWARD KESSELMAN

And to you, Dear Reader,

Thank you for allowing me this pleasure of being your storyteller. It is my most sincere hope that you have found here an enjoyable, educational, and enlightening experience.

As we part ways, I will now ask a favor of you.

In writing this book, I have taken the lonely path. I made no book proposal for a publisher, nor queried an agent before embarking on my journey. I let myself fall off the face of the earth, only to emerge from the wilderness a year later with draft-in-hand. Truly, this has all come from the heart.

Self-publishing is a great challenge, as I have no one to tell readers, researchers, or libraries about my work. As such, reviews on Amazon (or anywhere else!) play a crucial role. If you enjoyed this book:

- Submit a thoughtful review on Amazon, today
- Lend this book to a friend, next week
- Consider donating it to your library, next month

I certainly want to stay in touch with my readers, so feel free to follow me on Twitter **@eahonen**

elias@cryptonumist.com

In the odd case that you are not yet tired of reading, I do invite you to explore the *Encyclopedia of Physical Bitcoins and Crypto-Currencies Revised Edition*, which you can find at **www.cryptonumist.com**. You will find the crypto symbolism it explores deeply fascinating, and its large bright pictures will offer a welcome respite from this wall of text which you have now conquered.

Until next time.

INDEX

Cryptocurrency Concepts — Primary & Technical

Cryptocurrency Concepts — Secondary & Cultural

Cryptocurrencies

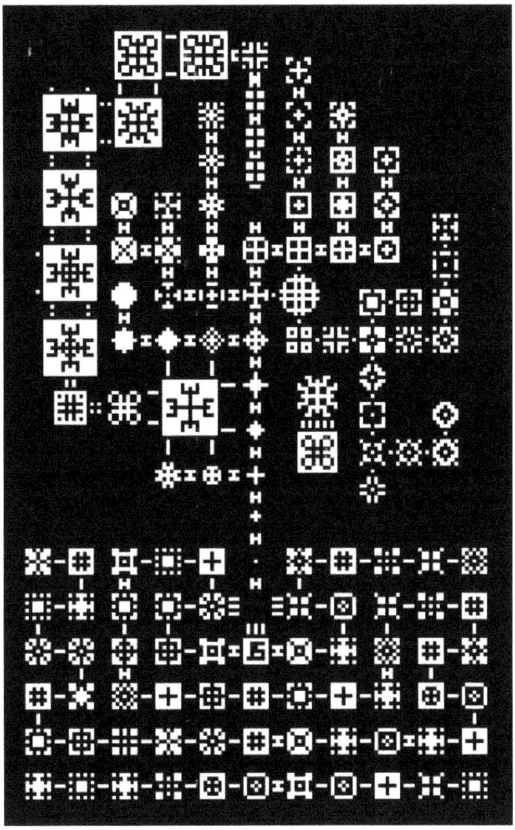

PUBLIC KEY

1FJ5X2YMTUjciJv5Xm5L9yGzztBPYQAmF

KxHPa1FRbAFtUuM51v4rvHA75nSG3G5VKSsNfd63dgtJnzYVPVeE

PRIVATE KEY

www.ingramcontent.com/pod-product-compliance
Ingram Content Group UK Ltd.
Pitfield, Milton Keynes, MK11 3LW, UK
UKHW020837290926
15470UKWH00004B/1409

9 780995 089969